Humphrey Carpenter

Humphrey Carpenter is the son of a former Bishop of Oxford. He has written the authorised biography of J.R.R. Tolkien, *The Inklings, Jesus,* and the widely acclaimed authorised biography of Benjamin Britten. He has recently published the fiftieth anniversary history of the BBC Third Programme and Radio 3 and is writing the authorised life of Dennis Potter. He has been awarded the Somerset Maugham Award, the Duff Cooper Memorial Prize and has been a runner-up for the Whitbread Prize for biography. Humphrey Carpenter is married with two daughters and lives in Oxford.

SCEPTRE

Robert Runcie

The Reluctant Archbishop

HUMPHREY CARPENTER

SCEPTRE

Copyright © 1996 by Humphrey Carpenter

First published in 1996 by Hodder and Stoughton
First published in paperback in 1997
by Hodder and Stoughton
A division of Hodder Headline PLC
A Sceptre Paperback

The right of Humphrey Carpenter to be identified as the Author of
the Work has been asserted by him in accordance with the
Copyright, Designs and Patents Act 1988.

10 9 8 7 6 5 4 3 2 1

A CIP catalogue record for this book is
available from the British Library

ISBN 0 340 66004 X

Typeset by Palimpsest Book Production Limited,
Polmont, Stirlingshire
Printed and bound in Great Britain by
Mackays of Chatham PLC, Chatham, Kent

Hodder and Stoughton
A division of Hodder Headline PLC
338 Euston Road
London NW1 3BH

'I get very angry when people blame Archbishops. No one asks to be Archbishop. It's a thankless task.'

Bishop Hugh Montefiore, talking to the author.

'I wasn't as interested in religion or the church as Coggan. Or Ramsey. I was ashamed that I got more delight from lecturing on a Swan Hellenic cruise than I did from going to some religious rally.'

Robert Runcie, telling the author why he hesitated to accept the Archbishopric of Canterbury.

Contents

List of Illustrations

Section I

Robert Runcie, aged two[1]
Nancy Runcie, Cunard hairdresser[1]
Father and sister Kathleen[1]
With his tank troop in Holland[1]
Runcie, Scots Guards officer[2]
A German helmet[2]
At Westcott House[1]
Wedding day[1]
A 'college codger' at Trinity Hall[2]
Entertaining Cuddesdon parishioners[2]
The new Bishop of St Albans[2]
The Runcies at home, St Albans[3]
Archbishop of Canterbury[4]
With Pope John Paul II at Accra[5]
A mission for Terry Waite[6]
With Graham Leonard at Walsingham[7]
A royal wedding[8]

Section II

With John Mortimer at Lambeth[9]
The pig-keeper[2]
Lindy in the *News of the World*[10]
With Hugh Montefiore[9]
With Richard Chartres and Terry Waite[2]
General Synod debate[9]
Lindy conducts the Guards[11]

Photographic credits

1 Rosemary Innes-Watson
2 Lambeth Palace archives
3 *Welwyn Times*
4 *Kentish Gazette*
5 Church Information Office
6 Robert Miles
7 *Lynn News & Advertiser*
8 PA News
9 Michael Ward, *Sunday Times*
10 *News of the World*
11 Press Association
12 Universal Pictorial Press & Agency
13 John Cogill
14 Tony Weaver, *Sunday Express*

Preface

This is both a biography, and a book about writing a biography. It tells its own story of its origin, aims, difficulties and excitements. All I want to add here is my thanks to all the participants, chiefly, of course, Robert Runcie (Lord Runcie) himself.

Besides those acknowledged in the text and in footnotes, I must thank: Ion Trewin, for commissioning the book before he changed publishing houses; Candida Brazil, for doing background research in the early days of the project; Vicky Clouston, for patiently typing interview transcripts; Jane Houston, for generous help with the Lambeth Palace archives; Anne-Marie Ehrlich, for skilled picture research; Rosemary Innes-Watson, for the loan of Runcie family photographs; Frances Charlesworth, Robert Runcie's secretary, for stage-managing my meetings with my subject; and Bishop Geoffrey Rowell, for giving me unrestricted access to the papers of Garry Bennett, whose executor he is. Margaret Body has played a vital editorial role very skilfully and Roland Philipps of Hodder & Stoughton has been overseer of the final stages, with the able assistance of Angela Herlihy.

Preface to the Paperback Edition

This book needs no introduction, since it already explains why, when and how it came to be written. At the time the first edition was published, Alan Watkins in *The Spectator* rather flatteringly described it as 'a Richard Rogers book, with pipes, ventilators and lift-shafts on the outside; not so much a biography as a book about writing a biography'. But, in view of the stir its publication caused, I think it deserves a postscript.

From my earliest interviews with Robert Runcie, it was clear that the book was going to be something unusual; and once he had spoken candidly into my tape recorder about the marriage of the Prince and Princess of Wales (this was in December 1993), I realised I was sitting on a hot potato. Indeed, in those days long before Princess Diana's tell-all *Panorama* interview, when the decay of the royal marriage was still largely a matter for speculation, I experienced a fleeting temptation to head for Docklands with the tape in my pocket, and invite bids. But of course this passed, and – incredible though it may seem – I had really almost forgotten about the book in the weeks immediately before publication.

During the five-and-a-half years since Runcie had asked me to write it, I had also been researching and writing *The Envy of the World*, the fiftieth anniversary history of the BBC Third Programme and Radio 3, which was due to come out almost simultaneously. I had been making unsuccessful efforts to get that book serialised in a newspaper. When the publishers of *Robert Runcie* rang to say that there were two newspapers bidding against each other for a serialisation of *this* book, I was slightly surprised.

The Times won the auction, and serialisation began on a Saturday in early September 1996; the first extract was a compilation of various bits of the book, showing Runcie's views on gay priests. This was not an issue that I had personally considered very important, but the paper devoted its lead story to it ('RUNCIE FEARED BETRAYAL BY GAY CLERGY'), and on Monday it gave the same treatment (serialisation plus headline news) to Runcie's remarks about the royal marriage.

The rest of the media had now woken up to the story, and by Tuesday morning all the front pages were carrying their own versions; for example, the *Daily Mail* led with 'FURY AS RUNCIE BETRAYS ROYAL SECRETS'.

The punning headline-writers got going – 'BOOK OF REVELATIONS' was quite popular, but the favourite was 'CANTERBURY TALES' – and the leader-writers began to pontificate. According to the *Daily Telegraph*, I had secured the interviews 'under false pretences', while the *Guardian* felt that Runcie had 'made the mistake of reaching a gentlemen's agreement with his new biographer ... in an era when gentlemen need legal contracts'. *The Spectator* said that my 'indiscretions' made 'a *Sun* reporter look like a Trappist monk'.

On an inside page of the *Guardian*, my fellow biographer Michael Holroyd generously sprang to my defence with an article pointing out that, since Boswell, members of our profession have never behaved in a gentlemanly fashion. Holroyd suggested that it had been 'vain' of Runcie to invite a biographer into his home, and he was now facing the consequences. Ben Pimlott in the *Daily Express* (himself then writing a life of the Queen) offered a kindlier interpretation of Runcie's behaviour, suggesting that the 'self-engineered profile', such as Runcie had in effect commissioned me to write, was 'temptation' that few people, who wanted to shape the way they would be viewed by posterity, could resist. Yet another biographer, this time a specialist in Church of England affairs, Michael De-la-Noy, quoted Runcie's complaint that he had only given me the interviews for 'background' rather than direct quotation, and asked: 'How is any biographer worth his salt expected to make use of such explosive material, freely given, as "background information"? There is no conceivable way he could have ignored the material presented to him on a plate.'

Many people suggested that I had behaved not as a biographer but as a 'mere' journalist, though Stephen Glover in *The Spectator*, himself a seasoned journalist, described me as 'mere' biographer (there's a topic for a good debate here). One of my favourite moments in that strange week was when a *Daily Mail* man – the kind who are unjustly described as hacks – congratulated me on my scoop, as one journalist to another.

I decided that the best tactic with interviewers was not to claim any moral high ground, and be honest about how much I had been paid for the book (not an enormous amount by the standard of the present literary world). This paid off – the honesty, I mean. A few days later, Lynda Lee-Potter wrote in the *Daily Mail*: 'Mr Carpenter ...[has] proved to be brilliant at coping with aggressive interviewers who accuse him of perfidy, treachery or betrayal. "You're absolutely right," he says genially, to which there is really no further question.' The non-existent Glenda Slagg, in *Private Eye*, charmingly called me 'Britain's ballsiest biographer'. Indeed, the women journalists were invariably the kinder; Lynn Barber wrote 'Runcie may have been a fool to waive all right to veto, but that doesn't make Carpenter a knave,' and Libby Purves guessed that God was finding the whole fracas 'hilarious'.

The *Daily Mail* tried to persuade several friends of mine to dish some dirt on me, and ran a story describing me as 'the jazz enthusiast who likes to play on sexual secrets', which also expressed disappointment that my history of the BBC Third Programme and Radio 3, about to emerge, had 'so far ... yielded neither sexual scandal nor political controversy'.

The religious affairs correspondent of the *Daily Telegraph* alleged that I was 'the man who brought belly dancing to the Cheltenham Festival of Literature' (not an achievement I recall), while her opposite number on the *Independent* managed to unearth a misdemeanour I had committed at school. Several papers offered any sum I cared to name if I would give them the bits that had been cut out of the biography. Fearful of burglars wearing green eye-shades, I wiped the original draft of the book off the hard disk of my computer.

Talking of schoolboy behaviour, A. N. Wilson attacked the book in the *Evening Standard* on the grounds that (in his opinion) its author was smelly: 'Humphrey dashes hither and thither, exuding sweat, halitosis and dandruff.' Being in possession of a letter from Wilson, threatening retaliation after an unkind review I had written of his book on Jesus, this caused me no surprise. Anthony Howard in *The Sunday Times* noted that Wilson was 'a former prospective ordinand ... See how these Christians love one another!' A lady from the *Sunday Telegraph* came to see me and told her readers that, though my hair wanted cutting, she could detect no strong odour.

Meanwhile leading churchmen were being given their turn to comment. Bishop Richard Holloway in the *Church Times* said the book had done for the Church of England 'what Princess Diana's *Panorama* interview did for the monarchy'. Graham James, Runcie's former chaplain and now a suffragan bishop in Cornwall, complained that the book was trivial because I hadn't read through the Lambeth archives. (I had, and there was very little that shed light on Runcie.) Edward Norman and George Austin wrote their usual sort of stuff. Jonathan Dimbleby, not a clergyman but Prince Charles's official biographer, stepped forward to say that Runcie's view of Charles was out of date – 'The remarks refer to an earlier period of the Prince's life when he was exploring a range of spiritual issues.'

The Runcies themselves had wisely kept mum during all this; Robert managed to be abroad, and Lindy told one reporter that she had taken the paper out of the fax machine, 'because I don't see why I should pay for people to send me questions I won't answer'. Ian Hislop revealed that he had recently interviewed Runcie at home for Channel 4, and had been puzzled that Lindy kept sticking her head round the door and hissing 'H.C.!' whenever her husband became too indiscreet. Hislop said he could now decode the initials.

By the end of the year it was all over and mostly forgotten, though round-ups of 1996 quoted Runcie's words 'I have done my best to die before this book was published' (they will probably get into the next edition of the *Oxford Dictionary of Quotations*). When journalists had asked me if I had remained friends with Runcie, I replied that I doubted I would still be on his Christmas card list. In fact two days before Christmas a card of *quattrocento* angels playing musical instruments arrived with familiar handwriting inside: 'Some liberal angels to hymn the season of forgiveness and good will. Robert and Lindy.'

Talking of post, I kept expecting nasty, squidgy packets to pop through the letter box, sent by furious old ladies accusing me of harming the Church of England. In fact all I got was amiable little notes from retired canons beginning 'I well remember your dear mother . . .' *Pace* Richard Holloway, the book seemed not to have shaken the Church of England one bit. One would hardly expect it to. It's an institution which has always prided itself on its excellent shock-absorbers, and I doubt whether, with the perspective of a bit of history, this biography will even have showed up on its Richter scale.*

Finally, would I do it again? When I began writing biographies, more than twenty years ago, most of the outstanding twentieth-century literary and artistic greats were waiting to have their biographies satisfactorily written. Looking back, I realise that I have consumed more than my fair share of them – J. R. R. Tolkien, W. H. Auden, Ezra Pound, Evelyn Waugh, Benjamin Britten, and (forthcoming) Dennis Potter. I cannot complain if the supply now seems to be running out. I have noted with interest that most of my fellow biographers have responded to the dearth of contemporary subjects by going back to earlier centuries; so that, for example, Peter Ackroyd has moved from T. S. Elliot to Dickens and then further back still, to Blake. Such distant figures hold no great appeal to me. Much of the fun of contemporary biography is engaging with living people whose lives were changed by one's subject. Engaging with the subject himself, as with Runcie, was an interesting variation on this. Yes, I would certainly do it again, if I could find the right subject. Volunteers please step forward – but please remember, there is no such thing as 'background information'.

---

* But it did make another appearance in the news in March 1997, when Runcie's successor George Carey accused Runcie of 'undercutting my ministry' by his remarks in the book about the Royal Family.

Part One

Part One

1

A steady job

On 4 January 1991 I received this letter from Robert Runcie, who was then in his last month as Archbishop of Canterbury:

Lambeth Palace
London SE1 7JU
3rd January, 1991

My dear Humphrey,

I am very busy preparing for my liberation at the end of January. An idea has recently occurred to me which I hope you might be prepared to discuss at some stage. If it has to be knocked on the head without more ado, the sooner the better.

For some time people have been pressing me to approach an official biographer. I realize that I am not a natural subject for you. On the other hand your books have meant a great deal to me and I am searching for a writer rather than a theologian or church politician.

I have suffered and will, alas, continue to suffer from the unofficial sort of book. There is a collection just out which could be consigned to the category of 'Hagiographical

Stocking Fillers'. There are more to come; but nobody has yet had access to any papers in the Lambeth archives.

I am not looking for a biography that has to come out in my lifetime. Maybe it would be better not. Anyway nothing in the next five years. Yet a biographer would probably want to spend some time with me before I decline into complete decrepitude.

I do not suppose I am a very good subject because I am not myself a writer. On the other hand I have been associated with a good deal of interest in the past decade. There have been a good many people surrounding me who are writers and I suppose that I hope for something like an Inkling book.[1] That is one of my favourites. If you thought it was worth a meeting, I would be very happy to give you lunch. Frankly there are hardly any spaces in my diary before I leave Lambeth. Maybe it could wait until afterwards, but I am at the stage of destroying material and have an archivist at my elbow wishing to pounce on every morsel and a librarian wanting me to sign documents about ownership.

Have you read Owen Chadwick's biography of Michael Ramsey? That is a very different terrain, but it scores high marks on readability and breaks with the old fashioned ecclesiastical melange of letters and documents.

I keep in touch with your father and hope to see more of him after retirement. Sister Frances Dominica has arranged for me to have an Oxford pied-à-terre in the convent. They have a spare little flat, so that should mean we will see something of each other whether this prospect I have advanced appeals or appals you.

Best wishes for 1991.

Yours ever,
Robert.

By the beginning of 1991, I had been writing biographies

[1]My book *The Inklings: C. S. Lewis, J. R. R. Tolkien, Charles Williams and Their Friends*, Allen & Unwin, 1978.

for sixteen years, but I had always believed that it would be impossible to write a satisfactory life of a living person. On the other hand, I had always wanted to write a book about that curious institution, the Church of England. My father had been an Anglican bishop, and I had been brought up as an Anglo-Catholic. At the end of my teens I had drifted away from belief, and a commission some years later to write a life of Jesus Christ,[2] while giving me some belated training in theology, had not made me return to Christianity. For some while I had hoped to find a project that would allow me to examine the culture in which I had grown up.

With this in mind, an invitation from an Archbishop of Canterbury to write his authorised biography would be hard to refuse. The offer of 'papers' was particularly tempting.[3]

Another factor was my liking for Robert Runcie. I had known him and his family in the 1960s, when he was principal of Cuddesdon theological college, just outside Oxford; the official residence of the Bishop of Oxford – my father – was just across the road. The college principal was also *ex officio* the vicar, so I had listened to many of Runcie's sermons in Cuddesdon parish church. They were lively and witty, and most of his students at the college seemed to think highly of him; I sometimes played the piano for their end of term revues, at which they would mimic his distinctive way of speaking, but the spoofs were always affectionate. I had not seen him since he became Bishop of St Albans in 1970. By the mid-1980s, my parents were living in a nursing home attached to All Saints' Convent in Oxford. Its Superior, Frances Dominica (founder of the Helen House hospice for children), was a great friend of Runcie's, and he had sometimes dropped in there. His visits and conversation had brought temporary relief to my father from the deep depression which blighted the end of his life, and I was grateful for this.

[2] *Jesus* (Past Masters series), Oxford University Press, 1980.
[3] Margaret Duggan's life of Runcie had appeared in 1983, and 1991 was to see publication of two more, by Adrian Hastings and Jonathan Mantle, but none of these writers had been given access to his official papers.

4 January 1991

Dear Robert,

Many thanks indeed for your utterly surprising and absolutely delightful letter and its invitation. Obviously you require a quick answer, and the quick answer is 'yes'. We can leave the details until you're a free man. A few random observations: (1) I think you ought to realise that I am no longer a practising and believing member of the church. A plain old-fashioned agnostic, in fact. I doubt whether this is necessarily a disqualification; I think a biographer always needs a certain distance from his subject. But you ought to be aware of it. (2) I am not sure whether it would be a good idea to wait a long time. I am inclined to say let's get on with it while your memories are absolutely fresh and a large number of people want to know about it all. (3) My only serious doubt is whether you should not write an autobiography instead. As to my own timetable and commitments, I'm in what I hope is the ante-penultimate stage of a biography of Benjamin Britten. I would love to pop in and talk for a few minutes. If I am to do a book, I would like to get a glimpse or two of your working conditions. Even if this project doesn't happen, it will be delightful to see you again . . .

A few days later, I had a telephone call from him, during which we arranged for me to come to Lambeth and Canterbury the following week. He also wrote me a letter on 9 January, in which he said he had 'no ambition to write my own biography', and added: 'I don't mind your failure to pass a test of Anglican orthodoxy. One always hopes that writing my biography might be a conversion experience. But I can't think it would be.'

On Monday 14 January 1991 I went to Lambeth. The first thing I noticed was a parish church at the Palace gates which had been closed and turned into a garden museum. I can't be the first person to wonder whether this is a symbol of the present-day Church of England.

An old-fashioned bell-pull summoned a friendly porter, who directed me under an arch and into a big quadrangle, resembling a college or public school. Cars were parked on the gravel. The big door under the main tower was open, and waiting for me there was the Archbishop's secretary, Eleanor Philips, a cheery middle-aged lady with the manner of a friendly doctor's receptionist. Inside rose a big ceremonial staircase, at the top of which stood Lindy Runcie, Robert's wife, putting flowers in enormous vases. We shook hands, I gave her a kiss on the cheek, and she snapped: 'I've been up since five-fifteen.' ('She *would* say that,' remarked Runcie later.) She looked scarcely older than when I had last seen her, more than twenty years before. I had of course followed the press stories, some years before, about the Runcies' marriage supposedly being on the rocks – highly unlikely, I had thought; I remembered Lindy from Cuddesdon days as brisk and no-nonsense to the extent that she was liable to be thought rude, but the marriage had always seemed to me full of vitality and very strong.

Eleanor Phillips took me along a corridor and into a big official drawing room, to wait. A notice on the Bechstein grand in the far corner said NO OBJECTS PLEASE ON MRS RUNCIE'S TREASURED PIANO (she is a piano-teacher and performer). The big windows looked out on the garden and the public park beyond. The room had framed photos scattered around: a few of Runcie, Lindy, and their children, James and Rebecca (who had been very young in Cuddesdon days); one of Runcie with the Pope; another of him talking to Solzhenitsyn, who was uncharacteristically smiling.

Returning, Eleanor Philips led me to Runcie's study, just along the main corridor. He was on top of us almost before the door was opened, grinning, affable, almost giggling, exactly the way I remembered him from Cuddesdon, but if anything even more relaxed, scarcely looking older. Almost his first words were, 'Didn't you meet your wife when she was playing the harp in a performance at Cuddesdon of *The Hunting of the Snark*?' How on earth did he remember that?

I noticed that when he talked to me he stood very close, almost embarrassingly so. Was it natural warmth or short sight, or a trick to win people over? (I had become aware that I was already asking myself what one might call 'biographer's questions'.) Later, I discovered that it was partly a strategy to cope with deafness.

We embarked on family news, and I reported that my father (then nearly ninety) seemed to think me most unsuitable as an archiepiscopal biographer, though he would not say why. Runcie recalled going to see him before setting out to meet the Pope, and slipped into an impersonation of Ian Paisley shouting abuse at him during the Rome trip. Much had already been written about Runcie's skill at mimicry, though what I remembered from Cuddesdon was (as I have said) his students mimicking *him* – his odd Malcolm-Muggeridge-style voice, later much beloved of *Spitting Image*.

He explained that this morning a bishops' meeting was going on in a big room along the corridor; he ought to be chairing it, but he was leaving most of it to the Archishop of York, so that he could take me on a tour of the Palace: 'A walk would be a nice change.' But he would have to spend a few minutes with the bishops, so he left me to examine my surroundings.

The study, a big comfortable room overlooking the garden, was more like a sitting room than an office, with a sofa (on which Runcie had made me sit, next to him) and two comfortable armchairs. A fake-coal gas fire was burning cheerfully, and there was coffee and biscuits. A couple of telephones were on the desk, and an in-tray; most of the bookshelves were empty because the contents had been packed off to St Albans, where the Runcies were to live in retirement. He had told me that the house they had recently bought there was not his ideal choice; his own inclination would have been to retire to 'a Northern seaside town with a university library', but Lindy had kept up friendships and work as a piano-teacher in St Albans, and wanted a modern house which could be easily looked after.

In a few moments he was back from the meeting, and he

gave me Adrian Hastings' book on his ten years in office, just published.[4] 'I'm going to the launch party tonight', he said. He threw the copy across the room at me, and laughed when I dropped the catch. He also gave me the David L. Edwards collection of tributes to him by his friends, and muttered about hagiography.[5] We set off on the tour.

'Archbishops have lived at Lambeth,' he told me, 'since just after Becket's murder. They decided that the Primate ought to be near Parliament after that, rather than out in the wilds at Canterbury. A mid-Victorian architect called Blore, who finished off Buckingham Palace, did the restoration here too, and when John Betjeman (who, when I arrived at Cuddesdon, announced that the new principal was "a jolly man with a very pretty wife" – he really took to Lindy) came up the stairs once with Princess Margaret, he looked around him and observed, "Good old Blore. You know, Ma'am, this is England's Vatican." To which Princess Margaret replied: "God forbid!"'

We passed an official dining room and went into a hall. 'The Guard Chamber. Yes, the Archbishop had a private army. Oh, they seem to be laying lunch in here for the bishops. That's a pity. I thought we'd be in the dining room.' I asked who made the domestic decisions. 'We've got two splendid girls who come in on weekdays and cook, and at weekends when we need them, but Lindy and I look after ourselves in the flat upstairs. I'll take you there later.'

We went downstairs to the Great Hall, a magnificent specimen. 'This was destroyed during the Protectorate, and when it was rebuilt under Charles II they put back a medieval-style roof. Pepys said it looked reactionary. They used to entertain here, but it was also where Wycliffe had his first interrogation.' He pointed to a bronze bust. 'That's Geoffrey Fisher by Epstein.' I mentioned that Fisher was Roald Dahl's headmaster, and the origin of a lot of nightmare figures in

[4]*Robert Runcie*, Mowbray, 1991.
[5]David L. Edwards (ed.), *Robert Runcie: A Portrait by His Friends*, Fount Paperbacks, 1990.

his books. 'Well, he was Michael Ramsey's headmaster too, and when Michael became Archbishop they had to put it out of sight, because he trembled like a leaf every time he saw it. But cunning old Fisher, he gave it not to the Palace but to the Library, because he knew that libraries never give away anything, and it was certain to stay here.'

We moved on to the Library, where a new Runcie Reading Room was opened during his archbishopric; then upstairs to the flat where he and the family had been living. The first thing we saw was a flat within the flat, a small guest apartment with a couple of bedrooms. 'This is where I slept when I first began here, before Lindy came up from St Albans to join me.' For the first time, I sensed that he was sad at leaving.

A broad corridor ran down the middle of the main flat. The rooms had high ceilings, but the furniture (the Runcies' own) was plain and ordinary, and their bedroom, with a rather narrow double bed, was fairly untidy, though this was partly due to the move, which had scattered cardboard boxes everywhere. A smart-looking lady was hoovering the sitting room, but Runcie said they had no live-in help. The kitchen was very modern, with formica worktops and a washing machine churning away. 'I cook for myself if I'm alone,' he said. I imagined him buying baked beans at a corner shop, but he explained that the cooks downstairs kept the cupboard stocked.

We went down to Eleanor Phillips's office, where I was introduced to the part-time Archivist, Jane Houston, whose help I would obviously need. She told me that during Runcie's time in office the incoming mail had tripled, so that they now received about ten thousand items per year. I wondered how one secretary could deal with it. Of course there were different departments within the Palace, but it all seemed to arrive here, and Eleanor was opening envelopes as we talked. Runcie now took me off to see the chapel, which had been excellently restored – 'I'm rather proud of that; we did it.' He pointed at an alcove. 'That's where Cranmer is supposed to have written the Prayer Book.'

I was to lunch with the bishops. Runcie disappeared for a while, and someone directed me down the corridor to where they were gathering. For a moment, I felt like a new boy at a public school who had suddenly been sent into the masters' common room, but there were several familiar faces – Mark Santer of Birmingham and Jim Thompson of Stepney, who were both on the Cuddesdon staff, and Eric Kemp of Chichester, an old friend of my father. Runcie appeared at the head of the table and said grace very slowly and carefully, as if he had just thought of the words and no one in the room had ever heard them before. Bishops *en masse* seemed just like any other gathering of middle-aged, middle-class men. Some were hearty and gossipy, some waspish, some muscular, some silent and depressive.

As we stood around drinking coffee after lunch, Santer asked Runcie how Mrs Thatcher had behaved when she had made a return visit to Downing Street a few days earlier for his farewell party – her first appearance there since her deposition. 'The stuffing seems to have gone out of her a bit,' Runcie answered. 'She said to me, "We ex's must stick together." One almost feels sorry for her. But one has so many feelings about her.' He recalled meeting Thatcher at a Lambeth reception: 'I said, "Prime Minister, this is Mother Frances, who has just opened the first hospice for children." And you'd think Mrs T would have wanted to ask her something about it. But no, she looked Frances Dominica in the eye and said firmly, "Now, the thing about hospices is—" as if *she* knew more about them than anyone in the world.'

I told Runcie I thought I had taken up enough of his time. He insisted on taking me to his study to pick up my coat, though Eleanor was at his elbow: 'The Bishop of Salisbury has been on the phone, and he's been on the radio at lunchtime too.' Had the much-expected Gulf war now begun? Runcie had muttered earlier that the BBC wanted him to do *Thought for the Day* if it did. I managed to leave, though he was still at my elbow, giving me firm directions about ignoring all the NO CARS signs when I drove to the

Old Palace at Canterbury on Saturday. It seemed rather odd to emerge through the Palace gates on to the Albert Embankment, with the traffic and the view of Westminster. I felt I had been at a party in a village hall.

The following Saturday, 19 January 1991, I drove down to Canterbury, to see round the Old Palace (the Archbishop's residence), and watch Runcie in action as he conducted one of his last services in the Canterbury diocese, the institution of a new vicar in the village of Borden. His chaplain, Graham James, whom I had met at Lambeth, had told me that some archbishops had tended to use Canterbury as 'a kind of retreat' from the pressures at Lambeth, 'but Robert has resisted that temptation most of the time, I think'.

I followed Runcie's instructions, driving through Canterbury's pedestrianised inner streets, and eventually came to the cathedral close. The Old Palace stood in one corner, behind gates rather forbiddingly labelled PRIVATE, but the house was milling with people, because Lindy had invited an ecumenical charity to hold its jumble sale there. Runcie explained that this was partly to clear out their own junk before they moved.

Lindy herself was in the kitchen, organising helpers. I spotted Mr Igglesden, the Steward of the Old Palace, whom Runcie had told me to look out for. He described him as a charmingly Jeeves-like figure: 'He likes to hoist a flag when I am in residence, and seems about to say, "You rang, sir?"'

He had just taken me into Runcie's study, which (like that at Lambeth) was very much a sitting room with an inconspicuous desk, when Runcie himself arrived from some sort of farewell ceremony at the King's School. They had given him a book, a history of the school. Of course at the moment he was engaged in getting rid of books. 'But I gritted my teeth and in my most sincere manner said, "This is one book I shall not be getting rid of."'

He remarked that the Gulf war, which had started since my Lambeth visit, had increased the demands on him, but he wanted to show me round the house. It was on the site of a palace that Becket had occupied, and part of the original building had been dug up in the garden. 'It's fun to drink tea sitting on top of it, and imagine you're in Becket's sitting room.' There had been many rebuildings, the last around 1900 in a rather William Morris style. Part of the house had been turned into flats, but there was a big sunny drawing room and a rather fine chapel, created at the time of the 1900 works. Runcie said he was going to miss living in houses of this sort (Cuddesdon, St Albans, Lambeth, Canterbury) where there was so much attention to architectural detail. The house they had bought for retirement in St Albans was completely modern. He said he would have preferred an older one they had found, with a romantic view over the water meadows, 'but Lindy quite rightly said I'd be hopeless if the heating system went wrong'.

We went over to the cathedral and began our tour in the crypt. He evidently had favourite spots everywhere. 'This is an altar where I particularly like to say Mass,' he observed of one of the side-chapels. The BBC were to televise their Sunday morning service here the next day, because of the war, and he would speak during it. He had not yet finished his sermon; he told me he would turn his mind to it after the afternoon's institution service. I began to sense that he had coped with what Graham James described as 'an intractable job' by just dealing with each task as it came up, and not thinking ahead more than was strictly necessary. The crypt had been rigged with vast numbers of TV lights, and two ridiculously inappropriate easy chairs had been set up in front of the altar rail.

We went up a spiral staircase and emerged at the place where Becket is believed to have been killed. A stone tablet had recently been let into the wall to commemorate the occasion in 1982 when Runcie knelt there with the Pope. 'They used to have a framed photograph, but this is rather good – one is proud to have become part of the fabric.' Then we went up one more level, climbing over a rope into the flat open space where Becket's shrine stood until the Reformation ripped it down. Here was the Chair of St

Augustine, a stone throne positioned above and behind the high altar, and quite separate from the ordinary bishop's throne which was down below. The Chair seemed odd and primitive, like some ancient emperor's seat of power. The view down the length of the cathedral from the Chair was stunning, and almost vertical, because we were on the highest of the three levels, designed to show off the shrine. Runcie explained that the Chair was not normally used, but he had sat in it on certain special occasions, such as his enthronement. He paused a bit to choose his words, and then said: 'One feels very small.' It seemed to me that small was the last thing you would feel.

We went back to the Old Palace, where the jumble sale was still being set up. Rebecca, the Runcies' grown-up daughter, down for the weekend from her London job, ticked her father off, in her mother's style, for going where he shouldn't – 'Not through *that* door, Dad.' Then David Maple, Runcie's chaplain at Canterbury, took me off for lunch in a pub while Runcie finalised his sermon for the afternoon. Once again there would be TV cameras, this time for a regional documentary on his ten years in the Canterbury diocese.

Borden, where the institution was to take place, about half an hour's drive from Canterbury, proved to be a traditional English village – thatch and church bells – buried in the suburban sprawl of Sittingbourne. The police were directing traffic, and local mayors and MPs were filing into the crammed church; very much the Tory-party-at-prayer face of the Church of England. The TV crew were not dressed for the occasion, but were hanging about in jeans and sweaters as if the whole thing had been laid on for their benefit, and we were privileged to be in the presence of television, the real god of the age.

Runcie conducted the service clearly and unpompously, slipping in a few words of explanation now and then. He pointed out that one of the things a newly instituted vicar had to do was to declare himself a 'loyal citizen' of this country – again, the Establishment aspect of the Church. Without looking at his notes, he brought into the sermon the names of the former vicar (who had just died), the new vicar, both churchwardens, and the new vicar's wife and children. I was impressed.

I had asked to see as much as possible of him in action before he retired from the archbishopric at the end of January 1991, and the following Wednesday night I went to Lambeth for Lindy Runcie's birthday party, which was also to be a goodbye to some of their London friends. It was quite a formidable occasion, with the Runcies receiving guests formally in the big drawing room as they arrived. They were then ushered into the Guard Chamber, where there were canapés and sparkling white wine. James, the Runcies' son, a BBC television producer and director (whom I remembered at Cuddesdon as a bouncy small boy), was an affable presence, making introductions, while Runcie himself went around being the perfect host, ensuring that most people met Princess Margaret. Other VIPs included Lord Hailsham and Neil Kinnock, but there were also ordinary people from Cuddesdon village, and Terry Waite's wife Frances, who looked as if she did not wish to be there at all. (Waite had now been missing for four years.)

Runcie introduced me to her and immediately moved on. What on earth was I to say? Fortunately at that moment someone made a speech. At the end of the party, Runcie and Lindy were positioned at the top of the main staircase to say goodbye to everybody. When it was my turn, he stood about two inches from me, as usual, and remarked conspiratorially, 'A very old friend of mine says that I have to tell my biographer that I knew Rosa Lewis' (the eccentric proprietress of the louche Cavendish Hotel, who is portrayed in Evelyn Waugh's *Vile Bodies*, and whom I had written about in a book on the Waugh circle). Had Runcie thought up this titbit especially for my departure? Was there something similar for all the guests – a verbal going-away present?

Two days later, on Friday 25 January 1991, I went to one of his very last official functions as Archbishop. Billed as 'The

Opening of the Vauxhall St Peter's Heritage Centre', it was in effect the closure of this church, which stands near Lambeth Palace, as a full-time place of worship. Runcie told me he had sometimes sat in the congregation there, when he was at Lambeth without a Sunday morning engagement; now, in the Heritage era, it was to become a craft centre, with just one church service a week.

It proved to be a splendid Victorian Gothic temple of Anglo-Catholicism. The service was a typical Anglican jumble of modern and traditional, the music ranging from a pop 'The Lord's My Shepherd' to an Elgar anthem. Runcie was the celebrant, and said the prayer of consecration in a monotone which indicated his ritualist upbringing. His sermon – which he read, with only a few ad libs – included an anecdote of a Sunday when he was in the congregation at St Peter's, and a man next to him confided that he had just come out of prison, and had nowhere to go. 'Then he looked enviously at my dog-collar, and said, "At least you've got a steady job."'

At the end of the service, Lindy came up and stood by him, and they were presented with champagne and bouquets. Runcie, thanking everyone, said: 'When I first thought about ordination, many years ago, I was inspired by a church like this. I thought of myself in a ministry in the Liverpool docklands. I've never been able to manage that. But it's lovely to be able to come to a church like this at the end.'

I reflected that it was not the end, only the beginning of a new phase in his life; and now he and I had to begin serious work on his biography.

2

I'm a performer

———————◆———————

'The best plan,' Runcie wrote to me on 19 February 1991, a few days after he had moved out of Lambeth, 'would be for you to come over to St Albans and we can go out to some discreet pub.' This was to discuss the biography. We did not manage it until 4 June. On that day I drove to St Albans to take both the Runcies out to lunch. I felt that Lindy's co-operation was essential, though Robert had seemed slightly put out when I added her to the invitation.

Despite his rather dismissive description of it, their retirement home, a modern house sandwiched between Edwardian villas in a genteel side-street, seemed to me good of its kind, well designed, with plenty of space. A big living room led via a 'picture window' into a garden which Lindy had already stocked. A small side-room housed the piano where she did much of her teaching; she was also taking pupils at local private schools.

Runcie was wearing a collar and tie. They had chosen a Spanish restaurant in the town centre, where there was loud canned music, and we were the only customers. Conversation was fast and gossipy. Runcie reiterated his hope that the biography would not appear in print for a long time, but

Lindy said: 'No point in leaving it too long, Robert, or they'll have forgotten who you are.' She told me she had had a dream in which Terry Waite came through a wall like a ghost and said goodbye – 'I'm sure that means he's dead.' Runcie made no comment on his wife's belief in dreams as prophecy, nor on what he thought had happened to Waite.

On the way back to the car, we discussed the idea that Runcie and I should visit his birthplace in the Liverpool suburb of Crosby, and meet people whom he remembered from childhood. He said: 'I'll stand on Liverpool Pier Head and say, "I didn't have enough sex."' Lindy, who was walking in front of us on the narrow pavement, spun round: 'Robert, what on *earth* are you talking about?' He explained that this remark was once made by John Betjeman in a TV programme, when asked what he most regretted about his early years.[1]

Later that day, after I had driven home, I began to wonder whether Runcie's thoroughly secular, gossipy manner over lunch might not be an example of his well-known characteristic of taking on other people's style, chameleon-fashion, when in their company. Maybe I was just getting a reflection of my own sense of humour?

Though he had shown some concern about the biography being published fairly soon, he had not discussed with me what sort of book it should be, nor had he asked for any sort of veto over the text. Knowing from personal experience how much difficulty such vetoes can cause, I said nothing.

We did not meet again until the end of 1991. I was finishing my Britten biography, and persuading the Britten Trustees – who had a veto – not to censor it; meanwhile Runcie was away on foreign trips, including lecturing on a Swan Hellenic Cruise. A letter from him on 15 August 1991 gave a few glimpses of an American visit:

We have enjoyed a mixture of business and pleasure in

[1] It was subsequently used in a TV commercial.

the States. We managed to see the Grand Canyon in an interlude from the General Convention. My address was jammed between 'Human Sexuality' and 'Inclusive Language'. However, I must not laugh too much as I was impressed by the enthusiasm of this inflated General Synod . . . I baptised a child in a service in a grottier part of Phoenix. It was immensely hot and I managed to stumble through the service in Spanish but preached in English. A small child was heard to say to her parents, 'Mom, his Spanish is okay but his English is terrible.' . . .

In some ways this is a defensive letter. I have returned to an immense amount of mail and . . . am under intense pressure to do programmes for the hostages. It will get worse as the news gets better. Everyone wants an up-date on the programme which they have in the can for the return of Terry.

Lindy's dream had proved misleading; Terry Waite was released in November, after nearly five years in captivity in Beirut. On 6 December I attended a party at which Runcie was to be guest of honour, at Shotover House, near Oxford, to celebrate his new title of 'Lord Runcie of Cuddesdon'. Among those there was John Garton, the present principal of Cuddesdon College. Looking conspiratorial, he described to me the sudden and dramatic appearance of Terry Waite at the college a few days before. Waite and Runcie had decided to meet for a talk – their first private one since his release – somewhere between St Albans and RAF Lineham, where Waite had been since arriving on British soil. 'And lo,' said Garton, 'where should Terry turn up but Cuddesdon, accompanied by a posse of what were clearly not RAF but MI6 men.' Waite and Runcie talked very privately for a while, and when they emerged Runcie said to Garton: 'I've told Terry that everything is going to be all right' – an intriguing remark in view of continuing press speculation about Waite's involvement with Colonel North, though Garton made no comment about this.

On 7 January 1992 I met Runcie in his 'flat' at All

Saints' Convent, Oxford – in reality just a bedsitter with kitchenette and shower in one of the shed-like outbuildings. He was putting books on the shelves and setting out family photos, not apparently having used the place before, though he had retired nearly a year earlier. He made Nescafé for us, and listed the people we ought to see when we went to Crosby; also those of his relatives I ought to contact for family background. He gave rather scathing, but not unsympathetic, word-portraits of several of the people he mentioned. Then he became rather embarrassed and told me, after some preamble, that I would in due course come across the matter of his letters to a Mrs Jenny Boyd-Carpenter, a great friend and supporter during his archbishopric. She wrote to him in playfully romantic terms and he, perhaps unwisely, had responded in kind. He said I was not to suppose that they had an affair. I recalled the tabloids' insinuations about the Runcies' marriage, but let the subject pass without comment.

The Crosby trip was fixed for 13–15 April 1992. By the time we set out, I had managed to meet Runcie's surviving sister and brother, Margery and Kenneth, and his brother-in-law Angus Inglis. Angus had been married to Runcie's sister Kathleen, the eldest of the four children, who had died a few years earlier.

The first thing that struck me when Margery (aged seventy-nine, nine years older than Robert) answered the bell of her flat in Nottingham was her soft Lancashire accent – the accent you would expect from somebody brought up on the edge of Liverpool. There remains scarcely a trace of this in Runcie's own speech.

Margery had frizzy grey hair, an attractive twinkle and a considerable sense of humour. Her brother Kenneth, who was staying with her, was tall and rather shy at first, but did not mind my tape recorder, and soon grew quite forthcoming. In contrast, Angus Inglis, aged eighty-four, living with an elderly housekeeper in an old rectory in Lincolnshire, seemed very much the Oxford man, scattering his conversation with names of celebrated church and academic figures whom I was expected to recognise. I learnt a great deal about Runcie's background and early life from all three, and was able to use this when I began to question him on the way to Crosby. When he and I set off up the M1, with me driving, I switched on the tape recorder and asked him what he knew of his grandparents.

'I hardly know anything,' he answered. 'I'm rather surprised at how uncurious I am and have been about it.' I said I knew that his mother's family came from Ireland, but I gathered she did not like being thought of as Irish. 'That's right. She was proud of the family she'd created, rather more than of the family from which she came. Her brother Billy made a brief appearance in my childhood, but she had been cut off by her family for some reason. She sent some cheque back home to them in Norwich, and it had been returned torn up. Then Uncle Billy Benson turned up. I can remember him saying, in a rather Norfolk accent, "Blood's thicker than water", and pressing a pound note into my paw. He was in charge of a ginger beer factory in Norwich. I thought, the Benson family must be rather better than I've been led to believe. But it didn't last. Something happened, and within months it was all off again.' He did not know what was the cause of his mother's rift with her family, but guessed it was 'marrying my father'.

Runcie's elder sister Kathleen wrote some notes on the family history, for Margaret Duggan's 1983 biography of him. These state that his mother, Ann Edna Benson,

was one of the five children of Richard Henry Benson & Sarah Gunning, a daughter of John Gunning of Dublin. They came over to England after they married & settled in Norwich where he was employed by Norman & Beard's the organ builder. There was disapproval of Sarah's marriage & consequent estrangement with the Gunning family. This meant little or no contact with the Irish side of the family.

So here we have an estrangement in the generation *before*

Runcie's mother broke with her family, which only makes the matter more puzzling. And what about Uncle Billy and the ginger beer factory? Kathleen's notes continue:

> Grandfather Benson was an independent & rather colourful character. In addition to his work at N & B he had a small mineral factory of his own where he also assembled parts of old organs & rebuilt them. In 1979 Mr Norman told me that there were small organs known as 'Paddy Bensons' . . . The younger son Billy [crossed out] William . . . took on the mineral factory . . . After our grandparents died in 1922, Mother did not have any close contact with her Norfolk family.

The transformation of Billy to William and the ginger beer factory to a 'mineral' business is apparently characteristic of Kathleen, whom Runcie describes as having a 'suburban respectability hang-up', though he adds that she was 'a person of great quality'.

On the subject of class-consciousness, I asked more about his vague belief that his mother had earned her family's disapproval for 'marrying my father'. Did he mean marrying beneath her? 'I don't know. I wouldn't have thought my father was a bad match. It may have been her going off and becoming a hairdresser, and also marrying too early, maybe, at nineteen – a nineteen-year-old girl leaving Norwich and marrying a Liverpool engineer – though how she met him I don't know.' He would only have to open the earlier biography of him by Margaret Duggan to find out:

> He [Runcie's father] had been in Liverpool three years when he went with a friend to the theatre where they met two girls, one of whom his friend knew. The other girl immediately attracted [him]. She was very pretty, slim and shapely, but it was her vivid auburn curls that made men look twice. She was introduced as Nancy Benson (her Christian names were Ann Edna), and she had recently

come from Norwich to live with friends at Rock Ferry and to finish her training as a hairdresser in Liverpool.[2]

After her marriage, Mrs Runcie did some hairdressing at home. Runcie's sister Margery told me that she worked as 'Madame Edna', and added: 'I always remember some little tot coming along and saying to my father, "Are you Mister Madame Edna?"' Kathleen's 'Notes' do not mention Madame Edna, and Runcie had never heard his mother's professional name until I told him (she must have abandoned it before his time). He was highly amused. 'Of course,' he said to me apologetically, 'it's a very suburban world. I hope you're not feeling, "Oh, crumbs, I'll never make anything of this."'

Kathleen also makes no mention of their father's antagonism to clergymen. Runcie explained to me that, at any early stage in his archbishopric, 'when people interviewed me about my father, and heard he was an engineer who didn't have much time for parsons or policemen, this – added to the fact that I came from Liverpool and went to a council school at first – led to some journalist suggesting that my father was a kind of Alf Garnett character.'

He said this had upset Kathleen, who was 'very concerned to protect our middle-class status'. Sure enough, Kathleen's account of their father stresses that he was 'chief electrical engineer' at the Liverpool sugar refinery of Tate & Lyle. Similarly Kathleen's husband Angus, when I went to see him, was much concerned to emphasise his father-in-law's gentility: 'He was a natural gentleman, he really was. He took on this very responsible job as electrical engineer for Tate & Lyle. He had a staff, and was middle management, I suppose, but he always identified with the working men. They elected him as president of their football club. He had such exquisite manners: this Scottish background of good manners and beautiful speech. I don't think I've ever heard anyone speak more beautifully.'

[2]Margaret Duggan, *Runcie: the Making of an Archbishop*, Hodder & Stoughton, 1983, p. 47. Hereafter referred to as Duggan.

This however, is not, the portrait of Robert Dalziel Runcie which emerges from Runcie's own recollections. I asked him if he knew why his father, whose family had been tailors in Kilmarnock, became an engineer and moved south to Liverpool. 'I don't know that. He was a keen engineer, though he also had poetical and lyrical sensitivities – a reciter of poetry, a singer of ballads. And a thoroughly delightful easy-going man. Infuriatingly contented (as I probably am myself). And I always remember, when I was small, my mother – who was an emotional person – rising from the breakfast table, taking a plate, and throwing it on the floor, taking my father's hat and throwing it at him, and storming in tears out of the room. And my father getting on with his oatcake and saying to me, "What a temper!" Not moving to comfort her or taking any notice of it.

'I loved my father; I thought he was a wonderful man. He was on the committee of a local club, the Waterloo Football Club, and also of a baseball club called the Crystal Club. He came home on a Saturday, had his lunch, and then he would put his feet up and have forty winks (as he called it), and I remember longing for him to wake up so that we could go out to watch football or baseball. We sometimes used to go to watch Liverpool or Everton, but mainly to this club, Waterloo, and we went in the dressing room afterwards. But I was always pushed outside. I suspect the language, and all those sweaty characters naked in baths, was thought to be inappropriate for a small boy. My father had that sense of decency, you know; he did keep me away from what must have been his men's club life.'

But what about his father's anti-clericalism, mentioned by Margaret Duggan and others who had written about the Runcies? It was 'undoubtedly there', said Runcie; and Joan Morgan, Kathleen Runcie's best friend in schooldays, whom we met during the Crosby visit, remembered Mr Runcie being 'scornful of clerics, really scornful. But then,' she added, 'he was brought up as a Presbyterian.' Runcie agreed with this: 'Definitely. He was scornful of the clergy, and would say, "Never trust parsons or policemen", but he wouldn't speak against religion (it wouldn't be like Lindy's father, who *would* speak against it). Hypocrisy he hated, cant. I can't remember ever having any religious discussion with him. We were very close, but I can't remember ever having that.'

He recalled spending childhood Sunday mornings going for a walk with his father to the edge of Crosby, where the open country began: 'It'll all be built over now, but we used to see a man in a greenhouse there – he was a market gardener. And my mother had obviously been told that we were going to buy sweet peas and things like that. But looking back, I can see the real purpose of the visit was the conversation in this hot greenhouse about which greyhound was going to win the Waterloo Cup. My father was very keen on the dogs, and he regarded this man as an astute tipster. You could never hear the man; he spoke in the huskiest voice, and always had a fag drooping from his lips. And I was set loose to wander in the fields, bird-nesting, whilst my father was in this greenhouse, or else in the pub nearby. It was a little area of Sunday morning which I thoroughly enjoyed.'

Mr Runcie was not often at home in the evenings: 'He went out every night,' recalled Runcie, 'to his club, a bowling and drinking club, of which he was President. He was a great clubman, a man's man. And we used to go for Sunday cricket to Ince Blundell, where there were rhododendrons, and I remember my father being embarrassed because we were having a cup of tea together during the tea interval, and some Scottish friend came and looked on us and said to my father, "Tea, Bob? That's a new drink for ye! To see ye drinkin' a cup o' tea!"'

Runcie recalls that his father spoke in a 'soft West Scottish voice', but knows very little about the paternal family background. Again, we have to turn to Kathleen for details:

James Runcie [Runcie's paternal grandfather] was a draper and tailor in Kilmarnock. By his first marriage to Isabella McKellar of Tarbet he had one son, Robert [Runcie's father], and two daughters, Catherine and Florence. The mother died when they were young children, and James married as his second wife Sarah Picken and had three more daughters. She died when the youngest was only three years old, and after his father's early death Robert found himself at the age of twenty the eldest of a family of five young sisters. There were two uncles who were prosperous flour merchants and within the family the girls were cared for, while Robert was apprenticed to engineering in Greenock, eventually leaving Scotland for Liverpool, where he settled for the rest of his life.

Runcie's second and third Christian names, Alexander Kennedy, were chosen from two of his father's Scottish friends. And how did Mrs Runcie fit into her husband's men's-club world? Runcie says he was 'rather conscious of my mother playing the soulful left-at-home from time to time. She went to the cinema at least twice a week, I think, and read avidly – detective novels and romantic novels. And I think he was the sort of man who went out and bought the Christmas presents on Christmas Eve, and spent too much on them to make up for the fact that he hadn't bothered until the last moment. And later in life, when things became difficult, I can remember my mother making much of the long hours she'd spent at home while Father was at the club.'

Yet she had her own social life, which may have been a greater threat to family stability than her husband's. Kathleen writes of this:

She went with a friend as freelance hairdressers on Cunard cruises during the early Twenties – one cruise in 1923 was round the world. This seems an extraordinary thing to have done at that time, to leave a young family to the care of others, but there seem not to have been unhappy memories for the children although the boys must have been affected by her absence.

Runcie provides more details: 'My mother had friendships

in the Cunard Line. She was friendly with a lady called Peggy Levy, her co-hairdresser, and they went round the world together. And when I was a small boy there was a man who came round, a steward called Bill Barnard who brought all the news from Cunard, and he was a regular, and used to arrive and bring wonderful American chocolates and Turkish cigarettes, and there was a kind of Bill Barnard smell to the house. He was obviously a favoured visitor. I have the impression that Father was tolerant of my mother's cosmopolitan, romantic world of San Francisco and Cairo – she'd been to these places, and brought back useless trinkets, some of which still feature in my house. It enables me, whenever I give an address in Yokohama, to say, "My mother was here, and I was brought up with a dream of one day coming to Yokohama."'

Her 1923 trip was made when Robert was not yet two (a great aunt came and looked after him). He has no recollection of his mother's absence, but Kenneth, who was ten, remembered feeling 'terribly forsaken, because it went on and on, for about four or five months. I resented it.' She was in her mid-thirties at the time of this world tour; Kathleen writes that she was 'considered to be beautiful with large brown eyes and red gold hair', and adds that her mother was 'somewhat indolent and a dreamer, not demonstratively affectionate'.

I asked Margery and Kenneth whether they thought there had been a strong relationship between their mother and Robert, her youngest child. 'No,' answered Margery. 'Mother was not that sort of person, really. Mother was marvellous and we loved her very much, but she was not what I would call a gathering-in sort of person, was she ?' Kenneth agreed: 'Oh no, not at all.' Margery added: 'But Father was. Very much.' Was it a happy marriage, as far as they could tell? 'Yes,' said Margery. 'That's why no one can understand why she went away. We never talked about it. I remember just taking it for granted that mothers went away. Though I never knew anybody else whose mother did go away.'

Runcie himself speaks of his mother in a more restrained manner than he uses of his father: 'Looking back, I find it quite difficult to do my mother justice. She expended a great deal of love and affection on us, but she was sentimental, and she wasn't a great organiser of the domestic scene, not a good manager. I've got no evidence for it, but I cannot believe that the Bill Barnard connection was not symbolic of a whole world of human relationships there. And I can't believe that my father's clubland was entirely innocent of other relations. (My father was apparently a very good dancer, and had a well-used dinner jacket.) I was never conscious that the marriage was under strain; the very fact that I was jolted by the breaking of the plate shows it was unusual. But I think my father and mother must have had quite a lot of separate lives. Tears were not infrequent. It wasn't an unhappy household, but there would be scenes. My mother would say things like, "Maybe I'll go out and throw myself under a bus, and then you'll be sorry." And I was always very embarrassed by this. And my father quite rightly picked up his trilby hat and went off to his club.'

We arrived at Crosby at lunchtime on 13 April, Runcie having talked tirelessly about his family all the way up the M1. Chris Price, head of English at Runcie's old school, Merchant Taylors', was going to show us round. We picked him up from his home, then checked in at the Blundellsands, the district's smartest hotel: red-brick baronial and, to my southern eyes, solidly north-country. Runcie had suggested that we stay there because he had done so a few months earlier on a visit to Merchant Taylors' to unveil his portrait. When I told the hotel he was coming back, they decided to put him in their biggest suite (while, mercifully, only charging me, who was paying, for two single rooms).

We had a bar lunch with Chris Price, and then set out on the tour, starting at 26 Queen's Road, where the Runcies lived for most of Robert's childhood. Crosby nowadays is just another traffic-ridden suburb, though it gets grander and more salubrious at the Blundellsands end, down by the shore, where the Mersey becomes the Irish Sea. Queen's Road is a cul-de-sac near a noisy road junction, with Victorian houses, largely run to seed. The present owner of 26 turned out to be a charming *Educating Rita* lookalike, determinedly getting herself qualified academically in mid–life. The house, an 1880s double-fronted semi with garden, was full of books, which had evidently not been the case in the Runcies' day – apart from Mrs Runcie's light reading, and her husband's copy of Burns. Runcie told me there were open fields behind it when they moved there from an earlier family home in Moor Lane. Judging by the size of the house, they were quite a prosperous family; they always had a servant (but everyone above working-class level did in the 1920s). Runcie peered into the bathroom and recalled 'Father shaving with his cut-throat razor, the while singing Harry Lauder songs'. He described the floor above as 'the nursery floor'.

He recalled amusing himself up there in childhood: 'I used to put on performances up in the attic of 26 Queen's Road, and invite the family up to my concerts. It was like my games-playing, which had to be with myself, so that I played for both sides.' (Kenneth was eight years older than him, Margery ten, Kathleen twelve, so he was brought up virtually as an only child.) 'And there was a toy saxophone that you could play, and I would be conducting, and playing it, and announcing: "This is Jack Payne and his boys, playing to you tonight from—" It was a performance. I'm a performer.'

I put it to him that the 26 Queen's Road household was not what we would now call cultured: 'No, it wasn't. And I've suffered all my life from not having read so many of the basic texts. Or I've come to them late in life, because my reading was done much more at school than at home. That's not entirely true; we had a well-thumbed copy of Shakespeare, and Burns, and Tennyson; it wasn't entirely without books. But when we went to the theatre, we went to Jack Hylton at the Liverpool Empire, and comics like Clapham and Dwyer, and Tommy Handley. And I had a passionate interest in jazz bands – Jack Payne and Ambrose and Harry Roy, and Orlando [*sic,* for Carroll] Gibbons at the Savoy. I can tell you more about that than about my reading list in those days.'

In his attic performances, did he do his own version of the comedians? 'Yes, absolutely. I was able to do' – he slips into a cockney accent – '"'Allo, 'allo, 'allo, I was walking along the road the other day, and met a man—" and all that kind of thing.' What did he want to be when he was a small boy? 'Oh, I think a bandleader.'

From Queen's Road we drove to Merchant Taylors' Boys School, which I found rather oppressive. The buildings have the look of a typical old-style grammar school, though these days it is independent. It was founded in the seventeenth century, but moved to this site in late Victorian times, and nothing is visible of its earlier history. When Chris Price started to name masters whom Runcie was likely to remember, Runcie launched into a series of impersonations of them – bad-tempered middle-aged men with a variety of speech defects. It made the place sound grotesque, but no doubt it was much the same as any other boys' school of the period.

Runcie's portrait, which hangs in the library, makes it look as if he is sitting on a sofa in the middle of Canterbury Cathedral. I would have thought it was rather embarrassing for him to be confronted with any portrait, let alone this, but he seemed not to mind, and suggested that it might benefit from being hung a bit lower. Later, he said that he is not keen on any of his portraits; yet there is one hanging in the Runcies' sitting room in St Albans.

Runcie told me he arrived at Merchant Taylors' when he was nine, but Margaret Duggan states that he was eleven. Obviously a check in the school records would clear this up, but the Crosby trip made me wonder how much this sort of detail really matters. When we left the school and Chris Price took us on a tour of the 'village' (as they still used to call it in Runcie's childhood), Runcie was unable to give the address in Moor Lane where his family had lived before moving to Queen's Road – he was very young when they left (Duggan says it was number 6). More remarkably, he did not know exactly where he had been born, nor did he seem interested. Kathleen's friend Joan Morgan said she thought it was in Little Crosby, a mile or so up the road (and still a village today), and sure enough when I got home and looked it up in Duggan, he was born there at a midwife's house, on 2 October 1921.

It is conventional for biographers to build up their narratives from this sort of detail. But what sort of 'truth' does it lead to? I realised I was responding to things about him which appealed to my particular taste – for example, his juvenile desire to be a bandleader, because I myself did become one, part-time, for a while.

After the 'village' tour, Chris Price's wife gave us a large tea, and then we drove down to the seafront, passing the sites of Coronation Road Primary School where Runcie had his first education, and the Methodist Sunday School which he hated. At Coronation Road he was taught by Jessie Gale, who was still alive when Margaret Duggan was doing her research. Duggan writes that Miss Gale 'knew Bobby Runcie as a quiet little boy, already tall and leggy for his age, with tightly-curled auburn hair the same colour as his mother's. He was bright and learned quickly.'[3]

Runcie himself had little to say to me about Coronation Road, except that 'the headmaster's name was Mr Ambrose, the same as the London bandleader'. He guessed that he had been sent to the Methodist Sunday School by his mother, who had been brought up in the Church of England, and 'thought that going to church was a good thing'. Kenneth had told me that she was delighted when he joined a local choir. 'She rather liked the idea of sentimental little cherubs, and she might turn up, just to hear her little boy sing out of tune.' All four Runcie children attended the Sunday School in turn, though Margery recalls that 'it was my sister Kath who started us going' rather than their mother. Why Methodist? Joan Morgan, who also attended it, says

[3]Duggan, p. 51.

that it served all denominations, and Margery confirms this: 'I think everybody bar the Catholics went.'

Runcie says he was 'terrified' by it: 'I hated the pictures of the sacrifice of Isaac, the hand that was going to sacrifice the child being stayed by the hand of God. They had a kind of gloomy religious-picture feel about them which frightened me. And so I gave it up, and nobody minded; in fact I'm not quite sure who made me go in the first instance.' Does he think it possible that Kathleen, rather than his mother, had enrolled him? 'Yes, I think that might be so, because Kath was, after all, twelve years older than I was, and she was quite capable of taking an initiative. She would have got into a crowd at school who were keen on Sunday School, and would have organised it.'

Margery, Kenneth and Angus all told me that Kathleen's headmistress at Merchant Taylors' Girls School, Miss Fordham, had persuaded Kathleen to become a churchgoer. Runcie agreed – 'Miss Fordham had a terrific influence on her' – and he recommended me to look at a book that the novelist Beryl Bainbridge had mentioned to him. (They had met at a 'Scouse lunch' given for fellow Liverpudlians by John Birt of the BBC.) This book, *The Merchant Taylors' School for Girls, Crosby: One Hundred Years of Achievement, 1888–1988,* by Sylvia Harrop,[4] records that Emily Fordham arrived as headmistress in 1922, aged nearly forty. She was 'a very large woman, heavy on her feet and severely and plainly dressed', with 'a lovely speaking voice, a beautiful rich deep contralto'.[5] The previous headmistress had been sacked for slack management, and Miss Fordham had an iron fist from the start. She dismissed most of the staff, replaced them with her own picked team, instituted a formal celebration of her own birthday, and inaugurated a Church Parade on Ascension Day to St Faith's, the local Anglo-Catholic church (her own taste being for high church worship). The Boys School also walked to church that day, but they went to the

[4]Liverpool University Press, 1988.
[5]pp. 79–80.

evangelical church, St Luke's – the original parish church for Crosby.

Margery, who was also at Merchant Taylors' Girls, told me she did not get on with Miss Fordham, but Kathleen had been one of the headmistress's favourites. Miss Fordham had introduced Kathleen to the vicar of another Anglo-Catholic church in the district, St Thomas's, Seaforth (by this time Miss Fordham had fallen out with the vicar of St Faith's), and Kathleen was confirmed and became a regular communicant there. Runcie agreed with this account, and said that Kathleen in turn 'went through the same motions with me', that is, stage-managed his becoming a churchgoer. Margery, on the other hand, said she had 'opted out from church, because my sister was a bit bossy, and I wouldn't be bossed!'

I asked Margery and Kenneth if all four children had been baptised in infancy. Margery answered: 'Oh yes, well, we presume so!' She laughed and added: 'Don't remember.' Kenneth added: 'I was certainly confirmed, when I went into the choir at St Mary's, Waterloo Park.' This raised the interesting possibility that Robert had never been baptised. I asked him. He said he was – 'I've got a record of it' – and when I told him that the others were uncertain, commented: 'That is rather curious, isn't it? Kath would have been twelve; she might even have influenced them about it' – that is, persuaded her parents to have the new baby baptised.[6]

His mention of Beryl Bainbridge led me to write to her to ask for her impressions of Crosby. She replied that she used to come in by train from Formby to go to school at Merchant Taylors' Girls in the 1940s, when the place had not changed much. 'It was sort of raffish, the kind of place that Mr Hulot went to for his holiday. I think it was already becoming run-down, though originally people settled there who had done well for themselves.' What about the Runcie household having almost no books? 'Nobody had. Though

[6]Duggan, p. 45, writes that he was christened on 22 November 1921 at St Luke's, Crosby.

very keen on education, one's parents thought books untidy. One or two houses boasted a glass fronted bookcase, but the key was always hidden or said to be lost. But we did go to the library a lot.'

After passing the sites of Coronation Road school and the Sunday School – both vanished now – Runcie and I reached the seafront. We got out to stretch our legs, and he was immediately approached by a man driving a battered ambulance containing another man in a wheelchair: 'My friend thought he recognised you.' Runcie went over and talked to the disabled man for about ten minutes, all the time keeping one hand on his arm. Meanwhile the driver chatted to me about the terrible economic climate in Liverpool: 'We've been in recession for twelve years.'

On the drive to Crosby, Runcie and I had discussed the previous week's surprise Tory General Election victory. He said he and Lindy felt very sorry for the Kinnocks, but the Majors had been very nice to them. 'I'm not really a political creature,' he added. 'I don't take political stands, I just get moved by individual issues.' He said he bought *The Times* by choice, 'for tradition rather than quality', but he found the *Daily Telegraph* (for which, since retirement, he had sometimes reviewed books) 'the best all round newspaper'. On Sunday he took both the *Sunday Telegraph* and the *Observer* to get a good balance. Lindy enjoyed the music columns of the *Guardian*.

After his chat with the man in the wheelchair, Runcie was immediately accosted by another man who had got out of a car, a working-class Catholic, who told us: 'I belong to the Labour Party at prayer.' Afterwards, I remarked to Runcie on his recognisability. 'I don't really mind,' he said, 'because I can get a lot from all kinds of people, whether they're Etonians or the opposite. And there's a side of one that would be rather sorry when people no longer recognise me.'

Going to bed that night at the Blundellsands, I made a note that he seemed to be more comfortable taking orders from other people than giving them – he was happily falling in with all my plans for the trip, even when I changed them as we went along. He had said to me that it was difficult since retirement having to plan his own life; he had been so used to being told what to do by his staff. Did that start in childhood with Kath organising him? Was he, I wondered, essentially a passive character?

3

Compartments

―――•―――

I had the same feeling at breakfast next morning in the hotel
dining room. He said he would just eat muesli, but looked
enviously at my huge cooked breakfast when it arrived, and
I easily persuaded him to accept a sausage, which he tucked
into a bun like a hot dog. He told me that he had been
rung at the hotel and asked to take the memorial service
for Earl Spencer, father of the Princess of Wales, who had
just died. He could not, as he was going to Armenia to open
a hospital.

After breakfast we set off to see Peter Gallant, whose
family lived in Queen's Road in Runcie's childhood and
who had never left Crosby. Over tea and scones (which we
both managed to eat a little of, despite the big breakfast)
the conversation turned to the Irish contingent of the Crosby
population in the 1930s. Runcie explained to me that, besides
Merchant Taylors', 'there was also St Mary's College, which
was the Christian Brothers' boys school. We weren't too
conscious of them; there was much more of a separation
between Prots and Catholics in those days, and it's only
now, when I speak to people like John Birt at the BBC,
or Roger McGough, who were both at St Mary's [some

years after Runcie was at Merchant Taylors'], that I realise
what a significant school it was. We always looked down
upon them.'

Kenneth and Margery had mentioned the Protestant-
Catholic divide, and Margery recalled that the family had
had an Irish Catholic maid, who 'used to take me round
to the Catholic church. Father used to grumble a little bit,
but I was always allowed to go.' Runcie produced a similar
recollection: 'There were people to help [in the house], and
one of them took me to the Catholic church, when I was
a small boy. I was taken into this church, which seemed to
be different from other buildings I'd been in, and I was told
that God was behind that curtain [the tabernacle containing
the reserved sacrament]. And I was always rather scared of
that building.'

Later in our second day at Crosby, we stopped outside
this church, SS Peter & Paul, in the Liverpool Road. Runcie,
who had not been inside since childhood, was rather moved
by what he saw when we opened the door. 'A place that
makes you want to pray,' he said. But before that, after
leaving the Gallants', we went to a mid-morning Mass
at St Faith's, the Anglo-Catholic church at which, thanks
to the encouragement of his sister Kathleen, he became a
communicant member of the Church of England. He had
outlined this story to me during the drive up the M1: 'There's
a man called David Mullineux, dead now, who was my best
friend at school, and keen on football and cricket, and it was
along with him that I went to be prepared for confirmation
– and didn't take it very seriously.'

Confirmation was part of the social scene in Crosby in
the 1930s. As Joan Fell, another of Runcie's friends from
those years, puts it, 'Your mothers made you have music
lessons, and dancing lessons, and you were confirmed. I had
a little white veil; and then we had a big family party with
the godparents, and a little Bible given to me, and a lovely
tea. It meant nothing to me at all.'

Runcie might have avoided this adolescent rite of passage –
Kathleen had only been confirmed because of Miss Fordham,

Kenneth because he had joined a choir – but Mullineux and other friends had signed up for confirmation classes at evangelical St Luke's, and Runcie tagged along with them, largely (as he admitted on *Desert Island Discs* while still Archbishop) because the group included a girl named Betty Cooke, to whom he was attracted. The newspapers made quite a fuss about this revelation, and Betty Cooke did not feature on Runcie's list of people to meet in Crosby, even though she still lives in the area under her married name; he seemed slightly embarrassed when I asked about her. However, we did see Audrey McCulloch, who vividly recalled his romantic appeal to the Merchant Taylors' Girls when she had been at school there. 'The girls were all very keen on him. And I said, "I must see this Bobby Runcie." We used to hang over the fence at Merchant Taylors' Boys, watching them all play cricket, and somebody said, "That's Bobby Runcie! That's Bobby Runcie!" He had gorgeous auburn hair.'

Similarly Joan Fell, who lived near the Runcies in Queen's Road, says she 'used to look at him from the bedroom window, because I had this crush on him – Bobby Runcie, with beautiful auburn curls, very tall and lanky and rather serious-looking. His hair was his main feature. He had really beautiful hair.' Towards the end of his time at Merchant Taylors' he took Joan to a school dance: 'One day he said, "Would you like to come to the Merchant Boys dance, Joan?" And it was *the* thing at the Girls School, if you were asked to go. I kept it to myself; I wouldn't tell anybody in the form. I thought, "Oh, I'm going with Bobby Runcie to the Boys School dance!" And he came for me in a taxi, and I wore a mauve taffeta bridesmaid's frock – but I don't think he danced with me much when we got there. I thought he was a bit of a dead loss!'

Runcie himself recalls the easy romantic atmosphere of those days – 'We used to meet in gangs on the steps of the public library, and you changed your girl friend every fortnight' – and seems to have had no sexual hang-ups in adolescence, though he freely admits to two brushes with homosexuality: 'I remember a male friend making advances on me once, which I didn't care for – nothing more than sort of fondling, nothing heavy, we weren't old enough (about thirteen or so). And I remember once I went by mistake to an evangelical camp, a varsity and public school camp, in the sixth form, and we all shared a tent. And there was a rather beautiful boy with whom I had a fight on the first night, a friendly fight, and I put my arms around him and said "I love you" or something like that, and began being amorous with him as a joke. And he came from some school like Westminster, and he said, "You're a bloody homo. I knew you were." And I was terribly shocked at this. But it was totally innocent.'

Having enrolled at the St Luke's confirmation class chiefly on account of Betty Cooke, he did not take the proceedings seriously. None of them did. 'It was a large class, and the man who taught us was standing in front of a mirror, so you could pull faces in the mirror at other members of the group. And I remember going to services at St Luke's, which had plush cushions in the pews, and a deep heavy red carpet, and a clergyman with a large moustache. I remember sitting in the free seats [those for which pew rents were not payable] at the back with David Mullineux and eating toffees and doing impersonations of the vicar. We tended to leave in giggles.'

His churchgoing might have ended then and there, if it had not been for his sister Kathleen. By then in her mid-twenties, she had taken a diploma in social science at Liverpool University, and become a social worker in Liverpool and then in the East End of London. Runcie 'can't believe she would have approved of my going to St Luke's', which was far too low for her Miss Fordham-educated religious taste; but, as it happened, the actual confirmation service for the group of local churches was held in St Faith's, the Anglo-Catholic church down the road, and Runcie, going there for the service, found that it had 'great atmosphere'. This made a 'big impression' on him, compared to St Luke's. (Duggan gives the date of the confirmation as Lent 1936, when he was fourteen.)

He would normally have been expected to make his first communion at St Luke's, where he had been instructed, but at this point Kathleen, who was at home for the weekend, stepped in: 'She said, "Why don't you go to St Faith's?"' And so, on Passion Sunday, he made his first communion there, alongside his sister. His parents, though they had attended the confirmation service, did not come to the first communion.

At this point, the very efficient machinery of St Faith's took over: 'A keen curate got hold of me that first Sunday, Passion Sunday, and said, "Come here for Easter. And you ought to join our Bible class." And they got their claws into me, so that in quite a short time I was put under training to be a server. There was Bible class on Sunday afternoon, and a club during the week – table-tennis and billiards – and a nativity play at Christmas. I was struck by the way I was put to work as soon as I touched St Faith's.' Possibly this was Kathleen's doing, too; Duggan writes that she had asked the vicar, John Schofield, to 'keep a special eye' on her brother.[1]

Though 'spikey' (ritualistic) in comparison to St Luke's, St Faith's was only moderately high church. Canon Bob Honner, who arrived as a curate not long after Runcie joined the congregation, says: 'It was not flamboyant. We were very rigidly Prayer Book – no Benediction, and certainly no incense. But we did have processions, and the music was superb. We had a daily Mass, but we didn't call it Mass, and we were referred to not as "Father" but "Mister"! We had a group of the older boys who were servers and leaders in the Scouts and so on who met in the upper room on a Sunday afternoon for instruction by the curates – a kind of continuing confirmation group; we called it the Upper Room. And twice a week we had a boys' club in the church hall. Robert Runcie was just one of the young people of the parish whom everybody liked, who was a very outgoing, friendly, stimulating person.'

The religious instruction Runcie had been given (and had

[1]Duggan, p. 58.

ignored) at St Luke's was not the first he had received: 'My mother taught me to kneel down and say my prayers at night – "Gentle Jesus, meek and mild, / Look upon a little child", and the Lord's Prayer – and I had intermittently done that.' So religion 'wasn't a totally strange world'; he had just not considered it seriously. Now, at St Faith's, 'I took more of an interest in my prayers. I served diligently once or twice on weekdays, and made my Confession three times a year. And I was rather careful to prepare for Communion, and I used my *Communicants' Manual*, and the Anglo-Catholic *St Swithin's Prayer Book*, and *A Prayer Book for Men and Boys*. Indeed, the prayers surrounding Communion – preparation and thanksgiving – were a nodal point in my prayer-life. The school assemblies hadn't meant much. I would like to think they began to mean a bit more now. But I don't know that that was so.'

There were about a dozen people in the congregation for the mid-morning Mass which Runcie and I attended at St Faith's on our second day in Crosby, the Wednesday of Holy Week. As a non-believer I muttered the responses and Amens uncertainly. Runcie, who sat next to me, has a voice which easily carries above a small congregation, thanks to its very individual timbre and his clarity of enunciation. To my eyes, as someone brought up at the very high church St Barnabas, Oxford, St Faith's seemed scarcely above 'middle stump'.

After the service, the present vicar, Richard Capper, and his wife gave us coffee (and more scones, and this time hot cross buns as well). Mrs Capper and I started to talk politics – as a governor of a local state school, she was incensed by the Tory election victory – but Runcie sat looking oddly adrift in this conversation. So I led the talk back to St Faith's in his day, and he began to recall such figures as Jim 'Pooh Bah' Parry, 'a tall man with a tum', who was master of ceremonies (chief server), and ruled the boys firmly – 'I was terrified one morning when I was due to serve and overslept.' On Friday nights the servers counted communion wafers, polished chalices, and read up any special rubric in the *Servers' Manual.* On weekdays which were festive, there would be a Sung Communion with choir at 6.15 am, which seems incredible now. Rita Woodley, another member of the congregation in those days, remembers young Runcie carrying the cross at the head of the procession, 'his hair gleaming golden in the sunlight'. A man would sometimes play a trumpet at the head of the procession, and Jessie Gale, Runcie's schoolmistress at Coronation Road, would sing 'O for the wings of a dove', in a hat. Runcie gave us a comic impersonation of this, and of a wobbly baritone who would often perform 'I know that my Redeemer liveth'.

Several times during the trip, he emphasised to me that his membership of St Faith's, important as it quickly became to him, was still only 'a compartment of a busy life. And I learned to live my life in compartments then. I had this St Faith's compartment, but it was a world which belonged neither to my family nor to Merchant Taylors', really.' This was borne out when we went to lunch with Raymond Fisher, son of the art master at Merchant Taylors', and a school contemporary of Runcie's. Here the conversation, prompted by a school group photograph from the late 1930s, turned at once to boys and masters (and never touched on church matters).

Margaret Duggan states that he entered Merchant Taylors' with 'a Harrison Scholarship, one of those which perpetuated the founder's original intention of providing free grammar school education for local boys of ability'.[2] Runcie himself gave me a different picture: 'I had to sit an entrance exam. And I passed that all right. But I didn't get a scholarship there. And I always suffered from being bad at Maths. I used to go to Miss Parker, in a flat in Blundellsands, for extra Maths on a Saturday morning. Her flat smelt of toast.'

The same picture, of someone not unduly able academically at this stage in his life, had been given to me by Melvin Watterson, one of Runcie's closest friends at Merchant Taylors'. 'In his earlier years at school,' Watterson told

[2]Duggan, p. 53.

me, 'he didn't appear terribly bright. He was competent, but that was it. It was only from the age of fifteen onwards, the year before School Certificate, that it started to appear. And in School Certificate [equivalent to today's GCSE] he got seven credits, including Maths.'

Runcie himself says he 'didn't have any academic ambition' during his early terms at Merchant Taylors'. Nor was he under any pressure from his parents to do particularly well at school; Margery and Kenneth had been allowed to drift through their education, and Kathleen had only done well because Miss Fordham had singled her out. On the other hand it was his mother who made him become a classicist: 'My mother went to some meeting at which Charles Russell, the headmaster, or somebody, was speaking, who said that the important thing was to have a classical education; that if you didn't know precisely what you wanted to be, then a classical education would give you the foundation to be anything. And my mother, who was easily impressed and moved by things, determined that her Bob should have a classical education. And so when the choice came for me to do Classics rather than the dreaded Maths which would be necessary for science, I readily accepted. That's how I came to be classically educated.'

It was a fortunate choice. Kenneth had opted for science, and left school at sixteen to work in an engineering firm. 'In Liverpool at that time,' he told me, 'with the Depression, it was *get a job*, at all costs.' At Merchant Taylors', 'most of the intake disappeared at sixteen,' said Melvin Watterson. 'They left school and went into places like banks (this was the top band), and then insurance companies, and people who didn't make that joined the Mersey Docks & Harbour Board! The headmaster did encourage people to stay on for the sixth form, but when Robert and I got into the sixth there were only four of us doing Latin, Greek and Ancient History. The majority of people who stayed on were scientists and modern linguists, and historians. On the Classics side they did get a number of scholarships to universities, but some people had to stay even three years in the sixth and upper sixth to make this possible.' Watterson added that, though Charles Russell the headmaster was a mathematician, he was keen to 'build up the classical side'.

Runcie himself told me of Russell: 'He was in holy orders; he was a rather good Cambridge mathematician; and he was a solemn man. He used to have a deep collar, and ride a high bicycle, and he was known to us as Creeping Jesus, because he walked very slowly about the school, with a soft padded approach, and had a habit of appearing without you realising he was there. And he was quite a beater. He'd been a master at Harrow, and he regarded the parents of Crosby with frank contempt. His idea was to rescue their offspring by introducing them to the public school spirit; and so he made us sing Harrow-style songs. I can still sing some of them now.' (He proceeded to sing two.)

Runcie was excellent at sport, becoming captain of cricket and playing in the first rugby XV and the first hockey XI, as well as being a high jumper, long jumper and hurdler. Harold Rich, son of the chemist on the corner of Queen's Road, Crosby, and another Merchant Taylors' pupil, says that these achievements and his good looks made him immensely popular: 'Bobby would be walking home from school when I was too. Sometimes I was alone; I think he hardly ever was. He was always the leading figure in a group of two or three, smiling and talking, lots of auburn hair. He was a kind of natural leader, but not a domineering one – leading by natural charm. Maybe it's a slight exaggeration, but I think he was the most popular boy in the school.'

Under Russell's headmastership, Merchant Taylors' played away matches against various public schools, including King William's College (Isle of Man) and Stonyhurst, and Melvin Watterson believes that this may have begun to widen Runcie's social horizons. Runcie himself agrees: 'Stonyhurst has a great atmosphere, with its Jesuit tradition. They had a swimming pool, and we had home-brewed beer for lunch, and you rubbed along with characters who were part of a bigger world.'

His first visit to London, in October 1937, for his

sister Kathleen's wedding to Angus Inglis, then a curate in Nottingham, was another social eye-opener. (The choice of London, where Kathleen was working, for the wedding, rather than her family home in Crosby, seems curious, but Runcie observes that 'she was already the slightly upper-middle-class member of the family'.) He recalls: 'It was the first time I'd ever been south of the Trent. And because Angus had all these social and academic ambitions (he was the don *manqué*), he'd asked Neville Talbot, who was his vicar, and had been Bishop of Pretoria to take it. And Freddie Hood from Pusey House assisted, and it was at All Hallows, Tubby Clayton's church. And we had the reception at the Waldorf Hotel in the Aldwych, in the palm court. It was rather a magical experience.'

His regular churchgoing had caused a certain estrangement from his father. 'I can remember him saying, when I started to go twice to church on a Sunday, that he was disappointed that this cricket-playing football-enthusiast that he'd brought up should show an interest in this unhealthy world. He said, "It's not natural for a boy to take such an interest in religion."' But there was no question of his father preventing him.

By the time he entered the sixth form, his father's health was beginning to break down. He suffered from mysterious pains which he called 'the screws'. No one could produce a diagnosis. Cures for rheumatism and arthritis were tried without effect, and Runcie recalls him shouting out, as he lay on his bed in pain, 'Christ Almighty! Hell's bloody bells!' Mrs Runcie, shocked at this language, would try to stop him. A spell in hospital seemed to make things worse, for his sight began to deteriorate, possibly as a result of wrong medication. Early in 1939, at the age of sixty, he went completely blind. He had to retire from Tate & Lyle, and 26 Queen's Road was given up for a smaller house.

'It was such a shock,' said Margery, 'such a terrible thing for a man like my father after this active and outgoing life. I just couldn't bear to see him fumbling for his food, but he wouldn't have any help.' He allowed Robert to take him to football matches and give him a running commentary, but Robert feels that he did really very little for his father: 'I was spending so much time in the St Faith's world, and the school world, that I was a fairly dead loss in doing much for the home world, which was under very considerable strain, but which didn't touch me unless I was prepared to let it touch me.

'Looking back, I'm surprised that I never tried to impose on my father's vulnerability by suggesting that he came to church, found consolation in the church. But it would have been unthinkable on my part – I would have loved him too much to mention it. And it's interesting that nobody came from the church to try and minister to him. I don't think he would have found it tolerable, but nobody came.'

By the time his father went blind, Runcie was working hard towards a scholarship, largely in consequence of his brother-in-law Angus's influence. Angus Inglis had been born into a poorly-off family, and had won a scholarship to grammar school and then an exhibition to Oxford. Runcie says that after his marriage to Kathleen, 'Angus was very eager to get a lodgement in this uncultured family. The boy specialising in Classics gave him an obvious opportunity. So he took an interest in me, because here was at least somebody who would understand the language he was speaking.'

Some time in 1937 or 1938 Angus and Kathleen took Robert on a brief trip to Oxford. Angus told me that he had judged it 'a bit beyond the Runcie family to think of Oxford for Bob', so he and Kathleen took the initiative. 'We stayed at Abingdon for a night, and went round Oxford, and I took Bob round gardens and my favourite bits, and into Christ Church hall, and showed him some of the pictures. And Bob began to go round in a kind of dream. And he said, "How do you get here?"'

Runcie himself does not recall this moment of sudden ambition, but says that Oxford certainly seemed 'magical'. Until this time, although he had had 'dreams of doing something more than those characters who were going into insurance or banks', there had been no focused ambition.

His involvement with St Faith's had given him 'a bit of distance in myself from the narrow horizons of the family', while even 'my mother's films, and reading Henty novels, had shown that there was a kind of wider horizon; I felt, I'm not going to be stuck here. But although I made my Confession, I didn't very often go to other people to ask for advice and help.'

Angus believed that 'Bob's father's plan was to put him into Tate & Lyle's. I wrote to Russell, his headmaster, and said, "Look here, this disaster must be averted," and Russell wrote back, and took an interest in him from then on.' Runcie says he did not know that Angus had made this approach to Russell, but remarks: 'That would explain the library visits.' He explains: 'Russell allowed me to come round and work in his library in his house in Blundellsands, because it wasn't easy to work at home, to read for a scholarship. I used to love to go along in the evening, and do my homework, and read. He was a collector of books, and I loved the smell of the pipe, and the trouble he took to show me something exciting he'd been reading.'

Talking further about Merchant Taylors', Runcie mentioned R. F. ('Bertie') Parr, another of his Classics teachers at school, who had introduced him and other boys to 1930s-style socialism: '"Joe" Parr, as he was called, after Joe Stalin, could easily be got off making you construe by the planted question – you would say something like, "Chamberlain seems to be doing well at Munich, sir," and that would be the end of Classics for the rest of the day. And he introduced the economic [i.e. Marxist] element into the teaching of Classics.'

Parr did not go down well in conservative Crosby, but he had at least a temporary influence on Runcie, who was soon bringing home 'those tangerine-coloured books from the Left Book Club'. This was 'really dangerous stuff', for though 'my father, I think, was not too worried about the pinkiness, and was easy-going', Mrs Runcie had always made the family stand up for the national anthem at the end of the

King's Christmas broadcast, and was wounded by Robert's attraction to socialism.

After lunch at the Fishers', Runcie and I drove to the edge of Crosby, trying to find the pub near the market gardener's greenhouse to which his father used to take him on Sunday mornings. We failed, and got lost in what appeared, from the churches and schools, to be predominantly Irish Catholic housing estates. We talked about Lindy, and I admitted that Angus had communicated some disapproval of her as an unsuitable wife for an archbishop. Runcie said what an enormous social asset she was on big occasions – she could keep everybody from Isaiah Berlin to Prince Charles entertained in conversation.

We drove back to the Blundellsands Hotel, and then walked the short distance to where Audrey McCulloch was living in an old people's home. Slightly older than Runcie, she had, as Audrey Ball, been a teenage girl in the congregation at St Faith's when he was a server. He described her to me as 'very flighty in those days – she wore green silk stockings, and showed me that religion and the adolescent preoccupation with sex weren't incompatible'. In her seventies, she proved to be still flirtatious, and we had a very amusing half hour with her. She had had a very difficult life; having lost her husband in the war, she was crippled by a lumbar puncture not long after the birth of her son Nigel, who eventually became Bishop of Wakefield. Although restricted by callipers and a neck brace, she radiated *joie de vivre*.

We discussed the ordination of women. Audrey was against it, but said she supposed Runcie agreed with it. 'On the whole, I do,' he answered, 'though there's an old St Faith's bit of me which doesn't like it, and is glad it didn't come in my time. But I think it's right that it should come.' We also talked about Miss Fordham, who was Audrey's headmistress too. 'When Kathleen said I'd got confirmed,' Runcie recalled, 'Miss Fordham summoned me, and I had tea with her, and she put me on to Father Basil Oddie, a Kelham priest who was a great favourite of hers, and who was working in the Liverpool slums. The story has got around that it was a walk along the beach with him that made me think of ordination. But I'm not sure it was quite like that.'

In this connection, he recalled an army cadet force inspection at Merchant Taylors': 'The inspecting officer asked a boy down the line what he was going to do, and he said something dreary. Then the officer came on to me, and I blurted out "The church." I hadn't really thought about it seriously until then.' Had he thought of it in reaction to hearing the others naming dreary careers? 'That's right.'

He could not say whether or not this incident preceded or followed his meeting with Miss Fordham and Father Oddie, but he explained that Oddie's community, the Society of the Sacred Mission, an Anglo-Catholic order based at Kelham near Nottingham, used to look for ordinands among lower-class boys. He then recalled an instant in his final year at Merchant Taylors', 1940–1, during which he lived in the school's boarding house, his parents having moved to Nottinghamshire so that Kathleen could help look after his father.

'The only real click I recall in my mind was at school one day, walking across to the main building from the boarding house. I'd thought about ordination, and pictured myself as a "slum priest" like Father Oddie, a heroic figure, with the Mass at the heart of my life, and wearing a cloak. Oxford didn't really play a part in that. And we were very short of cash, scrabbling together the money, so that I'd really wondered if I should try for Oxford – though Aunt Kate [one of his father's sisters] had offered help, and Angus was organising the finances of it. But suddenly I knew I *had* to get to Oxford, that it really was going to change my life. I said to myself, "I'm going to leave all this and go to Oxford and be an Oxford man."'

Joan Morgan, Kathleen's best friend from childhood, joined us for dinner on our second evening at the Blundellsands Hotel. Small and birdlike, she fussed about what to call Runcie – Robert, Bob, or Bobby? He seemed to have no idea. (He had told me that he was always Bob or Bobby till Lindy came along, then Robert.) I suggested she use Bobby, and she did.

Conversation during dinner was somewhat hampered by a young blind pianist playing deafening cocktail music in the otherwise empty restaurant. At the end of our meal, Runcie went over and introduced himself to the boy, and to his parents, who were eating at a table next to the piano, and requested 'Blue Moon'. That afternoon he had given Audrey McCulloch a blessing on departure which was memorable for its body-language – he really clasped her arm. I was becoming aware that he was supremely accomplished at this sort of personal encounter.

Another aspect of his character was touched on during dinner. He had been describing Margery and Kenneth as 'overshadowed and underestimated' in the family, and too inclined to be self-effacing. I suggested that he himself was far more self-effacing than most people realised, and Joan Morgan, who had known all four Runcie siblings well, was inclined to agree. 'None of you,' she said to him, 'has the forceful, critical aspect of character that your father had. I can't imagine any of you opposing or being hypercritical of anybody or anything, unless it was absolutely necessary and utterly right morally and logically. Whereas your father wouldn't hesitate.' Runcie was at first surprised at our assessment of him, but then recalled that, after a lecture he had given the previous week, 'Philip Howard of *The Times* said to me, "You're much more diffident than I'd realised."'

Towards the end of dinner with Joan Morgan, I asked him about the order of events relating to his decision to be ordained – if 'decision' was the right word, which I was beginning to doubt. Had Miss Fordham heard the rumour that he was interested in ordination? 'I rather think she picked up the idea that I was a keen Anglo-Catholic, and *she* thought it would be a very good idea for me to consider ordination.'

He said Miss Fordham had disapproved of his headmaster

Charles Russell as 'unsound theologically' – with some justi-
fication, for Russell introduced him to religious ideas which
were very different from those taught at St Faith's. Instruction
in the Bible class there, he said, had amounted to little more
than 'combative' definitions of where Anglo-Catholics stood
in relation to the rest of Christendom. There was scarcely
any exposition of scripture. Russell, however, 'introduced
me to the problem of suffering and pain, and how it was
possible to be religious and wrestle with problems rather
than find solutions'. This was during a term's study of
the book of Job, a text which Runcie agrees may have
had particular meaning for him at that time, because of
his father's disaster. 'And Russell introduced me to B. H.
Streeter's book *The Four Gospels*, which made the search
to understand how the gospels were written feel rather like
a detective story. Russell was a man for demolishing myths.
He was really an ordained agnostic.'

Other theological modernists were to be found at Liverpool
Anglican Cathedral, and by chance Runcie got to know one
of them quite well: 'At St Faith's we regarded the cathedral
with a certain amount of irreverent mockery. There was an
eccentric Dean, named Dwelly (of whom Stanley Morrison
the typographer once said to me, "Dwelly, now he was a
real Dean – never discussed a service without a bottle of
Bollinger on the table!"). And he gathered around him people
that at St Faith's were regarded as unbelievers, but actually
were very distinguished: Charles Raven, and J. S. Bezzant, a
high church modernist with a strong Oxford background. I
made his acquaintance in the sixth form, through a friend
who was going to be ordained and had been adopted by
Bezzant (who had a habit of getting a crush on young men
and becoming their patron). Bezzant would take us out to
dinner at a restaurant which was quite beyond our normal
experience, and talk about the high world of scholarship,
and tell ecclesiastical stories, and show how the modernist
case was common currency in places where people think.
He showed me that you could be unbelieving, uncredulous,
and still a good Anglo-Catholic.'

4

A perfectly charming Guards officer

As we left Crosby, and headed for the motorway to go south again, Runcie said it always slightly disappointed him that Lindy had never been there. 'She's never set foot in the school, never set foot in St Faith's. I think she has a kind of instinct that she wouldn't enjoy it, and that I might not like that.' He himself 'did not get nostalgic about the place until the 1970s, when I was a bishop, and St Faith's was proud of me and hauled me back'. By then, it was colourful for him to have a *déclassé* background, but in the 1940s he was simply glad to have escaped. ~~I tried Merchant — Tailed!~~

His first attempt at a university scholarship was at Pembroke College, Cambridge, where his headmaster, Charles Russell, had been a don. This was in December 1940 and, even in a wartime winter, Cambridge seemed immensely desirable: 'I was staying in somebody's rooms who was obviously a great socialite, and who had lots of party invitations on the mantelpiece. There were people bicycling along King's Parade in scarves, and a chap saying, "See you at the party, Diana darling!"'

Pembroke offered him 'a sort of bursary', but it was decided that he could improve on this, and in March 1941, aged nineteen, he tried for predominantly sporting Brasenose College, Oxford, with which Merchant Taylors' had a strong connection. 'A letter was sent to Brasenose saying I was a good games player.'

Brasenose, known as 'BNC', had surrendered its buildings for military training, and its undergraduates were billeted in Christ Church, Oxford's grandest college, where Runcie stayed for his interview. He was as impressed by the evidence of its social life as he had been at Cambridge. He was offered a slightly larger bursary, and Merchant Taylors' awarded him a foundation scholarship which would pay a further substantial part of the fees; so he went up to BNC – or rather, to Christ Church – at the start of the 1941 summer term.

He was given rooms in Meadow Buildings, built in Ruskin's version of Venetian Gothic – 'damp but remarkable', Runcie says. He quickly realised that Christ Church was 'a very big world to get into'. He has clear memories of the group of friends he made that first term, all of them from public schools: 'Derek Waters was from Cranleigh, though he came from quite a modest home, compared to Peter Moore (the Dean of St Albans today), who was at school with Derek but was well off. David Morgan was from Uppingham. Roland Wills, known as "Blast Me" Wills, because he always used to say that the whole time, was from Bloxham, a clergy son, and Michael Mouseley came from Wellington.'

I asked if there were freshmen from non-public school backgrounds with whom he might have made friends, and he recalled that 'there was a little posse of Manchester Grammar School people'. But that was not his chosen circle. 'I don't think I ever tried to distance myself from the grammar school boys; it was just that I admired the panache of the public school boy. Or if I did distance myself, I deluded myself that I could still get on with them all. But I was full of admiration for those public school characters throwing bottles and people into Mercury,[1] you know.'

---

[1]The fishpond in Tom Quad, Christ Church, at the centre of which is a statue of Mercury.

Surely he himself must have arrived at the college with a Lancashire voice, such as Kenneth and Margery retained? 'I suppose so, but I'm not conscious of when I developed such an upper-class accent; I suppose in the army. But I remember when I first went to the Otter household [Angus's friend the Rev. Tony Otter, who, with his wife had Runcie's parents to stay in their country vicarage during 1940] I remember thinking that they all talked in a very affected way, so that I must then have been speaking with a Lancashire or a Liverpool accent. And I suppose it's a bit of the imitator in me that I find even now, if I go to America for three weeks, that I'm speaking with a slightly American accent. If I'm in Scotland, I can pass as a Scot. The chameleon, I suppose.'

His desire to blend in with his Christ Church public school friends did not blind him to their oddities. He gave me very sharp character sketches of them, as they have become in later years, from an 'MCC genial easy-going stockbroker' to 'a kind of Waugh-like character who at one stage was living in the Turkish Baths in Jermyn Street, which he seemed to occupy permanently; an arrested undergraduate'. At another point the Otters, his parents' hosts at Lowdham in Nottinghamshire, came in for this sketching at some length:

'Tony was married to Dorothy Otter, known as Dodo. She was even more aristocratic than him. They'd adopted Kath as well as Angus, and they were educating her in cultured ways. I always felt that, though it was genuine in Tony's case, it was a bit affected with Dorothy. She was tweeds and sensible shoes, and would say "Come and look at my herb garden", and always baked her own bread. And they wore old clothes which were obviously originally very expensive tweeds.' He described his father struggling to survive in this milieu: 'He had to resort to devious ways of backing a horse and getting a glass of whisky.' I said that this description reminded me of the broken-down father in a similar predicament in Angus Wilson's *Late Call*. 'I'm rather keen on Angus Wilson,' replied Runcie.

A few weeks after the Crosby trip, I met one of Runcie's friends from Christ Church days, Michael Mouseley, who said he did not remember Runcie having a Lancashire accent, but recalled his ability to 'sink a pint of beer straight off'. On one occasion Runcie had spent an evening with his Merchant Taylors' friend Melvin Watterson, who was at St John's, and as he staggered back through Tom Gate at Christ Church the porter called out to Mouseley: 'Mr Runcie wants a bit of help.'

Apart from Mouseley, everyone else whom Runcie had mentioned among Christ Church friends seemed to be dead or untraceable – except the writer John Mortimer, who had rooms on the next staircase in Meadow Buildings, and whom Runcie mentioned several times to me. I wrote to Mortimer, who replied that he had no anecdotes about Runcie as an undergraduate, 'but I got to know and admire him more when I interviewed him'. This was for a newspaper profile in 1982; the interview is reprinted in Mortimer's *In Character* (1984):

> He had invited me to join him in a Campari and soda, and had reminded me of the distant time when we both had rooms in Meadow Buildings . . . He had greeted me with a warm handshake, and instant hospitality, but I was off in pursuit of a more enigmatic character who had never, as far as I knew, had rooms in Meadow Buildings . . . God . . .
>
> 'Why did an omnipotent God allow the murder of eight million Jews?' . . . Dr Runcie, with the best will in the world, was unable to help me. 'I'm an agnostic on that. I don't know God's reason, I do believe there's no human tragedy so great that it can't be redeemed in Christ.'
>
> 'But what does being redeemed in Christ mean if you're a Jew about to be gassed?'
>
> 'As I said, I'm an agnostic about God's purpose. But I believe we're responsible for the mess we make of His creation . . .'
>
> 'So how did you first meet God?' I was beginning to feel

uneasily that Dr Runcie might not have had such a long, or close, association with the Almighty as I had been led to believe.

'I had an older sister. I was much the youngest of the family, sort of autumn leaf. She took me to a service at St Faith's, Crosby . . . I think I'm the only person who was actually converted at his own confirmation service. But most of my friends were ungodly. I was at Oxford in the heyday of Freddie Ayer, and *Language, Truth and Logic*. It was quite hard to hold on to belief and I had many conflicts . . . When one is an Archbishop of Canterbury, one has to rally the troops. But I can't think of Jesus as a "pal". That just seems to diminish the mystery . . .'

'But you believe in an after-life?'

'Of course. I can't believe, when I see the promise of Christ expressed in a particular person, that that's all coming to an end. But as for the geography and climate of the after-life, well, I'm an agnostic about that too . . .'

He had the keys to Lambeth Palace, and led me out, past the wooden crosier in the umbrella stand, down the great staircase which led back into the world . . . Ex-Lieutenant Runcie had answered all my inquiries with honesty and great charm. But from his commanding officer, I thought as I looked up into the darkening sky over Waterloo Bridge, from the real subject of my interview, I had had, to most of the questions I had so carefully prepared, a great deal of 'no comment'.[2]

Runcie remembers John Mortimer in undergraduate days as being characterised by 'purple corduroys and beautiful girls, whom he had to tea. I always remember saying to my scout, "Mr Mortimer has rather beautiful ladies coming to see him", and he replied, "Mr Mortimer, sir, 'e's a man with wot you'd call a troublesome organ."' I use the spelling 'wot' because it represents the exaggerated working-class accent into which Runcie drops; he

[2]John Mortimer, *In Character*, Penguin, 1984, pp 27–34

never misses a chance of doing a funny voice when telling a story.

He himself took girls to dances at Oxford; they included 'the daughter of a socialist peer', and the 'exceedingly beautiful Ann Cumming Bell, who subsequently became Duchess of Rutland'. Keble College was 'full of delectable Foreign Office girls' (I corrected him: they were working for the War Office; my father was Warden of Keble at this time), and these were 'regarded as the best femininity available'. But this social life was 'all quite expensive', and money was a problem for Runcie, who soon found himself 'dangerously near to serious debt'.

He took vacation jobs, such as picking plums and teaching schoolboys to drive tractors as part of the war effort (he himself had received tractor training at the University's Department of Forestry). His twentieth birthday, in October 1941, fell during his second term at Oxford, and he was now of an age when he could be called up for military service. He seems to have felt no great apprehension on account of the war. 'I remember my scout waking me up one sunny day to tell me that Germany had invaded Russia. And I felt, "Well, that surely has sunk them; they're over-stretched now." I thought that was good news, really. I was rather astonished when people seemed to suggest we might lose.'

He did not know when his call-up would come; meanwhile his academic work was arranged so that it could be terminated at short notice. 'I took a thing called Sections, which meant you did an examination at the end of each term in order to clock up the requirements for a wartime degree. It meant that if you didn't get as far as Mods, you at least had something in the bank.'

In fact he had decided not to read for Classical Honour Moderations ('Mods'), the first part of the Oxford Classics course, which would have involved close study of Latin and Greek texts, but to proceed to the second part, Literae Humaniores ('Greats'), with its syllabus of Ancient History and Classical Philosophy. 'Instead of reading Mods, which I ought to have done – and have suffered all my life from not doing, because that was the language part – I went straight on to do Greats Sections. I was farmed out, so that my first tutor was a very famous Oxford epigraphist called Marcus Niebuhr Tod, who was at Oriel, a man of infinite courtesy. And I loved him, and he taught me, in my first term, Herodotus, and the early Persian history. And I was taught Philosophy by a man called Jimmy McKie, whose tutorials were astonishing monologues in which he walked around the room and sometimes climbed up the curtains, to a background of the bells of the University church across Radcliffe Square. At the end of my first tutorial, which I had with Derek Waters, he said, "And now let us have sherry." And this was quite new to me. A cut-glass decanter was brought out, and he went on talking, and this tutorial which started at twelve lasted until after two. And we emerged dizzy with sherry. And that was one of my first experiences of the Oxford educational system.'

He read a book by 'a man called Grundy' which had an 'almost Marxist view' of Ancient History, and 'tied in with my own left-wing tastes at that time'. He went to hear Harry Pollitt, secretary of the Communist Party of Great Britain, speak at an open air rally, and attended meetings of the Labour Club. This amused his public school friends, though Derek Waters 'had these interests a bit'. Meanwhile his participation in university church-worship was 'unfocused but quite active'.

He tried out different churches, doing 'a bit of tasting' of services and clergy. Christ Church Cathedral was 'full of interesting characters in those days, including a priest who was the only man said to have died of over-eating during the last war'. Charles Warner, the college chaplain, put Runcie on the servers' rota. Warner 'was very good with the aristocracy, getting hold of them by means of playing squash, and hard drinking, too; getting them to become ordinands, or to make their Confession. He used to play squash, have a drinks party, then take people down to the all-night soup kitchen on the railway station for soldiers and drifters, and when you were at your most vulnerable, he would say to you, "To think you're going off to fight in the next few months, and you haven't made your Confession." So he got men to be penitent converted Catholics. He was a bit of a gangster.'

Runcie sometimes went to St Mary's, the University church, where William Temple, then Archbishop of Canterbury, would come to preach for Dick Milford, the vicar, and Dorothy L. Sayers was among the visiting speakers – 'she chain-smoked, and was far too powerful to question'. He also tried the very high church Pusey House, whose principal, Freddie Hood, had been alerted to his presence by Angus. 'Freddie sent a little card asking me to come and have dinner. After that, I went occasionally. On a Saturday night they had a curious little service of preparation for Communion which Freddie used to describe as "What we all like". It was rather exotic – devotions to the Blessed Sacrament, which Freddie himself would accompany on the organ; we sang "O sweet sacrament divine". But I didn't somehow feel that I went down awfully well there. I was neither a gilded youth from a public school, nor a working-class lad, in which they also showed a particular interest. After the war, because of my brigade connection, Freddie became more interested in me.'

He also tried St Mary Madgalen, again very high church, but was put off by the vicar, 'a very old man called Father Hack'. He went to St Barnabas, 'where there was a man called Father Bisdee', tried 'the odd meeting of OICU [the Oxford Inter-Collegiate Christian Union, which was extremely evangelical], and took fright – it didn't take with me at all'. He did not enter the two popular evangelical churches, St Aldate's and St Ebbe's.

Meanwhile, one and a half days a week were spent in military drill, with the University's Training Corps. 'We used to meet in the back of the Town Hall – there was a kind of drill hall where we assembled – and then went out to different places, like Christ Church Meadow, or Port Meadow, or down by St Cross; quite fun. You might do drill, or grenade-throwing, or bayonet practice; you used to have dummy sacks, and people used to bayonet them. You might do an exercise which would take you up to Boars Hill or Shotover. And map-reading was taught to us by Edmund Blunden [then a Fellow of Merton College], in a very fey kind of way; you couldn't hear what he was saying most of the time. And the sergeant majors, who used to call the roll, gave everybody their titles. They used to say: "Mr Runcie? Mr Morgan? Lovat, the Lord? Mr Mond, the Honourable W. H. L.?"'

Runcie proved better at army written work than manoeuvres. He passed out 'nearly top of Certificate B' (the army exam for undergraduates) because he was good at 'getting up a set piece', such as a ten-minute lecture on the workings of the carburettor. 'My capacity for dealing with an actual carburettor today is nil, and Lindy is always staggered by this story. But I was able, by reference to a plan and illustrations, to introduce people to the carburettor and the petrol pump and so forth; though my ability actually to deal with a carburettor, then as now, was nil.' I remarked that it did not seem very improbable to me, because it demonstrated two skills he undoubtedly possessed: learning up a subject at speed, and delivering a convincing performance. 'That's right,' he answered.

Had he ever been nervous about giving a public performance of any sort? 'Oh, always! Perhaps not so much when I actually get started, but always very screwed up before it.' This surprised me. But I had noticed, sitting near him when he gave an address at the Classical Association, that he looked tense. 'I am very nervous before things,' he reiterated, 'and also if I haven't got command of the material, and if I haven't prepared it, I can get myself into confusion and lose my nerve a bit. In general, I'm not good at genuine spontaneity. I think I'm pretty good at calculated spontaneity, and at picking up something which a previous speaker has remarked, a thread, and playing with it, making it appear as if I've taken the whole thing out of what has just been said. And I can get up a brief quite quickly. But if I get something up quickly, I tend to forget all about it afterwards.'

I said that I had noticed at the institution at Borden that he remembered the name of the previous incumbent, of the new incumbent, his wife, his children, and the churchwarden. Would he have done that by carefully committing those details to memory? 'Yes, I would. But if you asked me who they all were now, I couldn't do it.'

In the Hilary Term of 1942, his third at Oxford, a few months after his twentieth birthday, he went to the adjutant of the University Training Corps to discuss his choice of regiment. 'I said my father was Scottish and I'd thought about the King's Own Scottish Borderers. And he said – and this was totally unexpected – "Have you ever thought of the Scots Guards?" The RSM was a Scots Guardsman, who wore a fancy Scots Guards hat, and one of my more aristocratic friends was going into that regiment, so I knew it was rather a classy thing, but it had never occurred to me, and I said, "No, because I wouldn't have the money." So he turned to the assistant adjutant and said, "I don't think you'd need any extra cash in wartime, would you, Bunny?" The other man said, "It depends where you are – old Tommy Pike hadn't got a bean." And they had one of those Wodehousian conversations about how much you'd need. And in the end he said, "Would you like to go up for an interview with the Scots Guards?" And I said yes, because the idea rather intrigued me. So I went up to Wellington Barrack, where I saw a group being formed up for the royal guard.'

I asked if the barrack was near Buckingham Palace, and he was astonished by the question: 'It's amazing you don't know – it seems to be a thing incredible that a man doesn't know that. It's right by the Palace.' It was the first time I had said anything that shocked him.

He was interviewed by Colonel Bill Balfour, who had come out of retirement in 1939, 'a rather splendid character with an expensive face, the kind of man who appears to be centrally heated – obviously used to living in large, draughty, wet, baronial castles. He talked to me on the assumption that I was going to join the regiment, and the sole serious question was, did I mind going into the armoured regiment, tanks, instead of the infantry? He said this was just starting, and it would be very helpful if I was prepared to. Obviously the fame of my lecture on the carburettor was already reverberating round the corridors of Whitehall. So I was recruited. I went back, dined that night in Hall, and there were pints all round on this amazing news.'

He could have declared an intention to be ordained, and not been called up for war service on account of it – the church was a Reserved Occupation. 'Some people thought I should do this. But I wasn't prepared to be such an ordinand as that.' He thinks it striking that Derek Waters, though definitely intending to be ordained, did not use this as a reason not to fight, but enlisted as a private.

Runcie was allowed to complete his fourth term at Oxford (Trinity 1942), and in June went to Pirbright Camp in Surrey. His Certificate B, taken at Oxford, had exempted him from basic military training, but this put him at a social disadvantage. Most of the other young men who had arrived at Pirbright with the intention of becoming officers in the Brigade of Guards were Old Etonians, who had gone straight from school to do basic training at the Guards' Depot at Caterham. 'Therefore their background was rather aggressive common Eton memories. And they were the sort of people who noticed that you'd turned up in a suit, rather than in country clothes. They were conscious that you hadn't got their sort of background, and they regarded me in a very funny way. A man called Tony Stevenson – ultimately to become a best friend in the regiment – was pretty sticky with me.'

In a genial telephone conversation with me, A. R. G. (Tony) Stevenson was keen to brush away any suggestion that snobbery had lain behind his and the other Etonians' treatment of Runcie: 'I don't think we were too beastly to him. If there was anything like that, it was much more to do with the fact that the rest of us had already been together for eight weeks at Caterham, and I suppose we felt we were old and trained soldiers. His different social background never appeared at all. In those days I don't think one thought about that sort of thing much. One was trying to get on with the war.' Others who had been at Pirbright told me the same. Nevertheless Runcie observed that 'very few people talked to me' in those first weeks of training.

He began to struggle with Scots Guards protocol. 'We were told some of the traditions of the regiment: that you never spoke of "going up to Town", always "to London"; that you never walked in London without gloves in the winter; that you never travelled on the Tube, and you never called it "the Tube", always "the Underground Railway"; that you never asked for "a Scotch", always "a whisky and soda" – all of which, I have to say, I assiduously keep to today, and I can't stop myself wincing when people reveal themselves in these ways. (But don't take me too seriously!)'

He also had to master the elaborate code which governed regimental life: 'You had to learn all the pipe calls, because we didn't have bugles. I can still recognise the call for tea, which was "The high road to Linton", and the reel played for Adjutant's Orders was "The De'il among the tailors". After dinner the piper would go round and play a set – a march, a reel, a strathspey and another reel – and if you were the orderly officer you heard the senior officer say, "Let's have 'Orange and blue'", or "Shall we have 'The Seventy-Fifth farewell to Gibraltar'?" And then they would say to you, "Orderly Officer, 'Seventy-Fifth farewell to Gibraltar', 'Orange and blue', 'Little brown jug' and 'The De'il among the tailors'", and if he came in and played the wrong things, it was your fault, and you would get an extra picket or something. One false move and you were finished.'

At weekends, the Etonians 'all rushed off to London, to the Bag o' Nails or the Four Hundred. I went off to Guildford where I was put up by Derek Waters' parents.' He also paid a visit to Miss Fordham, who was living in retirement near Salisbury, and was 'very proud' of his uniform. Meanwhile Angus, serving abroad as a military chaplain, was 'a bit worried that I was over-stretching myself with money' by going into the Scots Guards. But Kathleen 'was quite keen – it was socially good – and Mum and Dad were delighted'. Small postal orders would arrive from them to help him pay mess bills and buy train tickets. 'I was disgracefully glad to have them. They must have cost them a lot.'

The Pirbright course was chiefly drill and armoured training, 'duplicating what we'd done in Oxford, but on a much more serious, more coherent level'. Runcie and the others then moved on to the Royal Military College, Sandhurst, where they learnt 'how to command men, and how to command tanks – driving and maintenance, gunnery and wireless training'. The possibility of failing the Sandhurst exams loomed quite large, and a man who failed more than once would be sent to the ranks as an ordinary soldier. Runcie calls it 'amazing' that he passed at the first attempt, adding that 'Lindy says I never really knew how to drive until after the war, and that I still drive as if I was driving a tank.' (After the Crosby trip, Sister Frances Dominica asked me who drove, and when I said I did, she said, 'That was very wise.')

At Sandhurst, they were drilled by sergeant majors who did not always appreciate the kind of men they were dealing with, such as Harold Llewelyn Smith, who had been a scholar of Winchester and New College. 'Harold was treated with great veneration by all of us, because he was a mine of information; older than us, in his thirties, with grey hair; very much an uncle figure. One day we were tested on what was the motto of the Scots Guards, and a man said "*Nemo me impune lacessit.*" "And wot does that mean, sir?", pointing at Harold Llewelyn Smith. And Harold said, "Nobody harms me and gets away with it." "Wrong, sir, it means no one harms me twice." And Harold looked, with those grey academic eyes, and said, "But I know you're wrong and I'm right; *impune* means 'gets away with it'." "Put 'is name in the book for insolence!" And this Winchester scholar was marched off at the double.'

Runcie says that Llewelyn Smith, afterwards headmaster of Marylebone Grammar School, was 'the only man I really confided in about ordination'. Llewelyn Smith would sometimes precipitate a theological discussion by teasing the Scots Guards Presbyterian chaplain, George Reid, later Moderator of the Church of Scotland, 'a great but slightly academic preacher for guardsmen. In the mess he was hopelessly leg-pulled, and Harold joined in the mocking, but turned it into a serious question. He'd say: "What balls you were preaching this morning, padre", and quite often would get a serious conversation going.'

Runcie would not take Communion with the Presbyterians, 'on account of my high church ways', though Reid would willingly have administered it to him. Sometimes he would go to the Anglican Communion service, conducted for the Coldstream Guards by their chaplain, Tony Tremlett. Reid knew that Runcie contemplated ordination, and 'didn't look with favour' on this stand-offishness, 'but later in life, when I became Archbishop of Canterbury, he was quite proud of having been my chaplain. And when we had a great party at Lambeth, and had brother officers back, George Reid came, and I was very careful that he should be the chaplain of the occasion, and say grace, which he appreciated very much – even though he said a very long one, a rambling one of great rhetoric. And the microphone system didn't work, and there were cries at the end, on all sides, of "Bob buggered up the microphone to put George in his place!" And you had people like Willie Whitelaw, who by then was Home Secretary, and the Lord Chamberlain, Charles Maclean, to Lindy's amusement, all jumping up and down like small boys saying, "Bob buggered up the microphone!"'

I wrote to Lord Whitelaw, asking for his reminiscences of Runcie in the Scots Guards. He invited me to his office in the House of Lords, one morning during the summer recess. The small-boyish quality was very evident as he laughed over memories of officers' mess pranks, especially swapping George Reid's hat with the Catholic chaplain's.

He first encountered Runcie in November 1942, when Runcie and the others were posted to the Third (Tank) Battalion, Scots Guards, training on Salisbury Plain. Whitelaw himself had been in the regiment since 1939, and had joined the Third Battalion before it became armoured. He remembered his surprise, that with his family background, Runcie had got into the Scots Guards. 'He was said to be very good, but very shy and retiring. And at first he *was* terribly quiet, but he came out of his shell quite quickly. It wasn't long before he was one of the boys.'

Runcie and Tony Stevenson, the Etonian who had been stand-offish, were now going around together as friends. Stevenson says he soon found that Runcie had 'a great sense of humour'. Runcie recalls that there was 'a famous lady called Mrs Fox Pitt, who kept, for the benefit of Salisbury Plain guardees, a marvellous sort of night club – quite a respectable one, more a Four Hundred than a Bag o' Nails – at a thing called the Watermill, on the river at Salisbury. On one of my Saturday nights I went there with Tony Stevenson, with whom I was now a great chum, and we walked out of the Watermill, and it was totally black, and we walked towards our car, and I went past it and into the river. I scrambled to the shore, but my beautiful new guards officer's hat was lost! I needed it in a week's time – it was dress uniform – and I had to get a special replacement from Herbert Smith in London, for something like ten pounds, which was a lot of money then.'

In April 1943 the battalion moved to Yorkshire for battle training. 'We were deployed along Wensleydale – I enjoyed that hugely – and we did exercises at places like Hawes and Askrigg. That was where I last met Derek Waters, who had become a private in the Pioneer Corps – the sort of thing that guardsmen laughed at.' Margaret Duggan writes that Waters talked wryly to Runcie of 'the mockery he underwent in the barrack-room when it was known that he said his prayers and went to church. He endured it, but was sick at heart at the coarseness and brutality with which he was surrounded.'[3] In contrast with Waters, Runcie seems to have kept his religious life to himself, apart from confiding in Harold Llewelyn Smith. Whitelaw says that 'the mess would have roared with equal laughter had it been suggested that one day Bob Runcie would be Archbishop of Canterbury or that I would be Home Secretary'. Duggan suggests that Runcie was rather put to shame by the Waters parents, who took him to Evensong while they were visiting Derek in Yorkshire.Soon afterwards, Derek Waters was posted to Italy and killed in action.[4]

Meanwhile the Third Battalion of the Scots Guards moved from Yorkshire to the Dukeries. 'And of course,' Runcie says, 'this was a great Guards stamping ground, because they'd all stayed at the various houses there, and a lot of the nobs were still in residence in this hunting country.' The Third Battalion was stationed at Thoresby Park in Nottinghamshire, where a full-scale ball was arranged for the officers. Runcie had had experience of army dances when on Salisbury Plain. 'It was one of the duties of young officers to drag guardsmen away from women under arches, and make sure they got into the three-ton trucks which were bringing them back to camp. You certainly saw life there.' The Thoresby ball was a very different affair. 'I was accommodation officer,' recalls Runcie, 'and had to put up all these beautiful women in the Bell Hotel. One of the local characters who was just coming out was a teenager called Elizabeth Cavendish, daughter of the Duke of Devonshire. Lord Manvers, who presided over Thoresby Hall, was always very inclined to push her on us, and I got to know her quite well and have been a friend of hers ever since. I used to do a very good impersonation of Lord Manvers inviting us: "Will you look after the Lady Elizabeth Cavendish?"'

When Lady Elizabeth Cavendish (the great love of John Betjeman's later years) telephoned me in answer to my letter

[3]Duggan p. 71.
[4]Runcie told me that after the war, he went to Italy with Waters' parents to find their son's grave at Salerno. 'And that was the first time I ever went to Rome.'

about Runcie, she said: 'He struck me as a perfectly charming Guards officer. I wasn't aware of his being a grammar school boy. The thing that surprised me was when he went into the church.' Runcie admits that by this time he 'knew the language' of being a Guards officer. He says he had even become 'a sort of leader' in the life of the officers' mess. It was at this period that he sometimes stayed at Rosa Lewis's extraordinary Cavendish Hotel in Jermyn Street:

'Tony Stevenson, Teddy Cazenove [another officer in the Third Battalion], and a man known as "Pissy" (a kind of Irish aristocrat who drank himself to death), were *habitués* of Rosa's. Indeed I was present at Rosa's when Pissy was introduced to the estranged wife [actually mistress] of Augustus John, Mavis Cole, who subsequently married – or had she already? – Mortimer Wheeler. Anyway, she was a nymphomaniac, and she set about Pissy. She made love with such passion that she scratched and gouged great bits out of his back. We used to examine the scars when he came back from a weekend! And that was the time, when in London, that I regularly used to stay at the Cavendish. I was one of the sort of poor boys Rosa took a shine to. She was a kindly soul, getting on, and rather confined to the chair, but she still had those eyes.' (Rosa Lewis's rather mad-looking eyes are certainly a striking feature in photographs.)

Meanwhile Runcie paid occasional visits to his parents, now living in Angus's 'inner city vicarage' in Nottingham. He regaled them with 'amazing stories' of Guards life. His mother enjoyed his lists of titled names, and would go to the public library to look them all up in *Debrett*, 'which I must say I've never done. I've always been very vague about their relationships, which has sometimes got me into difficulties.' His father was 'not interested' in aristocratic life, but was 'pleased that I was a good soldier'.

By the end of April 1944, the Third Battalion was impatient to go into action. They moved to Kent to join the invasion force that was gathering in secret, and practised manoeuvering their tanks in farmland that resembled Normandy. On 30 May they attended a 'service before battle' at Canterbury Cathedral – the first time Runcie had been there – during which William Temple preached. D-Day came and went, and still they waited. Not until a further six weeks had passed were they moved, one night, along the coast to Gosport, 'and we embarked there for Normandy'.

5

The easy answer

————◆————

Conveniently, we reached the motorway exit for St Albans, and the end of our southbound journey from Crosby, just as Runcie had got to this point in his narrative. I dropped him off at his house – Lindy had gone away to visit her sister – and rather missed his company as I headed for Oxford, to write up my notes of the journey and to begin to track down the people he'd mentioned.

I got the same story from everyone who had been in the Scots Guards with him: that he was charming, witty, a good mimic, and had an eye for the girls; and that no one would have guessed he would land up in the church. 'If anyone had asked me what I thought he might become,' wrote one of them, Peter Balfour, 'I would have said either an academic or an actor.'

Two months after the Crosby trip, on 11 June 1992, I went to Cuddesdon, the village outside Oxford where my family had lived opposite the Runcies in the 1960s. A service of thanksgiving for the success of a big financial appeal was to be held at the theological college, with Runcie, its most distinguished living former principal, presiding. There were now women students (unthinkable in Runcie's days as principal), and the male student detailed to look after me said that they were very tense as they waited for the November vote in General Synod on the ordination of women.

There was no sign of any of the stars of Runcie's Cuddesdon days – Mark Santer, Jim Thompson, Mike Scott-Joynt, students from his era who are now bishops. All were too busy, presumably. Another absentee was Peter Cornwell, who had been on Runcie's Cuddesdon staff and was subsequently vicar of the University church in Oxford, but became a Roman Catholic amid much publicity half way through Runcie's archbishopric. I had recently met him in Blackwell's bookshop and he said he hadn't been invited to the Cuddesdon celebration. One old Cuddesdon man told me, at the party after the service, that he might have left his own Church of England incumbency and become a Roman Catholic if it hadn't been for the money – a Catholic parish priest gets very little salary after being provided with house, housekeeper and food. This man said that some Catholic priest friends of his had remarked that it was the economics rather than the theology which stops Rome letting its priests marry: 'It's a poor church, and simply can't afford to support wives.'

In contrast, Cuddesdon church was filled largely with wealthy-looking City men, whose trust funds had stumped up much of the money for John Garton's appeal. A City banker who helped organise the fund-raising said, in his speech at the party, that a lot of non-churchgoers in the City believed the Church of England was an important national institution. He made it sound like keeping an adequate defence force.

Runcie was the celebrant at the communion service, and preached, looking magnificent in chasuble and mitre. It being St Barnabas's Day, he began with this saint, pointing out that he had 'brought his private income with him into the ministry'; and 'the relationship between faith and generosity must be the theme of this service'. The sermon contained three jokes, carefully placed at beginning, middle and end. The briefest was about the dying Roman Catholic woman who said to him, as he clasped her hand, 'Father, you'd have made a wonderful priest.' At the party I met Margaret Duggan, who had vivid memories of trying to interview Runcie for her biography a decade ago, at Lambeth in the evenings. He was so tired that he would simply describe the day's events to her rather than let her ask questions (she did not use a tape-recorder, which is why there are no direct quotes from him in her book). I recognised this technique, and guessed that it was not altogether tiredness. I was beginning to find him elusive.

His letters – when I could get them out of him – were full of entertaining ancedotes, but it was becoming harder to pin him down so that I could get on with the book. Even Frances Charlesworth, his part-time secretary, did not reply as swiftly as before to my messages. I was beginning to pine for dead biographical subjects who could be researched in libraries and did not set off round the world just when I needed them – he was travelling extensively again this summer.

After the service he planted a commemorative tree, with some witty remarks, and talked at great length to endless old Cuddesdon men. I overheard him remembering names – or at least covering up lapses of memory – apparently effortlessly, with a constant supply of apposite and kindly questions. When I finally found myself alone with him, after the departure of most of the guests, I noticed that his *persona* was quite different from the genial but slightly bored individual with whom I went round Crosby, or the teller of good club stories during our motorway journey – he seemed much more alive and electric.

It was the week in which the press had been having a field day with Andrew Morton's book on the Princess of Wales, which alleged that she once threw herself downstairs in despair at her marriage. I asked Runcie if he had been involved with this – was he still acting as counsellor to the royals? He hinted that he was, and said something about the complexity of it all. Lindy had not come to the Cuddesdon event, and I ask if she was piano-teaching today. 'Yes, and

I'm categorically denying rumours that she's been hurling herself downstairs.'

He went to his car – an almost-new Rover, scarlet and very smart – to get his diary. His briefcase proved to contain a bottle of Moet & Chandon, 'a golden wedding present I'm dropping off on the way home'. He offered me a date in three months' time for our next interview session, but when I expostulated at the delay he brought it forward to one month.

On Tuesday 14 July 1992 I arrived at the Runcie house at 9 am. He had been celebrant that morning at an early Mass in St Albans Abbey. Talking of the crowdedness of his diary, he mentioned that a couple of Sundays ago he had preached at St Thomas's in Oxford, keeping a long-standing promise to Robert Sweeney, its vicar; but he and Lindy had been at a Rossini première at Covent Garden till 11.30 the night before, and had been invited to the BBC tent for the last day of Wimbledon on the Sunday. 'So I tore off my vestments, and drove at breakneck speed to Wimbledon, and found myself sitting next to Maurice Saatchi, though I didn't gather who he was till afterwards.'

Lindy gave me a cup of Nescafé, and, since she was about to embark on some noisy piano-practice for concerts during an American trip, Runcie and I went to his upstairs study, a tiny room with a prie-dieu, and lots of family photos. He sat in a swivel chair at the desk and I perched in a low armchair and kept an eye on the tape recorder, which was on a stool between us. Unlike the sessions in the car on the motorway, I was facing him; at the outset, eye contact induced a slight degree of self-consciousness in both of us, I felt. But once again he talked carefully and fluently, without any sign of tiredness, this time for two and a half hours.

I reminded him that we had left him on the tank craft, on a Normandy beach. What followed? 'A tremendous wait, sitting in apple orchards, with the smell of calvados, and some of the fire of calvados inside us! It was my first trip abroad, first time out of England, and I was conscious of that. My brother officers had usually been taken to Cannes for the summer, but to me it was the big thrill of being abroad. I enjoyed exercising a few French words on farmers, and was amazed to see them practically living with the animals – it was a very peasant area, between Arromanches and Caen. It was like Kent, where we'd been practising, only there were more orchards, and the sunken lanes were deeper. We had heavy tanks, and it was very difficult to manoeuvre them over that sort of country. It was quite a tricky business, planning to create an element of surprise in bringing into action heavy tanks, in an area where it seemed that only light tanks would be able to manoeuvre.'

He describes how life organised itself – with 'a certain cosiness' – inside a Churchill tank: 'There was one driver in the front, and a co-driver; they were lower down. Then there was a gunner on your left, and a wireless operator on your right, and you, the tank commander, normally had your head out of the top, so you were fortunate. It was only under fire that you put the lid down and looked through the visor. And then you felt less able to control what was happening, so you very often took the risk, even in battle, of keeping your head out.'

His rank was 'only a lieutenant – you didn't rise quickly in the Guards, because that was your appropriate rank as a troop commander'. Each lieutenant was in charge of three tanks, commanding one himself, with the others commanded by his sergeant and corporal. 'I had an easy-going sergeant, who was strange to find in the Scots Guards, because he was a typical Brummy, called Sandy Mildenhall.' These days, W. A. ('Sandy') Mildenhall still lives in Birmingham; he wrote to me: 'Bob Runcie's manner was that of a gentleman, and he was always willing to listen to any complaints that the troop brought forward, which was quite often during the campaign.' Another tank troop had Tam Shearer, a Scot, for its sergeant, who told me that Runcie was 'pretty easy-going – not as far as work was concerned, but some of the higher ranks were in the habit of making people jump. He wasn't of

that type, although he was perfectly able to do it. He wasn't
a strict disciplinarian. He tended to be a wee bit on the soft
side, we thought.'

Runcie himself says he was regarded as 'fairly soft' compared to some officers, 'but I didn't have difficulties with
discipline', even though the men were in some respects more
sophisticated than their commanders. They tended to be
older, 'and even if they weren't, on the Clyde they'd seen
more of life – they'd been apprenticed at sixteen, and were
married, or perhaps divorced and living with somebody'.
Runcie's own tank crew included a young Scots driver, 'just
a boy, really', and also a 'philosophical' radio operator.

On 28 July 1944, ten days after arriving in Normandy,
they moved up to attack the ridge of Caumont which was
held by the Germans, travelling all night, lying up the next
day, and at last going into battle early the following morning.
'It was all so unrealistic. I can remember, as we queued up
in the forming-up place, a wonderful, typical brigade officer
coming along the line and saying to me, "Better country for
an Irish hunter than a Churchill, I think!"'

Under German gunfire, they began their slow advance,
themselves firing at anything that might conceal enemy
mortars or machine guns. By evening they were four miles
inside enemy lines. It was only then, 'when we got into more
open ground, and the Germans realised what was happening
and wheeled up some heavy fire', that they came under
serious bombardment. Twelve of the Churchill tanks were
knocked out in a few minutes and their crews killed. Runcie
says it was 'killing other people rather than my friends being
killed' that shook him – 'a German standing up bravely
with a bazooka, and you training your gun on him, and
just blowing him to smithereens as you went through. That
was the first kind of "this is for real" feeling.'

He spoke about this in his 1982 conversation with John
Mortimer:

I have interviews with anti-blood sports campaigners, and
when they say: 'Have you ever killed an animal?' I say,

'No, I've only killed people.' ... When I'd been very successful in knocking out a German tank, I went up to it and saw four young men dead. I felt a bit sick. Well, I was sick, actually. The other time was when a German tank was shelling our position, and a very eager little man in specs came up to me and he said: 'Shall I go and discover where that tank is?' ... I said: 'Yes, why don't you go?' And I saw him shamble off ... Half an hour later, he was dead. I won't say that incident led directly to my becoming a priest, but it had a lot to do with it. I thought, 'I'll make up for that some day.'[1]

Talking to me, he emphasised that conditions in Normandy were not like what 'Wilfred Owen and people' had had to endure in the First World War, 'because you might sometimes stay at a farmhouse, wheel your tank alongside some habitation and take it over. And, frankly, you'd very often loot property, because the place had been deserted, and you would go in and take bottled fruit and that sort of thing.' Even during the push through Normandy, life consisted of 'ninety per cent boredom and only ten per cent panic'.

After Caumont came 'the fighting around Caen, which went on a long time. Eventually we moved on to the banks of the Seine, and had an opportunity to go to Paris, shortly after the Liberation [August 1944]. I remember going to all the places, living it up: the Georges V, the Folies Bergères – everything was alive again, and that, rather than pilgrimages to the Rodin Museum or to Chartres, seemed to be what people were doing.' He rejoined his squadron, and the tanks were loaded on to transporters which took them through newly-liberated France and Belgium.

The Guards' Armoured Division had played a large part in the liberation of Brussels, and had been rewarded by being allowed to establish a club in the city. 'We all went there for leave and weekends. Even when we were in Germany, in Schleswig-Holstein, you could drive back to Brussels

[1] John Mortimer, *In Character*, Penguin, 1984, pp. 31–2.

for a holiday.' During December the squadron was 'in the Netherlands, between the Meuse and the Rhine, and first of all up in the north, trying to link up with the parachute drop at Arnhem. Then we were switched, just over Christmas, because of a German counter-offensive in the Ardennes, to Valkenburg and Maastricht. It was then that we got to know a Maastricht family who had a country house near Valkenburg, and they had a Christmas ball. It was magical. It was in a castle, and there was a battle not very far away, and there we were with the girls in long dresses.'

At this point in the story Margaret Duggan mentions that one of the girls in this family was 'called Trees, a lively, sparkly girl who was a devout Roman Catholic and insisted, however late a Saturday night party, that Runcie accompanied her to Mass the next morning'. Duggan judges: 'Of all his girl-friends during these years, Trees . . . is the one he most probably would have married, if marrying had been thinkable at the time', adding that her son, who called on Runcie at Lambeth in 1982, 'is now a Brother of the Taizé Community'.[2] Runcie did not pick her out for special mention to me, merely remarking that 'they had six beautiful daughters, and Hector Laing and Archie Fletcher and Tony Stevenson and I became friendly with the family, and I'm still in touch with them today.'

Duggan provides a wealth of detail about his military movements during the first months of 1945, derived from the regimental history. Runcie himself is vaguer about it all: 'I think on the way to Munster we must have fought that battle at Winnekendonk, but it may have been the other side of Munster – I don't know.' Since it was at Winnekendonk that he won the Military Cross, his uncertainty is rather striking.

As he described his war experiences to me, I gradually realised that he was leaving out all mention of the medal and how it came to be earned. He had gone on to recall 'a time when I got too far ahead, and got out of my tank in

[2]Duggan, p. 79.

the dark, and found I'd gone right into German lines, and people were talking in German around me. That was the time when I really thought my last moment had come.' He 'battened down hatches, and crept away'.

Next, he came up with the story of how 'at Lütjenburg I was told to take over the surrender of the city, and the German commander had done the only sensible thing for a man in that situation – he'd had an enormous lunch, and was totally drunk. And when I tried to become very pompous, he put his arm around me!' Funny stories started to proliferate as he spoke. Yet he also mentioned passing through Belsen just after its liberation, and seeing 'the terrible, terrible grey skeleton figures'; but though I asked him to elaborate on his memories of this, he had nothing else striking to say about it; he was 'passing through pretty quickly – some people stopped, and did take stock of it, but I'd seen enough'.

He recalled 'a delectable village near the Baltic coast, in Schleswig-Holstein, the one part of Germany that was able to maintain its dairy produce, its standards of life and so on, and we got settled in the *schloss*, and the officers' mess opened, and the best of the food around was available'. Next, he brought out the story of arresting a German commander who had not surrendered, a distinguished elderly soldier who had been a hero of the First World War – except that Runcie could not remember the man's name. I remarked that it was striking, given the colourfulness of this episode, that he had not got the name at his fingertips. I added that he had also managed to skip over the action which won him the MC. He replied that he thought I was 'eager to get on' – as if his biographer could not be bothered to hear this crucial episode in his own words. But now at last he did tell the story:

'The previous day, again we'd gone a bit too far ahead, and were in a wood, and suddenly a whole lot of soldiers came marching either side of my tanks. I thought they were the infantry we were supposed to be supporting. In fact they were Germans whom we'd disturbed, who'd been sleeping there. Anyway, they were rounded up and captured. That was one of those times when I felt, I don't think I'm going to get out of this. I think I'm actually going to die. And also at the same time reflecting, How amazingly calm I am! You shut your mind to the ultimate, and just concentrate on the immediate, thinking, I'm not being brave, it's just that there's nothing else I can do. It's funny that people should be regarded as being brave in a situation like this, because it doesn't require any kind of reflected motivation.

'One of my tanks had been hit then, and it was on fire. And they all came tumbling out, and I said, "But where's Philip?" And he was stuck – the turret was stuck over the co-driver's lid, so that he was trapped – and the tank was on fire. It wasn't blazing; it was just smoking. Of course something might have exploded, but you don't think about that sort of thing.

'I had to get in first, you see, and then turn the thing round, so that it moved the turret. But he was confused, and we still needed to drag him out of the tank and bring him back to us.' And this was while they were under fire? 'Well, the tank had been knocked out – we'd gone out from the wood – we'd emerged from it – you can see this isn't a well-honed story. We were not under infantry fire, small arms fire, but we were under long-distance anti-tank fire.'

He said that this rescue was, perhaps, more important than what actually won him the MC. 'The rescue is mentioned, but only in passing. The main thing was the following day, or the day after, when we'd mounted an offensive to get hold of a place, and we had to advance with three tanks going forward, and three tanks behind to cover them. We were in the second group, and in front of us several went into the open and were knocked out, and some people were killed. To everyone's astonishment the Pipe Major was killed. And a man called Thomson, who got the Military Medal, the driver of another tank in my troop, located where the gun was that was firing on us, that was doing all the damage. So he manoeuvred his tank around, and said, "I canna see, sir, we'll have to go up into the open." And I took my tank out on to open ground with his, and we just had one shot at this thing, and knocked it out immediately.

'It was a mixture of tank and guncarrier. It had a big gun on it, and we knocked it out. It was critical, because it was surprising what this gun could do to anything we had. It was their last great resource. Of course there were other emplacements, but this was the troublesome one. And because we knocked that out, and things could move forward, that's the major reason why I got the MC. It's also mentioned that the previous day I'd rescued the character from the tank. That didn't make any difference to the battle, but knocking out the gun actually moved things on, and it came to the attention of my commanding officer, who subsequently had the reputation – because so many of us got decorated – of writing very good citations! So that's the story of that.'

I remarked that most people remembered the rescue from the tank. That was the story that usually got attached to him. 'I'm glad in a way,' he replied, 'because I feel that with the other one, actually we were in the wrong place! We shouldn't have been out there in view, and then the driver pointed out that that's where the gun was.' It was his suggestion? 'Yes. Although he did, on my recommendation, get decorated. I mean, *I* didn't expect to get decorated; I expected him to get decorated, because you don't write about yourself. And when the C.O. brought the news of my decoration – I remember it was a very cosy morning at this *schloss* at Panker, when the war was over – I was totally surprised. You think, my hat! That's extraordinary! One of those moments.'

I asked if he had seen much of Germany after the war was over. 'Ah, yes, now,' he answered, and began a story which made even more impression on me than his modest, hesitant description of the rescue from the burning tank. 'It was in Cologne that one was really aware of the devastation of the bombing – the cathedral was just a shell, and wonderful Romanesque churches and buildings were flat, and one was shocked at what the bombing had done. When I went back to Cologne I couldn't believe that they could rebuild a place like that. When I was there last, which was eight years ago, I went to try to find Weiden, because that was a place with great associations. We were there for a couple of months, and I had a girl-friend there, and she had an uncle who sang in the opera in Cologne. It was my first introduction to opera.'

Was this sort of fraternisation acceptable by that time? 'No, not really.' And what about the girl's side of it – a German girl going out with an English soldier? 'I don't think that would matter too much. We were quite discreet about it. But it was quite risky. You went with an army car, picked her up, took her to the opera, and then had dinner afterwards, and took her back. That was quite daring to do as an officer.'

I asked if it had been worth it. He replied by taking, from the window-sill, a framed photograph of a girl of Dietrich-like beauty. 'I brought that out specially for you. That's the girl.' Did they keep in touch after the war? 'Um, not really. It was my fault, really. She had been in the Nazi Youth Movement. Her boy-friend had been in the SS, and was killed in Russia. Her name was Marks.' What was her first name? 'Ingeborg. When I say Nazi, what I mean is, her world had gone. But she was a spirited girl who loved the opera, and worked at a photographer's. And when I left to go to Italy, I said I would keep in touch, but I wasn't very good at keeping in touch.'

He saw her again on a visit to Bonn after the war: 'I went to see her, and met her parents, who were very very keen to see me, and she said, "Come and stay." But I was so caught up in this conference [a summer school] that I couldn't. We had lunch together and a walk in Cologne and so on, but my mind was on other things, and it was just one of those things that went dead as a result of, I suppose, my self-interest, and she saw that there was no future with me. And when I was on this visit to Weiden [in the 1980s] I wanted to try to find her. Obviously I didn't like to make too much of it, being then an archbishop who was on an official visit! I mean, she was not exactly a pious Lutheran or anything like that! She was fairly anti-clerical. She always used to think it was extraordinary that I was religious, went to church and things like that. I said to somebody, "This is where she worked", and they tried so hard to trace her, and got as far as discovering where the family had moved away to, and even said, "This is the person!" – somebody who had married and got another name – and I dropped her a line. But it wasn't her.'

This seemed the moment to ask the question I had been steeling myself to put ever since his references to girl-friends back in Crosby days – the question of his sexual experience. What, I asked, were the habits of the army at this time, with this sort of affair, these short-lived romances? Were they expected to lead to bed, or what? 'Yes, in most cases,' he answered, 'but they didn't with me. I was having to rein that in, really. And it created a sort of tension.' Why didn't he sleep with her? 'I don't know why, really. My fellow officers, you know, would say to me, "I'm normal, you know, I drink, I fuck, I smoke," and that sort of thing. I remember a particular officer saying that. This was a sign of normality, you see. And they used to go to the Bag o' Nails, which was a great resort [in London, for prostitutes]. And indeed I've been to the Bag o' Nails myself, just out of interest, you know, and would go to the Four Hundred, which was more respectable, and couldn't afford any of these things, but was a tagger-on. Certainly I think I was unusual there. It may have been some effect of my religious commitment (knowing one would have to confess it), and some fear – I suppose it was more fear of getting the clap then.'

I suggested that his abstinence could hardly have been the effect of his upbringing, considering that his parents' fidelity was questionable. 'Yes,' he answered. 'I didn't realise it at the time, but I see now there was a question mark over it.' Nor was it as if he had been brought up in strict Presbyterian surroundings. 'No. And I mean I'd had girl-friends from the day when I first discovered what you could do in the back row of a cinema. But you have to take my word for this. I mean, I wouldn't be ashamed to tell you. In fact I'm rather ashamed of it, really!' And it did create quite a tension for him, in the relationship with Ingeborg? 'Yes, it did.'

* * *

The Third Battalion stayed in Germany till February 1946.
Runcie was was then sent to join the First Battalion keeping
the peace in Trieste. I asked him if his family hadn't been
expecting him back by this time. 'Yes, but the C.O. was
posted to command in Trieste, and he took some of his
favourites from Germany. And at that point I wondered
whether to stay in the army for a bit. Hector Laing and
I actually volunteered to go and be parachute officers in
Japan. But the Japanese war was soon over, putting an
end to such bravado!' It would have been triple bravado, I
suggested: staying in the army, Japan, and parachutes. Why
parachutes? 'Well, we were feeling rather sort of macho.
And we'd experienced most things, and we'd never jumped
in a parachute. But I went to Trieste, which was a much
more civilised battalion. I played cricket and tennis, and we
bathed, and I went to the first Salzburg Festival after the war,
on a truck with a driver – just went up there and saw Bruno
Walter conducting. Then I was put on the Italo-Yugoslav
Boundary Commission.'

It all seems, I suggested, to have been a good preparation
for life in the diplomatic or civil services rather than the
church. 'That's right. This four-nation commission – Britain,
France, the Soviet Union and America – was determining
the boundary between Yugoslavia, Italy and Austria, and
defining the nature of Trieste, a kind of Beirut of those
times, with bombs going off. We went round the country
areas, and the British delegation was minute. There was only
one secretary, and she had something of a breakdown, so I
had to do quite a lot of longhand taking of notes. You would
meet the head of the Communist party, the local Catholic
bishop, the mayor and so on. We went on to Venice, and
I really fell for Venice in a very big way. Those were days
when I did think what a good thing it would be to be a
diplomat. My tastes are those of a diplomat, really.'

But he took no definite steps in that direction? 'No. I think
I was marking time. I could have gone back to Oxford earlier
than this. I delayed my demob. But then I thought that time

was going on – it was 1946 – and I remember thinking, if I don't get out now, I'll have to give up Oxford altogether. And I thought I'd better get back there, and then I would make up my mind. So I came back from Italy and started at Oxford again.'

Peter Trafford, now Father Simon Trafford of Ampleforth Abbey, was in the First Battalion with Runcie in Trieste. He remembers him organising a shooting competition with scrupulous attention to detail, and playing cricket skilfully. He also recalls another officer saying, when he heard that Runcie intended to go into the church, 'What a waste.'

For a view of himself as a returning soldier who came up to Brasenose in October 1946 to resume his University studies, Runcie recommended me to Sir Richard Parsons, nowadays a retired diplomat and novelist, in 1946 an undergraduate with college rooms near Runcie's. Parsons described Runcie to me as 'an engaging chap, very jolly; a rather sort of smooth Guards officer, though I don't mean that in a nasty way. You'd have thought he'd gone to Eton; the manner was socially superior.'

BNC was 'a very hearty, sporting college', said Parsons, and Runcie quickly became very popular: 'He was elected president of the Junior Common Room, which is a real popularity contest.' On the whole the college was 'a celibate place', and Runcie's determination to acquire girl-friends 'rather stuck out'. Parsons describes the Runcie method: he would position himself opposite a pretty girl at a desk in the Radcliffe Camera (one of the Bodleian Library reading rooms) and at four o'clock would rise to his feet, bow, and say, 'Madam, my friend and I would like to invite you to tea.' 'I was the friend,' explains Parsons, 'and it was my job to buy the cream buns and put the kettle on.'

Parsons considers this skill at acquiring decorative girls the more impressive, considering that the majority of girl undergraduates in those days were 'frumpish like Margaret Roberts' – the future Margaret Thatcher, with whom Runcie now had his first contact. Writing to Angus soon after arriving for his first term back at Oxford, he reported: 'I take a mild interest in the doings of the Conservatives, and to show my broadmindedness have joined the Socialists so that their card should help to fill up my mantelpiece.' He was attracted by the stylishness of the Carlton Club, a Conservative club in Oxford of which he was a founder member when it opened in 1946. He took Conservatism seriously enough to be college secretary for, and on the committee of, the University Conservative Assocation. Margaret Roberts had just retired as its president.

This was my cue to ask Runcie for specific Margaret Roberts/Thatcher stories from those days. 'Well, I didn't take to her! I was in her company a lot – and I've always made sport of the fact that I had a minor job (I can't remember what it was now) on the committee, and she dropped me because of my rather frivolous attachment to politics. But it's true, because I represented the Carlton Club, against which she was rebelling. If she'd known that I come from the same background as she has, I think she would have been surprised, because she obviously associated me with those lordly characters who were getting Conservatism as a serious philosophy a bad name. She was a hard-working chemist. I always regarded her as rather tubby, with rosy cheeks. Not my sort of girl! I'm full of admiration for her, but it's like sitting next to electricity.' Then, or now, or both? 'Oh, both!'

As to the Labour Club, which he also joined, 'Shirley Williams was coming on as a young star, and there was Tony Wedgwood Benn.' Runcie made friends with a young married couple living in Wellington Square, John and Eileen Spencer, whom he describes as 'socialist and pacifist – they cultivated idealism as earnestly as other friends nourished my self-indulgences.' The Spencers went with him in the long vacation of 1947 to a summer seminar in Bonn, part of the British effort to heal relations with Germany. On this trip he met Merrie Middleton, a Scottish girl studying at Edinburgh University. He wrote of her to me: 'We became close friends and the Spencers encouraged this liaison. She went to France and when she came back supposed that we might pick up the relationship and even get married. In fact I had drifted apart while she was in France, since Oxford had claimed me too much. That is shorthand to what she will make into a huge and amusing story.'

I contacted her – she is now Mrs Mackenzie-Johnston – and she and her husband invited me to lunch in their house in Kensington. Runcie had suggested that she rather resembled Lindy, but I could not detect the slightest likeness of character. She turned out to be quiet, shrewd, with a warm regard for Runcie – she and her husband have seen quite a lot of the Runcies over the years, and she is James's godmother – but she told a very different story. She said she was not aware that Runcie contemplated marriage, and emphasised that she never did. Her Church of Scotland upbringing would have made it impossible for her to marry an Anglican (especially Anglo-Catholic) priest. 'And anyway I rather had the impression that at that stage he intended to be celibate.' She recalled that Runcie attracted the romantic interest of a German girl on the trip, who decided he was too 'cold-blooded' for her.

His father had died while he was in Trieste; Runcie had last seen him on a brief visit to Nottinghamshire about a year earlier. 'Strangely enough,' he told me, 'it wasn't thought that I should come back for the funeral. Funny, that.' He does not regard his father's death as any sort of watershed for him. His mother went to live with his brother Ken in Manchester, and Runcie would go up there in vacations and take a temporary job in the Central Reference Library, meanwhile reading hard to catch up on what ought to have been done in term time. 'I had such a full social life in Oxford, I had to work very hard in the vacation.' Denys Potts, another BNC man in those days, describes Runcie as 'a confirmed socialite, a great party-goer (and giver), whom one never seemed to catch actually working'.

His tutors were now K. J. Spalding and Michael Holroyd (no relation of the biographer). He describes Spalding as 'an oriental mystic, but a man of considerable wealth, and there was always the aroma of an after-breakfast cigar about his panelled room, and a lovely fire, and I thought, how nice to be a don!' Holroyd he describes as 'a lovely big teddy bear of a man' with a wife who was 'a great hostess of Boars Hill'. Holroyd's father 'had been a keeper of the Tate, and the house was stuffed with lovely things, and they rather adopted me a bit, and introduced me to a more civilised world. We used to go to the Playhouse. And there was a rather beautiful Czech refugee, they got me to look after her.'

He attended lectures by the eccentric philosopher Donald McKinnon – 'if you took down what Donald said, you couldn't understand it at the time, but you gradually worked your way into something which was really significant' – and by Russell Meiggs, who taught Ancient History, a 'really wonderful man'. But 'I got very little help from my tutors.'

It was now that he heard for the first time the name of Kierkegaard mentioned in lectures given as part of a mission to the University. Reading him, he found him 'congenial', because 'Kierkegaard thought religion had nothing to do with the rational part of your mind'. Runcie had been 'pretty well seduced by the arguments of the Logical Positivists', and was finding rational arguments for the truth of Christianity 'rather difficult' to accept. Now Kierkegaard, and also Wittgenstein, with 'his mixture of ascetic rationality combined with a sort of mysticism', suggested 'a way in which I could hold together a fundamental scepticism with religious devotion'.

This remark clearly required further exploration: did he mean a fundamental scepticism about rational proofs of the truth of Christianity? 'Yes. That's right.' But at the same time, in another 'compartment' (to use a term he himself had used in talking about his early life), there existed belief? 'Yes. Now, Stephen Neil [a Trinity don who lectured on Kierkegaard during the University mission] was one of those people who, for a moment, was able to make it cohere. There have occasionally been moments when there's been coherence in my Christianity.'

But only moments? 'Moments! And those moments of coherence are very valuable. The moments of coherence are, of course, the moments that make sense of it all.' What about the moments of incoherence? 'Oh yes, well, there are plenty of them! But I'm comforted because Luther said that he had more moments of despair and inexperience of God after his conversion than before. He makes this point that faith is experience plus decision; that most of the time it's decision to act by the experiences you've had, rather than any experiences you're having. I can understand that.

This was the time at Oxford when C. S. Lewis was in full fig. Wasn't Runcie attracted? 'No. He was entertaining and readable, and I used to go to the Socratic Club, where he gave endless papers. But he was too good to be true.'

Runcie's brother-in-law Angus now stepped into his life again. Margaret Duggan reports that in the summer term of 1948, at the end of Runcie's second year back at Oxford, he received a visit from the principal of Westcott House theological college in Cambridge, where Angus had been trained as a priest. This was W. D. L. ('Billy') Greer, shortly to become Bishop of Manchester, who called on Runcie while preaching in Oxford, at Angus's request, 'to discuss the matter of his vocation'. Greer found Runcie recovering from an all-night party: 'The conversation went on for some time with Runcie trying hard to remember just why he did want to be ordained. But Greer had a sure touch and knew his young men. "Oh well," he said as he got to his feet, "I think you would probably do very well for a parish in Manchester."'[3]

Runcie himself told me of this: 'The point is that Angus was nagging me, sort of saying, "You'll have to go to Westcott House" and so on. And a mixture of indolence, overactivity [in other spheres of life], and the question of whether I really wanted to go ahead with this, dogged me. I can remember one day going for a walk with Hugo Charteris, who was going to work on the *Daily Mail*, and he said, "I

[3]Duggan, p. 90.

could get you a job running the Ideal Home Exhibition – I could get you on the staff. A few years doing that, and then you can decide what you want to go in for." And also I had thought about the Foreign Office. But I thought, it's all I can do to concentrate on Greats; I can't really face the idea of diverting my time in order to do Foreign Office exams and interviews.'

He took Schools, his final examination in Greats, in December 1948, and got a First. Sir Richard Parsons, his BNC neighbour, remembers this as 'a great surprise' in the college, since Firsts were rare there. Just before the examination, Greer's successor at Westcott House, Kenneth Carey, called on him. According to Duggan, '"Are you still on?" he asked Runcie. "I suppose so," Runcie replied, preoccupied with his examinations, but also slightly cold round the feet now that his commitment to ordination was so close.'[4] Runcie himself tells the story much more bluntly: 'I went to Westcott and started on ordination training because it was the easy answer, you see, to "What am I going to do? Can't make up my mind." Saying, "Well, it's the easiest thing to do. I can always get out of it."'

[4]Duggan, p. 91.

6

I agree to act as if

———◆———

Towards the end of this conversation, Runcie remarked of the state of his diary and in-tray: 'I just feel a bit guilty that I'm so disorganised. I would really like to shut down, to proclaim that I'm having an illness of some sort for a month.'

His wish was granted. During August 1992, he and Lindy set off for another American trip, a combination of duty and holiday. I soon heard that he had been taken seriously ill in Salt Lake City, and was in intensive care. Lindy had returned to St Albans to make preparations for looking after an invalid.

I rang her at once, and she explained that though initially it looked like heart failure, it was a recurrence of a rare condition called cellulitis, which he had contracted years ago. He was about to be flown home in the company of a nurse, and would have to have a bedroom downstairs. He would be forbidden to stand, let alone walk or carry out engagements, for at least the rest of the year, 'otherwise he'll lose a leg, and I don't want a voluntary Long John Silver around the house. Thank God it didn't happen in Uganda or Armenia or most of the other places we've been recently, or he'd be dead. He'll be bored out of his mind with nothing to do, so I hope you can come over and get him talking.'

I kept in touch with Frances Charlesworth, his secretary, and when I gathered that he was well enough to see me, I asked for a date and was offered one a few days later, a great change. On 6 October I drove to St Albans, listening on the radio to reports of the Amsterdam air crash – two hundred and fifty people were feared dead after a plane had ploughed into an apartment block.

The front door was half open when I arrived; Lindy was out teaching, Runcie pottering about with one trouser leg rolled slightly up, and walking a touch more stiffly than usual, but otherwise looking quite unravaged. (So much for Long John Silver and 'no standing'.) A workman was putting finishing touches to a shower which had been installed downstairs for his use, but when I asked to use the loo, he took me upstairs himself. His bed was in the sitting room, but I could not see why. He said that standing for a long period was bad for him, but he needed to keep on the move.

His brother-in-law Angus had just died, and he had been to take the funeral, and was talking of going to Australia to lecture in the New Year. He wanted to make tea for the workman, and only reluctantly let me do it. He sat on the sofa and put one leg up (his left) while talking; but when the phone rang – which happened often – he went spryly across the room, threw himself on to the bed (next to which was the phone), and picked it up with the 'Yes, good morning?' which I had noticed was how he always answered a call.

He told me that the cellulitis was originally caught while blackberry-picking with James on a Cornish holiday in the 1960s. It probably came from a thorn which had crop-spray on it. He was ill for several weeks then, and apparently it remained dormant in his bloodstream, probably being triggered off again during the American trip when he drove a splinter into his foot. He described how he began to feel ill while conducting a combined baptism, confirmation and communion service:

'As we moved into the church there was one of those

American ladies, peroxide blonde, with huge sunglasses, and as the long procession set off she leant across to me and said [he drawls] "Have fun!" I didn't have fun, because I began to feel shaky. I managed the sermon, and to baptise ten babies and confirm a number of people, and I got through the prayer of consecration, but by the time I had communicated myself I said, "I'll have to go out now." A doctor and a nurse in the congregation seized hold of me and took me up the road to the cardiac unit. At first they thought it was heart failure or a clot on the lungs.'

There was a 'slight difference of opinion' between him and Lindy as to which of them first guessed it was a repeat of the cellulitis. He was given 'quantities of antibiotics' intravenously, and when he was well enough to travel he flew back in the care of the 'slightly up-market nurse' who had been in the congregation when he collapsed – evidently a senior nursing officer for the area – who stayed for a week, when they arrived at St Albans, 'because Lindy can't touch a foot with flaking skin, you see, or bear the thought of removing a bottle in bed. For a lady who's borne children, she's amazingly un-nurselike! But on health insurance, and altering the house, getting the best price from plumbers and things, she's amazing.'

He admitted to 'quite a sense of release in just leading a quiet life' since the illness had struck, and wondered whether he should follow James's advice to stop being a public figure 'and watch television with Mum' instead. On the other hand a BBC camera crew was arriving the next day to record him for a programme on portraits at the Tate Gallery. Runcie was to speak about a painting of Randall Davidson, Archbishop of Canterbury from 1903 to 1928.

'It's by de Laszlo, and it's interesting because he's a painter who's got a reputation for impeccable accuracy but little psychological penetration. The interesting thing is that Davidson wasn't a deep man, really, so you don't need much psychological penetration. What comes out is a good man, with honesty and Scottish good sense. He's the last of the Victorians and the first of the twentieth century, and he's got around him all the accoutrements of the Establishment: the Cross of Canterbury, which was given to Archbishop Benson by the clergy of the Southern Province; and he's wearing the Royal Victorian chain, and peeping discreetly out is the Garter Star, which I don't think he should be wearing because he only had that when he was Bishop of Winchester. So he's got all the kit, and seems to carry the accoutrements of position rather well. People were always telling me I was a sort of Davidson character.'

The same thought had occurred to me. But before I could develop this theme, he had returned to his recent hospital experiences. 'At Santa Fe and in Salt Lake City, the Episcopal church had a female rector, and it's actually the first time I've received the sacrament from a woman priest who was the sole celebrant. And I wondered why we'd been fussing about it. The hospital was Catholic – in Mormon territory – and the chaplain, a rather saintly amazing man called Dave, gave me the sacrament each day. So that was the first time I've ever received what – as an Anglo-Catholic – I've always wondered might be the real thing.'

I asked what the Roman Catholic church's attitude to allowing Anglicans to communicate was these days. 'It wouldn't be allowed formally. But things of that sort happen much more in a country where the Anglican Communion is thought to be an ally, and no threat. I think there was a feeling in the hospital that you were either Mormon or Catholic. I remember once in the Carribean, the local Catholic bishop coming to a Eucharist at which I was presiding, and receiving the sacrament from me.'

Talk of the American woman rector prompted me to ask whether his ear was close to the ground for the General Synod vote on women priests the following month. He replied that no one could be certain of the outcome, 'though personally I would put my money on it passing. It won't pass by too many votes, and that will be awkward, but I would have thought it would get through.' And if that happened, what would he put his money on coming next? 'Oh, I think some will leave, but not that many. If we'd forced it through – this is Runcie's defence! – in the early 1980s, perhaps two thousand clergy would have left, out of a total of fifteen thousand. But I think that now, if fifty leave, that'll be all. I think people have just got used to it, and of course the ministry of women deacons has been really acceptable. But this is the Davidson defence! The Church of England deals with the maintenance of tranquillity.'

Since I had last seen him, I had been in touch with many of his friends from Scots Guards days, and they had all recalled their astonishment when he went into the church. Now, I asked him about this, and he agreed that 'amongst some friends' there was certainly amazement, but said that his more serious acquaintances at Oxford, like John and Eileen Spencer, the socialist couple who lived in Wellington Square, had known all along. (I met the Spencers a few weeks later, and they confirmed this, adding that he also told them he intended to be a celibate priest; the impression he gave to Merrie Middleton.) Runcie summed up these different impressions he made on different people with: 'I just suppose that I kept them in separate compartments.'

I put it to him that a reader of this book, contemplating the indecision, or at least lack of other plans, which seems to have made him go in for ordination rather passively, would want to know whether, looking back, he now felt he had been providentially guided, or whether it just seemed the way things had happened to fall out.

Runcie: Well, I do have a sense that there have been moments in my life, not when I've suddenly been converted, but have had a click in the mind which said, now, I'm going to do that, and that's going to be important. When I was at Oxford, a great deal of moral philosophy was taken up with the difference between act, intention and motive, all that linguistic stuff started by G. E. Moore, who had the idea that goodness was a colour, like yellow. I used to believe (I don't know where I got it from, but there was a philosopher called Campbell at Glasgow who had certainly advanced some theory) that we choose between sorts of life. At a certain level of maturity we build up a kind of life into which particular actions fit, and others don't. And it's no use saying that certain acts are good in themselves, only that certain sorts of life are more worthwhile than others, and particular actions fit into them.

I think that in my serious moments of thinking about life I had been sophisticated by the linguistic analysts and hadn't allowed the Bible (which I would read devotionally) to shape my attitudes, with the result that I would never quite shed the opinions that I had in those final two terms at Oxford. And when I went to Cambridge and was introduced to theology proper, the theologians and writers who appealed to me had to fit somehow into those categories. I could defend my faith and my vocation not by systematic theology, or metaphysics, but by philosophical attitudes, which were convinced that knowing *how* was prior to knowing *that*. It was an attitude that would proceed from the particular to the general. You'd take hold of a particular action, and it would fit into a certain sort of life. But you would begin with the action and then discover that it was fitting.

HC: I'd like to pretend that I followed you. I don't think I do; or if I do, it's on such a hesitant basis that I'd like a recapitulation. I think this is very important.

Runcie: Did you see in *The Times* on Saturday an interview with Iris Murdoch? It was on the priority, the sovereignty of good; saying she believed in the good but not in God. She thought religion was the most important thing because it kept certain values in play. She didn't believe in God, but she went to church from time to time. (I know she does because I've seen her.) But the point is, she said in a very Oxford way after a time, 'But you can see I'm hopelessly confused.' And I'm afraid I've sounded hopelessly confused. But you may have heard me tell the story of the logical positivist called Braithwaite, a don at King's, who belonged to the Freddy Ayer group, and who to everybody's surprise was baptised and became a Christian. And it was alleged that he made a pact with the Bishop of Ely – this was gossip – that he could say *sotto voce* before the Creed: 'I agree to act as if I believe in . . .' Logical positivism insisted that no metaphysical statements could be made.

I remember having lunch in a British Restaurant in Oxford with Merrie Middleton and John Spencer, and a man came in who had been in Bonn with us, and he was reading Theology, about which I knew practically nothing as a mental discipline. There was some mention of history, and he said 'Ah, but it's a question of what is history.' And I said, 'What do you mean by that?' And he said, 'Well, is it an act of God, like events in the Old Testament?' And I thought, good heavens, is this what they do in Theology?' I felt immensely superior, and thought, when I read Theology, if I have to believe that, I'll have to change quite a lot.' I remember that particular moment, this man saying, 'History is the working out of God's purpose.' I thought, it doesn't mean anything to me, 'the working out of God's purpose'.

On the other hand, clicks in the mind are the way in which to discover the wider claims you make about God – a truth understood is a truth enlarged.

HC: That doesn't sound like logical positivism – 'A truth understood is a truth enlarged.' Can you give an example?

Runcie: Well, Jenner noticing the complexion of the milk-maids, and being led on to find a cure for tuberculosis. And Archimedes in his bath. A small step leading to a larger. Because a logical positivist deals in particularities rather than in generalisations or absolutes.

HC: And the Braithwaite thing makes some sense to you, because if you say, even *sotto voce,* 'I agree to act as if . . .' and you do act as if, and you then find that acting as if works . . . ?

Runcie: Yes, that's right. It works, because it fits into a sort of pattern of life. Faith is made up of experience plus decision plus gathering of evidence as you go along.

HC: And in your own case, by taking the step, for whatever

reasons, right or wrong, to go for ordination, you were putting yourself in a situation where—

Runcie: Yes, where it will justify itself by the way it sort of fits the next stage.

HC: Not very different from conducting a scientific experiment just to see if it works.

Runcie: That's right. There was a great deal of 'It's worked up to now, and I'm confident it'll work if I trust it.'

Let's move from there to an example I've used before in my ministry. Suppose I were arguing for life after death. Now, my own philosophical understanding wouldn't allow me to say that there's a sort of bit-in-the-machine that goes on after you've died. From a philosophical angle I would find it difficult to sustain an argument for immortality. On the other hand, the promises of Christ are ones that create the pattern that I've gradually built up as my choice of a way of life. And to discover that at the heart of it there is something bogus or false in the promise of 'Though a man shall die, yet shall ye live in the Resurrection' – that I would find unacceptable. So that my trust in the Communion of Saints, and the language of life after death, is not grounded in any philosophical arguments, because I don't actually believe them. But they must be grounded in trust in this sort of life.

HC: You wouldn't believe in any philosophical arguments for it? You can't imagine there being any?

Runcie: I wouldn't put it quite as strongly as that. But if it were the philosophical argument alone, that would be something I would find difficult to sustain. I wouldn't be able to sit with a person and argue the immortality of the soul from Socratic dialogues, or extra-sensory perception.

HC: But you can only talk about 'the promises of Christ' from within the theological system.

Runcie: Yes, but you've committed yourself. I remember somebody making sport of the theologian Christopher Butler, who was chaplain of Keble but then became a Roman Catholic, and was a Catholic bishop here in Hertfordshire. Somebody said how shocking it was that

Butler had said he wouldn't believe in the resurrection unless the church told him he had to.

HC: And do you agree with him? If the church didn't tell you to believe in the resurrection, would you?

Runcie: I don't know!

HC: But this click in the mind, it's something that everybody experiences. It's a totally secular thing.

Runcie: Do you think that? The clicks in my mind I'm able to relate to the practice of religion.

HC: Because you're within the system.

Runcie: Because I pray – in a not very advanced way – and have a few disciplined rules about the sacrament, and having a spiritual director and so on: the clicks in the mind therefore fit into that. But I heard, the other day on Radio 4, Ludovic Kennedy talking to John Selwyn Gummer, and all my sympathies were with Kennedy.

HC: Taking the atheist point of view against Gummer?

Runcie: Yes. Gummer was saying things like, 'Well, the only thing I can say is, you just miss an awful lot in life, you know, if you're not a Christian, and I feel really sorry for you.' I find that sort of thing excruciating. It makes me wince. Religious know-alls tend to put me on the side of the unbelievers. And I don't feel that if you're not a believer, you're somehow inadequate, or don't have anything to teach us who do believe. Yet at a subliminal level, that's probably what I *do* feel. Because belief sort of holds things together.

HC: I read John Mortimer's interview with you, in which you said, of the purpose of God behind the Holocaust, 'I'm an agnostic on that.' Now, my mother was always telling me, in childhood, that everything was meant for the best; whatever happened was always somehow assumed into her system of Christian belief, and I think that this probably did more to put me off the Christian religion than anything else (my father never did it). Now, if you chose to regard these clicks in the mind, on a crude storybook level, as the workings of Providence – and I'm not saying you do – then how do you cope with a Providence which also allows a jet to plough into a block of flats in Amsterdam, and kill we still don't know how many people?

Runcie: Um, yes. But the click in the mind is something which relates to *my* attitude to things that happen, rather than determining what things should happen.

HC: This is the Oxford philosopher talking again, surely?

Runcie: Yes!

HC: Splitting split hairs.

Runcie: I would certainly have to find some reason for denying that something like an aeroplane flying into a block of flats in Amsterdam was the will of God. I would have to find some reason to rebel against that. But I think that in the Cross, you see that suffering is God's burden, not God's will. The stable and the Cross and the empty tomb are particularities which, if worked at and lived with, give you sufficient evidence to – how shall I say? – live appropriately with what happens in the world. They give you some kind of way to respond to what happens in the world.

HC: But this sounds terribly armchair. We can sit here in front of a comfortable fire, and there are people in Amsterdam digging with their hands in the rubble.

Runcie: Yes, but we're in armchairs now, talking about these things. I mean, when you're digging in the rubble, you're digging in the rubble, and if you have decisions to make, decisions about whether to save a child or loot a house, then it's the particularities of the sort of person you have become which makes it instinctive for you to have a certain sort of reaction.

HC: What matters is the particular moral decision they make at that moment?

Runcie: That's right. And they make it instinctively on the basis of – putting it crudely – all those acts of Communion, all those Confessions. They should theoretically make you into the sort of person who instinctively does what is more worthwhile than you would otherwise have done.

HC: But you said the opposite in your sermon at Cuddesdon a few weeks ago. You quoted Charles Moule saying, of this question of whether Christians are intrinsically better than non-believers. He said, 'Oh dear, no we're not, but—' . . . I've forgotten the next part.

Runcie: He said, they carry about with them a sense of gratitude.

HC: But isn't it reducing Christianity to a kind of Boy Scout training in ethics, which, after all, you can get in plenty of other establishments? I mean, most people, I would suggest, are going to behave well in a situation like the Amsterdam crisis?

Runcie: Yes, but you're just asking me about a moral decision. There's much more to Christianity than how you behave in a moral sense.

HC: Of course, but what I'm trying to get to is the old problem of making the Christian religion compatible with all the suffering in the world. Apparently it wasn't a problem that debarred you from faith at any point? Because it was the big thing with me in the end.

Runcie: And it was obviously the big thing with John Mortimer. The fact that I didn't give him any sort of firm answer about it left him finding me an agreeable but not converting sort of person. I suppose suffering hasn't been for me the big difficulty. Maybe it's because I've had a fortunate life. In the war, it wasn't easy, and my Dad went blind, but those things weren't catastrophic.

HC: They don't, for example, compare to what a priest in Oxford whom I knew well experienced. His son disappeared for quite a while, and later his daughter-in-law killed her children, his grandchildren. He seemed to keep his faith, but I can't think how. You've never experienced anything remotely on that scale, obviously.

Runcie: Absolutely not. And I'd rather be silent than use some of the well-honed illustrations I've been using. For example, when I was a curate, I used to go to the children's section of a mental hospital, and I used to think, what's the point of all this? But there was a nurse who'd been on that ward for about twenty years, and the only sign of humanity any of those beings were capable of showing was their affection for her. And I can remember using this as an illustration, and saying – and I'm ashamed of it now – that what might have been sheer tragedy had become a family through a Christian nurse. I feel terrible now. But actually that's Graham Greene at the end of *Brighton Rock,* isn't it?

HC: I can't remember how it ends.

Runcie: The terrible Pinkie had been responsible for creating a saint.

HC: The girl?

Runcie: Yes, the girl becomes a saint. I always slightly distrusted that ending, but there we are.

HC: To my mind, Greene's best book is *A Burnt Out Case,* which is an absolutely brilliant study of depression. Is that something which you recognise? Depression? The dark night of the soul?

Runcie: That's interesting. I remember saying when I was at Cuddesdon, to Anthony Bird [the chaplain], that I was very fortunate because I didn't ever have depressions, and I wouldn't be mentally ill. And he looked at me with astonishment, and said, 'How can you be so sure?' And my depressions have been expressed in things like an inability to function effectively, and weariness, and being unable to sleep after four in the morning. And some of the pressures at Lambeth created what was a depressed state.

HC: I'm surprised you slept at all when you were at Lambeth. But I think that's quite a different matter – the sheer wear of managerial responsibility.

Runcie: Yes, but I remember the doctor saying to me, because I could never understand the difference between pills which were anti-depressants and tranquillisers – because I occasionally had to take tranquillisers – and the doctor used to say to me, 'I won't put you on anti-depressants.'

HC: But you were put on those because of the strain of insomnia and the worries of an enormously responsible job, which is perfectly normal.

Runcie: Yes, and he said, 'When you don't have it, you won't need them, so you needn't worry.' And Lindy's thing was

'Be humble enough to take a pill.' But I've not had a clinical depression in the sense of appalling blackness and meaninglessness. I don't think I've ever experienced that.

HC: You'd know if you had. You were just exhausted, run down.

Runcie: I wasn't really 'clinically depressed'.

HC: To put it another way, you've never had the experience of total self-doubt, total loss of faith in yourself?

Runcie: No, I haven't. But since I said that to Anthony Bird, I've had a sort of feeling that perhaps I could have. And then I comfort myself by saying, 'Well, I never *have* had.'

7

Work to be done

On 18 October 1992 the *Sunday Telegraph* printed an extract from a forthcoming book, *Hostage: the complete story of the Lebanon captives*, by its chief foreign correspondent, Con Coughlin. In this, Runcie was quoted at length – his first public statement about Terry Waite since Waite's release:

> Terry misled me . . . he had been working independently of me, which was something he should never have been allowed to do . . . His love of publicity and lack of sophistication about what was being worked on him by the Americans were the cause of all his difficulties . . . I think both Terry and I recognised that we would have to part company.

A few days later, I met John and Eileen Spencer, Runcie's Wellington Square socialist friends from his undergraduate days. He had suggested that I might get a sceptical view of him from John Spencer (who has held chairs in English Language and Linguistics in various parts of the world), so I asked if they felt that he might be an essentially frivolous character. 'No,' answered Spencer. 'I think he's a very typical Oxford product, like we all are. We can be irreverent about everything, and serious about everything. And people who listen to our conversations tend to be rather puzzled by this. They can't quite pick up the signals when we move from one mode to the other. And Bob is very characteristic of that.'

He was certainly in the frivolous mode when I arrived at St Albans for our next session on 5 November 1992. The bed had been removed from the sitting room, and the only remnant of the illness (beside the new shower in the downstairs lavatory) was a surgical cushion, connected to an inflating machine, on which he sat while talking, 'because otherwise I get a sore bum'. He said he had turned down an invitation from the BBC to be a studio commentator on the General Synod vote on the ordination of women on 11 November.

'They wanted me to be a Jimmy Hill,' he explained, and put on a Jimmy Hill voice to give a football-style commentary on the debate (complete with interviewer): '"Well, how's the debate going?" "Well, McLean made a very good opener, but I don't think they've got their act together . . . Yes, this is a great day for the Movement for the Ordination of Women!"'

I brought up the Coughlin book, and his feelings now about Waite.

'Waite was initially a good friend and a good companion, and we worked well together. But he always enjoyed centre stage; he was what Oliver North once called "a grand-stander" – but forgivably so. Of course it was totally absorbing to him, but if he was going to be an international negotiator he oughtn't to be on my staff. I thought Terry should pack it in and come back to being on my staff, or leave and set up on his own. I don't think he knew about the Irangate thing, but I think he would now recognise that he was being used by the Americans.

'Since he's come out, we've got on better than we ever did, because he's come through the incarceration in a remarkable way – he's united to his family, which he wasn't before, and there's a lot which endears him to rather critical fellows of Trinity Hall [where Waite had taken up residence to write his book]. If the Professor of Genetics' daughter is knocked off her bicycle on the way to school, she gets a little note from Terry, saying he's sorry to hear it. And this is all genuine; I have many examples of the way in which his thoughtfulness has been extended to a remarkable variety of people in the time since he returned. Of course, he's been on a lecture tour, collecting honorary degrees from Yale and all that, and has had big financial advances to write this book – it's going to be translated into ten languages, and all that sort of thing . . .' I realsed he would have much to say about Waite later on.

We turned back to Runcie's training for ordination at Westcott House, from January 1949 until December 1950. Margaret Duggan describes the theological college, which stands in the centre of Cambridge, as having a reputation as a 'charm school',[1] a place designed for gentlemen amateurs rather than serious theologians, though it had consistently produced more bishops than any other Anglican seminary. Its style had been set by B. K. Cunningham, principal from 1919 to 1944, and Runcie agreed that under Kenneth Carey none of this had changed.

'Ken Carey was a B. K. Cunningham update. Although he was passionately interested in developments in Theology, and encouraged John Robinson and Hugh Montefiore and people like that when they were his students, he was a snob. He was a spiritual man, but I remember one August bank holiday he remarked, "B. K. always used to say, 'The worst thing about a bank holiday is that you can't get the lower orders to do anything.'" And in order to illustrate the overcoming of the division between sacred and secular, he would talk about B. K. having promised to pray for a young man in hospital in London; and he was shooting game, but while his eye was on the partridges in the butts, his prayers

[1]Duggan, p. 91.

were still able to be raised for Tom in hospital! There were some terrible cringe-making things like that.

'John Betjeman came to give a talk, which had a great effect on me – it was very funny, and it had got a kind of heart to it – about what a church was for: a little bit of eternity in time. And Ken introduced him, saying, "John and I haven't really met since we both swung ungirded hips over the Marlborough Downs." And John looked at him and said, "I can't remember a thing about my time at Marlborough, and anything I do remember I try to forget." And this was a terrible blow, because Ken was very much a Marlburian. I think his own moments of poignant encounter with God had been at Evensong in Marlborough Chapel.

'Ken could be good company, though, and had an enormous influence on people: Pat Rodger, Kenneth Woollcombe, John Habgood, Stanley Booth-Clibborn, Stephen Verney, Richard Hare – the bishops who were produced from "his boys" (he would talk about "my boys"). But he had this assured public school background – his father had been a housemaster – which seemed to me much more snobbish and cut-offish than anything I'd experienced in the Scots Guards. I felt that the public school boys were closer to him. And this, together with my military and Oxford arrogance, made me feel slightly superior to them.'

What about the obviously homosexual atmosphere? 'I wasn't conscious of it. I was amazingly innocent about the gay world, amazingly ignorant. I remember Richard Hare saying that Ken must be constantly torn by his physical reactions to handsome young men, and it had never occurred to me. The different bits of me found different associates at Westcott. Simon Phipps – another one of the future bishops – was very amusing, a friend of Princess Margaret, who appeared in Footlights smoking concerts, and wrote amusing songs, like "I want to be a line or two in *Crockford*". Very amusing, sophisticated.

'There was a magnificent production, which Simon was responsible for, of *Androcles and the Lion*, in which I was the Emperor, and he cast Bill Vanstone as Androcles.' Very

much his interpretation of their respective characters? 'Very
much so. Bill was a terrific scholar – he was my hero,
really, at Westcott. Not a public school character at all;
a working-class background, a double First in Mods and
Greats at Oxford, and about to get a starred First in
Theology at Cambridge (he didn't slacken off as I did).
He had no time for the sloppy emotionalism of Westcott.
And I also made common cause with a group that was in
opposition to it, led by somebody who became my suffragan
bishop when I was at St Albans, Vic Whitsey, who was from
Lancashire, and was prepared to start putting the knife in.
There was a termly news bulletin, the *Record,* and Vic and
Bill were responsible for editing it one term, and Vic wrote
in it, "Do you belong to Athens or Jerusalem?" – a protest
against the homosexual atmosphere.

Was this his first encounter with the element of homosexuality in the Church of England? 'It was, really. But I don't
think there was any physical expression of it, no going to
bed together. I think not, though I can't say for certain.

'Ken was quite proud of me, because I was somebody who
had "had a good war" and, though I say it myself, I belonged
to a group of rather promising characters who had academic
honours. But I was never really close to Ken. I was much
closer to the third member of the staff, Harry Williams. He
was Anglo-Catholic, very amusing in conversation, and the
best of the three lecturers. You could say anything in Harry's
company and he'd laugh it off. He hadn't had his breakdown
yet.' When it came, what caused it? 'His relationship with
his family, and his homosexuality, and his rage at the way
he hadn't been able to express himself. All this is charted in
his autobiography, which has created great scandal because
he's so open about his homosexuality. It's called *Some Day
I'll Find You.* It's an amazing document. You ought to
read it.'

I borrowed it from the library a day or two later. It
was published in 1982 with the author's name as 'H. A.
Williams, C.R.' – the initials standing for Community of
the Resurrection at Mirfield, of which Williams is nowadays

a member. I found it unputdownable. Williams trained at Cuddesdon and became a curate at All Saints, Margaret Street. He describes himself at this stage of his life as

God's blue-eyed boy or – perhaps a better description – his lady companion . . . This God of mine forbade me to be three-quarters of what I was . . . The elimination of sex was one of the most important clauses in the contract I had made with him . . . Even mildly attractive people God regarded as his sexual rivals . . . And since sex and emotion are so closely bound up together, there were whole realms of feeling which were also frozen. God wanted me to be an emotional dwarf so that I might give my stunted heart wholly to him. And I used to tell him that my heart was stunted because I didn't love him as much as he deserved. How delighted he was by that admission. I could almost feel him patting me on the head.[2]

Williams joined the staff of Westcott House in his late twenties, just before Runcie arrived there. His description of Ken Carey is much the same as Runcie's: 'a supremely good principal . . . within limits. For if a young man was not particularly attractive physically and came from a lower-class background, then Ken was no use to him at all.'[3] Williams moved on from Westcott to a Fellowship at Trinity College, Cambridge, where he 'fell hopelessly' for a male colleague, and was soon experiencing a severe nervous breakdown. When he finally achieved recovery, he chose a sexually liberated way of life: 'During the next years I slept with several men, in each case fairly regularly. They were all of them friends. Cynics, of course, will smile, but I have seldom felt more like thanking God than when thus having sex. I used in bed to praise Him there and then for the joy I was receiving and giving.'[4] He continued to officiate as a priest,

[2]H.A. Williams, C.R., *Some Day I'll Find You*, Mitchell Beazley, 1982, pp. 131–2.
[3]*ibid.*, p. 139.
[4]*ibid.*, p. 197.

was the Dean of Chapel at Trinity, and became a monk at Mirfield when he was in his fifties.

I wrote to him to ask for his memories of Runcie at Westcott. He replied at once and at length, saying it was difficult to distinguish recollections of him in student days from friendship with him later – 'having kept up with him during the whole course of his career', but that he recalled one thing for certain:

R showed himself at Westcott as very sensitive to this or the other atmosphere, to what made people tick, to social set-ups, to people's prejudices and points of view. With this sensitivity went an ability to adapt himself in accordance to the circumstances he found himself in . . . With regard to the specific question you ask about sex and snob appeal: Carey certainly treated R as one of the sheep rather than of the goats. He wasn't dazzled by R as he was by some of the student grandees . . . And R was not the sort of person whose physique etc. attracted homosexuals. But, as you say, he had been in the Scots Guards; he had a pleasant personality; and he had a First in Greats . . .

I found when talking to him that he had a far deeper spirituality than was common among the students. It was totally unostentatious. It was never explicitly paraded, but I felt that he was a man of God. He was in the best sense a jolly person, a superb mimic and always full of fun. I took him with nine other students on a parish visit to Wigston, a suburb of Leicester . . . R was billeted on a couple who had a daughter of seventeen. When he left, the couple thanked him for 'bringing her out'. We teased R afterwards, saying that the couple were unable to get their daughter in again.

Talking to Runcie about the sexual atmosphere at Westcott, I mentioned that John Spencer had told me that he intended to become a celibate priest. I added that Merrie Mackenzie Johnston had reported the same thing, when the topic of her possible marriage to him came up. Did that ring true?

'Yes – that's what Lindy says. It's right. I didn't have any thought of getting married in those days, and believed that I would be content to be unmarried, though I preferred female to male company. No, that's too extreme in the second regard, because I was clubbable and enjoyed male company, male societies and so on. There was a crude economic element in it: I never had any spare money to marry the sort of girl who I found good company. Does that make sense?

HC: Yes, up to a point. You'd had lots of girl-friends, and we talked once before about the problem of repressing sexual desire in the relationship with Ingeborg, when you knew that sex would have been welcomed. And yet you really could imagine yourself leading a celibate, chaste life into the foreseeable future?

Runcie: I know that it sounds odd, and I think that it was perhaps something that never got resolved. And it was only when I got married that I realised how foolish I had been, how enjoyable it was. And yet Lindy would still say today that I'm three-quarters bachelor, really. Because there's a great deal of retiring into books, and retiring into the male club – whether the church male club or the academic male club or the military male club – because I'm so at home and protected there.

HC: People have sometimes interpreted you as having, if not a homosexual private life, then a sort of—

Runcie: Yes, I know.

HC: Somebody said to me, 'I've always heard that Runcie was gay.'

Runcie: I'm always astonished – I always think that Richard Ingrams imagines that I'm gay.

HC: And the *Spitting Image* version of you is immensely effeminate.

Runcie: Yes, that's right.

HC: One reason for opting for a bachelor existence can be shyness, that one actually doesn't want to give oneself totally to other people. I wonder whether, for all your clubbability, you aren't possibly a much shyer person than you seem to be.

Runcie: Insecure, I think. My earliest memory of going to parties as a child was getting halfway up the stairs and discovering that I was so terrified that I couldn't speak. And trying to establish myself in school and in the regiment and in Oxford and then theological college was always an anxiety to me. But because I had the kind of gifts that were clubbable gifts, I was quite good at it – a mixture of anxiety about it, and yet an interest in other people.

HC: Your brother Ken didn't marry for a long time, did he?

Runcie: No, and my father also married very late. He was ten years older than my mother.

HC: The gap between you and Lindy is the same – ten years again. But the desire to be celibate wasn't particularly a sort of monastic vocation?

Runcie: It was bound up with my priestly vocation, but it wasn't a very monastic sort of thing. I would tell people that I wanted to be celibate, but the connotation of that word was more on the bachelor side than the monkish side. And I wasn't particularly encouraged by my mother to get married. But Vic Whitsey, the Lancashire lad, used to say that I ought to get married 'Looking after your money and sexual licence will be your problem.'

HC: You'd be hopeless with money without a wife to manage it?

Runcie: Yes. And being attractive to girls would get me into trouble unless I got a wife. I don't know whether I ever rationalised it, but I think I felt that if I did get married, it would be rather dangerous, because I would go on being attracted to girls.

HC: You felt that marriage might be risky because of that? That innocent flirtations might continue?

R: Yes. But Vic Whitsey discerned the difficulty of maintaining the innocence.

He turned to the topic of his theological studies at Westcott, saying that he 'didn't work very hard because I was rather weary'. Eric Heaton, subsequently Dean of Durham and then Christ Church, and only a year older than Runcie, taught the Old Testament to Westcott students at Caius College. 'Eric was liberal, and interpreted the Bible through the prophets, and saw belief as inseparable from moral action: that to do justly is the way to understand the doctrine.' That suited his current state of mind? 'That was very congenial. And I went to hear Noel Annan and David Daiches, and was on the fringe of the E. M. Forster circle. I remember walking through the streets of Cambridge with Forster one evening, and him saying, "It's the sense of sin, it's the sense of sin. I'm so against it, so against it." A lovely Cambridge evening. He seemed to be a slightly fragile and frightened person. The only theologian that I really attended to was a nonconformist, a man called H. H. Farmer, who taught the History of Doctrine.'

In other words, he preferred to learn Theology historically, in a rather detached manner, rather than as living belief. It seems that he was making quite an effort to distance himself from the party line? 'Very much so. So that I hitched on to a man who, in retrospect, was a bit bonkers, the logical positivist R. B. Braithwaite, whom I mentioned last time – "I agree to act as if".' Braithwaite, a philosopher, did not belong to the Theology faculty? 'Not at all, though he became a Christian. So I was this mixture of Catholic devotion and radical philosophy, and I don't think I've changed much in that respect.'

So this fear he had had while at Oxford, that when he came to read Theology he would be in an alien world, did not come to pass? 'No. Because I didn't ever enter into it, really.'

Unlike many of his contemporaries at Westcott, he chose not to read the Cambridge Theology Tripos, but took a shortened course called the Cambridge Diploma. 'I got distinctions in that all along, so people said, "Why didn't you read the Tripos?" But I suppose I was frightened of failing.' Or maybe he did not want to immerse himself in Theology to that extent ? 'I was quite bored by it sometimes, quite bored by some of the lectures at Westcott. But I didn't find myself at home in philosophy either, in pure creative philosophy.' His study of philosophy, at Oxford, had been historically based, too.

What about the more practical sides of training for ordination? 'Ken Carey was responsible for lectures on pastoralia, which described his rather limited parish experience in County Durham – rather amateur and anecdotal – and yet it covered how to baptise and marry and bury, and counsel the bereaved and visiting in hospital.

'I found reading books about prayer and the spiritual life quite a labour, not very absorbing. But I did find the necessity of learning to pray by receiving and recognising the goodness and integrity and loveableness of people who prayed. There was a man on my staircase from South India called M. A. Thomas. I thought he was a holy man. And one or two people who came to talk to us backed up my old-fashioned slum priest image, like John Groser from the East End. They didn't disappoint me. And I certainly learnt some practices, like the value of saying the offices, which have stayed with me.

'So I was carried along by that, and by the feeling that there was work to be done, because there was a world to rebuild – rebuilding church life after what had been dismantled during the war, and industrial missions and worker priests, who were becoming fashionable at that time, and new religious orders, with the beginning of Taizé. All these things rather put in the background the sort of questions that eventually surfaced with John Robinson and later – much more acutely, it seems to me – with Don Cupitt and people like that. So that when they put their questions, I was aware how significant they were, because they were my questions, which had never been resolved, because I had been totally overwhelmed by the enthusiasm of meeting needs and working with people who impressed me.'

On 20 November 1992 we had our next meeting, in Oxford. It was just over a week since the General Synod had voted to let women become priests. Runcie was staying at the convent in his tiny bedsit. Sister Frances Dominica was there when I arrived, running to fetch a packet of milk for him so he could make coffee for me. He talked fluently as usual, and when he finally looked at his watch it was too late for coffee.

We spoke about the vote; the majority was of the size he had predicted. 'I listened to some of it on the radio,' he said, 'and watched a little on the television. Since the vote, I have been surprised at the emotional disturbance of people who have consulted me. I do have a possibility of helping individuals, because there's an air of neutrality about my position, which of course is interpreted on both sides as weakness or inability to make up my mind. But I've never doubted what my feelings were: that it's possible to ordain women, but not worth it if it means destroying the Church of England. But people like [he named an Oxford college chaplain, one of the leaders of the opposition to the ordination of women] have been here for an hour, weeping – literally weeping for an hour. And there's a great deal of tears about, people in an emotional state I couldn't imagine myself getting into over something like that. It may be a sign of how church commitment isn't so deeply in my bones and in my blood, isn't the totality of my life as it is with somebody like him. Do you think that's it?'

He meant commitment specifically to the Church of England? 'Yes. I mean, I should miss it. But I suppose this must be a weakness in an ex-archbishop and a priest, that it doesn't form the totality of my being. There are those who've said to me – and they're good people whom I respect, not people playing games or intriguing – "I feel I've been grieving for two days; everything in life seems to have been taken away from me." Even if I was a hundred per cent an opponent of the ordination of women, I can't imagine myself feeling that.

'And of course I wouldn't have any difficulty in being a Roman Catholic. It's just that all my affections and history and loyalties are Anglican. But if twenty years ago somebody had said, "You've got to live in France for the rest of your life," I'd have become a Roman Catholic for convenience.'

It was with some effort that I wrenched the conversation back to his early career. Westcott House liked to send its young men to the industrial north-east to serve their curacies, and Runcie had been introduced to John Turnbull, vicar of All Saints', an Anglo-Catholic church in the Newcastle suburb of Gosforth. Turnbull (whose memory Runcie reveres) agreed to have him as a curate, and he was ordained deacon on Christmas Eve 1950 by the Bishop of Newcastle.

I asked him about Gosforth. 'It was huge and unmanageable, with a vicar who was very suspicious of Westcott House and had never been much south of the Trent – it was a very un-Oxbridge set-up. And a church which seemed to have no atmosphere at all, a suburban church with great spreading estates north of Newcastle, about sixty thousand people. And I said, "I'm going to get away from posing, from all this play-acting; I'm going to get away from thinking I'm an academic, and recover the original vision," and so on.

'It was a time when there was a degree of optimism, born of church growth. Where we laboured there are now five churches and the seeds were sown in those big estates. We certainly planned the creation of two of them while I was there. There was a great demand, huge confirmation classes, a large youth club, some services crowded, and you could see new people coming in. And you didn't really have time to reflect on what it was all about, because everything was growing.

'I was responsible for a huge Sunday School, with about twenty teachers, who formed a preparation class on a Tuesday night. On Sundays there was an eight o'clock Communion, a nine-fifteen parish Communion, which was the main thrust, eleven o'clock Matins, and one of you had to go to the mental hospital, where you would have a congregation of hundreds dragooned into a great barnlike chapel with warders on the door.

'Sometimes you had to come back at twelve-fifteen for a late morning communion service for the fur-coated people, and then you collapsed with a huge gin and tonic in a private school next to the church, which was presided over by a man called Mr Salmon. It was the best and most expensive private school in Newcastle, and the headmaster was a fully paid-up socialist! The gin and tonic carried you through, and then you had to turn out to face a churchful of over two hundred for the Sunday School. And you might have a tea engagement, and then you'd have Evensong at half past six, and then the youth club. And for two years I gave myself as I've never given myself to anything, and largely put out of my mind speculation about the faith, because there was so much to get on and do.'

8

A college codger

On 7 January 1993, I telephoned Frances Charlesworth in the hope of getting a double appointment with Runcie and Lindy to talk about how they came to get married. Frances told me that Runcie had just had an accident. He had fallen out of the loft, the ladder having parted company with the lintel, and had broken several bones in the heel of the leg which had the cellulitis, and which had swollen up in consequence. He had gone into the loft to get a suitcase to go to Australia. Lindy, whom I rang to express sympathy, told me Frances heard the crash and called out, 'Are you all right?' Robert had not only fallen many feet, but suitcases had crashed on top of him. 'Yes, thanks,' came the answer. 'Very English,' remarked Lindy.

On 20 January I rang Frances again, in the hope that Runcie might be ready to see me again now. She said he was on the move again, in plaster, and had been to see his brother Ken, who had been ill and staying at All Saints convent in Oxford. But she thought he was not quite ready to contemplate seeing me yet. He was fed up and miserable at not going to Australia. It occurred to me, after I rang off, that this would have been a chance to observe him with his defences down, and not on good form, which I had never yet done.

On 15 February, I arrived at St Albans to find the bed back in the sitting room and Runcie walking around on crutches. P. D. James, an old friend, had written him a poem on the occasion of his falling out of the loft, 'Lament for the Archbishop's Heel', and he recited this to me:

> Come, seers and poets, sweep the lyre,
> And with united voice conspire
> To tell a tale of dreadful woe!
> Our good Archbishop is laid low.
> An evil sprite with jealous frown
> From ladder high has hurled him down,
> And on the Magi's blessed feast
> Dear Robert could have been deceased . . .

There was a good deal more of it.

Lindy had gone to America to give a piano recital and had left a lookalike behind to cope with Robert, a woman with the same bossy and energetic style, and the same short dark hair. 'She's an ex-Cuddesdon wife,' he explained, 'estranged, a divorcée. She'll be splendid.' While he was in the loo, I examined the two Valentine cards I had spotted on the mantelpiece. One said briskly: 'Robert – with much love from Lindy.' The other was unsigned, and said: 'I HOPE YOUR LEG IS BETTER – XX.'

He told me that his brother Ken had now died. 'It was obscure to me whether it was liver, or a blockage in his gullet, but anyway he had slight stroke, and that hastened his end. I had the business of co-ordinating at the crematorium. I'm rather an expert on co-ordinating the obsequies of those about whom there is conflict over what would be appropriate. Ghyslaine, Ken's wife, who's rather vigorously anti-religious, said, "We're not having a religious service." Miff [the family nickname for Runcie's sister Margery] was outraged by that. So in the end we had something which was very decent, I thought, and a surprising gathering of rather worthwhile people, who'd come from Manchester, particularly, and a couple from Morley College with whom he used to make jewellery, and things like that.' So there was more evidence of a life than you might have expected? 'Yes. He was a loyal brother, without a shred of envy. He'd failed in one sense, to an external observer, whereas his brother had succeeded. But it's real gospel stuff, really. I mean, he was the weak member of the family, who found contentment, whereas all us competitive, striving characters, you know— !'

Since we had last met, the Prince and Princess of Wales had announced their separation. I had heard at second-hand that, shortly before the announcement, Runcie had been spotted looking furtive in the car park of Clarence House, just after the Queen Mother and Princess Anne had also come out of the building. I reported this to him. 'Ah yes, but that wasn't a crisis meeting. It was only an annual fixture which I have with Norman St John Stevas. We have a Christmas lunch party with the Queen Mother. I'm sorry to disappoint you.'

I was keen that in this interview session we should get as far as the start of his own marriage. On a previous occasion he'd described how he had first met Lindy while he was a student at Westcott House; though the story really began with her sister, Jill Turner, whom he had known at Oxford: 'Jill belonged to the Conservative set; she was a very attractive Lady Margaret Hall undergraduate, very much in the social set of that period – she acted with Ken Tynan, and all that sort of thing. She was the most beautiful member of the family, an absolute honeypot, and bright. The tragedy of her life was that nothing ever matched up to Oxford. She went through two able husbands, and became a very good barrister, and outside court her life was a tragedy, an emotional disaster. And she was always in some chronic state of ill health or emotional breakdown, so nobody really bothered at first when she said she'd got cancer.

'I felt guilty, because I ought to have done more for her.

Anyway, the only good thing I did for her – because she belonged to the Turner agnosticism – was that, when she was lonely and living in Lincoln's Inn, I rang up a character who had been Dean of Johannesburg, and was at St Vedast's, and said, "Look, there's somebody not too far from you, and it would be marvellous if anybody could look after her, and she might take it from you." And his only question was, "Does she drink gin?" And I said, "Yes, that sometimes has been one of her troubles." And he said, "Then that's all right!", and he invited her round for gin, and got her baptised and confirmed, and she became attached to that little congregation. And when she died, he gave one of the best little funeral addresses I've ever heard.'

Though he had seen a lot of Jill in undergraduate days, 'I never had a sort of girl-friend relationship with her. She belonged to a class of beautiful girls without enough animal presence.' He first met Lindy when he went to Westcott House, and Jill told her family to look after and entertain him. He was then aged twenty-eight, and Lindy was eighteen. He thought of her as Jill's 'nice kid sister'.

He particularly remembers meeting her with Jill at the Oxford & Cambridge match at Lords in the summer of 1952. The two sisters were 'looking very smart, with parasols and things like that', but Runcie now felt out of touch with the gilded social world he and Jill had inhabited at Oxford. He had begun to 'despise Westcott House, and to despise my past', and to identify completely with his role as celibate priest at Gosforth. Nevertheless it was shortly after this that he returned to Cambridge and a job at Westcott House.

'The puzzle that I find difficult to explain,' he told me, 'is why I decided to go back to Cambridge.' It was in the autumn of 1952, after he had been at Gosforth for nearly two years, that Ken Carey telephoned to offer him the job of chaplain at Westcott, replacing Alan Webster, who was going to a parish.

HC: It's always seemed to me quite extraordinary that

vice-principals, chaplains and teaching staff of theological colleges should be so young – should have had so very little experience since they were ordained themselves. You had young people on the staff when you were principal of Cuddesdon, and of course you were very young and inexperienced when you went to teach ordinands at Westcott. Why does that happen in the Church of England?

Runcie: It was thought that you'd be absolutely fresh, and that you'd inspire people. But I think you've exposed a flaw, a fault line which runs through the Church of England: that clergy tend to be very happy in their early years, and then there's a sort of 'sickness that destroyeth in the noonday'. If you get through that, you have quite a happy old age and retirement.

HC: So it's unwise to use the middle-aged as the trainers?

Runcie: Some priests who were very good when they were young and active are rather pathetic in middle age, and even those who are cheerful in latter years can seem pathetic, because they're trying to repeat the experience of their early days.

HC: Trying to forget the mid-life crisis, to pretend it hadn't happened?

Runcie: Yes. And I think that's a fault in the training system – though I suppose it's been corrected to an extent in continuing education; theological colleges only start you off.

HC: Corrected by in-service training for working priests?

Runcie: Yes. In my day it was rather like a camel being filled up for two years, and then it was expected to keep him going for the next thirty or forty!

John Turnbull, Runcie's parish priest at Gosforth, was not keen that he should go back to Westcott so soon; and the Bishop of Newcastle, Noel Hudson, said to Runcie: 'I could have wished you'd stayed at least the full three years. It will, of course, show in the rest of your ministry. But I can't withold my blessing if you really want to.' I suggested

There's another — an
with fault an awful anticurshion.

to Runcie that he had accepted Carey's invitation because it was flattering. He replied: 'Yes. I hadn't expected it; I didn't think I was a favourite. I was very surprised.'

When Harry Williams, who had taught Runcie at Westcott House, wrote to me about him, he recalled that Ken Carey had consulted him about appointing Runcie to the staff:

He came round to consult me, listing the pros and cons of the appointment. Among the cons was the fear that R was 'too much of a chameleon'. I answered that R's adaptability was much more of an advantage than otherwise. I said that I had never known it to lead to any compromise of principle, but that it made R capable of understanding and getting on terms with all sorts of different kinds of people.

His fellow Westcott House student Bill Vanstone, whom Runcie had described to me as 'a terrific scholar [with] a working-class background', and who is generally regarded as the most intellectually brilliant of that Westcott generation, received similar invitations to return to academic life. But Runcie explained that he did not accept them: 'Bill, who was my hero really, the person I most respected, this brilliant scholar, he went off to Lancashire, and within the first two years or so he turned down seven academic invitations, and never went back – and never really wrote anything, but spent a great deal of his time making lists of boys to play football on Saturday mornings, because it was one of those big Lancashire parishes with seventy men in the Bible class, and four football teams, and all that sort of thing. He eventually did write two beautiful books, very small, *Love's Endeavour* and *The Stature of Waiting*. He said, "I've learnt all this theology; it's very important, but there are only one or two things which apply to my pastoral work, and that's what I'm going to concentrate on." And there was an element of that about me, but I wasn't such a whole-hogger as Bill, because he went off and lived it out entirely – what my original vision was, the celibate priest.'[1]

Returning to Westcott House in January 1953, Runcie took up his duties as chaplain alongside Ken Carey as principal and Hugh Montefiore – a year older than him – as vice-principal. A year later, Montefiore moved on, and Runcie took over the vice-principalship. 'I was responsible for a ridiculous amount of teaching. When I look back, it was slave labour. I had to teach what had to be taught, which meant the Old Testament – I didn't attempt to teach the New Testament; that was Hugh's, and he was a proper theologian – and great tracts of the middle ages and the Reformation and the nineteenth century. And liturgy – I was a great expert on liturgy! [He laughs.] I was constantly "getting up" Luther, or Newman.

'I really spent from 1953 to 1956 "getting up" things, racing around, keeping the show going. And it was the period when I gained fame from students, like Garry Bennett, of being more approachable and ready to jolly-on those who found life at Westcott difficult. Quite a lot of people who went to Westcott in those days think, well, old Bob kept me sane, that sort of thing. I remember Hugh's wife Elisabeth once taking me aside and saying, "You don't know how your popularity with the troops hurts Hugh." And this amazed me, because I knew Hugh was a real theologian. He could knock spots off me in the teaching.

'Angus thought there was a very dangerous liberal trend at Westcott, not so much in the days when I was on the staff, but when I was a student there with Pat Rodger [future Bishop of Manchester and then of Oxford] and Hugh and Simon Phipps and so on. It certainly has had an effect on

[1]Vanstone, writing about Runcie, describes him as 'my oldest friend', and says: 'I have sometimes heard Robert described as, and criticized for being, "a liberal archbishop". If "liberal" means "woolly-minded", the description is absurdly inept: for his mind, in comparison with that of his typical critic, is razor-sharp.' *Robert Runcie: A Portrait by His Friends*, edited by David L. Edwards, Fount Paperbacks, 1990, p. 21.

the Church of England; I think there's just a measure of truth in Angus's charge that we were a generation that lacked bottom. Harry Williams, although he'd gone off and had his breakdown at Trinity, was enormously influential on me in those days, in telling people Jesus wasn't concerned that we should be religious, but more that we should be fully human. The gospel of the day was "fully human", and the pendulum swung too far on that one. It did release a lot of people from their inhibitions, but on the way created all sorts of other problems. For instance there was a chap who went off with another student's wife, but didn't marry her. Ken got into a great steam-up about this.'

Runcie was now, presumably, having to run so fast to keep in the same place, with so much lecturing, that he had no time to consider his own future with any great concentration? 'That's right. So when Owen Chadwick came round and said, "I'm leaving Trinity Hall [the Cambridge college where Chadwick was Dean], and some of the fellows would rather like you to succeed me", I thought, "Ah!" I was tired, and feeling the strain of not having a home – you had meals during term time at Westcott, but were sort of thrown out in the vacation – and I was always living out of a suitcase, staying with friends, and not being paid enough.

'I was pretty convinced that Trinity Hall was the escape route that God wanted me to take, because I felt intellectually shabby at Westcott. I mean, I can be quite a con man in presenting things which I've made my own, but I did feel shabby by the end of my time at Westcott, churning out this stuff and doing so much teaching. And I thought I would be able to have a quieter life at Trinity Hall. And I went to see the fellows, and had drinks with them, and that was my interview.

'And then I was walking across the Backs, and I saw Lindy, and we hadn't met for ages, and I said, "How's the music?" – she used to send me little notes about concerts. And she said, "You never come to any of my concerts." And I said, "Well, I've got news for you. I'm going to be Dean of your dad's college." And she said, "Do you want a secretary? I'm looking for a job." And she obviously said something to Tony Tremlett, who was chaplain of Trinity Hall, because he said: "And you're going to have Lindy Turner as your secretary." And I said, "Well, I haven't got round to—" "Yes," he said, "I've fixed it all up. She's marvellous. She's just had a bruising love affair, and she really needs a job because her music isn't enough for her."

I was now anxious to book a time with Lindy, to begin to record her side of the story, but she was still away in America. Meanwhile I wanted to meet Alan Webster, who had been on the Westcott staff when Runcie was a student, and had eventually become Dean of St Paul's. We arranged to talk over coffee in the Palm Court of the Ritz in London, where my band used to play at weekends. I felt this to be an appropriate place.

It was. Webster proved to be a rather Trollopeian figure, in a dog-collar and clerical black, though he had been retired for some time. He described Runcie in student days as 'curiously unassured' for someone with such a war record, and brought up the matter of Runcie's failure to contribute to a book on the question of Anglican relations with the non-episcopal Church of South India, a hot issue of the early 1950s. Runcie had told me that he wrote nothing for the symposium, which was being edited by Ken Carey and had essays by Hugh Montefiore, Bill Vanstone, and Webster himself (among other Westcott men), because 'I was convinced that what held a true church together was the scriptures, the creeds, the sacraments, and the historic episcopate structure' – in other words, his views were too conservative for the others.

Webster, however, took a more caustic view of Runcie's failure to write anything. He described the South India business as 'a kind of test case for reunion with the Free Churches', and suggested that Runcie's failure to contribute demonstrated his typical inability to commit himself, rather than a passionate belief in the historic episcopate. He added that Runcie's habit when Archbishop was to get others to supply material for many of his sermons and speeches for him, and that when he heard this, his predecessor Michael Ramsey remarked, 'I have never said anything in a speech which I didn't write myself.'

Webster agreed with me that Bill Vanstone was an *alter ego* or reverse image of Runcie – from a similar Lancashire background, but an ascetic scholar who refused glamorous appointments. Webster guessed that Vanstone had refused to go back to academic life because, unlike Runcie, he admitted to himself that he couldn't square academic philosophy (he had read Greats at Oxford, like Runcie) with Christian belief, and was not going to risk it. 'He was always being offered academic jobs,' said Webster, 'but he turned them down. And I had always thought he would end up as Archbishop of Canterbury.'

On 6 March 1993 I went to St Albans Abbey to hear Lindy, back from America, play Mozart's Piano Quartet in G Minor, as the concluding item in a concert by the Chilingirian String Quartet, in aid of an appeal for Armenia with which the Runcies had strong links. After the performance, Runcie, who was in the audience with his son James's wife Marilyn (a BBC radio drama producer), told me that Lindy had risen from a sickbed with a temperature of 103 degrees to play the Mozart, which presumably explained one or two slightly uncertain passages. But it was mostly very impressive, given that she was having to perform alongside top professionals.

I telephoned her to say 'well done', and asked if I could take her out to lunch – without Robert – so that I could catch up with her side of the story. She readily agreed, showing no compunction about leaving him at home with a tin of soup, and we made a date for 19 March. Runcie agreed to give me a session earlier that morning.

He was back to normal, with just a slight limp, and made me a cup of coffee. He had told me that he had just given a speech at a lunch of 'a group of clubby people in the inner circle called "The Old Gang" – the Queen's secretaries and Downing Street secretaries' – and his subject was the Establishment of the Church of England. I asked how it had gone. 'It was quite well received, but I thought it was a bit waffly, and it was a bit shot down by Dahrendorf [head of the London School of Economics]. He was taking a fairly simple continental line, that the things of God are the things of God, and the things of the State are the things of the State, and if you get them muddled up you can't really exercise a proper sort of autonomy.' *Good old Two Kingdoms' stuff*

Didn't he agree? 'No. It's a typical example of the logical taking precedence over the human and personal. My thesis was that the fundamental unit in society is, from a theological point of view, a person in communion. Not the isolated individual, nor the collective. The isolated individual is enslaved to himself and his instincts and the dark continent within him. And the collective is the impersonalising of how things are, the deterministic view. But a person in communion with himself and with God and his neighbour, and with the natural world to which he belongs, is how we should regard the human enterprise. I think that the State needs the church because it's in danger of falling into one or other of those polarities.'

But does the church need the State? 'Yes, because otherwise it's inclined to become an episcopal sect. I remember Alan Watkins in the *Observer* writing, quite early in the 1980s, "Mrs Thatcher is wrong to fall out with the Church of England, and she'll live to regret it." And it's true that all sorts of *Daily Telegraph* readers in Bath and Leamington Spa were influenced by what church people were saying about the injustices that were being perpetrated in order to get the economy right.' *And Now Labour profit from it.*

We took the coffee into the sitting room, and returned to his days as a Cambridge don, from the autumn of 1956. He displayed his usual talent at portraiture: 'The Master was Ivor Jennings, a great constitutional lawyer, but a dull man, because his main staple of conversation was constitutions. He lived with the idea that the Westminster parliamentary democracy was transferable to different parts of the world.

He had written the constitution of Pakistan, and of Malaysia, and of Sri Lanka, and no sooner had they been implemented than there was a coup and they were torn up! Ivor Jennings was a man who got up and wrote books from about half past four or five in the morning, and chain-smoked. I quite liked him, but he was universally regarded as a bore.

'But of course the interesting fact is that Lindy's father was the Senior Fellow, still adored by Lindy – that's the love of her life, her dad. And he had been Bursar of the college since he came back from the First War. And Charles Crawley, who was the Senior Tutor, was my boss, but Cecil Turner, Lindy's father, didn't greatly like him, though on the face of it they were friends. And there had been a Dean of the College called George Chase, and those three in the 'twenties and 'thirties had rather ruled the college. And Lancelot Fleming, the chaplain, had been the person who kept the undergraduates happy, and knew them all, and that sort of thing.

'It was still quite a small college when I was elected a fellow – I think there were twenty fellows – and Turner was by then over seventy and was still teaching, and had an enormous influence on generations of lawyers. Then there was H. R. Dean, the Master of the college before Jennings, who was still Professor of Pathology, and he was eighty, and was famous for making the great remark [puts on an accent]: "I've lived to be an anomaly; I expect I shall be a scandal; and I hope I shall be an outrage before I die." And he wouldn't retire. So when he became rather ga-ga, I had to keep "Daddy Dean" (as he was known) happy, and look after him a bit.

'There were only three tutors in those days, and we divided the college between us. I had as tutorial pupils all the natural scientists and the medicals and the engineers. For Medicine, Dean was Director of Studies. But he didn't bother too much about them, and I had to do things like getting them into their London hospitals, and making sure they were entered for pharmacology, and that sort of thing. Even now there are distinguished consultants who were once my tutorial pupils.

Above left, Robert Alexander Kennedy Runcie, aged two. *Above right*, his mother, Nancy Runcie, on one of her Cunard cruises, as a hairdresser. *Below left*, Runcie as a Merchant Taylors' schoolboy, in the garden at Crosby. *Below right*, Runcie's father with his eldest daughter, Kathleen, on her wedding day in 1937.

Above, Runcie (left) with his tank troop in Holland, October 1944. *Below left*, 'A perfectly charming Guards officer'. *Below right*, on the back of this photo, Runcie has written: 'Taken in a French farmyard at Bacqueville, on the Seine – I suddenly discovered this old German helmet, popped it on my head, and David Banks took my photograph.'

Above left, at Westcott House. *Above right*, Rosalind and Robert Runcie at their wedding, 5 September 1957. *Below left*, Runcie at Trinity Hall – 'a college codger'. *Below right*, 'I'm a performer': Runcie entertaining Cuddesdon parishioners, with Lindy at the piano.

Runcie (left) with Archbishop Michael Ramsey, who had just consecrated him Bishop of St Albans on 24 February 1970.

The Runcies at home in Abbey Gate House, St Albans; Rebecca, Robert, James and Lindy.

Runcie leaving his service of enthronement as Archbishop of
Canterbury, 25 March 1980.

...ve left, with Pope John Paul II at Accra, 9 May 1980 – 'He was
...g me up, I think.' *Above right*, Runcie gives Terry Waite a letter
...e Ayatollah Khomeini, before Waite's departure to Iran, 1980.
...w, Graham Leonard, Bishop of London (left), with Runcie on a
...singham pilgrimage, May 1980. 'I never found personal relations
...h him difficult,' says Runcie.

Runcie marrying the Prince and Princess of Wales, July 1981. 'We thought it was an arranged marriage, but my own view was, "They're a nice couple, and she'll grow into it,"'

'Graham Storey became a great friend of mine, a bachelor don who edits Dickens' letters, and wrote the definitive history of Reuters. He was my best man, and James's godfather. And I was friendly with Geoffrey Kirk, the Professor of Classics, who would disappear to Yale for a term and leave me to do some of his teaching. Now, although I was the college's Director of Studies in Theology, I felt a bit bogus at that, and I farmed out all the theology teaching except Church History. Don Cupitt [radical theologian] was there, but I never taught him anything – I claim the credit for his First, but I didn't teach him anything! And Moses Finlay, a Jewish refugee from the McCarthy witch-hunt, who was Professor of Ancient History, got me to lecture on Ancient History for classicists and historians and on Church History for theologians. I began to think I was a real scholar.

'But I wasn't doing any research, and Tony Tremlett, the chaplain, was for ever saying to me, "You must get a book written – you must write a big book." He knew that if you were doing a lot of lecturing and teaching, you were in danger of becoming an acceptable college codger, but you would never become a professor, you would never go from the University to being a bishop. He was a great man on all that.

'And I knew this was true, but I hadn't got either the inclination or the capacity. And yet I was haunted by it. I was very happy; life was full. They were in many ways the happiest days of my life. I got married to Lindy after a May Ball proposal in the garden. James was born. She, of course, hoped that I'd stay in Cambridge for ever. But I was haunted by this thought, that it would be very nice, but I would become a college codger.'

I asked about the position of dean in a Cambridge college in relation to the chaplain. 'The dean is in charge of the religious life of the college,' he explained, 'and the chaplain is hired, as Tony Tremlett used to say, "to get 'em for God with buns" – a sort of pastoral appointment. The chaplain wasn't a fellow.' And the tutors were what Oxford would call moral tutors, concerned with undergraduates' general welfare, as opposed to teaching them their subjects? 'That's right. But you were tutors for admission as well. The three of us were responsible for the whole range of entrance and scholarship exams. I used to set the general paper – "What is gold?" and "Why hasn't water been nationalised?" I also examined in the Classical Tripos, in Part I. That's where I discovered Mark Santer first, this brilliant classical scholar. And in order to pick up money I used to examine in Religious Studies at the Oxford and Cambridge Joint Board. That was a sideline for the summer holidays.'

He did no teaching in Theology? 'I did Church History. It was a real mish-mash of jobs, but quite a lot. And also you did your bit in the external world, being examining chaplain to a bishop or two, sitting on selection boards. You'd go away in the vacations to do things, like Holy Weeks, to keep up your duties towards your priesthood outside.'

But what, I asked, about the engagement to Lindy, which we seemed in danger of skating over without elaboration (as with the award of the MC during the war)? In reply, Runcie recapped the story of Lindy offering to be his secretary – with a new twist:

'Tony Tremlett was very keen on supporting her, because she had had a big romance which had ended in tears, and she'd rather collapsed on Tony. And he wanted to help her, initially by suggesting that she should be my secretary. But I think he had the thought, from the very beginning, that she should be my wife. Tony died last year – you just missed him, unfortunately. He was terrifically good with people in high income brackets. You wouldn't call him gay, because he never came out, and I don't think he went to bed with people, but he certainly cuddled them. And he had a great Cuddesdon discipline. At Trinity Hall, we had absolutely regular daily Mass, and meditation afterwards. I don't think people have that discipline nowadays in college chapels.

'Tony had got on well with Owen Chadwick; he worshipped Owen, and hoped that I would follow in his footsteps. And he knew what had to be done in order to become different sorts of people. And Lindy was on the rebound from her Indian; and I was a person who ought to be writing a book and settling down, and therefore Tony encouraged our relationship.'

According to Margaret Duggan, she was the only member of the Turner family who took much interest in the church. 'That's true,' said Runcie. 'She had had a hopeless person to take her for confirmation, who didn't answer any of her questions. Lindy's always questioning, a great questioner, likes to know the details. When you've told a funny story, Lindy's never content with the punchline. It's always, "Now, what happened to— ?" Despite this, she was going to the college chapel. Tony Tremlett had got her there. I think it was because Trinity Hall was her whole life. She was part of the furniture. So she became my secretary. And I became quite dependent on her. And I was surprised to find that I fell in love with her. And she had a love for me, and that's, I suppose, how it happened, really.

'But although I was keen on her, I'd been keen on girls before, and I had no intention of marrying and having children. That still didn't appear in my immediate intentions. I just didn't think that I would be able to settle down and cope with it all. And it was her determination that made me look at it gradually from a different angle, and see that it was possible. I hadn't got the money, and I couldn't imagine it happening. And yet she made it all seem possible. And when we eventually got married, and went on our honeymoon, I thought, "Well, why haven't I done this before?"'

He had not mentioned romantic friendships, girl-friends, since the end of the Oxford period. 'Well, I usually had a girl-friend in tow. When I was a curate at Gosforth, there were lots of flirtatious characters about in the youth club, and one had to be careful. And there was a lovely character – but she was too good for me! I felt, you know, "This is marriage material or nothing." And I didn't persist in it. But she would have been a real priest's wife, because she was a great idealist. But she was too good, too morally good for me.'

The crucial factor with Lindy, then, was her determination? 'I was rather frightened, because I thought she imagined that I was very assured and confident, and would steer things, and she didn't realise what a fragile character I was under the suave exterior. But it did me good, because she brought me into a dimension of coping with domesticity. But you'll find out from Lindy what she thinks about it.'

9

No one asks to be Archbishop

———◆———

Lindy erupted into the house promptly at 12.30, in a tracksuit and trainers, having spent the morning selling bric-à-brac at a St Albans charity shop for the Runcie Appeal for a hospice day centre. 'Ooh, I am exhausted,' she exclaimed, describing the morning's sales. 'We were *busy*. I mean, it takes some time to decide whether you really want something for 10p or not. We managed to sell a baby's pushchair – instead of twenty pounds it went for fifteen, so she felt she'd got a bargain. And someone was deliberating about a necklace, and she wanted something else, so I said, "I'll tell you what, the two for one pound fifty." I must have had a barrow boy as an ancestor some time. I'm going to make myself look more respectable. It's rather a smart place we're going to.'

She went upstairs, and Runcie remarked: 'Lindy isn't a bursar's daughter for nothing. That was another feature of Turner. A very agreeable character, but a very materialistic man. Not offensively so, but keen on, you know, good accountancy to your own advantage. And justice. And integrity. I remember when a certain Lord Lieutenant was making quite a good story of how he had cheated in an exam, Lindy silenced the lunch table by saying, "I'm rather shocked by that, you know." And everybody looked uncomfortable. Justice, more than forgiveness, is characteristic of the family.

'Mrs Turner was a great manager with money. She came from a humble sort of family in Devon. Father was much better connected, quite a dandy in his youth, a good soldier and all that sort of thing.' I asked about the father's agnosticism, which Margaret Duggan says developed from his days in the trenches. 'Yes, according to Lindy. I can say that I never had a serious conversation with him about it. He didn't like talking to clergymen – talking about religion. He was very polite and very correct. Tony Tremlett used to say that he was quite religious, but the experience of chaplains during the war turned him right off clergy and religion. Of course, when my engagement was announced, he fell silent. It was a terrible blow to him.' Solely on account of Runcie's being in the church, or on financial grounds? 'I think mainly the church. I mean, the other fellows were amused, and that was a bit difficult for him, I suspect. Old Dean, the former Master, said, "I think it would be an act of kindness if the fellows were to club together and buy Turner a Book of Common Prayer!"

'I asked to see him, and it was one of the most painful interviews, to ask him whether I could have his approval for it. And he said, "Well, it's her decision, not mine." That was the burden of the answer – "I don't see that it's got anything to do with me."' Very like Runcie's own father's attitude to the church, surely? 'Yes, but my father would have wanted to treat it with humour and warmth. Whereas it pained Turner.'

Over lunch (in a manor-house hotel on the outskirts of St Albans) Lindy agreed that her father, to whom she was devoted, was indeed a very reserved character. She did not always get on with her mother, who would not speak to her for days at a time if she was cross. She could not say where her own forcefulness had come from, but emphasised that she had not always been like that.

She went to the Perse School, Cambridge, and liked it, but was so naughty that, when her form elected her as their monitor, the authorities overturned the election. She was sent off to boarding school in Bedfordshire in her early teens, and hated it so much that she would not eat, and the school got worried. She eventually coped, by being tougher than everyone else. For example, when she was put in charge of gardening, she made everyone garden like fury.

She attended confirmation classes at school because she did not want to stand out from the crowd by refusing. 'I believe in God,' she says, repeating an often-quoted remark, 'but I'm not sure I believe in the Church of England.' Not liking theology, she becomes 'ratty' whenever Runcie tries to explain some theological point to her. 'He puts on *that voice,* and I can't stand it.' But she generally enjoys his sermons, and argues points from them, in adversarial fashion, with him afterwards. 'He says to me, "Ah, you've picked on a weak point there . . ."'

She went to the Guildhall School of Music in her late teens, and was very happy flat-sharing in Chelsea. But she did not aim for a career as a concert pianist: 'You really have to be a man to succeed at that.' So she went back to Cambridge and began piano teaching from home. 'I paid my mother rent.'

I said that Runcie had told me there was a bruising romance before he came along. 'Huh!' exploded Lindy. 'It wasn't "bruising". I've seen him once or twice recently. I mean, he's very like Robert, same sort of lost little boy, you know.' A lost little boy? 'That's what women fall for. I mean, Robert's not allowed to go on a Swan's Hellenic Cruise without me! And even so, I have had to step in. These lonely widows, or divorcées, and so on. Some of them are an absolute pain in the neck.' They think he fancies them? 'Well, he's so kind, and he looks at you with those blue eyes – Ol' Blue Eyes! – and you feel he's really interested in you. Of course, he's thinking of something else at the same time, or wishing they'd go away. And if one of them is making a complete ass of herself, I've said to her, "It's so sad because so-and-so thinks she's madly in love with Robert," knowing that they are themselves. This is my devious way of dealing with it. "It's such a pity," I say, "because really he's not interested in anybody – except me!"'

I had already come across an example of this. At a North Oxford Christmas brunch party, I had found myself next to a woman whose name I didn't catch, who lived at Cuddesdon. She had met Runcie when he came to take a funeral about two years earlier. 'He clasped my hands with incredible warmth, looked me in the eye, and said, "I must come and see you some time soon." I went home and told my husband, "Guess who's fallen in love with me? The Archbishop of Canterbury."' She added that a number of people in politics, including Michael Heseltine and (rather surprisingly) John Major have this mesmeric manner with women.

I asked Lindy about Runcie's declared intention of being a celibate priest. 'My sister told me he'd said that. I was about sixteen, and I said, "Has Robert Runcie got any girl-friends?" "Oh no," she said. "There've been a lot who've been mad about him, but he's going to be a celibate priest." I didn't know what "celibate" meant, so I looked it up – under "S". When I found it, I thought, what a waste of a nice man.' She was mildly interested in him by that point? 'Oh yes. He'd had the same effect on me. And then when he became Dean of Trinity Hall, I was his secretary for a bit. I think he was quite lonely there at first. He used to ring me up. And of course it's the way he says your name which is quite something. Because he's genuinely interested in speaking to the person he's with, and making you feel at home. But then – well, I think it's not so with men, but he gets bored with women.'

Here, then, is a sociable person on the outside, with a lost little boy at the core? 'Yes, he is. And work still comes first. He used to say to me, "Are you all right?" And I used to say, "Supposing I'm not? What are you going to do about it? Are you going to stay in this evening rather than go out?" "No, I've got to get on." So I did my own thing. I decided I was not going to mope at home. I was going to go out and meet friends.' But he was surely not an ascetic where people were concerned? 'No. But his work does come first.'

I said he had given me the impression that Lindy was more determined than any of the other women he had known. 'I *didn't* push him into marriage,' she answered, 'because I was still told that he was a celibate priest.' The age gap (ten years) did not worry her because she had no expectation of marrying him. 'And at that stage there were three men who were very keen on marrying me, and he said about one of them, "You'd better go and marry so and so." So I said, "I'm not being directed like an old boot to go and marry so-and-so." (He was a bore, actually, but we don't say any names – he's quite well known.)

'From September 1956 I typed for Robert, and he gave me a Christmas present, and I gave him one. And then he said, "Would you like to come to the May Ball?" So I said, "Do you mean on my own or with a partner?" because I didn't understand what he was talking about. I said, "Do you mean to bring a partner in your party, or what?" "Well," he said, "if you want to, you could come with me" – in a very vague sort of way. Apparently he did want to ask me, but didn't quite know how to. And he never actually asked me to marry him. He said, "I suppose I ought to buy you a ring." "Why?" I said. "Does that mean you want to marry me?" "Well, I suppose I do," he said.' She described him as 'very proud' – not daring to risk being turned down.

What about her father's pained response? 'Well, I think I was also his "little girl". And I think my father didn't want me to be hurt by all sorts of things. People hurt the clergy and their families.' Did she worry about being a clergyman's wife – did she know enough about the clergy to know what was in store? 'I didn't know anything about clergy wives. I had imagined I was going to stay in Cambridge and be a Dean's wife. What nicer job could you have? I reckoned I'd hit the jackpot. I had loads of piano pupils, all sorts of academic children. Of course, Robert hadn't got any money at all then. In fact he had debts. I found this bill he just hadn't bothered to pay – threatening legal action, practically. I was furious. After that I took over the money.'

I noticed that she always called him Robert rather than Bob. 'I hate "Bob",' she explained. 'And he was "Robert" at Oxford, and Jill [her sister] called him Robert.' At the end of lunch, I mentioned that he had told me he never suffered from depression. 'Don't you believe it,' she said.

Alan Webster had told me that he was a member of the Crown Appointments Commission which had chosen Runcie as Archbishop of Canterbury in 1979. He was the first Archbishop to be picked by this newly created body; previous appointments had been made by the Prime Minister, who still had the final choice from two names submitted by the Commission.

It had met at a conference centre in Leicestershire, under the chairmanship of Sir Richard O'Brien, head of the Manpower Services Commission, and (said Webster) a 'solid churchman'. Webster himself had already written to several people, canvassing their opinion, and Mervyn Stockwood, Bishop of Southwark, wrote back that Hugh Montefiore, who had recently become Bishop of Birmingham, should be chosen. Montefiore had recently got into trouble by remarking that Jesus might not have been 'the marrying sort' – that is, homosexual – but Stockwood thought the Church of England could forgive this. He said that if Montefiore was unacceptable, then it had better be Runcie, but was worried about Lindy's unsuitability for Archbishop's wife.

The Commission, said Webster, 'laboured for a day and a half', then made up its mind that Montefiore's name should be one of the two submitted to the Prime Minister. The procedure was that they would sleep the night on this decision, then get up, take Holy Communion before breakfast, cast the official vote (a secret ballot) and go home. But the next morning the Prime Minister's Patronage Secretary suddenly produced a whole list of objections to Montefiore. Webster suspected that the Secretary had reported to Mrs Thatcher by telephone late the previous night – she always worked at night – and that she had expressed her mind. Montefiore's name was duly dropped. 'It left a bad taste in my mouth,' said Webster.

In view of this, I wanted to talk to Montefiore. A year older than Runcie, he had retired from the bishopric of Birmingham in 1987. He was due to be in Oxford on 26 April 1993, and came to tea with me that day. One of the first things he talked about was Runcie's announcement of his engagement. 'I remember him inviting me to tea in the Cambridge Senate House, and saying, "Hugh, I've got engaged to the most marvellous girl in the world. I hope she won't interfere with my priesthood." And that's always stuck in my memory, because it seemed such a remarkable way of introducing one's fiancée.'

I said that Runcie had hinted that Lindy piloted him into marriage, and he did not recall any conscious decision. 'That's rubbish,' responded Montefiore. 'I mean, he was thrilled. If he was cajoled into marriage, he gave a marvellous imitation of someone who wasn't. But I thought he was a celibate. He was very much regarded at Westcott as in the Catholic tradition, and Harry Williams was his great – I wouldn't say idol, but model, who wasn't perhaps celibate, but wasn't a marrying man. I got the impression that it was a case of a person who'd always intended to be celibate, but was rather overcome by the unexpected emotions of being in love.'

I said that Runcie felt that Tony Tremlett set up the marriage. 'Tony Tremlett would set up anything,' answered Montefiore. 'He was a splendid manipulator (he set me up too).' I was beginning to feel that without manipulators, the Runcie career might have amounted to very little. 'Isn't that entirely reasonable?' responded Montefiore. 'I would have thought a good priest would go where the Lord sends him. I certainly didn't have any career planned. You wait till events unfold. But I never thought of him being a don. He never took theology seriously until he had to chair the Orthodox commission, and then he realised he was pretty illiterate in it, and he got interested. He

was an historian. He became quite a good theologian at
the end.

'He was an intelligent archbishop, but he was a great sitter
on the fence. I always felt he would never say or do anything
that would imperil his career. I have to say that. I mean, it
was very much true about the ordination of women. Until he
saw which way the wind was blowing, he wouldn't commit
himself. He did in the end, but not very strongly. I must say
I always felt this was constitutional. It wasn't his fault, and
no one could blame him. He didn't ask to be Archbishop
of Canterbury. And he did very much better than I thought
he would. He was more decisive than I ever imagined he
could be.'

I said I could imagine him having become a diplomat. 'So
could I,' answered Montefiore. 'I quite agree with you. He
always thought diplomatically rather than theologically. I
mean, one sees the difference now, at Canterbury [with
George Carey as Archbishop]. There's a personal conviction,
but no finesse. Whereas before we had a great deal of finesse,
and a very moderate conviction! I don't mean that Bob
wasn't a devoted priest, but there was still a very moderate
conviction. Do you agree about that?' I said it was exactly
the picture that was forming in my mind.

'You mustn't blame him,' continued Montefiore. 'He is
what he is. I get very angry when people blame archbishops.
No one asks to be archbishop. It's a thankless task.'

I now told Montefiore about Alan Webster's allegation
that he was in fact the person chosen for Archbishop
of Canterbury by the Crown Appointments Commission
– or was about to be, before Mrs Thatcher's supposed
intervention. Did he know that? 'Yes, because Alan Webster
told me! As a matter of fact, I would never have been made
Archbishop, and I couldn't have done it, I couldn't have done
it! I'm too sensitive, too sensitive about what people say to
me, about me, and so on. And – I would have had a very
different style.'

Webster had said Montefiore was not sensitive enough –
in the sense that he would have been willing to do things from

which Runcie held back. 'Oh yes, that's true!' responded
Montefiore. 'That's my problem! I would do all the things,
and be terribly hurt. I think Bob made a much better job
of it than I would have. And I'm very glad. And the other
thing was, I don't think my wife could have managed – I
don't know whether it would have been Elisabeth's style, at
Lambeth. But anyhow, I don't think there was the remotest
chance. Of the two names put forward, I would never have
actually been appointed.'

The Commission had to put forward two names, so I
asked whose was the second that was put forward, alongside
Runcie? 'Oh, well, who am I to know? But I'm almost sure
it was Geoffrey Paul, who at the time was suffragan Bishop
of Hull. He became a diocesan, Bishop of Bradford, for a
very short time before dying of cancer. In 1979 he was
only a suffragan, but Coggan was terribly keen on him,
and was pushing him all the time. But I don't think, he was
a starter.'

I had recently met David Hare, whose play *Racing Demon*,
about the Church of England, had featured Runcie promi-
nently on the poster when it was performed at the National
Theatre. Hare told me he had attended a General Synod
debate, to get copy for the play, and had come to the
conclusion that Runcie was 'a man haunted by his own
lack of spirituality'. I mentioned to Montefiore that I had
been speaking to Hare. 'I take a dim view of David Hare,'
he remarked, 'because I was Bishop of Kingston on Thames
at the time that he wrote *Racing Demon,* and it's all about
the Bishop of Kingston on Thames!'[1]

[1]*Racing Demon* is set in a team-ministry parish in South London. The senior
member of the team is sacked by the Bishop of Southwark (who threatens
to leave the Church of England because of the ordination of women)
because he refuses to make the sacraments his priority, but concentrates
on preaching left-wing sermons; a Tory cabinet minister is a regular member
of the congregation, and has objected. The Bishop of Kingston on Thames
(Southwark's suffragan) reneges on his promise that the priest's job is secure.
The play portrays the Church of England as in terminal decline because of
division between high churchmen and evangelicals, and because of the erosion
of doctrinal certainties.

I repeated Hare's summing up of Runcie as 'haunted by his own lack of spirituality'. Montefiore paused for a long time, then said: 'Well, I'm interested that he should have thought that. I wouldn't have thought that there was a great deal of spirituality in Bob, but I've never noticed him as being haunted! Bill Vanstone was someone who rather fascinated him – who was in a way what Bob would have liked to have been. Here was a man with every talent in the world, with a First in Part III in Theology and God knows what else, who went off to be a celibate priest in Lancashire, where he lived his whole life. And in a sense I think Bob recognised something in Vanstone which he would probably have liked to have been himself.'

10

He still had his L-plates on

O n 24 May 1993 my father died, aged ninety-one. A few days later, Runcie was the celebrant at the Requiem Mass. My father, with typical self-effacement, had forbidden any kind of sermon or panegyric, but Runcie ingeniously got round this by composing a set of intercessions which described my father's character and achievements – and which, typically, he submitted for my approval in advance. I particularly liked the phrase 'His lack of pomposity, self-righteousness or vanity – and his distaste for shoddy thinking, spurious piety or self-promotion', the latter half of which seemed to apply just as much to Runcie himself.

My father, as Bishop of Oxford and chairman of the governors of Cuddesdon College, had in 1960 played a crucial part in Runcie's next career move (though by the time I came to work on this book he was already too unwell to remember much about it). However, once again the prime mover was Owen Chadwick, as Runcie himself recalled:

'Owen Chadwick again was the man who came round and said, "I'm on the governing body of Cuddesdon, and Harry Carpenter thinks you ought to be the next principal." And he said, "Of course I'm very fond of Trinity Hall, and wouldn't want you to leave here. But also I'm very fond of Cuddesdon, and I'm bound to think you would do very well." And I remember thinking, "This is a vote to leave the open society and go to the closed society, and will I be able to stand it? And will Lindy be able to stand it?" I think what chiefly motivated me was the feeling, "I can't go on being a sort of second-rate character in Cambridge." And I think Lindy also knew that she'd had a sheltered life. She didn't know what she was in for at Cuddesdon, of course.'

This was in the spring of 1960, two and a half years after Runcie had married Lindy. They were living in a flat in King's Parade, in the middle of Cambridge, which Owen Chadwick had previously occupied. In May 1959 James, their first child, had been born.

Correspondence in Cuddesdon College archives shows that Chadwick had consulted Tony Tremlett, then a parish priest in Westminster, who suggested Runcie for the principalship on the grounds that 'Bob is not going to write books & be a proper Dean of T[rinity) H[all]'. Writing to me, Chadwick himself made the same point: 'Bob has and had all the qualities to be a real scholar if he wanted. He showed no sign of wanting to get on this bandwagon.'

Cuddesdon theological college stands in the village of that name, about ten miles on the London side of Oxford. Lindy had 'never heard' of it when the offer came, and asked Owen Chadwick what the salary would be. 'It was eight hundred pounds a year,' she recalls. And I said, "If you think we can live on that, we won't go." Robert said: "You can't complain about the money if it's God's will." I said, "Ask Owen Chadwick if *he* would go there for eight hundred pounds a year." It moved up to twelve hundred and fifty.'

Runcie told me how Lindy's heart sank when they both visited the place, with its Victorian Gothic buildings – the house in which they would live dated from 1852 and had twenty-six rooms – 'and the fish pie and the general air of enclosed piety. But maternity was occupying her, and she did accept that she'd had a sheltered life. Looking back on it, she was very courageous, really.'

The departing principal of Cuddesdon was Edward Knapp-Fisher, an unmarried man who was leaving to become Bishop of Pretoria. Peter Cornwell, subsequently on Runcie's staff at Cuddesdon, was a student there towards the end of the Knapp-Fisher days. 'Most of us had done national service,' he says, 'and we came there keen to get on, highly motivated. But there was a broodingness about Knapp-Fisher; it was very sepulchral, and people were beginning to get a bit restless. It was a time when we were becoming aware that the Church of England in that post-war period had become a little bit sleek and complacent. A lot of people went to church, but there was a slight feeling that beneath this placid surface things weren't quite right – there wasn't enough questioning.'

Some of the twenty-six rooms in the Vicarage (as the Principal's house was called, since he was also vicar of the parish) were occupied by students, and Runcie tells an anecdote which illustrates the spartan lifestyle in Knapp-Fisher days: 'There was one student who crept down in the night, and was filling a hot water bottle. Well, there was silence after Compline every night, and Edward Knapp-Fisher came into the kitchen, saw this, and said nothing. But the next day he said to the student, "Come for a walk" – he was a great one for silent walks – and they walked for nearly an hour without his saying a word. And his opening remark, finally, in the conversation was: "Getting a bit soft, Tom?"'

One of the few relaxations permitted to students was the performance of an end-of-term revue, known as *Bright Hour*. But Runcie recalls that even this caused problems: 'Edward Knapp-Fisher had a rather childlike, prankish sense of humour, and he liked dressing up. One year a student who was in charge of *Bright Hour* was in the middle of all the preparations, when Edward decided it would be very funny to dress up as a tramp. And just when tension was at its height, and the curtain was about to rise, there was a knock at the common room door, and there was this old tramp: "I 'ear there's a concert we can all come to." And the student, not recognising Edward, said, "No, it's private." "But I 'ear it's a theological college, and very kind to strangers. And I've got some money, I'm prepared to pay." And the student said, "Well you can't come." And Edward kept on at him, and finally the student lost his temper completely, and shouted: "Oh, fuck off!" And Edward took it terribly seriously; the man was summoned next morning. In fact he didn't get ordained.'

Whereas at Westcott House wives and girl-friends of students and staff had been made welcome as guests, Cuddesdon under Knapp-Fisher almost totally excluded women. No wives or fiancées might live within two miles of the college, and the students had to attend all meals, with the exception of Saturday lunch. The only concession was that those partners who attended the parish Communion on Sunday morning were given coffee in the vicarage afterwards by Knapp-Fisher's mother.[1]

Runcie points out that Knapp-Fisher's rigidity in this was partly a reaction to the 'very relaxed' regime of Kenneth Riches, his predecessor as principal. Yet at first, on taking office as principal in the autumn term of 1960, Runcie changed nothing. Why? 'Before I changed things, I had to show that I could be just as good as Edward. There was a sense in which I didn't have his sense of intensity. And perhaps my priesthood had become a bit loose through the

---

[1]Bishop Edward Knapp-Fisher writes that neither of Runcie's anecdotes is wholly accurate: 'I never went for a walk with a student without saying a word for nearly an hour! Such a remark ("Getting a bit soft, Tom?"), if made, would certainly have been jocularly spoken. I remember the *Bright Hour* incident clearly. I put on the act on the suggestion and with the connivance of a student. I do not recall that it went on unduly long or that it provoked anything but amusement. I cannot believe that a student lost his temper and shouted the words alleged. The implied suggestion that because of a single incident he did not get ordained is absurd.

'As Robert Runcie suggests, the austerity of the College regime in my time was in part due to reaction against the relaxed atmosphere of my predecessor, and in response to the express wish of Bishop Kirk, who appointed me. In retrospect I recognise that the austerity may have been overdone, but I was keen to emphasise the self-sacrifice and discipline needed in preparing for the priestly ministry. A source of encouragement to me has been the number of old students, including some of the more recalcitrant, who have written to say: "Then, I couldn't see the point. Now, I understand and am grateful."

expansive life of Cambridge. There was a feeling that this was something I really ought to do, because it would be good for me.'

Lindy, however, did not take kindly to being totally excluded from almost all her husband's daily life – for he followed Knapp-Fisher's practice of remaining in the college (a hundred yards across the lawn from the Vicarage) from early morning until late at night: 'I got so fed up, because he didn't eat a single meal with us in term-time. And in the holidays he worked just as hard, as the vicar. And I said, "I can't stand this! I'm leaving if you don't look after me. I didn't marry to be in an enclosed order."'

The no-women regulations were soon changed. 'I had about a year,' recalls Runcie, 'living in the image of Edward; and then people like Richard Harries [future Bishop of Oxford] were trail-blazers – he was allowed to have Jo [his fiancée] visit regularly for the weekend, and I think he was allowed to marry and stay in the village. And quite early on I opened the doors to fiancées and wives being able to come during term time. There used to be a weekend for wives at the beginning of term. I was very bad at conducting that. I've been all right at befriending clergy wives, I think, in my ministry; but I've never been very good at instructing them in their own piety, affirming them in their own subordinate role, and all that sort of thing. Lindy was meanwhile at the nappy-changing stage of things.'

Their second child, Rebecca, was born in August 1962. Besides bringing up the children, Lindy was doing part-time music-teaching in local primary schools, to enlarge the family income. 'God, that was hard work,' she says, 'but I did it. I mean, what was it? Ten bob an hour. But it was something. And I managed to get somebody to wheel James out in the afternoons, and then I got an *au pair* girl and so on. And some of the students were wonderful. I started playing bridge, and one of them was a great bridge player. He taught me a rather sneaky hand, which I've forgotten now, because Robert doesn't like cards. And on Saturday nights I used to have the boys in for bridge.'

Sabine (Bin)
Now Sauter "

Though the majority of the students had girl-friends, fiancées or wives, Runcie became aware of 'the influence of a homosexual group' among his students – much less marked than at St Stephen's House, the high church Anglican theological college in Oxford, but none the less perceptible.

Runcie: It wasn't sufficiently overt to become a problem. But I've never found dealing with homosexuals very easy. I've enjoyed their friendship, but I've always been conscious that they might stab me in the back because I wasn't one of them.

HC: What is your feeling about practising homosexuals among the clergy?

Runcie: I generally take the line that heterosexual relationships are the norm for Christian behaviour, so that the young should be brought up to believe that genital sexual activity is something between different sexes. But of course I do recognise that there are people for whom that's impossible, and that there must be some tolerance of same-sex affections having a physical character. Yet there are one or two quite outstanding clergy, now happily married, who were homosexual when Cuddesdon students. One of them was seriously at risk with the police for going out to hunt for partners. And yet, with treatment, and with the right sort of girl determined to marry them, they're happily married and have children.

HC: Surely the reality is that the church has a large percentage of clergy who are homosexual by inclination, and in many cases discreetly practising?

Runcie: Yes, but oddly enough – and you may think this is very naïve of me – until I became concerned about it, because of the campaigning of people like Richard Kirker [Secretary of the Lesbian and Gay Christian Movement], I didn't realise the extent of homosexual clergy. I think, mind you, that it is exaggerated now, because of the availability of the London clergy to grab the headlines. I honestly don't think that in good old-fashioned dioceses like Newcastle it is a huge problem. But yes, I'm not comfortable at ordaining somebody whom I know to be a practising homosexual, and I tried to hold that line. I reckon now it's a difficult line to hold.

During his second year as principal of Cuddesdon, two members of his teaching staff moved on to other jobs, and he was able to make his first appointments. Peter Cornwell, who had gone to a curacy in Hull, was called back to fill one of the positions. He found things much altered from the previous regime: 'It had become a cheerful place where people laughed. The heavy oppressiveness of the Knapp-Fisher dogmatism had gone. Here was a man of liberality, who would go for asking questions.' Yet Cornwell was also struck by elements of conservatism in Runcie: 'I think he felt very much that he wasn't there to cause a revolution. He always said that "Cuddesdon is bigger than its principals", that there was a way of life which principals ought to be respectful towards, a basic pattern, a tradition. And so little bits of conservatism remained throughout his time there. I always got irritated by the saying of long Latin graces, and I said an English grace every now and again, and Robert was always irritated by that.'

Besides displaying elements of conservatism, Runcie could be as tough with the students as Knapp-Fisher had been. David Stancliffe, now Bishop of Salisbury, recalls a specific instance, when his father – Michael Stancliffe, then Vicar of St Margaret's, Westminster – and mother were about to celebrate their silver wedding. 'It happened to be on a Friday night, so I asked Bob, "May go to that?" "No," he said. "Absolutely not." My mama was immensely cross, and had to be restrained from writing to him.'

Stancliffe has more to say about this apparent contradiction: 'There's this fascinating mixture between the lover of the bright lights, and the re-assertion of the true heart of Tractarian spirituality. He clearly does hover between those two worlds. He would love to live a disciplined life of prayer, and yet it doesn't somehow quite come naturally. I think the anxiety of what people might think, and the sense of wanting to do the right thing, has always militated against it. I think he's one of the most insecure people I know. But that's probably one of the things that endears him greatly to others.'

In other words, the substitute for a spiritual side is a lack of self-confidence which makes Runcie successful with all kinds of people, because he hasn't got a determined, tough view of himself? 'Yes,' says Stancliffe. 'There's no doubt that he gave a lot of time at Cuddesdon to spiritual exercises, but he always came out at the end of them looking more agonised than when he went in. Some people have a kind of walking serenity which seems inaccessible and unchallengable, but he did not. And in a way I find that more attractive.'

Stancliffe talks about spiritual exercises. What does he mean specifically? 'Getting into chapel early in the morning, slumped with his head in his hands, before anyone else arrived. But it didn't look as if it was working.' I told Stancliffe that Hugh Montefiore said that he did not think Runcie was someone who was worried by his own lack of spirituality. 'I think it *did* worry him. Like it worries all of us who haven't got something we think we ought to. And in a way, that is the heart and root of prayer; not that you possess God, but that you'd love to. That's what draws people to God. And in a sense it's also what draws people to Bob. Because they recognise somebody who longs for things, and yet knows that you can't always get there.'

Peter Cornwell takes a similar line on the question of Runcie's spirituality: 'I find I get more and more sceptical about spotting "spiritual" characters. I mean, some people are actually born looking "spiritual". They've got that sort of face. And Robert hasn't. But my suspicion is that the people who look that way are not quite as "spiritual" as they seem. And that people who don't look it are perhaps more so than they appear. Robert's was a sort of spirituality of struggle; it wasn't easy. And yet it was all very honest. We used, at Cuddesdon, to have half an hour of meditation between morning prayer and the eucharist; we were there in chapel, in the early hours of the morning, the entire college.

We all sat for half an hour. And what did Robert do during that time? He prayed a lot with his diary – looking at the concerns that were coming up. He was a sacrament of the present moment sort of chap. I don't think he lapped up the silence with ease. But I think he felt it was all very necessary.'

Cornwell was impressed by Runcie's lectures at Cuddesdon for much the same reason: 'Edward Knapp-Fisher's lectures on prayer were *ex cathedra*. But when Robert spoke about it, you felt that he still had his L-plates on – we're-all-in-the-same-boat sort of thing.'

Runcie himself is typically deprecating about his lectures: 'I had to get up subjects which were unfamiliar to me. I had to lecture on prayer, the ascetic life, because Edward had done this – it was competitiveness! I had to be able to give a course of lectures on St John of the Cross and St Teresa, and the spiritual life, which was not really my line. And I had to lecture on pastoralia, had to become the man who knew what it was to be a parish priest. I had never been a parish priest, you see!' But now he found himself working as one, thanks to the double nature of the principal's job at Cuddesdon.

At the beginning of his time there, he enjoyed the parish work 'much more than the college'. The local population was mostly at the extremes of the social scale, with (in his own words) a few 'nobility' living in scattered manor houses, 'the working-class culture in microcosm' in an estate of council houses opposite the college, called Parkside, and nothing much in between. He recalls that the chief power in the village was the garage proprietor, Arthur Smith:

'It was reckoned that he was the man who allocated council houses and so on, because he was a county councillor. He was in active hostility to the college, on which he depended for quite a lot of his income. And he had always put in some pliant aristocrat to be chairman of the parish council. Colonel "Trotty" Bowes, who lived at Chippinghurst Manor, was the current chairman when

I arrived. And then he suddenly died. Arthur Smith had to choose the nearest thing to an aristocrat who would be pliant, and wouldn't have too much time to interfere with his machinations. And that's how I got elected. Nobody had a copy of the constitution; Arthur kept it locked up in his safe. And he used to whisper to me: "If anyone starts talking about the constitution, slap 'em down! And don't worry, Vicar, until hand-to-hand fighting breaks out."

'It was great fun being chairman. And at one time I was also chairman of the village hall committee, and that was a matter of dealing with the vandalism of somebody who'd kicked in a piece of hardboard, or who'd been undressing one of the Parkside girls in the back cloakroom. And of course you dealt in generalities. You said, "Now, it's very distressing, this vandalism," and everyone knew we were talking about Mrs C.'s son, but Mrs C. was there, and you had to talk round it. It was an education in human beings.'

Though I myself saw very little of Runcie as principal, I regularly heard him preach in the parish church. I told him my mother used to remark that he always seemed happier and more relaxed when addressing the tiny village congregation, when the college was on vacation. He agreed, but remembered that 'you could never tell who was going to greet you. I remember going to Evensong on a sunny August evening, and discovering that your father was there with the Archbishop of Cape Town, Joost de Blank. So there was old Fred Sellar, Mrs Hicks wittering away on the organ, and a general who lived at Chippinghurst who had a hearing aid which whistled (it used to be reckoned that he made it do this if some member of the college staff was uttering left-wing sentiments), and old Mark Carpenter-Garnier, who'd been Bishop of Colombo and lived at the Old Vicarage. I used to get little notes from him.

'We had an evening Communion for the college, and he sent up a little note saying, what arrangements were being made to keep the fast before Communion? And he would very often enclose some faded little pamphlet, with gothic twirls on it, by Father something-or-other, SSJE,[2] on *Fasting Before Communion in the First Three Centuries*.

'A very good example of how the Tractarian teaching on such things had, over the years, seeped into the subconscious of the lay people of Cuddesdon was exhibited by Gwen Stanley, the college cook. There was an American student at the college, and he thought he couldn't manage to get to church first thing in the morning without having a little cup of coffee and a bun. An urn of coffee used to be put out, ready for afterwards. And he was secretly having his bun and coffee when suddenly Gwen came round the corner, and said: "Mr ——! God's body on the tongue first thing in the morning!" The man fled, and told me this story.'

The old Bishop of Oxford's palace, opposite the college, stood in large grounds, partly wooded. It was demolished after being badly damaged by fire, and only a part was used for the new episcopal house, into which my parents and I moved in 1962. The Church Commissioners decided to build on the vacant land, and Runcie recalls that he told them: 'What we need is to create a little Guildford in this wood. It mustn't be too large; it mustn't swamp the village. But we need a middle class, and if you can build some middle-class housing, it will bring some sort of leadership into the village.' The proposal was acted upon, and soon a cul-de-sac of quite substantial new houses had been erected, and given the name Bishop's Wood. One of the first householders there was Bill Saumarez Smith, the Archbishop of Canterbury's Patronage Secretary, a recently-created job, as Runcie recalls:

'Bill was, I think, the second-ever Patronage Secretary – there are two key people nowadays, the Prime Minister's Patronage Secretary, and the Archbishop's Patronage Secretary. And it was his business to build up a whole stock of knowledge about people's *cursus honorum* and career – a career structure for the upper clergy. It's never quite worked.' With the holder of this job on Runcie's doorstep, did he find himself being consulted by Saumarez

[2]Society of St John the Evangelist, the official name of the Cowley Fathers.

Smith? 'No. Bill was immensely discreet. And also a bit humourless. The students used to take the mickey out of him. As Bill would be going up the churchyard path, somebody behind would say loudly to his neighbour: "I hear that Montefiore is going to Birmingham – it's a very well attested leak." You could practically see the back of Bill's head quivering.'

According to Peter Cornwell, Runcie himself was now being spoken about in this fashion: 'Here was this lad zooming up, making an almost inevitable progress, and being spotted as a "likely lad". So that even when he was principal of Cuddesdon, people began to murmur, "Canterbury, Canterbury".'

What David Stancliffe calls 'various bits of external recognition' began to come Runcie's way. In 1963 he was invited to join the Cell, a small self-electing group of Anglican clergy who met now and then for a week-end of prayer and discussion on a pre-arranged topic. It had no official status within the Church of England, but its members tended to be, or to become, bishops. Stancliffe says that there was now 'a good deal of respect' for Runcie within the church. 'And he always was, in his wonderful self-deprecating way, an extremely powerful operator.'

In September 1963, Mark Santer, a twenty-seven-year-old Cambridge graduate with a brilliant academic record, who had gone on to study for ordination at Westcott House, was brought by Runcie, straight from being a student there, to become a Cuddesdon lecturer and curate to the parish. Margaret Duggan explains: 'He had not actually met Santer when the idea of inviting him to Cuddesdon occurred to him. While at Trinity Hall he had marked the examination papers of some of the undergraduates [in other colleges] reading Classics, and the papers submitted by one of the students had so impressed him that he had made a point of finding out who was this bright lad ... [who] ... got the best First Class degree that year.'[3] Santer went on to achieve a First in Theology at Westcott as well.

Cuddesdon's bachelor ethos was a rude shock to the newly-wed Mark and Henriette Santer. Talking to me not long after his wife's death from cancer, Santer remembered this period with some bitterness: 'Robert maintained the old regime; he humanised it, but there were aspects of it which Henriette certainly found very hard – the effects on people newly married of the husband having to have all meals in college. And the wives being very much on the fringe of things. As I look back, I'm astonished at Henriette's resilience at not having a nervous breakdown. It seemed like a madhouse in many ways. What was particularly hard for her was that she was a professional woman [a psychologist], and had been national president of the Dutch Student Christian Movement, a reflective Christian. And there she was in a place where all sorts of interesting people were coming, whom she'd have loved to meet, and she was never allowed to meet them or hear them, to come to any lectures. This denial and exclusion of a contribution that an articulate lay Christian could make, she found very hard indeed. I would say it took years before our marriage recovered from those initial patterns.

'Against that, I would want to set an enormous affection for Robert; and Henriette was always very fond of him. And by maintaining the old forms, he did help Cuddesdon to survive the 'sixties. So it was not all negative. But I really do think more thought ought to have been given to what it meant to married people. And of course there's a curious symbiosis between this and the pattern of Robert's own marriage – I don't know how far Lindy wanted to be left outside it, or it legitimated her being left outside it; but everyone else had to pay the price of their following that pattern.'

The appointment of someone as young and inexperienced as Santer raised few eyebrows, for Runcie was merely

[3]Duggan, pp. 132.

continuing the Westcott practice. Santer himself, however (according to Jonathan Mantle), was heard to remark that the college was 'run by a man and three boys'.[4] This was said to his successor, Mike Scott-Joynt, who went straight from being a Cuddesdon student to becoming a member of the staff. David Stancliffe, however, defends the practice in much the same terms as Runcie himself: 'Most people of middle age and beyond have not remained in touch with the academic subjects to the required level. And people coming out of college aren't sullied by the disillusionment of unfruitful parochial experience, nor by just having gone rusty and not being able to read. Most of the interesting clergy that I know have not gone on being high-powered theologians.'

Stancliffe describes Mark Santer, who was on the staff during his own student days at Cuddesdon, as 'a tougher character altogether' than most of the men Runcie appointed there. 'Mark was the person who made me work. None of the others really did.'

Runcie's chief innovation on the academic side at Cuddesdon was the regular stream of visiting lecturers he invited, many from Oxford. Among these was David Jenkins, then chaplain of Queen's College; but the net was spread wider than theology, as Runcie recalls: 'Tommy Balogh came and talked about the economy. And Lucy Faithfull [then director of social services for Oxford] helped me to run a course called "Introducing the Social Services", so that every fortnight we had either a probation officer or someone from the prison service and so on. Littlemore [a local psychiatric hospital] was then presided over by a Jewish agnostic called Mandelbrote, and students were put on a course there. I had Noel Annan to talk about the Tractarians from a different angle. I like to think we stimulated intellectual curiosity.'

Peter Cornwell remarks of this that Runcie 'was by nature a don, and he liked college life, so he didn't have the great desire of Edward Knapp-Fisher to distance us from the

[4]Jonathan Mantle, *Archbishop: The Life and Times of Robert Runcie*, Sinclair-Stevenson, 1991, p. 67.

university'. He adds that David Jenkins, later to achieve notoriety for his radical theology as Bishop of Durham, proved 'a very good guide through the *Honest to God* debate'.

John Robinson, Bishop of Woolwich, published his short book questioning the nature of the deity in March 1963, and was surprised by the public outcry it caused. To Runcie, however, nothing in Robinson's book was a surprise: 'I remember Hugh Montefiore saying to me, "My God, John Robinson's written a book which is going to cause mayhem – he's going to tell the world the sort of things *we* believe!" David Jenkins was lecturing in all this radical stuff to my students, so it wouldn't be a big problem for them, but Hugh said *Honest to God* was going to be a big problem, and very prophetic he was.'

Runcie sums up the Cuddesdon ethos, as it had become under his principalship, as 'detached, slightly amused liberalism', and remarks that his brother-in-law Angus was wary of it: 'Angus used to say, "I don't really trust people who are funny, who mock the things they are actually doing." And I think the more solemn students found themselves unhelped by the sophistication of the place.' Did some drop out in consequence? 'Some, but on the whole a smaller number than at other places; very much smaller than at Westcott in those days. I tended to err on the side of generosity, and occasionally supported (against my staff) some people who I don't think would ever have made the course at another theological college. People like Richard Chartres – who is now [1993] a splendid Bishop of Stepney.'[5]

The 'detached, slightly amused liberalism' is of course Runcie's personal style,[6] though Cuddesdon students were

[5] He became Bishop of London in 1995.

[6] Or so it seemed to me when I wrote this chapter. Gradually I have come to see that, while he is theologically a liberal, in most other respects he is innately conservative, or at least a traditionalist who has no appetite for change, and greatly respects institutions. I suspect that the liberalism of Cuddesdon was hugely influenced by Mark Santer, Peter Cornwell, and other highly able young liberals who were on the staff and among the students. Runcie's conservatism is discussed in the last chapter.

also aware of his uncertainty and insecurity. David Stancliffe singles this out as a virtue rather than a weakness: 'I think people who are watertight in their systematic theology, impregnable in their spiritual life, and unassailable on personal grounds, make very unconvincing ministers of the gospel. It is manifestly absurd to go around saying things that you don't actually fully understand, or aren't quite sure that you believe, at any rate as expressed in that kind of terminology. It's intellectually dishonest, and it doesn't in the end allow you and what you are preaching to be integrated. Some bishops spout about believing in this, that and the other, and you know perfectly well that they don't. You don't need to challenge Bob about belief; he challenges himself the whole time. He has a pragmatic, cobbled-up structure for dealing with a multi-layered community. Push any bit of it too hard, and the ceiling leaks. But when you don't push it too hard, it actually succeeds in keeping the rain out.'

11

Now your troubles start

Terry Waite's autobiography, *Taken on Trust*, was published in August 1993. I paid my next visit to Runcie on 9 November, and remarked that the book had had a very hostile reception on the whole – most notably from Robert Fisk in the *Independent*, who suggested that Waite knew about the arms-for-hostages deal all along. 'I find that difficult to believe,' said Runcie. 'He was very close to them all [the Americans], of course. But I've talked to Terry about it. It's quite difficult for me. I want to support him.'

With which we turned to his departure from Cuddesdon in 1970 to be Bishop of St Albans. I asked whether, considering that his two predecessors at Cuddesdon had become bishops, he had assumed that this was a likely next step for himself.

'It's difficult to think back,' he answered. 'I suppose it was in my mind. I had an invitation to be Dean of Guildford. I was rather attracted by the thought of being a dean. I used to say that if I let ambition have its run, Dean of Durham would have been my desire. But Michael Gresford Jones was retiring [from the bishopric of St Albans], and after a meeting of the Cell he said to me, "You know, you're at risk for this diocese." Something slightly stirred within me, so I think I mentioned it to Lindy, and quite quickly afterwards I got a letter from the Prime Minister.

'I remember Bill Saumarez Smith came round and had a little talk with me in the garden. And he passed me a remark by Harold Wilson, who didn't really know me – we'd only met once – but Bill made much of this: "We're sure that St Albans is exactly the right diocese for you" (and I thought he was going to mention the new towns and all their challenges) "because it's exactly halfway between Oxford and Cambridge!" I took Lindy over, and she could see that the house was manageable – slightly smaller than Cuddesdon; a Georgian house with Victorian additions.

'But I didn't know very much about it all. Nobody told me what the job involved! It was all in sharp contrast to the three months' sabbatical which people have now when they hear they're going to be a bishop, and they have induction courses and things. We've entered the era of the Management Church, you know – "Except a man be evaluated every other year, he shall not see the Kingdom of God!" '

Lindy had a letter from Runcie's sister Kathleen, saying she would have to learn to be a bishop's wife. Her reaction can be imagined. Runcie says there was also some 'ill-disguised envy' from at least one other senior cleric. Then came the business of getting 'kit and clobber', with Lindy determined that they should not spend more than the Church Commissioners would reimburse. In the midst of all this, says Runcie, 'there wasn't a huge amount of time for spiritual preparation, though I did manage a week's retreat at Burford convent'.

His consecration was in Westminster Abbey on 24 February 1970. 'I asked Harry Williams to preach, and he preached at what he describes in his autobiography as "sadistic length". It was forty-one or forty-two minutes, and I remember Michael Ramsey, at the end of practically every paragraph after the first quarter of an hour, picking up his mitre – and then putting it down again! And Ian Ramsey of Durham, the most relevant and lovely of bishops, was off to

a meeting at [puts on Yorkshire accent] the Boony Cloob.'
'The Bunny Club?' I repeated unbelievingly. 'Yes,' explained
Runcie, 'it had just opened, and Ian, who was never one
for turning down an invitation which would perhaps enable
him to communicate a sort of penny-dropping disclosure of
God, was going to some meeting there. And I remember
him rushing into the reception and pocketing a number of
sausage rolls, and saying, "In case I don't get anything at
the Boony Cloob. I told them I was having loonch here.
But I didn't expect that sermon." And somebody said to
George Reindorp [Bishop of Guildford], "That sermon
should be published", and he said, "Yes, as a book!"
But I remember Jim Thompson saying, "You notice how
frivolous and dismissive they are of the sermon because of
its length. That's because it was too near the bone."'

Lindy 'did all the refreshments herself' at the reception,
Runcie explained; 'she bought a whole lot of Yugoslavian
white wine, because London catering was so expensive. And
we stayed the night before the consecration with Michael
Ramsey at Lambeth, and Rebecca was about eight, and the
first course at dinner was cold consommé, and Rebecca took
a mouthful and wouldn't eat any more, and said, "Tastes
like sick!"'

After 'the kind of theology we were pedalling at Cuddesdon',
Runcie's first impression of the St Albans diocese was of
intellectual shallowness and complacency: 'I remember a
woman saying to me in the Abbey congregation on my
first Sunday here, "You must be frightfully pleased to be
coming to a cathedral like this." And I remember a couple
of cathedral women were giving me tea, and the way they
talked about some clergyman from a dreary parish in Luton –
the cosy distanced conversation of ecclesiastical households.
I was very shocked by that – my sort of Liverpool distaste
for it all.

'I tried to get round those places. I tried to become a
friend of Luton, tried to reach characters who in the past
hadn't got much of a hearing; like the industrial chaplains
– they were Cinderellas. Also I inherited the business of

trying to rationalise resources. This was distasteful to me temperamentally. It meant persuading worthy rural parishes in Bedfordshire to merge with others, when in my heart of hearts I knew they were all little Cuddesdons!

'It was difficult for me to engage in strategic thinking, since I knew so little about how to organise such a framework. But in my enthronement sermon I had preached this idea of a believing, a caring and a prophetic church. Those were my three targets. First, to make it more aware of questioning, better able to give a more sophisticated account of how our beliefs related to the discoveries and choices of the world – David Jenkins stuff, really. The sheer fact is that, in their heart of hearts, less and less people year by year believe in God. What are we doing about that? The second thing is that clergy, when it comes to social care, are amateur, anecdotal and generalised; whereas in social work people are professional, succinct and specific. What are we doing about that? And already I was on about the big problem – the gap between the rich and the poor of the world. I was keen to challenge the fact that we had so many of the resources that were not so much needed where we were, but in places that were having a hard time – if you couldn't look further than Luton and Bedford, then you had to start there.'

Michael Gresford Jones did not have a chaplain. Runcie appointed one, choosing Nicholas Coulton, who had been one of his students at Cuddesdon. 'It was the first example of my cronyism,' Runcie admits, alluding to the frequent accusation that, as Archbishop, he tended to appoint people he already knew. 'If somebody has already proved themselves,' he answers, 'then that's the name you tend to think of. And has any of them been a disaster?'

But what about the accusation that they all had the same kind of churchmanship as him, and the same intellectual style – liberal, with a sense of humour? Surely this excluded a lot of people? 'Bill Vanstone would say that the best people never get beyond being a parish priest. It's a bit of an exaggeration, but there are a whole lot of people overlooked.'

Is it right, I asked, that the church should operate on

the passive system of appointments, by which nobody must apply for promotion or try to further his career, but wait to be asked? 'There's more advertisement of jobs now, and much more interviewing.' But can you actually apply for, say, an archdeaconry, or anything at that level? 'No. By the time people have reached that level, you tend to know the pool.'

This surely means that promotion is in the hands of certain crucial people, who have enormous amounts of power? 'Yes. Looking at it from the outside now, I realise how much that is the case. Nicholas Coulton came to my mind because he had been at Cuddesdon. He had been a solicitor, and he was a good administrator. He was the seed of my cabinet-style of government. He's now Provost of Newcastle.'

The next addition to the 'cabinet' at St Albans was a priest called Eric James. Runcie had known him from his Cambridge days, when James was chaplain of Trinity College, under Harry Williams, who had moved up to be dean there. He was, says Runcie, 'the kind of man who knew about the boys who'd come to Trinity from Bermondsey. When I went to Cuddesdon, Eric sent quite a number of people to me. And also he came and was quite a good Quiet Day conductor. And he became very much in demand as a preacher at public schools, where he would entertain them by denouncing them! He disapproves of public schools, but he also likes the champagne and the company. He's somebody who enjoys being in on privilege and power, but has a prophetic ministry to denounce it!

'Eric went to Mervyn Stockwood at Southwark [as a Canon of Southwark Cathedral], and in some ways he was a Stockwood man, but in other ways he disliked Mervyn's dictatorial way of running a diocese. He has always been one to stand up for blacks, the poor, gays – all the fashionable causes of the 'sixties, but none the worse for that.'

Runcie invited Eric James to St Albans because he had had a big row with Stockwood. 'He actually preached a sermon in the University church at Cambridge against Mervyn,' explains Runcie. Stockwood had appointed a young priest as Director of Education for the Southwark diocese, and there had been a disagreement with Hugh Montefiore, who was then suffragan Bishop of Kingston and Chairman of the Board of Education. The Director of Education resigned. Eric James was so incensed by the matter that he handed in his own resignation, and made public allegations.

I suggested to Runcie that it was not like him to offer a job to someone as controversial as James sounded. 'Oh, on the contrary, I had quite a reputation of rescuing people from obscurity or persecution, because I thought they were able, and others wouldn't touch them. I think Eric would say I was quite bold in taking on some of *his* lost sheep.' What did Mervyn Stockwood have to say about his taking on Eric James? 'There was a bit of coolness!'

Canon Missioner was a job largely invented by Runcie, though the St Albans diocese had previously had a priest who had 'set up a lot of clergy cells around the diocese', to look after their morale. 'But he had been rather conservative. And Eric inflamed them! And some of the things that he proposed were difficult to take. But he had *one* idea, which I was slow to accept, but when I decided to take it up I did so firmly, and was loyal to it (rather as with Waite, later on). The idea was that, if you were going to close a parish down, and take away a full-time parson because you were short of clergy, and you were going to employ part-time non-stipendiary clergy,[1] then you need four non-stipendiaries for one full-time. Therefore – and this was a great Eric James phrase – "We need it now. We need to have a training programme, based on this diocese, which will produce a large number of non-stipendiary clergy very very quickly." It was against my feeling that "Cuddesdon is what people really need", but we started the St Albans Ministerial Training Scheme. And that was quite pioneering, a break-through.'

The non-stipendiaries were mostly working in full-time or part-time day jobs. 'And the difficulty was that the needs were in Luton or multi-cultural Bedford, but the volunteers

[1]That is, clergy who receive no salary.

came from Radlett, Harpenden, Berkhamstead and so on.' So the closure of the overstaffed country parishes was part of the same movement to redeploy? 'Yes. I'd felt discomfort at the closing of churches, but Eric's idea was "*No* churches need to be closed. They're all supportable if we train a diocese much more to own its own ministry." Each parish would be asked to seek out among its members the sort of people that God was calling. The training would be for three years, and there would be a support group for each candidate – somebody from his place of work, somebody from his parish, somebody who knew his family, somebody who represented the diocese, and so on. It was a very good idea. I think nobody has ever really carried it out fully. But I think the St Albans diocese is in good condition because this sort of thing was happening. I mean, it's significant that it keeps producing leadership. It's produced lots of bishops and spokesmen in the General Synod.'

I met Eric James at the Reform Club in Pall Mall and took him to have lunch in a wine vault in an alleyway opposite St James's Palace. Despite Runcie's description of him as something of a firebrand, he turned out to be a rather diffident uncle-figure, wearing a collar and tie. His accent puzzled me a little, until he mentioned that the wine vault reminded him of the bonded vaults on the wharf where he had worked as a lad on Thames-side. He explained that he was 'not at all the Guards officer like Robert', but had been born in Dagenham, left school at fourteen, and eventually, thanks to night school, managed to get to King's College, London (at the age of twenty-one) to read Theology.

He told me that, when they first met in Cambridge days, 'Robert was always saying to me,' (he puts on the Runcie voice), '"I've got a lecture to write. Can you take Lindy to Ladies' Night at Trinity?" In fact it was almost always Lindy that I took, while Robert stayed at home writing his lecture and looking after the baby. And I don't know whether I saw James before Robert did, at his birth, but I think I may have. Robert said to me: "Lindy thinks she's started labour.

I don't think she has. I've got to go off and give a lecture. If she has to go to hospital, can you go and see her?" And I did.' Yet he describes the Runcies' marriage as marvellously successful.

In their St Albans days, he was often at the Abbey Gate House, the episcopal residence. He calls it 'my bachelor home', and says he was 'often there in the evenings, watching telly with Lindy and the children' while Runcie was at work. He is by no means uncritical of Runcie, observing that he 'operates on different levels' (the 'compartments' as Runcie himself put it), but clearly has considerable warmth of feeling for him.

His departure from the Southwark diocese was even more dramatic than Runcie had given me to believe. He was persuaded to go away for six months, to get a perspective on things, and on his return discovered that it was rumoured that he had had a nervous breakdown on account of a homosexual affair. His response was to attack Montefiore and Stockwood in a sermon at Great St Mary's, Cambridge, of which both men were former incumbents. Talking to me over lunch, he cast doubt on Alan Webster's story that Montefiore rather than Runcie was the first choice for Archbishop. Yet he showed no malice towards Montefiore, praising his devotion in recent years to his wife, who has Alzheimer's; and he mentioned that he himself had played a crucial part in Montefiore's career.

At the 1967 conference of the Modern Churchmen's Union, Montefiore – then still at Great St Mary's – explored the question, quite open-mindedly, of whether Jesus Christ (though celibate) could have been homosexual in orientation. This provoked public outrage, and allegedly the Queen was so upset by it that she would not agree to Montefiore becoming a diocesan bishop. About two years later, Eric James, then Chaplain of Trinity, Cambridge, was asked by the Master, Lord ('Rab') Butler, if he could do something about 'poor Hugh'. James spoke to Mervyn Stockwood, who shortly afterwards chose Montefiore as his suffragan Bishop of Kingston, a step which would make it almost certain that in time he would become a diocesan. (Incidentally, when I mentioned David Hare, Eric James said that Hare had consulted him for 'local colour' when writing *Racing Demon*.)

When James arrived in the St Albans diocese, and the ordination course for non-stipendiary clergy was proposed, Runcie 'gave his mind and his official signature, but I never convinced him. He was very reluctant that we should train anyone who might not have become a Cuddesdon student' – that is, anyone of an ability and character that would disqualify him for Cuddesdon.[2] Eric James, on the other hand, would cheerfully have seen Cuddesdon and the other theological colleges dismantled; he would have preferred many ordinands to go into full-time secular jobs, and work as spare-time non-stipendiary clergy.

He went on from this to compare what he calls Runcie's 'serial theology' – 'a chunk of academic study, followed by practical experience' – with his own outlook: 'My theology is worked out on the hoof. It's a continual ricocheting between ideas and experience.' In passing, he spoke scathingly of Runcie's intellectual cast of mind as 'Sixth form scholarship'. Yet he went on: 'Robert's appreciation of other people comes out of what he knows he can't manage himself,' and emphasised that there was a very considerable humility inside him.

He compared Runcie's rescue of him from the Stockwood-Montefiore disaster with the case of Alan Wilkinson, principal of Chichester theological college, who was resigning this post because his marriage had broken down. Runcie invited him to become director of what became the St Albans Ministerial Training Scheme, which helped Wilkinson greatly, and also provided the scheme with a trainer of

[2] After reading this, Runcie commented: 'Not true! I was enthusiastic, and sold the scheme to the diocese. But I did think that full-time priests needed residential training. And I had a built-in doubt about the part-time priesthood, and the part-time training for it, being put on a par with the full-time. I've since been proved right, since we are now seriously short of young full-time properly trained priests.'

considerable distinction. Eric James cited this as an inspired piece of management.

He also mentioned Runcie's canny handling of clergy who got into trouble – financially, sexually, or in some other disastrous way. 'One of your jobs,' Runcie told him, 'is to keep these people away from me.' His technique was exactly the reverse of Mervyn Stockwood's in a similar situation: 'Mervyn would growl, "Before you or I say a word, I want your resignation in writing. Sign here." But Robert wanted me to handle it so that it could all be unofficial – so that officially he knew nothing. He'd tell me, "You can consult me if you really need to, but not as the bishop – just as Mr Runcie or something."' This meant that a lot of tricky cases were handled delicately and successfully.

A personal case of a quite different sort, which required careful handling, was that of Richard Chartres. He had arrived at Cuddesdon as a student in 1969, but had left before completing his ordination training, which he eventually finished at Lincoln theological college. In 1973 Runcie was to ordain him to a curacy in Bedford. Eric James saw him during the ordination retreat in St Albans. 'We went into the garden, and he simply couldn't speak – his teeth were chattering with nerves. And when I asked him what was the matter, he ran indoors, and went up to his room, and shut himself away. And I saw Robert, and told him that one of the ordinands seemed to be in a bit of trouble, and he said, "Don't tell me who – I know, it's Richard Chartres. Well, I'm going to go ahead and ordain him. I believe that the grace of Holy Orders will work on him." And it did.' Eric James saw Chartres a year later, when he came to be ordained priest, and Chartres – who had had a difficult family background – told him that a year of being 'loved' by the old ladies in his parish had worked wonders.

James was describing Chartres and his wife, the tough-minded daughter of a merchant banker, in terms that recalled the Runcies. I ask him if he thought Chartres would go far. 'If he lives,' he replied, 'he'll be Archbishop of Canterbury.'

I raised the point that many people assumed that Runcie

*He's Now
Bp A London!*

was gay. 'The word "gay" is so complicated,' James answered. 'Just consider how many things "heterosexual" can mean. If you said "Robert is not gay", you'd be cutting out a large part of him.' Not that he means that Runcie is a practising homosexual; merely that many elements can be found in his sexual psychology.

Summing up Runcie, Eric James is the first to be aware of the weaknesses: 'Everyone at Cambridge was always putting him down, saying that he was second-rate. But there's a type of person who mixes together gifts and abilities which may not be striking individually, but which produce an extraordinary mixture. He's one of them.'

I listened to another character-analysis of Runcie when I met Professor Gillian Stamp, head of the Individual and Organisational Capabilty Unit at Brunel University, which conducts research in management theory and finances itself from services to industry and public bodies. Although not herself a Christian, she is immensely knowledgeable about church affairs, having worked since the mid-1970s at St George's House, Windsor, a study centre which brings church and business people together, and runs management courses for clergy. She came into contact with Runcie when studying organisational procedures in the Hitchin deanery of St Albans diocese for her doctoral thesis.

I listened while she talked about the weakness in the Church of England's central management structure. She said she felt a grave mistake had been made when synodical government had been adopted in the 1970s: 'The General Synod is a legislative body, but it has no executive.' This was the root cause of the Church Commissioners' disastrous investment policy: it was like leaving Whitehall civil servants to make policy decisions which ought to have been in the hands of ministers.

She regards the Church of England as a managerial mess, and is constantly reminded of this when running training courses for new bishops: 'These poor people really haven't the foggiest. And they're faced with a really horrendous financial situation now.'

Now she turned to Runcie. 'I'm an expert on structures and strategies of organisations,' she explained, 'and on people's capabilities within them. And I have learnt, over the years, that there is a certain type of individual who has a capacity to see any issue as part of a wider and more complex canvas than most people can perceive. You can find such people in all walks of life – they occur among black South Africans and aboriginal Australians. This capacity for wide-ranging judgement is totally unaffected by family background, race, or even educational attainment.'

She explained that people with this kind of capability may get far in life, but more often than not they don't fit in. 'By the time they're thirty, their CVs look a mess – it seems as if they've hopped from one thing to another. In fact they've seen the limitations in one particular job or form of study, and have moved on, restlessly.'

In most contexts, having this detached and judgemental view of the world will not, she said, help you to get on with other people. You will essentially be a loner, with maybe one or two friends at the most who really understand you; with most people, you will have to keep your perceptions under wraps.

She believes Runcie belongs very clearly to this type: that it was the kind of intellectual restlessness she describes which carried him away from Crosby and on and up in the church; but, crucially, that this restlessness is accompanied by a huge vulnerability to boredom, and she believes – indeed knows – that he has suffered almost cripplingly from this. She says he wasn't a good diocesan bishop, because the job was too easy for him. 'Indeed, crazy as it sounds, I don't think the archbishopric of Canterbury was a big enough job for him.'

So she would guess that, at heart, he was, and always had been, deeply bored? 'Bored, yes, and very, very lonely.'

I told Runcie about this the next time I met him. He laughed, and admitted: 'I *was* really rather bored with these

endless weekend conferences to discuss the management
structure of the Hitchin archdeaconry – when good laymen
were taken away from tennis or their families in order to
discuss whether a lay chairman ought to be regarded in the
same way as a rural dean, and what was the relationship
between a lay member of the synod and the traditional
churchwarden's.

'Now, churchwardens are ancient, pre-synodical. The
people elected their churchwardens, and because churchwardens could determine the sort of stone you could have in
the graveyard, and things like that, they took trouble about
whom they elected, in a way they didn't if it was diocesan
synod representatives. And when I wanted something done,
such as a new stewardship movement that wouldn't be
caught up in jargon about "needs and resources", I simply
assembled all the churchwardens in the cathedral, and said
to them, "Now, you're the characters who really matter." I
outwitted all that synodical nonsense. I did the same when
I went to Canterbury, and we had a crisis in the affairs of
the diocese. And when I wanted to sell *Faith in the City,*
and get people to contribute to the Church Urban Fund, I
did the same. The successful clawing-in of eighteen million,
or whatever it was, I regard as partly due to my suggesting to
all the bishops to go for the churchwardens. It wasn't Gillian
Stamp management orthodoxy, but I'm not as conscientious
as she was.'

I met Nicholas Coulton, the former solicitor who had
been Runcie's first chaplain at St Albans, in the lobby
of Church House, Westminster. When we went for a cup
of tea he gave me an armful of legal-looking documents
which proved to be a selection of Runcie's addresses to
the St Albans diocesan synod, and back-numbers of *See
Round,* the diocesan magazine, which Coulton had edited
as part of his role in overseeing communications within the
diocese. In the September 1975 issue, just as Coulton was
about to quit as chaplain and take over a parish in Bedford,
Runcie wrote:

Nicholas Coulton has managed to overcome his Victorian title of domestic chaplain – it sounds as if he ran my bathwater! Though adept at juggling with books, mitres, crosiers, minutes of countless meetings, and the moods of his employer, he has chiefly helped outwards, in communication with people ... My new chaplain is to be Richard Chartres. He comes from Hertford and is now a curate in Bedford. Those who already know him will be aware that he also combines an ability to listen and to communicate without dangerously uncritical or humourless deference to his boss.

Chartres was on my list of topics when I went to see Runcie again, on 24 January 1994, intending to cover the remainder of his years as Bishop of St Albans. I said I'd seen Eric James, who had talked a lot about Richard Chartres. Runcie recalled his first meeting with Chartres, at Cuddesdon:

'I always remember his arrival there [as a student]. I'd been out somewhere – it was a hot Saturday afternoon – and a man in a dark suit and a bowler hat, with an umbrella on his arm, was ringing the doorbell when I got home. And I thought he was an undertaker or something. And he took off his bowler, and said, "Good afternoon, sir." And that was my introduction to Richard.

'He was very right-wing. These were the days when students were going off to turn pots in Indian ashrams, but Richard eventually went to Franco's Spain, and joined the staff of the International School in Seville.

'He was a product of a grammar school in Hertford. His father was works manager of a pharmaceutical company. There was a brother was was severely mentally handicapped. Richard had a tremendous capacity to relate to the upper classes. An original Young Fogey. And behind it all was a shrewd, observant, discerning mind, a very good turn of phrase, and a very considerable presence and fluency. Another man would perhaps have tried to solve Richard's deep problems, but at that time I think he preferred that

I should enjoy the Richard who presented himself, rather than delving.

'He had got a scholarship to Trinity, Cambridge. His family were not religious, but he was greatly influenced by a most eccentric man, Max Bryant, the vicar of Northaw, just outside Hertford. He was the man who scythed nettles on the graves and made homemade wine from them, which he bottled as "In Memoriam"! And he was a mixture of disciplined, old-fashioned Anglo-Catholic, who managed to get people into church on saints' days at half past six in the morning, and extreme intellectual scepticism, which he didn't conceal. I couldn't quite take Max as Richard did, particularly when you'd go after a confirmation to have lunch with the local bigwig, and Max would take his claret glass and say, "Here's to Our Lord!" And all these county magistrate types would look frightfully embarrassed.

'Richard powerfully dominated Cuddesdon when he became a student there, because he had opinions shared by nobody at the place. He believed in old-fashioned terrifying religion. I remember David Painter getting a note from Richard which said: "Dear Painter" – he was a person who still called people by their surnames – "I hope you will have a truly terrifying ordination." He was miserable about the trivialising of the faith, and believed in the great established orders. What really upset him was one day when Ken Jennings, the vice-principal, preached a sermon attacking the Maundy ceremonies "A sham," Ken called it. Richard was very upset about it. And Ken disapproved of Richard. When I left, Richard was still there, but he left soon afterwards, without proceeding to ordination for the time being.'

Lindy – who was at home, recuperating from a hip operation – came into the room at this moment, and remarked: 'I always stuck up for Richard Chartres. Because I thought he was genuine.' Despite all the posing? 'There was a lot of posing at first,' admitted Runcie. Lindy said: 'I liked his sense of humour. I think he had a lot of compensating to do, because of his brother. And very little money, so he bought those funny clothes from the second-hand shop at

Mornington Crescent. He's one of the few people I know that have galoshes!'

Given that Cuddesdon and Chartres had parted company, how had he become ordained? 'Eventually he went to Lincoln theological college,' explained Runcie. 'Alec Graham, the principal, was a bit more discerning than the Cuddesdon characters, and saw there was real profundity in his religion. I wrote to Alec and said, "Look here, I want this man in the diocese." And we found a curacy for him in Bedford, and immediately he became the best possible curate, a dream curate. He got on well with his vicar, who wasn't his cup of tea at all, really. That was always Richard's amazing quality – he would go out (when he was my chaplain) and form a friendship with a trade union leader and his family, a man who at that time was taking the press barons for a ride. And Richard became a terrific friend of theirs, and persuaded them to have their child baptised, and he was its godfather. And he knew the highways and byways of St Albans in the most amazing way. I had been regarded as mad for appointing him, but he never let me down. Indeed, he enhanced my reputation for wisdom! He once said to me that he had no ambition for personal position, and I believe that to be true. But I think he liked to be near power.'

Didn't his outlook clash with Runcie's theological liberalism? 'That was a great advantage! We clashed completely, but he greatly influenced me more than I influenced him. He moderated my liberal position, and nourished the roots of my innate conservatism. His attitude to me was, "You're not a liberal. Liberals are phonies – and you're worse. You're a phoney liberal." He believed in the offices that I held, and he thought that I had it in me to be something rather better than a canting liberal, as he put it. He was the ideal chaplain in the sense that wherever you were in the world, you'd go into a great big room, and when you talked to him afterwards, he would have noticed the significant person, the telling remark, what was really going on, whether it was a happy place or not.'

The original plan when Chartres took over from Coulton

at St Albans was that he should drive Runcie to engagements. But he did not learn to drive until he had taken on the job, and (recalled Runcie) 'after one terrible moment – Richard going off at high speed down the wrong side of the M1, or something like that', this was dropped. Like Coulton, Chartres lived in the Abbey Gate House with the Runcies. 'At first I think he found the way we lived, with the family and the lodgers, and at a slightly high tension,' said Runcie, turning to Lindy, 'with your refusal to be, how shall I put it, a mere supporter in the episcopal outfit, or fully sharing in His Lordship's ministry – I think he found that a bit strange.'

Lindy quickly sprang to her own defence: 'How much does Caroline [Chartres' wife] join in, I ask myself? I did at first. But Rebecca was seven, and we had to go to smart things on Sundays – country houses – that poor child! And I just said, "I'm not going to do that!" After that, she and I went to the same church, sat in the same place, and saw the same people every week. And that's what she needed, a stable home, rather than touting around, wondering when Dad was going to finish.'

I said that I knew the predicament of a bishop's wife from my mother's experience. I asked Lindy if eyebrows had been raised at her refusal to travel round with her husband. 'Who cares?' she answered. 'And the other clergy wives said, "You've freed us."'

'It was a break with the trend,' agreed Runcie. 'Lindy's predecessor at St Albans, Mrs Gresford Jones, was an old-fashioned person who fully shared her husband's ministry, and went around and adorned occasions. And of course they had a private income. And at Lambeth, both Mrs Coggan and Mrs Ramsey had been as if glued to their husbands. Not only did Lindy have a separate life, but at Lambeth she refused to give information to the staff as to what she was doing.'

'Well, why should I?' she answered. 'I had a lot of homosexual friends who used to ask me out. If one of them said, at a quarter to seven at night, "Like to go to a concert?", I'd say "Yes!" It was ten minutes down the road to the Festival Hall, and they knew they didn't have to give me dinner. They also knew they were perfectly safe with me – and I with them!'

At this point I decided to take advantage of the rare presence of both Runcies at once, and ask them about Jenny Boyd-Carpenter. When I had begun work on the book, Runcie had referred rather coyly to his correspondence with this lady.

I asked Runcie how they had first met. 'Well, she was going through an interest in religion at the time, and it coincided with my beginning to make an impact on the St Albans diocese. She was married to Mike Boyd-Carpenter, a stockbroker who was very successful at that time, in the early 1970s, and had made a lot of money which they'd put into buying a big country house. They had five children, who were beginning to stand on their own feet, and she was looking for fresh fields to conquer. She had a great gift as an embroiderer.'

'She was a model, too,' added Lindy. 'She was very attractive.'

'Oh, very attractive,' agreed Runcie. 'She quickly established herself with the archdeacons, and the clergy, and with the laity,' he went on, 'because she was quite stunning! And so she got elected to everything – on visual grounds!'

'Ah, but she was a worker-beaver – she did work,' said Lindy.

'Oh, she did, like anything,' Runcie agreed. 'She could write very funny and very discerning letters.'

'You had a whole drawerful,' said Lindy. 'But I always liked her, actually.' Had she not found her threatening? 'No, because Robert gets tired of people who try too hard. I knew this, because we'd had it before. And I liked her husband. He had a hot temper. I mean, he's an Aquarian – absolutely fiery temper.'

Was I hearing that Lindy was a believer in the Zodiac? 'Yes,' she said. Did Robert share this? 'No, of course he doesn't.'

'Not at all,' he said, 'but I've learned to live with it.'

'He's a real Libran!' interjected Lindy.

'Feckless,' suggested Runcie. 'Kind to everybody, generous to a fault.'

'No,' snapped Lindy. 'Can't make up your mind.'

I asked if Jenny Boyd-Carpenter had invented the pig-keeping business which had delighted the popular press through the St Albans years.

'No,' said Runcie, and told the story in full. 'During the war, when I had some leave, I used to go to Lowdham, where my sister Kathleen was. And there, and after the war at Cotgrave, they kept a "pig for victory". And Angus used to say to me, "Berkshires are the only sort of pig to have." The Berkshire is a very fine black pig. And I always used to be very interested in that pig, and say, "I'd like to keep a pig." And when I was at Cuddesdon, I used to get bits of pork from Fred Sellar, and say, "Oh, if only I could keep a pig." Lindy would say, "If you kept a pig, I know who'd have to muck it out." Well, when I was at St Albans, I said once to Jenny Boyd-Carpenter, "I'd like to keep a pig." Now, she was a lady who went into action, you see, and she said, "What sort of a pig do you want?" And I said, "A Berkshire." So she went and purchased three pigs and installed them at their house, where there was plenty of room. And she read up all about pig-keeping, and talked to local farmers. And then we had to get a boar to service them. We tried a local man, whose boar wasn't good enough. There was a service called Rent-a-Boar, which sounded like something for the General Synod; but we couldn't do that, so we bought a boar. I went halves, and that was quite a big expense.

'She did it all, and she used my name shamelessly in order to get things from people. She was the sort of person who could persuade a local poacher to come in and do any emergency stuff. And we started the industry. And really it did very well. We had about sixty of these black pigs at one time. They were under arcs which she had installed, so they were free-range. And pork was produced – a little business. And Runcie began to be famous as a pig-keeper, because everything was done in my name. I remember the *Express* had a cartoon of me at the altar – rather a good cartoon – with a cope with pigs embroidered on it, and gumboots protruding underneath, and all the choirboys holding their noses.

'When I went to Canterbury, the Home Farm Trust, which is a farm for the mentally handicapped, wrote to me. They'd heard of my pig-keeping, and asked if I'd like to give one of a litter to start up their new Home Farm, at Lympne in Romney Marsh. I remember Richard Chartres, who never really took the pigs seriously, said, "It'll be better for your image that the pigs are looked after by the mentally handicapped in Kent than by some glamorous Bo-Peep in Hertfordshire. So why not give them all to them?" So I wrote and said, "You can have them all." They went, and Jenny was happy about that, because she was struggling with them. But they're still mine.'

Lindy recalled that he used to let Jenny Boyd-Carpenter drive him to official engagements now and then. I asked what this had done for his reputation in the St Albans diocese, when Lindy was resolutely not participating and the bishop turned up with another woman, an ex-model who smelt expensively. 'I was so unconcerned,' said Lindy. 'I don't think it mattered. And she was often plunged down to here' – indicating a low neckline – 'amazingly provocatively dressed. Sort of Nell Gwynne outfits.'

Wasn't Runcie aware of ripples of astonishment going about the place? 'She caused more than ripples when she got elected on to the General Synod. There was a little bit of gossip about the place. But Richard Chartres used to say, "The thing about Jenny is, she's not a carnal person."'

I wrote to Jenny Boyd-Carpenter in France, where she was now living, proposing that we meet on her next visit to England. She replied that she had 'no present plans to return to the UK. As to Dr Runcie, I make for [*sic*] a number of famous men, & chaps chat to their "Vestry hens" in the same indiscreet manner ladies gossip with their hairdressers. One can't repeat it, even if one did remember it – not if one wants to keep one's friends, let alone stay in business!' But she invited me to write again 'if there is any particular fact you want verifying'. What I had wanted was not facts, but to meet her.

In 1992 Richard Chartres had been consecrated Bishop of Stepney, to succeed Jim Thompson, Runcie's former student and staff member at Cuddesdon. The *Church Times* photograph of the occasion showed an apparently benign, bearded figure standing alongside George Carey, Runcie's successor at Canterbury, flanked by his wife Caroline, who seemed to bear a certain resemblance to Lindy, as Eric James had hinted.

Early in 1994, I wrote to Chartres, asking that we should meet. He replied in a thick, elegant script that might have been fashionable in the 1880s. We arranged to meet in a Japanese restaurant in Soho.

I looked forward to our meeting slightly apprehensively. It was on a snowy February day, and much of the London Underground had been paralysed by signal failures and bomb scares, so I was surprised and impressed when a tall figure stepped into the Fuji in Brewer Street two minutes before the appointed time. Very tall – as tall as Terry Waite, with a trim beard and a domed forehead, and very, very sharp eyes.

Nicholas Coulton had worn a collar and tie when I met him at Church House, and still looked like the solicitor he had once been. A few weeks before meeting Chartres, I had been looking at Holbein drawings of Tudor statesmen and court politicians in the National Portrait Gallery. Chartres, who was wearing official dress (a dark suit and a purple stock beneath his clerical collar), could have stepped out of one of those portraits.

We sat down and ordered. We were both a little tentative about the choice of Japanese food, but when I suggested wine he plumped unhesitatingly for red, and I think would have got happily through much more than the rather mean half-bottle with which I provided him.

I thought he had dangerous eyes, like an actor's – or was

it Machiavelian? He spoke with slightly uneasy joviality at first, always referrring to Runcie as 'Bishop Robert' when talking about something that happened in St Albans days, or as 'Archbishop Robert' or 'the Archbishop' – very formal, and differentiating between the two jobs.

I told him that early in the project I had taken Runcie to Crosby. Chartres said he had accompanied him there too, and they had been to Coronation Road Primary School, where Runcie had been a pupil. Before they went in, Runcie told Chartres that he knew exactly how to handle the children: '"I shall ask one simple question which they can all answer, and that will break the ice." And we went in,' continued Chartres, 'and he took out his crosier, and held it up, and said, "Now, can anybody tell me what this is?" And no one's hand shot up at all, except a boy in the front row, and the Archbishop said, "Yes?" And the boy mumbled a reply, and the Archbishop, who's rather deaf, as you know, couldn't hear it. So he asked the boy to speak up. And the boy yelled out [slips into Liverpool accent]: "Mister, it's for whacking bums."'

As the raw fish and noodles arrived, I asked Chartres about his stormy Cuddesdon days. He told me that he had left because he was disaffected by student power (this was 1970). After leaving, he had worked in Spain and briefly in a Sainsbury's warehouse before finishing his ordination training at Lincoln.

Recalling the days in which he had lived *en famille* with the Runcies, he said not a word against Lindy, and described it admiringly as 'a marriage in which each allows the other to be impossible when they are out of the public eye'. He portrayed Runcie as very much the competitive statesman, determined to out-manoeuvre adversaries, whose favourite phrase was 'We mustn't be outwitted.'

He suggested that it was Runcie's insecurity which made him so sensitive to the character and intentions of others: 'He's always looking out for ambushes.' He also emphasised that Runcie had no ideological drive, and was always used to taking ideas from others (which entirely corresponded to what I already knew). So it must have felt strange to Runcie, I suggested, when suddenly he found he was in the top job with no commanding officer above him. Chartres agreed, and added: 'One of the best things about him was that he never really believed he was the Archbishop of Canterbury.'

Chartres traced much of Runcie's insecurity back to the young Guards officer who had never lost his social anxieties. He brought out the story of Runcie going to some formal dinner in a London hotel when the invitation had told people to wear both dinner jackets and military decorations. Runcie was certain that this must be wrong – absolutely not etiquette. But did as he was bid. He and Chartres were getting out of the car in Park Lane when up loomed some Guards acquaintance of Runcie's who *wasn't* wearing decorations. Runcie immediately became furious and ripped his off and stuffed them in his pocket. Chartres accompanied him into the banquet. The next person who loomed up *was* wearing medals. Runcie, now livid, plucked his from his pocket and attempted to pin them on again, pricking his finger in the process ('He's got very poor motor co-ordination'). Chartres thought all this was absolutely ridiculous, but could understand it.

I began to be astonished at Chartres' swift rise in the church – because it was becoming increasingly obvious that he had wielded a huge influence over Runcie. Here was someone who in 1971 had failed to complete ordination training. Four years later, he was the right-hand man to a diocesan bishop; five years after that, he was trusted to make policy decisions – I had no doubt about that – on behalf of the Archbishop of Canterbury. (In 1995 he was to become Bishop of London.) Towards the end of lunch, he remarked to me that Runcie belonged to 'the last generation of ten-talented men who thought they could change the world by being ordained into the Church of England. During his lifetime,' Chartres continued, 'that belief has become totally implausible.'

Chartres afterwards told me that he had wished the medals

story to be off the record, and felt that it – and my record of our conversation – misrepresented his esteem for Runcie: 'He has a very considerable gift of discernment, and knows which ideas to back and which to block. At the same time he creates conditions in which things can happen and has given a succession of members of his personal staff the scope and freedom to do significant work.' He also disputed my assertion that he had influenced Runcie: 'During my time with Lord Runcie, I believed and still believe that my work reflected his attitudes and wishes. When I moved to parish life after eight years as his chaplain, there was no noticeable change in either the tone or policy of his archiepiscopate.'

In 1974, when Donald Coggan went from York to Canterbury, Runcie was tipped to succeed him, and I gathered that he had been offered that archbishopric. 'Yes, we went up to York,' he admitted to me. Lindy explained: 'I said no.'

Runcie began to tell the story in full: 'We went up to York, and we had fish pie, and Evensong in the Minster, rather badly sung, and a night at the Railway Hotel. And I was keen on York. I thought it would be a return to the North, a New World. But Lindy was in tears at breakfast.'

'It was a terrible house,' she explained. 'Robert had been offered it, and we went on holiday the next day, and I was still crying. One of Robert's staff said, "If God calls you, it's your duty." And I said, "I don't think God is calling." And Rebecca? She was twelve years old, we'd just got things established for her, and it would have meant her boarding, or me driving every day to a girls' school miles away. Ugh. Horrible!'

How did Runcie feel about Lindy's resistance to York? 'Quite a lot of me wanted to go, but I felt that it wouldn't work. I mean, I did care for my wife, and it wouldn't work. And somehow it didn't linger long as an opportunity missed, or anything like that.'

'I said I wouldn't go,' repeated Lindy. 'We went on holiday, and I hid in the garden where we staying, and drank gin! Weeping to myself. And George Reindorp [Bishop

of Guildford] wrote and said, "You mustn't betray his God."
And I said, "Well, if that's his God, I don't want Him."
Wrote to her or to Robert? 'To Robert, saying it was all
my fault, and I'd have to go there. They were nasty about
me, and Robert said, "You don't understand about Lindy.
She needs roots, and when she's put down roots she doesn't
want to move." I don't know what it is about me. I wept
when I went to Lambeth. I wept when I had to tear up
Lambeth and come here. I wept when I went everywhere.
Now I am ensconced here with my garden and my family
and this *lovely* house.'

Had she seen the archbishopric of Canterbury coming up
on the horizon? 'No.' But surely by the end of the 1970s
it was looking pretty likely? 'But don't forget I had dished
him before, over York. You know, they were having odds on
[the candidates for the Archbishop of Canterbury in 1974],
and I said, "I think it's disgusting for an important church
matter to be turned into a horse-race." The result of that
being printed in the *Mirror* was that Robert went from eight
to one to twenty to one! And I said, "I'm only going out
of Abbey Gate House feet first!" Because I loved it, it's a
gorgeous house.'

'I was tempted to go to Oxford,' explained Runcie. 'I was
offered Oxford, you know, after Kenneth Woollcombe went
[in 1972].' It would have meant living in Cuddesdon again,
and Lindy told him: 'Never go back.'

What was their first reaction in 1979 when the Downing
Street letter came, offering Canterbury? 'Horror!' answered
Lindy. Runcie recalled: 'We had been to dinner at the BBC –
it's an oft-told tale – and Richard Chartres was in a dressing
gown – and a fez! He gave me this letter. We'd just come in
from a very good party, and he said, "Now your troubles
start." I always remember those dramatic words.'

Margaret Duggan records that the letter from the Prime
Minister, Mrs Thatcher, arrived at the Abbey Gate House
on Thursday 19 July 1979, and that it took Runcie a very
long time to make up his mind whether to accept the
Archbishopric. When I asked Richard Chartres whether the

offer had come as an entire surprise to Runcie, he said he thought that Canterbury had been 'not entirely absent from his mind' as Coggan's retirement approached, adding that his turning-down of the bishopric of Oxford may have been a calculated move. 'But the reluctance to accept Canterbury was real,' Chartres added, 'because there was a real sense of the cost.'

'You took six weeks to decide,' Lindy reminded Runcie when I was asking them about this. 'They were getting very worried.'

'I went to see Mrs Thatcher,' Runcie said, 'and I was intending to refuse.' Was he really? 'I think I was. I said, "I feel that I'm so uncertain, it's wrong for me to do it." And she said to Colin Peterson, her Appointments Secretary, "Colin, why does it have to be now? Why can't it wait until after they've had a holiday?" And he said, yes it could. And she said, "Go and have a holiday and come back and tell me." And so we went off to Italy. Where Lindy cried most of the time.'

'Well, it's quite a lot to take,' said Lindy. 'And everybody said, "Lambeth's dreadful, but you'll love Canterbury." And it was the other way round.'

I asked her if the offer of the archbishopric of Canterbury sent her down the garden with the bottle of gin again. 'Not quite. It wasn't that bad. I said, "I will go if you want to. I will not refuse this."'

'Yes, she did say that,' agreed Runcie. 'And the children were quite participators by this time.' He told them he had been offered it? 'Yes.'

'Rebecca was at Haileybury in the sixth form,' added Lindy, 'so it wasn't a question of finding her another school at a vital time. James was at university.'

Why was Runcie so hesitant, I asked him. He paused to think before replying. Lindy interjected: '*I* know why it was. I didn't want our private lives to be taken away.'

'Yes, I didn't like that idea either,' agreed Runcie. He could see this coming? 'There'd been a certain amount of it already. They'd been unkind to Coggan. I realised I couldn't easily be an archbishop and have a private life which was uninvestigated.' But was there anything to investigate? He laughed when I asked this. 'No! But I mean, you couldn't have a private life.' But besides that practical doubt, what did he feel on the spiritual level? Again, there was a long pause before he replied.

'Well,' he said at last, 'I didn't think I was good enough for it. I wasn't spiritual enough. And I thought that people over-rated me considerably. I knew that I had, from time to time, impressed in a sort of way. Only six months before that, I had to give an account of some trip that I'd taken to the Orthodox patriarchs, and it was at a meeting of the bishops, and I knew that they were bored with Coggan's rather dull chairmanship, and I was asked to give this talk – a very dull agenda – and I entertained them hugely. I could see that it went down like cream. And I thought, the reason why they want me to be Archbishop is they want that sort of sparkle. But I'm only capable of putting that out from time to time, in an area with which I'm familiar. In between, there are huge areas of boredom, of inability to be enthused by the business of ministering the faith to the country. I wasn't as interested in religion or the church as Coggan. Or Ramsey. I was ashamed that I got more delight from lecturing on a Swan Hellenic cruise than I did from going to some religious rally.'

Lindy reminded him that he had gone to consult John Turnbull, his former vicar at Gosforth. 'Yes,' he said. 'That was the most dramatic part of the advice I got – driven there by Jenny Boyd-Carpenter, oddly enough! She drove me up to Ripon, with a beautiful picnic. John was really dying, but quite coherent. He said, "You'll have to pace yourself. You tend to wear yourself out doing things that aren't top priority" – you know, simple things like that. And he said, "In my experience, if God wants you to do something, he gives you the grace to do it." And I talked to my sister Kath, and to Angus. And they were keen on my accepting, but they were very worried about Lindy.'

I had come across this attitude to Lindy when talking to

ws wer 4th at Bossey in 1953

Patrick Rodger, who had been Bishop of Manchester and had then moved to the bishopric of Oxford after Runcie had turned it down. Rodger described his own wife (now dead) as 'the perfect bishop's wife in every way, there all the time supporting you', and obviously found Lindy extraordinary.

Runcie was quoted in the *Sunday Telegraph Colour Magazine* (3 February 1980) on his decision to accept the archbishopric: 'I would get up in the morning and say, "No, I won't do it." Then, over lunch, I would have second thoughts and say, "Yes." But by the time the evening came, I would decide to put it off until the next day.' Another factor in his indecision may have been a fear of having to commit himself to firm opinions; he told Michael Charlton on Radio 4's *Analysis* (30 January 1980) that what frightened him was the prospect, as Archbishop, of having to produce 'an instant word' on important topics.

I asked the Runcies if they had heard Alan Webster's story that Runcie was not the first choice for the archbishopric – that it was Hugh Montefiore. There was a stunned silence.

'I don't believe it!' said Lindy.

Did they not know that? 'No!' said Runcie. I heard it was – somebody else.' But he added: 'Alan Webster should know, because he was on the Crown Appointments Commission.'

Eric James, who had heard the story from Webster too, was very doubtful of it. So was Richard Chartres when I told him. He suggested that it was possible that Webster had imagined the feeling of the Commission was for Montefiore, whom Webster himself had perhaps championed.

'I don't find the story that I was second choice impossible to believe,' Runcie told me, 'but I find it impossible to think it was Montefiore It was the time when his "Was Jesus a homosexual?" was still reverberating.'

Some months later, I went to see Donald Wright, who had been Archbishop's Patronage Secretary at the time that the new archbishop was being chosen. He too had been on the Crown Appointments Commission. He told me that Montefiore was near the top of list, but at the top was Geoffrey Paul, the other name Montefiore had mentioned, at that time suffragan Bishop of Hull, who had done remarkable work in South India and at an evangelistic centre called Lee Abbey. 'A brilliant theologian,' said Wright, 'a wonderful teacher, and a scholar with the common touch.' (He is now dead.) Wright said that they also considered one or two people from the Anglican Communion overseas. 'But in the end we felt it had to be an English diocesan bishop, even though none of them was absolutely right.'

Wright cast doubt on Webster's story about the Prime Minister's Patronage Secretary (Colin Peterson) consulting Mrs Thatcher by phone overnight, and over-ruling the decision next morning: 'Colin was Harold Wilson's appointment to the job, and she always looked on him with suspicion.

Wright lent me a number of papers that he had selected from his files, including the confidential report he had drawn up for the Crown Appointments Commission on Runcie's suitability as archbishop. This noted that more people were in favour of his candidacy than against, and quoted a selection of comments that had been made about him, by several different, unidentified people. These included: '*Positive*: Sophisticated, not flippant. A man of extraordinary self-knowledge and ability to mock at himself. *Negative*: He has impressed me only as a showman, even when he is most serious. Although he has social ease and personal attractiveness, there is something wrongly academic and curiously detached about him.'

Once Runcie had been chosen, and told, Wright was summoned to St Albans by him. Lindy met him at the station, in a dreadful state: 'You've heard about this bloody thing that has happened?' Meanwhile Runcie kept saying, edgily, 'This isn't my job.'

Eric James recalls that, just as the appointment had been announced, 'we were holding the St Albans diocesan triennial clergy conference, and by chance this year it was at Canterbury. So we all trooped down with Robert, and arrived just in time for Compline at the cathedral. And we were kneeling there in the candlelight, looking up at where the light fell on St Augustine's Chair, and we were all glancing across at Robert, praying with his hands over his face, and I know we were all thinking, "That poor bugger!"'

Part Two

12

What the job is

————◆————

It was just over three years since Runcie had written to me asking me if I wanted to be his biographer. At last, we had reached his appointment as Archbishop. 'I think we should open some champagne,' I remarked to Runcie and Lindy, adding that the original time schedule for the book had been torn up (I had been due to deliver the manuscript about four months earlier).

'How many indiscretions are you going to put in?' asked Lindy.

This was indeed a crucial question. Soon after the Crosby trip I had tried writing the opening of a conventional biography ('Robert Alexander Kennedy Runcie was born on . . .'), but it had felt false. For the first time, I had realised how much biographers bend their material, and use conjecture just as much as fact, in order to achieve a seamless narrative. With my subject still walking around, living his life and talking to me about it, I had begun to understand how untidy, unformed and fluid is most people's view of their own lives. I could not pin Runcie down to a conventional biographical text like a dead insect. So I had thrown away that first attempt, and written up an account of our meetings and conversations just as they happened, beginning with my trip to Lambeth in January 1991 – not so much writing a biography, as keeping a diary about writing one. This version virtually wrote itself. But how much of it could I print? And, since Runcie had never asked for a veto, or enquired after what sort of book was emerging, should I give him any hint that it was not turning out to be the weighty official biography I felt he expected?

I left Lindy's question unanswered. And Runcie seemed to have no curiosity about it.

'What I would like to do,' I told him, 'is to begin looking at the papers at Lambeth. But if you don't want me to see anything there until you've looked through them yourself, fair enough.' He had recently been showing some unease at the prospect of my having free range through the archiepiscopal papers, and had vaguely expressed the intention of looking through them himself before they were released to me. But when I told him that Jane Houston, the Lambeth archivist, had warned me there were several hundred boxes, he looked horrified, and swiftly lost interest in this plan. So I made an appointment at Lambeth.

In the three years since I had been there, nothing seemed to have changed at Lambeth. Eleanor Philips, still the Archbishop's secretary, gave me a cheery greeting, and still seemed to have all the time in the world to chat. Jane Houston took me down to the basement passage where some of the Runcie papers were being stored in cupboards, and I began to wade through the first dozen boxes, covering part of 1980, his first year as Archbishop.

The first thing I found that interested me was a note from John Miles, Information Officer at Church House in Westminster, to Richard Chartres, Runcie's chaplain, dated 31 January 1980, about two months before Runcie's enthronement as Archbishop. It was a comment on one of the radio interviews he had given:

The answers seemed to be long and with a little more

experience they could come across with far more impact and interest. There is still that tendency to try and give both sides of an argument without appearing to answer the question . . . There is still a clicking noise which I cannot trace. Is it teeth or something else?

Chartres had told me that virtually no staff remained at Lambeth from the Coggan era when Runcie and he arrived from St Albans, apart from Michael Kinchin-Smith, whom Runcie had known at Christ Church, and whom Coggan had employed as his 'lay assistant'. Chartres described him as 'immensely genial and deferential – a most marvellously courtly person' – but says he was not the sort of man to give Runcie the firm guidance he needed temperamentally. 'The Church of England has a terrible management style,' remarked Chartres. 'People get some problem into a terrible tangle, then deliver it, still tangled up, to the Archbishop, and say, "What is your mind in this, Your Grace?"' Being new to the job, Runcie was usually incapable of giving clear answers. Chartres recalls: 'Michael would emerge from the Archbishop's study and say, "I don't know what he wants."'

Immediately after Runcie's enthronement, it was announced that Ross Hook, Bishop of Bradford, would be resigning his diocese and coming to Lambeth as Runcie's 'chief of staff', also known as 'the Bishop at Lambeth'. Chartres explained that this was an upgrading of the post of Senior Chaplain to the Archbishop, intended to create a 'class one paper-pusher, capable of relieving the Archbishop of trivial things' (in 1980, for example, the Archbishop was still required to sign minor documents relating to planning permission in the diocese of Canterbury). In Chartres' opinion, Hook was a large personality who was mis-cast as an administrative assistant. He was succeeded in 1984 by Ronald Gordon, former Bishop of Portsmouth.

But the real problem, according to Chartres, was the administrative structure of the Church of England. It has a legislative-consultative body (the General Synod) meeting only at intervals, and a civil service (the Church Commissioners), but, says Chartres, no actual government. 'The result,' he continues, 'is constant chaos and demoralisation. The Archbishop of Canterbury can expand into that governmental vacuum. But the only real solution would be to make the House of Bishops [in the General Synod] into the government – give them portfolios like cabinet ministers.' Meanwhile, explains Chartres, the actual role of the Archbishop remains absurdly undefined: 'There's been very little shrewd thinking about what the job is or isn't. There aren't any policy documents setting it out. And there's nobody to turn to for advice.'

Since Runcie was faced with an undefined job, and somewhat hazy briefing from his staff, his capacity for decision-making (says Chartres) was put to severe test. 'His antennae were very, very sensitive, but when so many contradictory signals began to be received by them, things started to get clogged.' He was helped, Chartres emphasises, by his 'fantastically strong physical stamina', and indeed Chartres discouraged him from taking too much rest, feeling that he could come to less harm if his mind was constantly having to turn to the next task: 'I was always against, at Lambeth, there being any real time off, because I feared that otherwise the anxieties would surface in an ungovernable way.' (It struck me that, here at least, the chaplain seemed to have been giving the Archbishop his orders, rather than the other way round, or at least managing him skilfully like a statesman handling a tricky monarch.)

Chartres describes Runcie on a rare afternoon when he had no appointments, wandering around the offices and dismaying the staff by trying to tinker with decisions. Donald Wright, Archbishop's Patronage Secretary at the beginning of Runcie's archbishopric, has a similar story, which he was told by Douglas Cleverley-Ford, the Archbishop's Senior Chaplain who had been replaced by Ross Hook: 'Cleverley-Ford's office was next to the Archbishop's study, and Donald Coggan had always left the door ajar, so they could communicate easily. But he said to me that

Robert Runcie always kept it shut. "I don't mind that, but I do need to know where he is, for phone calls and things. One knew where Coggan would be at any hour of any day; he was very methodical. But sometimes you go in there and Runcie's nowhere to be seen. The other day I had to search for him all over the building. He'd just wandered off. Eventually I found him downstairs in the Great Hall. He was just standing there, looking at the pictures."'

Chartres continues: 'We got management consultants in at Lambeth, and they were utterly dismayed. But it wasn't a management structure at all. It was, and is, a court. And one's experience of Tudor court politics' (Chartres read history at Cambridge) 'was of more use than anything Coopers & Lyebrand could tell us. Terry Waite was well aware of that. When he first arrived, his office was in the basement. He knew he had to get to the ground floor, where the power lay.'

Waite's appointment as Archbishop's Assistant for Anglican Communion Affairs – another new job – was announced a month before Runcie's enthronement. The job description in the Lambeth files specifies that it will include

a Research element addressed to evolving a general strategy for the Archbishop's visits to the various provinces of the Anglican Communion and providing adequate briefing to ensure that he goes not just as a tourist but with the clear understanding of the opportunities to be grasped ... also ... a 'trouble shooter', a low profile emissary for the Archbishop to send to places where he is asked to intervene . . . It would be difficult to think of anyone better equipped for this complex task than Terry Waite ...

Chartres told me that the Anglican Communion – the loosely affiliated fellowship of Anglican churches outside Great Britain – had been largely neglected in the years immediately preceding Runcie's appointment as Archbishop. It had been (Chartres explains) an enthusiasm of Archbishop

Fisher in the optimistic post-war years: 'Fisher was a kind of ghost we kept running into when we went overseas. A policeman in Chicago remembered him bouncing out of his hotel like a schoolboy, jumping on to the cop's motorbike, and making *vroom, vroom* noises.'

Waite, who had been globetrotting for some years in various lay ecclesiastical jobs, had been recommended as a revitaliser of the Archbishop's relations with Anglican churches overseas by Oliver Tomkins, Bishop of Bristol, for whom he had once worked as a Lay Training Officer. He came for interview to St Albans. 'Lindy was in the room,' recalls Chartres, who was there too, 'and she and Terry were very dubious about each other before a word was said.' In his account of the interview in *Taken on Trust,* Waite makes little mention of Lindy, but calls Chartres 'shrewd and incisive', and gives the impression that he, rather than Runcie, did most of the interviewing.

'Terry,' comments Chartres, 'combines being the Cheshire policeman's son with the feline antennae of someone who's fascinated with Jung.' He recalls that, at spare moments on Anglican Communion tours, he would come across Runcie and Waite reminiscing enthusiastically about their boyhood reading – the *Gem* and the *Magnet.* 'At Lambeth, Terry was immensely restless, and padded around the corridors, usually ending up in my office.'

On 3 March 1994, armed with the notes I had taken at Lambeth, I arrived once again at Runcie's front door. As often before, he had asked at the last minute to postpone our meeting, saying he desperately needed the time to write something that he would shortly have to deliver – in this case, a series of retreat addresses. But this time I had dug in my heels, though as a concession I arrived at 8.30 am so he would have the remainder of the day free to work. (This became the pattern thereafter, necessitating a very early trip along the M25.)

I observed that he obviously still didn't find writing things any easier than he had in the past. 'No! I got into the way, at Lambeth, of depending upon somebody to give me a sort of draft, and then I was all right. It's a funny thing – I could even cross the whole draft out and start again.'

I said I had already observed his use of ghost-writers when going through the 1980 papers. Chartres had mentioned it to me, too, admitting to a major role in the drafting of Runcie's enthronement sermon. I had discovered that Owen Chadwick had also supplied some of it. On 29 April 1980, just over a month after he had been enthroned as Archbishop in Canterbury Cathedral, Runcie wrote to Chadwick: 'Thank you for all your good wishes and for coming to the Enthronement. One or two phrases in the sermon will have been familiar to you and I am grateful for the way in which you tidied up my draft.'

As well as my Lambeth notes, I had brought with me some recent press cuttings about the finances of the Church of England. 'Parishes to pay price of church property debacle,' announced the *Independent* on 16 February 1994, over a report on the likely consequences of 'the Church Commissioners' catastrophic property speculations which lost them £800m in the late 1980s'. Hugh Montefiore had just written to me about this, putting some of the blame on Runcie – or at least on what he called 'Bob's reluctance to make painful decisions'. Montefiore's letter continued with an explanation of the appointment of the various Commissioners:

The First Estates Commissioner has to be a layman, and the Second Estates Commissioner an MP, but the post of Third Estates Commissioner is in the Archbishop's gift, and when it fell vacant, considerable pressure was put upon Bob, I am told in particular by Jim Thompson, a member of his 'Cell' and then the Bishop of Stepney, to appoint Derek Hayward to the post. Archdeacon Hayward was well known to us, because when Bob and I were both on the staff of Westcott House, Derek flew in from India (where he had been making the famous, or infamous, Hayward's Gin) in order to train for ordination. Derek, besides getting a First in Theology in Part I, is a genius with money, and for many years has been General Secretary of the London Diocese. In 1984 he had published a pamphlet, *The Diocese of London's Reply to the Commissioners' Report on the Historic Resources of the Church of England*, in which he had questioned the Commissioners' self-congratulation on the conduct of their affairs.

Bob, I am told, refused to appoint him as Third Estates Commissioner because he would be bound to brush up against Sir Douglas Lovelock, First Estates Commissioner; and Derek told me that Bob had written him a letter to explain why he had not appointed him. Had Bob been prepared to make an appointment which would certainly have resulted in some conflict, I think it very likely that the Church of England would not have lost one fifth of its historic resources.

I summarised this letter to Runcie. He commented: 'It isn't the normal practice to put in a Third Estates Commissioner who would have the effect of undermining the First Estates Commissioner. The Third Commissioner is the pastoral person who largely has to deal with local parish situations. Hayward thought he could have reorganised things. But if he'd been appointed, I suspect he'd have gone over rather to the establishment.'

How much was it Lovelock's personal error of judgement, and how much the sort of thing that was happening widely? 'I think it was happening all over the financial world. Douglas Lovelock was a kind of scapegoat, but it was the independence of the investment panel rather than him personally. He was in Customs & Excise before. He was put in as Mrs Thatcher's person – very much a Thatcherite appointment. He did his bit by explaining to the Synod what was going on, but there were certain areas which were kept to the financial experts. Choices were made, and some people made the Thatcherite choice that if you wanted to maximise profit you had to be in on the new enterprise – and he overdid it. It's easy for me to say that now, but I can remember saying, "Ought we to be investing in things like the Gateshead Metro shopping centre?" And I always got the reply, "It's creating jobs – you want jobs, don't you?" That was always the answer I got. And of course I had no qualifications in investment.'

Richard Chartres had talked a lot about the absence of a job description for the Archbishop of Canterbury; though I found someone's attempt at writing one in the files, dated 6 September 1979, six months before Runcie's enthronement:

1 The Archbishop is a Diocesan Bishop of the diocese of Canterbury . . .
2 The Archbishop has responsibilities towards the National Church . . . presides over the General Synod, takes the chair of some Synod Committees, presides over the Church Commissioners and the general meetings of important Church Societies . . .
3 . . . the Archbishop . . . remains one of the chief spokesmen for the Church of England . . . to offer an informed and searching commentary on events and controversies . . .
4 The Archbishop also has an international role . . . The Churches of the world-wide Anglican Communion . . . now number more than 65 million members . . .

Chartres had emphasised to me that there was really no system of government in the Church of England. The Lovelock investment crisis to some extent reflected that lack. Did Runcie agree that there was no proper structure for making top-level decisions? 'The investment crisis,' he answered, 'reveals that there were no relationships of a cross-fertilising character between the House of Bishops and those people who were handling the major part of the church's money. But it would be interesting to know how they do it in the church of Rome.' There is probably not much democracy there, and equal errors of judgement? 'Yes. The incompetence of spiritual men, who don't have much contact with these things, giving it over to financiers who have no wish for any sort of interference.'

To continue with the comparison (I said), the papacy – the Pope plus his immediate retinue – was a dictatorship, running on the totalitarian principle; whereas the archbishopric of Canterbury had no power of that sort. And didn't the Archbishop have to be a number of different things in different contexts?

'Absolutely,' replied Runcie. 'You could say he's Bishop of the diocese of Canterbury. He's Chairman of the General Synod. He's President of the Anglican Consultative Council. He's a whole number of things, and it's impossible to formulate a job description, to allocate the amount of time he should give to any one function at the expense of another. He may choose to spend a great deal of his time in the House of Lords, and become a great spokesman for the church there, and never go around his diocese. Contrariwise, he might take the diocese of Canterbury over-seriously, and not really pay attention to committees in London. He can stay in England, or he can spend almost all his time – because he's always wanted overseas – all over the world.'

I suggested that these uncertainties were compounded by the fact that a new archbishop brings or appoints his own advisory staff when he comes to the job. There seemed to be no team corresponding to the permanent senior civil servants, who give continuity of advice to the Prime Minister and the Cabinet. 'Well,' replied Runcie, 'you've got the General Synod, you've got Church House, you've got the Secretary-General to the Synod. The idea is that Church House is Whitehall, and Lambeth Palace is Downing Street.' But surely they operated separately, and with a degree of rivalry? And there had really been nobody in Runcie's early months at Lambeth to give him top-level advice? 'That's certainly the case. So I was in the hands of Bishop Say.'

Richard Chartres had told me that David Say, diocesan Bishop of Rochester from 1961 to 1988, had exercised a considerable influence over Runcie when he first arrived at Canterbury. Runcie said of him: 'He has always been an adviser, and like most advisers, thinks himself the total adviser! He worked very, very hard at it. And then the Bishop of London – a good man, Gerald Ellison – was definitely the Church Commissioners man. He was soon taking the chair at the Church Commissioners instead of me; Donald Coggan used to go every month to the Commissioners, but I didn't go at all to start with, and then it seemed a considerable burden. So I put the Bishop of London in the chair to be my deputy. Therefore I did not have so much acquaintance with the day to day running of the Church of England. But being Chairman of the Church Commissioners was a huge responsibility, if you were going to treat it as a hands-on chairmanship.'

I gathered from Chartres that it had been Say who persuaded Runcie to take on Ross Hook as Chief of Staff. 'Yes, now, that was a mistake, from which Richard derived a certain amount of amusement. But I used to quote Eric Abbott, saying "No man can get more than seven out of ten appointments made right, and his character lies in his ability to live with the other three!"'

In June 1980 it was announced that Richard Third, Bishop of Dover, one of the suffragan bishops in the diocese of Canterbury, would take responsibility off Runcie's shoulders for all diocesan affairs. 'Richard Third was very, very conscientious, and pastorally excellent,' Runcie told me, 'but I was, you know, tending to make sure that I was still the Archbishop.' So it would almost have been easier to have done all the diocesan work himself, or to have nothing whatever to do with it? 'That's right. I enjoyed the times at Canterbury. But Lindy didn't settle there. You were entering quite a close-precincts world.'

It is evident from the files that the Runcies took time to settle at Lambeth. 'Lindy bicycles to Billingsgate and begins to get hospitality under control,' Runcie wrote to Owen Chadwick on 16 May 1980, 'but we still have not moved everything into our flat . . .'

I had asked Chartres how the new Lambeth jobs created by Runcie on his arrival – Terry Waite's and Ross Hook's in particular – had been funded. He said that Sir Hector Laing (now Lord Laing) had provided a lot of the cash. Laing had known Runcie since they were in the Scots Guards together. He became chairman of United Biscuits and joint treasurer of the Conservative Party. At his home in Chelsea, he described to me his involvement with the Lambeth finances:

'Between the end of the war and his marriage I only met Bob occasionally. But I saw him quite a lot at St Albans. And as soon as he got up the hierarchy of the church, I recognised that those who give a service to the church are, compared to a lot of us, poor as church mice. I was appalled to find the state that Lambeth Palace was in. Blackout curtains on the windows, cork tiles on the floor of that great drawing room, and so on. So I put that right, because it ought to have been done years before. He then said that he needed help with his staff, and I funded that for a bit. Quite serious sums. And then one day I can't have been looking very well, and Bob said, "Hector, I think we should put this on a more permanent basis, in case you peg out!" And so the Lambeth Fund was set up. One of Bob's great chums, Ewan Harper, joined in, and I went to a lot of chairmen and said, "You can't get the church on the cheap," poking them in the stomach with my stick. And all I asked them for was ten thousand pounds each. And a lot of them gave it. And then John Sainsbury's trust gave a hundred thousand. Now the Fund stands at a million. And we need to raise another million.

'It's to help archbishops past and present. We fund Bob's secretary – the present one, Frances – which the church should do, but doesn't, and wouldn't. And we also help George Carey in various ways.'

Shouldn't the Church Commissioners have been footing

all these bills? 'I would rather not say anything about the Church Commissioners,' answered Laing. 'I think they've been simply terrible! But I wouldn't have asked them. Bob was a chum, and I wasn't hard up for a penny or two. And one liked to help when one could.'

Runcie gave me some examples of how Laing's money was used in his early days as Archbishop: 'Lambeth was terribly primitive in terms of telephones and intercoms. There were old-fashioned typewriters, no word processors. It was very antiquated. And I had begun by sharing a press officer with the General Synod, John Miles. He'd had a very close relationship with Michael and Joan Ramsey. But he was stretched, because he had to cover *all* Church of England things. He had an idea that press relations were column inches, that if he got things in the tabloids – the Archbishop going down a watershoot with children, and that sort of thing – that was good stuff. He had started as a journalist on some local paper. We decided to set up our own press office at Lambeth, financed by the Lambeth Fund, in order to show the Church Commissioners what could be done, so that they should then take it over. The appointment of Eve Keatley as press officer [later in Runcie's Archbishopric] began a great split with John Miles, which led us into all sorts of difficulties.'

The acquisition of his own press officer seemed to me indicative of his need, which I had perceived elsewhere, to build up his own *familia* in order to operate effectively. He agreed: 'I tried to do that even more than I achieved it. I wanted to have a sort of penumbra of people who came in from positions in the outside world, with whom we would enjoy easy relations, and they in turn would bring in others.' I had found evidence of this in the files, part of a transcript of an unidentified interview given to the BBC by Runcie six months after becoming Archbishop:

I am trying to create a repository of advisers. For example, I am trying to grapple with the nuclear question, and I find it difficult to understand all the questions involved. Hence,

I have formed a group of people – like Neil Cameron from the Defence Staff, Solly Zuckerman, Mary Kaldor, Frank Allaun, and somebody from the Foreign Office sometimes, and we talk about it together . . . I aim to get out of it a capacity to say something constructive even though I am . . . not a unilateralist . . .

Talking to me, he recalled a gathering of these people: 'We had a very good evening on unilateral disarmament – probably the most top cross-fertilising group that ever sat round a table. They came to supper at Lambeth and talked about the deterrent. And that was valuable. All sorts of spin-offs. We had a similar thing on penal reform, in which we had judges and probation officers. The idea was that this group of people would enable the Archbishop to listen to what was being said, and then draw up a speech for the Lords, or a statement to be made in Synod. And that worked, a bit, for penal reform, for unilateral disarmament. And that was the way in which I hoped to handle what Richard was always saying we needed to make up our mind about – "the leadership line for England". He used that phrase when I tended to get interested in going round the world. He said, "What we lack is a leadership line for England." But frankly we were totally overwhelmed by events – by Thatcher, by the Falklands. We were always up against the next thing.'

This think-tank on disarmament reminded me of what Chartres had said to me about Runcie: 'He's a genuine liberal because he can see *all* sides of an argument.' But surely it had made it even harder to form his own opinion on these issues if he had all these presumably conflicting expert voices to listen to? Did he feel he came out of the experience more decisive, or merely all the more aware that opinions conflicted?

'I wouldn't say that I came out of it decisive, but I came out of it understanding.' Understanding the impossibility of being decisive? 'That would be one way of putting it. The other would be that I was aware of diversity and doubt when the country was being governed by people who thought there was *no* diversity and doubt.'

In his letter to Owen Chadwick thanking him for help with the enthronement sermon, Runcie added: ' If you have any thoughts about what I should say to the Pope ... don't hesitate to pass them on!' His first meeting with Pope John Paul II was on 16 May 1980.

The Pope was visiting Africa; Runcie was attending the enthronement of Archbishop Ndahura (who had been a curate in St Albans diocese) in Zaire. Waite and Chartres had noticed the conjunction of the visits and had acted swiftly. The two church leaders came face to face in the Papal Nuncio's house in Accra.

'We met early in the morning,' recalls Runcie. 'He was sizing me up, I think. He told me about his lack of understanding of much that went on in western theology, and in western attitudes, when he had spent all his ministry in an atheistic country, Poland. He made it quite clear that he regarded atheistic communism as the enemy in the East, and self-indulgent consumer hedonism as the equivalent in the West. I was impressed by him as a man of spiritual quality surrounded by this enormous staff and retinue – I was terribly envious of that! And I was very impressed by a man who subsequently was useful to us, Cardinal Casaroli, his Secretary of State, who was good on Waite, good on orthodox things, very quiet in the background. Also the Pope had a very genial Irish American as his secretary, and we made friends with him. So we made good contacts. It was rather amusing, because we had obviously been fitted in – we only had about an hour with him, and then he flew off to Kinshasa.'

Did they use an interpreter? 'I don't think so. But to the end, I always felt that he spoke English better than he understood it. And then there was an amazing drama when I was flying out to Nairobi, and he was flying back to Rome. He'd done with me. But his plane was delayed by two and a half hours, and my plane had been advanced, so we were both at the airport at Accra. It was a small airport, and there didn't seem any possibility of keeping us separate. I distinctly remember that I was in a telephone box, and Waite was getting a sandwich – we were all hiding round a corner lest we ran into the papal party. Then we actually *did* meet them, face to face! You could see it registering on the Pope's face – "I thought I'd done with this lot" – because he'd already had a hell of a day. And we had to explain. And it was then that I realised he didn't understand at all.'

Runcie's foreign visits were being planned by a committee which included Michael Moore and Christopher Hill, his Counsellors on Foreign Relations, as well as Chartres, Waite, and Sir Derek Pattinson, Secretary-General of the General Synod. A few weeks after the meeting with the Pope, they noted in a minute:

> The Archbishop of Canterbury has invited the Pope to visit him at Canterbury Cathedral . . . The Pope has also invited the Archbishop to Rome, but the Pope's trip to England must come first. It was felt that at the next meeting between the Pope and the Archbishop, a serious attempt should be made to get down 'to business'.

The same meeting noted that, in Accra, 'At times [the Pope] was obviously inadequately briefed.' Runcie's briefings for speeches, at this date, were being organised by Michael Kinchin-Smith. To give some idea of the range of occasions on which the Archbishop was required to speak, I noted these examples during Runcie's first few months in office:

1 A service for railway enthusiasts in Canterbury Cathedral, celebrating the 150th anniversary of the Canterbury & Whitstable line. Runcie's sermon included a reference to the Ealing Film comedy *The Titfield Thunderbolt*, in which the Rector of Titfield comments sadly on the closure of the Canterbury & Whitstable: 'Perhaps there were no men of sufficient faith in Canterbury.'

2 A speech at the Free Church Federal Council

Dinner. Runcie told them: 'I spent four years in a Scottish Regiment with a Presbyterian padre, and will never forget his preaching of the Word.' He also recalled the influence of the theologians C. H. Dodd and Reinhold Niebuhr during his time at Westcott House: 'Those were days when we irreverently stated the Commandments as "Thou shalt love the Lord thy Dodd and thy Niebuhr as thyself."'

3 A service at RAF Biggin Hill to mark the fortieth anniversary of the Battle of Britain. Runcie quoted from Richard Hilary's *The Last Enemy* (a first-hand account by a fighter pilot) and said: 'It was a book that had a profound effect on me in 1942; the other day, I read it again ...'

4 An address at a seminar on the Brandt Report on the Third World. This speech contained no personal material, and was drafted by a team.[1]

5 A talk at the Media Society on the subject of the state of the press (*The Times* and the *Sunday Times* had just shut down because of a dispute with trade unions), moral responsibility in broadcasting, and similar topics. This speech was written by three people, including Angela Tilby of the BBC's religious programmes department.

6 The presentation of Mary Whitehouse's Viewers' and Listeners' Association award to the BBC's *Songs of Praise*. 'From time to time Mrs Whitehouse and I may not have agreed on every point. But today is the chance for me to say ... how much admiration I have ... for her courage and her consistency ...'

JSH always wrote his own sermons & speeches.

Even the jokes, Runcie's hallmark, were sometimes supplied by other people. Or at least they tried. The draft of a speech for the Ecclesiastical Insurance Office dinner in November 1980 has an accompanying note by the anonymous speech-writer: 'I have tried very hard to find

[1]Runcie says he used the prepared text as a basis for a chiefly *ad lib* speech.

I suffered some
illustration to a cancer
at Birmingham!!

an amusing story about some aspect of the EIO's work,
but no one has been able to find one for me.'

When I went to see Runcie on 28 April 1994, it soon
transpired that he was worried. He should have been in
South Africa, as part of a group of observers monitoring the
country's first all-race election, but he had gone into hospital
at Easter for a prostate operation, had developed alarmingly
high blood pressure (to which he is always prone), and after
surgery had been told some bad news by the consultant,
formerly one of his undergraduates at Trinity Hall.

'He came in to tell me I could go home the next day,
and he said, "The histology's not good, because you've got
some cancer in the material we've taken away." And then
he explained that he'd start me off on some treatment. But
he's a little bit in awe of the man who was once his tutor,
so he's very correct and professional, and I didn't altogether
understand the choices he was giving me – you know, you
don't when people say, "Would you like to have it by pills
or injection, or you could have a scan." I said, "Well, look,
Peter, you're the man who knows about these things. I'll do
whatever you recommend."

'And Lindy was told. And I thought, I'll just tell the family,
otherwise people will make a big do of it. And I told one
or two close friends, people who pray for me, like Frances
Dominica. One of the reasons I didn't want a great deal of
publicity about it is that I've been putting a lot of energy
into the creation of a hospice care centre. I've raised over a
million pounds for it, and it's been a huge local success, and
on May the sixth it's being opened by the Duchess of Kent.
It's going to be called the Runcie-Macmillan Care Centre –
just down the road here. And there's a Runcie wing – a
geriatric wing! The Mayor of St Albans, who is a good deal
younger than me, had cancer during the year, and she said:
"I want everybody to know that I've had cancer and that
I'm going to work for good causes for cancer." And that's
all right eventually, you know, but it's a bit hard on your
family. Because it would be such a media focus, and the

drama of opening the thing I'd built and now might need to use myself.'

I suggested that, though some malignant cells had been found, it scarcely amounted to full-blown cancer. 'Yes, you're right – I went to see my doctor yesterday, and he said, "I'd like to tell you that I've got patients who've been coming to me for years and years for this injection. And you're not to fold up."'

I told him that I had had another session at Lambeth, and had finished the 1980 papers and begun 1981, his second year as Archbishop. I had spotted a substantial printed document headed *Towards Visible Unity: Proposals for a Covenant*. Published in June 1980, this was a report on an attempt by the Church of England, the Methodists, and the United Reformed Church to 'recognise and accept one another's Churches and ministries' – in other words, a very tentative step towards unity. During the 1960s my father had been co-chairman of an earlier and abortive attempt at Anglican-Methodist reunion. The Covenanting scheme was much more cautious. The report stated: 'It is not a scheme inaugurating a union of Churches, but a way to enable the Churches to work more closely together as they grow towards visible unity in life and mission.'

I admitted that I had had some difficulty in keeping awake while wading through the Covenanting material. Runcie sympathised: 'The difference between myself and Graham Leonard [Bishop of London] was that he would sit up in bed at night, reading all the documents, and producing ideas about how to deal with Methodist objections to this and that. I remember him doing that when we were in Russia. And I admired him for it, and felt a bit guilty about it, but I was much more interested in getting to know the Metropolitans and going off to see icon museums. I thought there were people who were good at these things, and I trusted them and tended to be swayed by them. I was very much inclined to move as they wanted to move. I mean, your dad convinced me that it was all right to believe in the Anglican-Methodist scheme, and John Habgood [Archbishop of York] taught me

Runcie should have been _more honest_ about the Covenant.

that it was all right to believe in Covenanting.[2] But I suffered! And at one stage in the ordination of women debate, I spoke in favour of the motion, but incorporated such a (said he modestly) clever understanding of the arguments of the opponents that it undermined my own case!'

The Covenanting proposals were linked with the issue of ordaining women, since the Church of England was the only participating church which did not. In April 1981, interviewed for the magazine *Woman's Realm,* Runcie characteristically put the case for both sides:

> There are arguments which I respect both for and against, but I think the best arguments for the ordination of women are these – if priesthood is to represent God to mankind and mankind to God in days when an exclusive male leadership is no longer the case in most walks of life, it's hard to justify the fact that men alone can represent God to mankind and mankind to God. I therefore now think that the best arguments are in favour of opening the priesthood to women.
>
> But there *are* arguments on both sides and I have opposed the ordination of women simply because I think unity among Christians is more important than the ordination of women as a particular topic – a topic that can arouse strong feelings both ways.[3]

Runcie told me that he had behaved the same way on another issue that the General Synod was debating in 1980–1, remarriage after divorce: 'They were told to go away and bring back better proposals. And they said that they brought back the proposals that I had asked for, but that when I spoke in their favour, I put the opposition's case!'

[2]Habgood writes: 'One of Bob Runcie's great strengths has been his readiness to consult with others. That this should have been interpreted by some as evidence of weakness represents an extraordinary failure to understand what leadership actually entails.' *Robert Runcie: A Portrait by His Friends,* edited by David L. Edwards, Fount Paperbacks, 1990, p. 61.

[3]*Woman's Realm,* 4 April 1981.

While this infuriated some people, a memorandum among the 1981 Lambeth papers indicate that his fence-sitting, or tendency to express both sides of an argument, sometimes had the approval and encouragement of his advisers:

The Archbishop of Canterbury's role in the 'Covenanting' Debate: a personal note for discussion at the Lambeth Staff Meeting, 22nd January 1981

The Archbishop appears to be slowly moving towards a more favourable opinion of the proposals contained in *Towards Visible Unity*. However he clearly has a number of remaining anxieties and is unlikely to be an enthusiastic supporter of the proposals. In any case strong support (or fervent opposition) would alienate a significant number in the Synod and beyond and jeopardise the Archbishop's leadership in sections of the Church. He has to deal with 'catholics', 'open synodmen', 'evangelicals' and Free Churchmen for the rest of his archiepiscopate! *Whichever* way he votes must not be felt to be party . . . Spiritual leadership is not exercised by *simply* telling people which way to vote. It is the more profound task of an Archbishop to articulate the *true* mind of the Church amid the conflicting voices of debate. This is frighteningly difficult when issues deeply divide the Church and clergy. In view of the above I think the Archbishop should exercise his leadership judiciously . . .

The memo is signed 'CJH', the initials of the Rev. Christopher Hill, who had been appointed Archbishop's Assistant Chaplain on Foreign Relations six years before Runcie came to Lambeth, and in 1982 became his Secretary for Ecumenical Affairs. I asked Runcie about him. 'Christopher Hill was a good lieutenant. He was Catholic in his fundamental stance, but fair-minded in ecumenical affairs. And I was very dependent on him for theological and ecumenical opinion, because he had a tremendous gift as a drafter, and he would be admirable in coming and

y hni Verdict on 165
in Reflection 1932–1956 .

talking over what our stance would be on something. He wasn't as original as Richard, nor stylish, but very plugged in to the facts of the case and the various options; one of the most enlightened bureaucrats I've ever come across. He's now Precentor of St Paul's.'[4]

The most explosive issue I found in the 1981 files at Lambeth was the appointment in March that year of Graham Leonard as Bishop of London. *The Times* of 31 March reported:

> An extraordinary tug-of-war between the Prime Minister aided by the Leader of the Opposition on the one hand and the Queen and the Archbishop of Canterbury on the other ended yesterday with the announcement that the Bishop of Truro, Dr Graham Leonard, is to be the new Bishop of London – a victory for Margaret Thatcher.
>
> Dr Leonard was not the first choice submitted by the Crown Appointments Commission of the Church of England, it was clear yesterday.[5] The archbishop, Dr Robert Runcie, is chairman of the commission, and spent some time with Mrs Thatcher, urging her to accept its advice. Dr Leonard, a controversial figure who has doggedly opposed several recent trends in Anglicanism, including the ordination of women, had most of the dignatories of the diocese of London ranged against him . . . The favoured alternatives included the Bishop of Durham, Dr John Habgood, and the Bishop of Wakefield, the Rt Rev. Colin James.

I asked Runcie about this. 'I wish I had a stronger memory of it,' he answered, 'and also, of course, it's a privileged area. But I can say that there was intense lobbying on the part of the high church section of the London diocese to get on to the Crown Appointments Commission, in order to represent their views. And my recollection is that Graham Leonard

---

[4]In 1996 he became Bishop of Stafford.
[5]However, next day Clifford Longley reported that 'opinion in the diocese of London [is] 70 per cent in favour of Dr Leonard'.

was one of the names put forward, by reason of their vote, but not the first name. I never found *personal* relations with him difficult, but I found his absorbing ecclesiastical preoccupations uncongenial.'

Was it Margaret Thatcher personally who over-rode the first choice of the Crown Appointments Commission? 'I think it would be her decision, yes. But she was within her rights.' She was presented with a list of names, and she chose? 'She used to regret that she didn't have more say in these matters, but she played by the rules. But it did seem to me that there were characters like David Sheppard [Bishop of Liverpool from 1973] who were unlikely to get preferment.' She had a simple political preference for somebody whose sympathies were obviously towards the right? 'When I look back on that decade, I sometimes think we should have been tougher. But somebody to whom I said that replied, "You didn't fight with their own weapons, you didn't play their own game."'

Nevertheless the Church of England under Runcie was popularly perceived as having set itself in opposition to the Thatcher Government. The first instance I had found of this in the Lambeth files was Runcie's own action following the Brixton riots.

On 15 April 1981, Runcie wrote to the Home Secretary, his fellow Guards officer William Whitelaw:

Confidential

My dear Home Secretary,
The events at Brixton over last weekend have made me very conscious of the enormous burden which you carry. You have been much in the thoughts of all of us during these difficult days. I am off to the United States on Tuesday, and will not return until May 12th. Before leaving, I want to send you a brief message of good wishes for what you are trying to do to solve these intractable problems.

I have been trying to inform myself about the troubles

at Brixton and it may be helpful if I let you know that yesterday I invited six leading clergy from that area to come to see me. Four were white and two were black. All have been deeply involved in community affairs in Brixton, and I was impressed by what they said to me.

They had two main anxieties. First, while welcoming the decision to set up the Scarman Inquiry, and the speed with which this was done, they feel that the situation is still very precarious and volatile. The Inquiry is bound to take time, and their concern is about what could happen in the meantime. They believe that it would help if the Government was seen to be listening in other ways also to what the community leaders want to say. The Brixton Council of Churches has a good record of trying to build bridges and, if you wanted to talk privately to someone, I can recommend to you the Vicar of the parish in the centre of the troubled area – The Revd. Robert Nind . . . I have known Robert Nind for a good number of years and I regard him as a man of some intellectual and spiritual stature.

The other anxiety concerns the problem of police/community relations. These clergy feel that these relations have seriously broken down and that their re-establishment is a matter of great urgency. They think that the clue must lie with the local force – and reported that there is a great deal of criticism of the decision to bring in so many outsiders; and particularly of the reliance on younger officers who have little experience of this kind of situation . . .

One other point which they stressed was the extent to which social programmes have constantly been changed and tampered with. This has caused great frustration and negatived much of the good that could have come from the expenditure which was mentioned in your television interviews . . .

In passing on these comments, I am sure that I am telling you little that you do not already know, but you may find it useful to have these grass roots reactions . . . You can imagine that I am also under some pressure to give a moral and spiritual lead in what may become the central issue for our society in the coming months and years. I am eager to respond but not by rushing into generalised and unconstructive comments on highly complex issues.

Nevertheless, I regard this letter to you as a first step in my responsibility for spiritual leadership in the face of a deteriorating situation in community relations which is not confined to Brixton.

With best wishes,

Yours very sincerely,

[Carbon not signed]

Whitelaw replied on 27 April

Personal and confidential

My dear Archbishop,

Thank you very much for your kind, and helpful, letter to me about the events in Brixton. It will be of enormous value if, over the coming months, you can direct some of your personal concern and the authority of your office to binding together again a community so apparently torn.

I am in no doubt about the delicacy of the present situation. It was because of that that I asked Lord Scarman to inquire into the events at Brixton, and their causes, so urgently. I know he himself will wish to draw closely on the experience of local community leaders, including the Brixton Council of Churches, and I very much hope they will be ready to put their views to him. Although that must be a first priority, I should of course be happy to talk to them, and especially to you. Perhaps we could meet early on your return from the United States.

Yours sincerely,

William Whitelaw

On 18 June, Runcie and representatives of the Brixton Council of Churches met Whitelaw. Runcie wrote to him the next day:

My dear Willie,

Thank you so much for giving us generously of your time and listening so obviously to the points which you must have heard many times before; but I can see that you are sensitive to how those points are put and the background of experience which enables people to make them. I can say that the Brixton group were enormously encouraged by the reception they received, and whatever they may still think about some aspects of policing, Government policy in the area and the Nationality Bill, they are in no doubt about your own integrity and determination to pursue some long term answers in all those fields.

With best wishes,

Yours ever,

[Carbon not signed]

The following November, Runcie made a public statement about the Scarman Report:

This Report deserves to be widely read ... I believe that the Churches and especially their members in inner city areas have a vital contribution to make in the rebuilding of trust and confidence. The recommendations are being studied very carefully by the Churches together and I hope that we may be able to make a joint response about the part which we can play.[6]

I told him that I was rather surprised that he had taken action so quickly after the Brixton riots. 'Well, there seemed to me to be a need for immediate action. I summoned round the vicar of St Matthews', Brixton, practically the next morning.' It was really his own initiative? 'It's very difficult to tell in retrospect what were one's own initiatives and what were not. I tended to be better at choosing between options rather than inventing options.'

[6]Text in Archbishop's papers, Lambeth Palace.

Presumably Whitelaw received them courteously? 'Yes. And I remember going up to Toxteth [the district of Liverpool where riots also took place] as well. Have you ever been attacked in a way which made you feel sort of cold and prickly? I went to express concern, and I thought, you know, that I was being rather a good man, really. And a vicar got up, an evangelical, and said: "There are two things that disqualify you from talking to us today: one, you were born in Crosby, and two, you were born before the war. The fact that you were born in Crosby makes you think you understand Merseyside. You don't. And you think you've got experience of Merseyside, but it's changed out of all recognition. You represent the Church of the Shires, and we shall never make progress here as long as we are wedded to the Church of the Shires." He was very eloquent. It made me feel sort of goose-pimply.'

By late 1981, in his Christmas sermon at Canterbury, Runcie was taking what was beginning to look like an anti-Thatcher line. This sermon, reported in the *Daily Telegraph* on 27 December 1981, referred (without mentioning Mrs Thatcher or her Government) to 'hearts that have been hardened in resentment or unimaginative complacency . . . contempt for working people, neglect of the hungry'.

I asked Runcie whether, when he first arrived at Lambeth, there had been a dinner invitation to 10 Downing Street – were social doors opened, so that he and Mrs Thatcher could communicate informally? 'To a certain extent. Actually she wasn't very good at inviting one round. But she used to say, "Why does he sound off like this? He knows that he can come round and warn me that he feels like this." That was her defence.

'People like Geoffrey Howe used to invite me round. But none of them ever said to me, "You're terribly wrong." Willie Whitelaw and my other friends would say, "You've got to remember it's all very difficult." They would go out of their way to be friendly to me because the press was hostile to me about it. I remember Jim Prior used to say to me, "It's not that she initiated the attacks on you in the papers, but she could have called them off at a moment's notice." And I always remember Nigel Lawson being really very convivial with me. I think they all felt, "We're not going to make the sort of noises that Runcie does, but they ought to be made!"'

He was, I suggested, on the most congenial terms possible with the majority of her ministers. He agreed. 'I used to laugh about this. There can't have been an archbishop in this century who was on such friendly terms with the Foreign Secretary (Peter Carrington), with her Chancellor of the Exchequer (Geoffrey Howe and then Lawson), and with Jim Prior and people like that.' The Guards, of course, had provided the common background. 'It was a bizarre state of affairs, that here was I, portrayed as hostile to this government, and on terms of friendship such as no archbishop has been this century. Norman St John Stevas was another one.'

The Lambeth press cuttings had reminded me that 1981 was the year in which Runcie conducted the wedding of the Prince of Wales and Lady Diana Spencer. I had found some drafts of his sermon for the royal wedding in July 1981. With its much quoted opening, 'Here is the stuff of which fairy tales are made', this had done Runcie's public image a lot of good. Correspondence found with the drafts indicated that at least two people, including Gerald Priestland, BBC Religious Affairs Correspondent, had contributed ideas to this sermon. We had talked about the royal marriage in December 1993, prompted by an article in *The Times* by George Austin, Archdeacon of York, saying that Prince Charles should not succeed to the throne – or at least become head of the Church of England – if (as it was then beginning to seem) he had committed adultery with Camilla Parker-Bowles.

Runcie: In my view, it's a terrible reflection on the state of public life that someone like Austin – who was in the St Albans diocese when I was bishop – should become a household name in the current debate about the state of the monarchy. I was indiscreet about it at Jeffrey Archer's party last week. There was a man with whom I let off steam about the difficulties of the Prince of Wales and then I saw him go off and start talking to Andrew Knight and Charles Moore [of the *Daily Telegraph*]. He said, 'What do you think about it?' And I said, 'It depends whether the Prince wins his way with the British people over the next five to ten years. Also, it would quite help if he loved the Church of England a bit more.'

HC: You don't think he does?

Runcie: That's one of the things that I found disappointing – that he was so disenchanted with it. But he didn't have a consistent view, because he would go in with the *Spectator* gang on 'the lovely language of the Prayer Book', but then he would say, 'Instead of interfering with politics, the church should be creating centres of healing in the inner cities – ought to be bringing together the spiritual, the intellectual and the architectural.' But these were only conversations in passing, not seriously sustained argument. He would, under pressure, respond to being asked to do something about my 'urban priority areas' – go and open a Jobcentre. But I think he'd given up on the Church of England before I arrived.

HC: Why?

Runcie: I don't know, because he was quite pious, and was cultivated by John Andrew [chaplain to Michael Ramsey], and was confirmed by Michael Ramsey, and had a sort of relationship there. When he came to Lambeth for his pre-marriage talk, I remember he said in a kind of nostalgic way, 'I came and served here sometimes.' But it was rather something that had passed away. And I think he was deeply into the Laurens van der Post spirituality. When it came to his concern to do something about the state of the country, I don't think he took the Church of England very seriously.

My relationship with him was friendly, but I couldn't get much in depth out of it. He was very nice to

Lindy – he appreciated her bubbling conversation that is totally without any affectation. He liked that. One of the difficulties for me was that, when things began to go wrong in the marriage – when things were very unhappy for Diana – he invited me to lunch with her.

HC: With him as well?

Runcie: With him as well. On the basis of 'It's been rather a lot for Diana, because religion hasn't stuck much with her. And we feel we ought to mention it to you, because you married us.' And the arrangement which he thought was good was that I should see her from time to time. She was happy about this. I had her private telephone number, and she had mine. And I then gave her what amounted to two or three – I forget how many – not very successful confirmation talks. That's what he thought she needed: a bit of instruction. What I quickly saw she needed was some encouragement, and some 'Are you all right, girl?' When you began on abstract ideas, you could see her eyes clouding over, her eyelids become heavy. But it was a matter of encouraging her through talk about people, about personalities. And she was very receptive to that. For example, she would always write a very prompt and thoughtful thank-you letter – she had that sort of gift. But they were difficult times. About a year after this I was at some state banquet, and I said, 'How goes it?' And she said, 'Well, I'm still as thick as a plank up here,' tapping her forehead, 'but I've really got it down here now,' tapping her midriff.

HC: Got more guts?

Runcie: Got more guts. And the big moment was when she went on her first tour with him. And I remember having one of my sessions with her when they were packing. I never saw him again in relation to Diana – all my relationship with him was inner cities or official things; I could never get him on to Diana again.

HC: Did you try?

Runcie: Not really hard. Diana felt she had a separate relationship with me, because I took her brother Charlie's

So much for confidentiality!

wedding, and baptised his children as well as hers. And I became, and remain a friend of Frances Shand-Kydd, her mother, who is really rather an underestimated person. So I'm in a way, I suppose, associated with that camp. Then her grandmother I knew very well, Ruth Fermoy, and Ruth used to see me, and I felt – typical Runcie – on both sides, because Ruth was very distressed with Diana's behaviour. Ruth was a gentle and lovely person, a great encourager of music, and she was totally and wholly a Charles person, because she'd seen him grow up, loved him like all the women of the court do, and regarded Diana as an actress, a schemer – all of which is true, of course.

HC: Is it?

Runcie: Well, it can be. Very competitive. I don't know what will become of her. Sad, really, and I feel a desire to support her.

HC: When the stuff about the marriage began to come in the press, did it seem familiar to you? Charles and Camilla Parker-Bowles?

Runcie: Yes.

HC: You knew about that already?

Runcie: I knew about that already, yes. That was what worried Ruth Fermoy, about his needing a woman to love and be cared for by. And also that Diana would never be under control until she fell in love with someone.

HC: Were you nervous about the marriage from the start?

Runcie: I remember Richard Chartres saying – a very observant man – when they came to see me for the first time, and there was general conversation, with Richard present, about the arrangements and things, Richard said to me, 'He's seriously depressed. You can tell from his voice.' We thought it was an arranged marriage, but my own view was, 'They're a nice couple, and she'll grow into it.' They weren't casual about their preparation for marriage; I remember that we had a private Communion service together, and Charles encouraged her a lot when she looked a little anxious and wan about it. But she was very tender, very unformed. And yet had a sort of shrewdness, and was tremendously observant, always very observant of anything about you. I used to go and see her at KP [Kensington Palace], and she'd see me to the door, and I opened the door of the car and a packet of cigarettes fell out, and she said, 'Oh, you have a fag between sessions, do you?' And she came to Canterbury once, and she wrote to somebody and said she'd been to lunch with me, and she said, 'Guess what, we had grilled sole!'

Charles is highly sensitive – that's what everybody says. I could quote so many examples of personal letters or hidden acts of kindness to individuals in need, or unglamorous but worthwhile causes. But he is a mass of contradictions – almost as much as I am! He's punctilious in being Colonel-in-Chief of the Welsh Guards, but he also wants to be friends with the Greenham women. He's on about the grandeur of our cathedrals and the epic language of the Prayer Book, but he wants to be exploring Hinduism with people in inner cities. He hunts regularly, but is a great man about the environment. So that the public don't really know where they are. There are people who have all sorts of conspiracy theories. The most amazing was that Diana would become a Roman Catholic, and lead the return of the Stewart royal house!

The person I do admire is the Queen. She's the only person who has the abilty to rise above it. I don't fully understand her, but that's part of her secret. At moments of either high drama or pressure on me, like the papal visit or the coal miners' strike, she always went out of her way to encourage – it may have been indirectly, by an invitation to do something; it may have been by a chance word. But I've always felt that she regarded it as part of her responsibility, though he was never to be regarded as a member of the court or a private chaplain, to encourage the Archbishop of Canterbury, and to listen to what he had to say – to ask him his opinion about things. Now, I never managed to strike that sort of relationship with the Prince of Wales.

It's a strange family, the royal family, because conversations aren't followed up. I think it's also that survival is the over-arching priority, and you have to prove yourself as a safe person with whom to be a friend, not a man who enjoys boasting about his position with them.

HC: But the Queen has to have some responsibility for their appalling public image?

Runcie: When I said I admired her, I meant that she managed to combine the mystique and informality which sprang from her own deep sense of vocation. This meant you knew where you were, even though you were often uncomfortable, because her shyness makes it hard to relax in her presence. She creates a feeling of uncertainty. I remember the first time I met Diana was when I sat between the Queen and her at the Privy Council meeting summoned to confirm the engagement. Diana was terrified of her. She'd obviously been told that it was very important that she made it, so to speak, and she was anxious to make sure that, if I ought to have been talking to the Queen, I wasn't talking to her.

They're people of formal personal piety, of course, people who intercede, who say their nightly prayers. Diana said she found that this was something that Charles couldn't share. She used to say to me, 'He's very deep, Charles' – this is the little girl talking in the early days – and Charles had said, 'I like intercession a great deal, and there's always new things to pray about, so it's very difficult, your intercession list gets longer and longer.' My line was to get on her side, under her skin a bit, really, and say, 'Don't worry about all this religious vocabulary to start with. You may have more spiritual insight than your cerebrally inclined husband. The trouble is that you believe that to be religious you have to be capable of handling ideas, religious ideas. But that's not necessarily true at all. The inarticulate is just as valuable in the eyes of God as the articulate, maybe even more so. And I have a wife who is very very bright, to my mind, but she's not an ideas woman – she hates an idea when she sees one!'

HC: You didn't get involved, I imagine, in the Andrew–Sarah marriage?

Runcie: We got on rather well with Sarah, and she was very open about it all. I remember having tea with her and the children in a very lofty corner of Buckingham Palace where she had a flat, and she'd just come back from some public engagement, and was trying to live in that echoing place, and I felt sympathy with her. She was the one who was most uninhibited about calling you by your Christian name, and embracing you and all that sort of thing. And she said, 'I just can't take the stiff upper lip syndrome. And the you-are-never-ill syndrome. And that's what's got Diana.'

13

A sort of mastery over me

———◆———

I did not manage to get an appointment to discuss the next major events in Runcie's time as Archbishop, the 1982 papal visit to Britain and the Falklands war, until the beginning of August 1994. The Runcies' daughter Rebecca had been married in June, and then they had been on a Swan cruise.

I found him looking well and relaxed, in an aertex open-necked shirt, and it was so sunny that we sat outside the back of the house, where Lindy had now created what Runcie described as 'an Italian garden', including a fountain.

'My sister Margery has died,' he told me. 'That left me with some feelings of guilt, because I ought to have seen more of her. She was a quiet, good woman. She was hoping to live to come to Rebecca's wedding. She didn't manage it, and she died two days later. I went off on the cruise, leaving the arrangements to Angus's son Richard, and I flew back from Malta (by the arrangement of Swan) one day, took part in the funeral in Nottingham on the next day, and then flew back to Tunis and Carthage and carried on with the cruise. So that's been another reminder of mortality, but I'm quite cheerful, really.'

I said that the last time we had met, he seemed to be convinced that death was waiting round the corner. 'Yes. And then I had a pain in the back, so I thought, oh, it's got to the bones now, I'm finished. Then I got a bronchial cold on the cruise, and I thought it had gone to the lungs. Then suddenly I was aware that, it having gone to the lungs, I no longer had a pain in the back! And the cough seems to have gone. I "suffer from evil imaginings", as the Prayer Book says. But my doctor calls them neurotic obsessions!

'Lindy has fixed for us to have a fortnight in New Jersey, and she's always anxious that I should work my passage across. I was asked to be a celebrity lecturer on the *QE2*. I had visions of a comfortable cruise in a sort of 1920 Claridges afloat, but the reality is clearly not like that. Lindy is quite shocked that we have to pay our own bar bills! And I have to give two talks. I thought I'd just give something on the Grand Tour – Hellenic things. But Jeffrey Archer, who's done it, said, "They won't be interested. You've got to win them from the gaming tables!" So off the top of my head I produced two titles, which he thought were absolute winners: "Religion and Diplomacy: an Archbishop Abroad" (that will be what Rajiv Ghandi said to me, and that kind of thing, and it'll deal with Waite); and the second one will be "Religion and Politics: an Archbishop at Home during the Thatcher Years". So if you've got any ideas – anything you've discovered that I don't know in those fields . . . ?

'I had a word with Waite last night. He rings me up for comfort from time to time. His book is a world best-seller, and the paperback is coming out, and it's already in a second edition before it's been published. But he reminded me – for this lecture – about when we were in Vancouver (I think it was in 1981) for the World Council of Churches, and talking with a South African delegate, and asking him about the situation there, and about getting more profile for Desmond Tutu. And I asked him about the diocese of Johannesburg, where a pupil of mine, an Englishman, was then the bishop. And I said: "I think he could possibly come home now. If we were able to engineer a vacancy for him in England, could you, do you think, get Tutu elected Bishop of Johannesburg?" And he said he thought they could. And I said, "And if you manage that, do you think that when Philip Russell, the Archbishop of Cape Town, retires in two years' time, you could get Desmond translated there?" And he thought they could. So I managed, through the Crown Appointments Commission, to persuade the diocese of Portsmouth to accept my man, Timothy Bavin, who's been an enormous success.[1] And they got Desmond elected to Johannesburg, which gave the ANC someone who was in a position to communicate that the party wasn't a bunch of communists. Now, Waite said last night, "That was an example of what other people might think was intrigue, but it was good diplomacy" – it had a big effect on world affairs.'[2]

I said this was highly relevant to my current research, because I had come away from two more sessions with the Lambeth papers under the impression that he had not taken much initiative in matters like the papal visit to Britain, which seemed to have been largely engineered by others.

Things had started to happen as soon as Runcie and John Paul II had met in Accra in May 1980.

Geoffrey Fisher was the first Archbishop of Canterbury to meet the Pope; he paid what was described as a 'courtesy visit' to Rome in 1960. Bruce Kent, the former Roman Catholic priest turned disarmament campaigner (whom I met shortly after going through these papers), told me he was secretary to Cardinal Heenan, leader of the English Roman

---

[1]Three months after this conversation, Bavin was 'outed' by the organisation OutRage, which alleged that he was homosexual. In January 1995, at the age of sixty, he announced that he would resign as bishop and become a monk. Runcie says he was 'an enormous success' in his diocese, and had already decided to resign.
[2]Tutu has written of Runcie's support for him: 'There was no fence-sitting here for Robert.' *Robert Runcie: A Portrait by His Friends*, edited by David L. Edwards, Fount Paperbacks, 1990, p. 146.

Catholics from 1963; and that after Fisher had retired in 1961 he would ring Heenan up and criticise things that Heenan had said or done. (Fisher did this to Anglicans, too; my mild-mannered father was often goaded into fury by him.) Kent said he could see the back of Heenan's neck going red as Fisher barked at him, in his headmaster's voice, down the telephone.

Michael Ramsey and Donald Coggan both went to the Vatican to meet Pope Paul VI when they held the arch-bishopric, in 1966 and 1977 respectively, and the Ramsey visit resulted in the setting up of the Anglican/Roman Cath-olic International Commission, which had been meeting at intervals ever since to discuss reunion. It was due to deliver its final report in the spring of 1982. But no Pope had ever been to Britain.

In July 1980, two months after the Accra meeting, Runcie went to see Lord Carrington, the Foreign Secretary, to discuss the possibility of a papal visit. Michael Kinchin-Smith's note on this meeting reports that Carrington accepted that a visit was 'likely to happen in due course', but 'saw no advantage in attempting to hurry it'. (Did Mrs Thatcher feel nervous at the prospect of a public personality even more than powerful than herself setting foot on British soil? Certainly Carrington gave no reason for his lack of enthusiasm.)

Runcie replied that he knew from his conversation with the Pope in Accra 'that such a visit was not at the top of his priorities and was most unlikely until 1982 at the earliest'. He expected that the Roman Catholics would want to programme some special event into the visit, such as the beatification of Cardinal Newman.

The plan was for the Anglicans and the Roman Catholics to issue a joint formal invitation to the Pope; but before this had been drawn up, Basil Hume, Heenan's successor as Cardinal Archbishop of Westminster, and Derek Worlock, Roman Catholic Archbishop of Liverpool, happened to be having a meeting with the Pope at Castel Gandolfo, on 23 August 1980. During this, 'rather on the spur of the moment',[3] Hume asked the Pope if it might be possible for him to come to England.

The Pope replied that forty-seven other countries had recently issued invitations, whereupon 'it was decided there and then by the Cardinal and Archbishop Worlock to invite him'. The Pope accepted on the spot. 'The summer of 1982 was agreed,' says a note in the Lambeth file by Christopher Hill. 'The Pope asked about the ecumenical implications of a visit and requested the Cardinal to consult with the Archbishop of Canterbury in particular.' On his return to England, Hume informed the Queen, the Prime Minister, the Foreign Office – and of course Lambeth.

Runcie, meanwhile, was away on a Greek cruise, as a guest of the Swan company ('I didn't do any lecturing for them while I was Archbishop, and this was a special trip'), and it was Christopher Hill who received a message from Hume that the Cardinal would like to see the Archbishop. Hill himself went to Archbishop's House, Hume's Westminster residence. Hume apologised for the failure to issue a joint invitation, as planned, but said that it had 'appeared to raise problems'; also 'others (including Norman St John Stevas) had been inviting the Pope to England'. Hill 'expressed sadness that the joint invitation had been aborted by events', and was alarmed by Hume's feeling that a public announcement of the visit should be made almost at once. 'I asked,' writes Hill, 'that this should not be done until after the Archbishop of Canterbury's return.' Hume said he had 'drafted something of a press release', which emphasised that the Pope hoped to meet the Archbishop of Canterbury during the visit. Hill said he would look at Runcie's diary so that a date for the visit be fixed soon.

After leaving Hume, Hill decided that it was 'very important not to lose an Anglican initiative'. Next day he was told by one of Hume's staff that Hume intended to make a press announcement in five days' time, before Runcie returned

[3]Unless specified, all quotations are from papers concerning the papal visit in Lambeth Palace archives.

from holiday. Hill 'could not see the reason for haste', but told Hume that Runcie 'would probably wish to send an immediate message to the Pope' saying he would welcome him in England, and reminding the Pope that in Accra they had discussed making a joint pilgrimage to Canterbury. Hill also suggested to Hume that 'an immediate reply' should be obtained from the Pope so that this could be published along with Runcie's letter. Hume was 'very happy' at this suggestion.

Accordingly Hill drafted a letter to the Pope on Runcie's behalf, and tried to send it to Runcie's ship via maritime radio. 'Eventually the person in charge admitted that the Greek ships often failed to respond to signals! The ship was regularly called for eight hours before I decided to send the message on my own initiative in the hope that the Archbishop of Canterbury would approve.' Hill had already alerted the Foreign Office. He also left a message for Richard Chartres, who was at Canterbury, to check that he approved of the draft. Chartres rang back and agreed that it could be sent without Runcie's approval. In fact, before it was sent, the message did get through to Runcie's ship, and he telephoned Hill and 'cleared the message to the Pope'. The message was then sent to Rome via the Foreign Office; meanwhile Hume contacted the Vatican and requested an immediate reply from the Pope, which was forthcoming by 29 August. A press release containing both Runcie's letter and the Pope's reply was then issued simultaneously by both the Anglicans and the Roman Catholics.

I recalled that among papers which Donald Wright had lent me was a note of a meeting between Wright and Basil Hume on 25 June 1979, when Wright was consulting a wide range of people about the type of person who should be chosen as the next Archbishop of Canterbury. It seemed to me fairly remarkable that the leader of the Roman Catholics in England should have been among those consulted.

It was a delightful occasion [wrote Wright] totally relaxed, and [Hume] began by showing himself willing to talk about two recent meetings with Pope John Paul II ... [who] was particularly interested in the Church of England and the Anglican Communion, conscious of the fact that he did not know enough about either (having come from Poland) and [Hume] believes that the Pope will want to give reunion a big shove. So what [Hume] is hoping for in the new Archbishop of Canterbury is a man who will give reunion an equally large shove ... What we need, he said, is someone who will come with us and grapple with the difficult issues in an open way.

I suggested to Runcie that one benefit – it may have been only a temporary one – of all the high-level contacts preceding the papal visit was that people from both churches got to know each other – particularly himself and Basil Hume. 'Yes. And the Pope, eventually, though I think he is quite difficult to get to know personally. One of the problems is that so much is done for him by his Secretary of State. You talk about everything being arranged for *me*, but when you stay in the Vatican – !⁴ If he's going to perform, it takes so much of his energy. He has to learn to say mass in Russian and Swahili, and so on, and his day is full of welcoming the clergy of Brazil, and pilgrims from the diocese of Perugia, and giving an address to the Sacred Commission on the Arts. And you wonder what he *does* think himself. But being with him in Accra, and then in Canterbury, and in Rome, did give one some sort of sense of the man.'

So what impressions does he give? 'I think that he's a man of genuine devotion. A man who's had to struggle. He's a very attractive human being – an attractive university chaplain for many years. He's had to struggle with his own masculinity. I mean, he must have had many people fall for him. And I think that he has the discipline of the priest. And yet the warmth of the good host, and a person who understands human beings well enough. But

⁴As Runcie did in 1989.

he *is* a hardliner – on women in the ministry, and on contraception – because he thinks the pace is being set too much by a gospel of self-fulfilment, disastrously affecting the West.'

This is surely the key to the Pope – having fought against one enemy for the best part of his life, he then looked for another when he came westwards? 'Yes. And therefore he doesn't, it seems to me, appreciate the moral ambiguities which arise from living in a free society, and the further responsibility that God puts into our hands.' Does Runcie see the Pope as personally to blame for the great oppression which the Catholic church has exercised in some areas? 'If you are going to be a world evangelist, then you can't really mind the shop. I think the people he has had to leave to mind the shop are very often Mediterranean male conservatives. But he goes along with them. For me, staying in the Vatican was very agreeable, like being in an Oxford common room. But when you realise that these are the people who are laying down ethical standards for Polynesian women and so on, then you pause and think it can't be right. But I still stand by my view that you need a focus for the Christian community – and therefore an ecumenical Primate. The present Pope has never taken that seriously; his ecumenism is strong on rhetoric, but not very good on substantial steps.'

The Archbishop of Canterbury's letter to the Pope, written by Christopher Hill, speaks of the 'good news' of the Pope's acceptance of Hume's invitation, and assures him that he will be 'warmly received with real affection in England by Anglicans and other Christians, as well as by your own Roman Catholic community'. It reminds the Pope that in Accra they 'spoke of the possibility of your making an Ecumenical Pilgrimage to Canterbury', and invites him to do so, 'with a profound sense of the tragedy of human divisions and the belief that the unity of Christians will offer real hope for the reconciliation of mankind'.

The Pope's reply – a very grand-looking document with an embossed crest – says he is 'deeply touched by the warmth with which you associate yourself with the invitation extended to me by Cardinal Basil Hume', and declares that 'it will be a joy and a privilege for me to meet members of the Anglican Church'. There is no mention of the Canterbury pilgrimage. The letter, of course, had not been written by the Pope at all; a draft was shown to Richard Chartres and Michael Moore by Monsignor Mario Oliveri of the Apostolic Delegation to Great Britain on 30 August 1980, the day after it had supposedly been sent; they expressed discomfort at one phrase – 'visiting the Catholic people and meeting members of the Anglican Church' – and this was changed before the letter was published.

On 12 September 1980, Runcie – back from his Greek cruise – met Basil Hume for a 'Summit Meeting', with no one else present. Afterwards he made some notes:

> It is very important that we keep some initiatives:
>   1 I think the Pope should experience *Anglican Worship* – preferably at Canterbury.
>   2 Do something about both lots of martyrs . . .

He also began to consult bishops as to what might be made of the visit. Cyril Easthaugh, former Bishop of Kensington, told him that in 1961 he had suggested to Cardinal Heenan that Anglicans and Catholics should 'organise two penitence processions, the RCs to Smithfield, & Anglicans & others to Tyburn' – places where many martyrs were executed. Heenan had replied that 'he saw the point but thought it should not come to the point of public penitence. Anyhow people in those days were like that and did that sort of thing so it would be better to forget it.' Easthaugh commented: 'You would have a better deal today with Cardinal Hume, I think.'

David Sheppard, the left-wing Bishop of Liverpool, wrote to Runcie that he had a 'dream' that 'you and the Pope together might do two or three great public meetings', at which 'a Free Churchman of appropriate stature' would appear on the platform with them. But he was concerned about the Pope's ultra-conservative stance on 'human relations and sexuality' and on 'Schillebeeckx and Küng' (liberal Catholic theologians disapproved of by the Vatican). Sheppard's 'dream' may have influenced a suggestion which Runcie passed to Basil Hume in a letter of 17 November 1980:

> Dear Basil,
> . . . I know that you are anxious for the kind of ecumenical contact which will reveal to the Holy Father the realities of the mission of the one Church in this country and I wonder whether this would not be better achieved by an intimate meeting of the dozen or so Christian leaders of real account in the British Isles, including yourself, under a neutral roof. Leeds Castle, a place of great natural beauty where the first Rhodesian Conference was held, might be a possible venue half way between Canterbury and London, for a confidential meeting which would permit substantial conversation, over a dinner of Papal proportions, on the evening of the second day . . .
> Yours ever,
> Robert

Hume replied that this was 'very much on lines with which I would agree'.

A week later, Hugh Montefiore wrote to Runcie that the Pope's visit put him in 'something of a dilemma'. On the one hand he wanted to 'foster true ecumenism' and welcome 'the world's foremost Christian leader'. On the other hand:

> before I was enthroned as Bishop of Birmingham . . . I recollect very well swearing on oath that 'no foreign potentate or prelate hath any jurisdiction in this realm of England'. And therefore I feel that I cannot just simply dance attendance on the Pope . . . Also, I would feel a certain revulsion at finding myself present at a Papal allocution in which there was wholesale condemnation

of abortion, contraception, re-marriage, or the marriage of the clergy.

Runcie reassured him – 'I have a great deal of sympathy with what you say' – and agreed that, on the matter of the Pope's conservative views, 'the omens are not too good'. The Apostolic Delegate to Great Britain, Archbishop Heim, said much the same when he visited Runcie on 1 December 1980. 'The Delegate very much hoped that the Pope would stop speaking about sex,' noted Christopher Hill, who suggested that there might be 'some discussion' between the two churches 'about what the Pope might speak about when he comes to England. The Delegate thought this an excellent idea.' Four days later, Hume wrote to Runcie, saying he hoped they could get together before Christmas for further discussions. 'I despair at the moment of being able to do anything but deal with the immediate, and I suspect that you are in the same situation. Yours ever, Basil.'

The discussions about the visit were leading to the airing of sensitive and important topics. In 1896 the then Pope had condemned Anglican holy orders as invalid, and this had never been repealed. On 4 December 1980, Christopher Hill had lunch with Hume's Adviser for Non-Diocesan Affairs, Monsignor George Leonard, who 'wondered whether there would be any chance of Anglican Orders being "opened up", that is, recognised by the Pope at last. We agreed that Rome should be pressed on this . . .'

Leonard liked Runcie's suggestion of a summit under a 'neutral roof', but told Hill that 'Leeds Castle savoured too strongly of political summits'. He remarked that Hume suspected that the Queen was 'rather cool' about the papal visit, and wondered if Runcie could do anything about this.

Meanwhile the Lambeth staff were discussing what sort of service the Pope should attend at Canterbury. Hill felt that 'the actual experience of an Anglican Eucharist can be converting for Roman Catholics . . . Evensong would create less problems, but have less significance.' St George's House, Windsor, was suggested as an alternative to Leeds Castle, but the Pope's overnight presence in Windsor could embarrass the Queen.

Hume had suggested that the visit should take place 'between Wembley and Wimbledon', and the dates were now fixed for Friday 28 May to Wednesday 2 June 1982. It was also agreed that Henry Chadwick, Regius Professor of Divinity at Cambridge (and brother of Owen Chadwick), should go to Rome to discuss directly with the Pope – who had recently escaped an assassination attempt – the nature of the service which would be held at Canterbury.[5] Meanwhile a visit was paid to London by Archbishop Paul Marcinkus, described by Christopher Hill as 'officially head of the . . . Internal Vatican Bank . . . unofficially the Pope's bodyguard on overseas visits . . . a likeable but tough Chicago Catholic.' The *Sunday Mirror* (28 March 1982) reported that during the Pope's 1979 visit to Ireland, the six-feet-four-inches Marcinkus, spotting 'a sinister figure who was getting too close to the Pope', had administered 'a swift knee to the parts that Catholic priests should not reach'. The victim 'turned out to be a member of the Irish Secret Service'. Near the time of the papal visit to Britain, Marcinkus caused considerable annoyance through what the organisers considered his excessive demands for security, refusing to expose the Pope to the slightest risk.

Henry Chadwick arrived in Rome on 4 January 1982, staying for four days. On his return, he sent Runcie a lengthy report on his experiences at the Vatican. The General Synod's Standing Committee had strongly felt that the ideal form of service at Canterbury would be eucharistic; Chadwick thought the Pope most unlikely to feel able to consent to that. Cardinal Hume had already pointed out that

for the Pope to assist (without any question of inter-communion) at an Anglican Eucharist would cause deep

---

[5]Runcie says that this came about because Cardinal Daneels from Belgium, on a visit to Canterbury, suggested to him that they should 'get someone into the Pope's study, who could talk to him as one theology professor to another'.

division among English Roman Catholics, who would
feel that his presence could carry an implicit public
recognition that an Anglican Eucharist is neither heretical
nor schismatic . . . While some English Roman Catholics
would of course welcome this implication, others (and
not all those being of the extreme right wing) would be
caused great pain.

Chadwick 'nevertheless felt bound to press the question' of
the Canterbury service being a Eucharist, and was eventually
able to put it to the Pope himself:

The Holy Father replied that he was sure many things
could be achieved within a Liturgy of the Word [i.e.
some other service than the Eucharist]; that the intensity
of feeling with which the request for a Eucharist had
been put to him required him to defer a decision on that
until he had given thought and prayer to the question
and felt able to respond with an equal intensity; and
that he felt confident that Our Lord Jesus Christ would
guide both Pope and Archbishop to the right decision in
the situation, which would be for the good of Christ's
Church.

   This dialogue did not take place during my private
audience, which was cut short to about ten minutes,
but over a luncheon in the Pope's private dining-room,
which was also attended by Fr Duprey, Mons. J. Rigali,
Fr John Magee, and a Polish priest who is the Pope's
private chaplain and whose name I did not catch. There
were some preliminary discussions in which . . . the Pope
asked me if Anglican theologians rejected or read with
sympathy the medieval Catholic theologians. I replied . . .
that Anglicans read them with much sympathy, especially
Anselm . . .

   The Pope also asked about the position of the Queen
as 'head' of the Church of England, and the relationship
of Church and State. John Magee clearly thought too that
the Establishment of the Church of England would be a

major obstacle to a restoration of communion between Canterbury and Rome. I ventured to reply that I doubted if this was a correctly focused view; that the disestablishment of the Church of England was more likely to be regarded as a further step towards secularisation than as a liberation of the Church; that the Prime Minister certainly had a power of veto and a limited power of choice in episcopal appointments but that here the Prime Minister's actual power is far less than that exercised by the French Government over nominations for bishoprics in Alsace (still under the old Concordat!).

I explicitly mentioned that we had Protestants opposed to the Holy Father's visit. The Pope also asked me in what kind of honour Anglicans held the saints. I replied that we dedicated our churches to them and decorated them with likenesses of the saints in stained glass and in statues and other representations; that we celebrated the saints in our Calendar; that the Blessed Virgin Mary was celebrated in this way; that there were Anglicans for whom the honour of the Blessed Virgin was very important in their spiritual and devotional life, and others for whom this was not the case. I mentioned Walsingham.[6] It had at one time been suggested that the Pope's visit to the UK might include a visit there, but the project was abandoned in view of the logistic impossibility of finding room for the many visitors who would come to so tiny a place. The smallness of the site made a Papal visit impracticable. The Holy Father accepted this judgement with an obvious regret . . .

In my luncheon conversation with the Holy Father he was visibly moved when I happened to mention in passing that it was quite common practice in Anglican parish Eucharist's for the celebrant at the prayer for the Church to bid intercession not only for the Metropolitan [i.e. the Archbishop of Canterbury or York] and the Diocesan Bishop but also for Pope John Paul.

[6]Where there are two shrines of the Virgin, one Anglican, the other Roman Catholic.

During the lunch, the question was raised of the Church of England's moves towards the ordination of women. Chadwick 'said nothing, of course, to suggest that it would be an easy matter to reverse engines in those provinces [of the Anglican Communion] which had accepted women priests . . . The Pope is aware that in England we have no women priests. I said we had no objection to women deacons; this aroused no comment at all.' Chadwick felt that the Pope was very unlikely to agree to a Eucharist at Canterbury, and added:

I came away from my interviews at the Curia with the impression that Anglicans have come to seem a bore to the top administrators of the Roman Catholic Church . . . The Curia fear either that we shall take them for a ride in a fast car and end up by publicly urging inter-communion in terms they are bound to reject, or that we shall trample on their corns in hobnailed boots, as they feel was the case in the unilateral decision [by several provinces of the Anglican Communion] to ordain women to the priesthood without prior ecumenical consultation. Our apparent insensitivity on this issue continues to astonish them, and confirms suspicions that we are at heart simply Liberal Protestants in our ecclesiology.

At the discussion over luncheon with the Holy Father, I mentioned that the ordination of women in America and Canada had been done before the Vatican Declaration against the practice (*Inter insigniores*), and had been fostered with a great deal of encouragement from Roman Catholics in these countries who hoped that the Anglican Church could give their own Church a lead in honouring women's rights. This information did not seem welcome to my audience . . .

It turned out to be a difficult week beset by very high tension . . . There remain many dark clouds. The Holy Father frankly confessed to me that he could not at present imagine what kind of unity we could have with one another which would not entail some kind of surrender of principle by the Roman Catholic Church . . . The Curia . . . must, I think, be tempted to wish we would go away and get lost! And yet personal contact at the right kind of level is obviously extraordinarily congenial to them. We may irritate Rome, but we also fascinate Rome too – at some moments a diabolical Doppelgänger or counterfeit and rival Catholicism, at other moments 70 million believers whom it would be so good to reconcile in one communion and fellowship with the see of Peter and Paul. Though the Holy Father must regard any eucharist I celebrate as invalid, he sent me away with the gift of a most beautifully embroidered white stole![7]

On 8 February 1982, a month after Chadwick's trip to Rome, this letter was sent from the Vatican:

To His Grace
The Most Reverend Robert Runcie
Archbishop of Canterbury

Through your letter of 27 December last, I received the welcome news that Professor Henry Chadwick would be arriving in Rome at the beginning of January. On 7 January it was my pleasure to receive Professor Chadwick and to speak to him at some length. I am sure that he has subsequently reported to Your Grace the details of our two meetings.

Professor Chadwick not only conveyed to me your fraternal greetings, but he spoke with evident satisfaction

[7]Chadwick adds, in a letter to the author (1 February 1996): 'I myself thought the most remarkable revelation of my visit was the evident pressure being put on the Pope by conservative English Roman Catholics to cancel the visit to Canterbury (as mixed bathing with heretics and schismatics), and the resistance of the Unity Secretariat to any suggestion of cancellation. Top Cardinals in the Curia reasonably feared that there might be some unscripted confrontation, humiliating the Pope. My assurance that the Archbishop of Canterbury wanted everything agreed in advance reassured them, and the opposition died.'

about the widespread and growing desire for unity that is found throughout the Anglican Communion today. I indeed give thanks to the Holy Spirit, who does not cease to enlighten the minds of the faithful and to guide their hearts according to his purpose.

Professor Chadwick also spoke to me about the actual form that our common ecumenical service in Canterbury might take. In particular we discussed the central action of that service, and it is principally to this question that I wish to make reference in this present letter. Professor Chadwick presented your views and listened carefully to my own. He spoke with great intensity of ecumenical sentiment.

I assured him that, after prayer and reflection, I would send my response to Your Grace. In the meanwhile, I have also had further consultation with some of the Bishops of England, including Cardinal Hume. While appreciating the desire of Your Grace to be able to celebrate the Eucharist on the occasion of my visit, I would rather propose a Liturgy of the Word, in accordance with your alternative suggestion and my own desire to centre the celebration within the context of God's holy word. This Liturgy of the Word would, I hope, emphasize to the whole world our common faith in the divinity of our Lord and Saviour Jesus Christ, as well as the inestimable gift of our common Christian Baptism. It would likewise be evident in the service how much we wish to continue our ecumenical commitment – 'speaking the truth in love' (Eph. 4:15) – to the very end, fulfilling completely the will of Christ for perfect unity. I would further hope that our common veneration of the word of God, expressed in a festive Liturgy of the Word, would be seen as implying the need for a common witness to the demands of the Gospel for charity, justice and peace.

I am entrusting this letter to Bishop Ramón Torrella Cascante, Vice-President of the Secretariat for Promoting Christian Unity, who, I trust, will be able to plan with the appropriate authorities of the Anglican Communion the text of a Liturgy of the Word that could then be submitted to Your Grace and to myself.

I wish also at this time to thank Your Grace for the special concern that you have shown for the suffering people of my homeland. I am truly grateful to you for having asked the prayers and solidarity of the entire Anglican Communion for the Christians of Poland.[8]

In presenting this letter to you, Bishop Torrella will assure you once again of my earnest desire to continue along the path of unity, being guided always by the Holy Spirit.

As I did in the presence of Professor Chadwick, I would now renew my confidence in the powerful grace of God, to whom I offer the expression of our common trust and praise: 'To him who by the power at work within us is able to do far more abundantly than all that we ask or think, to him be glory in the church and in Christ Jesus to all generations, for ever and ever' (Eph. 3:20).

With these sentiments, and looking forward to our meeting in Canterbury, I greet Your Grace once more in the love of our Lord and Saviour Jesus Christ.

From the Vatican, 8 February 1982
[signed] Joannes Paulus PP.II.[9]

Chadwick had spoken to the Pope of Protestant objections to his visit. These had been raised from several quarters during the preceding months. In April 1981, Enoch Powell had written to Runcie, saying he hoped the visit would not compromise 'the royal supremacy and the authority of Parliament'. A letter from the Church of England Evangelical Council expressed fears that 'the Roman Catholic diplomatic and propaganda machine' would attempt to make 'capital' out of the visit. The Free Church of Scotland regretted

[8]Chadwick had mentioned to the Pope that Runcie had spoken about Poland, then under martial law, in his Christmas Day sermon.
[9]I am grateful to the Apostolic Nuncio to Great Britain for permission to quote this letter.

that Runcie proposed to discuss 'relatively trivial' matters with the Pope, and observed that 'the claims of the See of Rome are incompatible with the history of the early church'. And Runcie's successor as Bishop of St Albans, John Taylor, wrote in the parish magazine inset *Home Words*: 'I do not think we need fear that Lambeth will sell our Protestant heritage down the river . . . Nor do I fear that a few days of papal over-exposure will sweep Anglicans unthinkingly into the arms of Rome: the Englishman is too canny to let that happen.' Catholic complaints about Taylor's phraseology were received at Lambeth, and Runcie delicately administered a rebuke.

On 11 March 1982, Runcie was on a visit to Liverpool, and was about to preach in St Nicholas' church to a congregation which included Bishop David Sheppard and the city's mayor, when Protestant demonstrators who had smuggled placards into the church began to make themselves felt. Margaret Duggan takes up the story:

He started to speak, and . . . his theme being Church and State, he touched on the church's earliest history and mentioned Pope Gregory. That started the jeers and cat-calls. He asked for calm and tried to carry on, but the boos and hisses grew louder, and there were shouts of 'Judas' and 'traitor'. After another paragraph or so it was clear that he would not be allowed to speak from his script, so he picked up a Bible and said he would read from it, choosing to read the Beatitudes from the Sermon on the Mount, but he was interrupted by jeers . . . Then . . . he tried to lead the congregation in the Lord's prayer. Even that was raucously interrupted . . . He then said . . . that Christian discussion had become impossible and that all he was now concerned about was that the church should not be further desecrated . . . He left the pulpit to further jeers from the placard-bearers and applause from the congregation . . . He walked up to the altar and knelt before it in silent prayer for several minutes and then, to ever more vindictive abuse, he walked slowly down through the church with members of the congregation reaching out to him all the way to shake his hand.[10]

The demonstration had the opposite effect from that intended, causing most evangelicals in the Church of England, and members of the free churches, to dissociate themselves from such extremism, so that objections to the visit swiftly died down in the remaining weeks before it. But it now began to come under threat from the Falklands war.

As I followed Runcie's public pronouncements on topics other than the papal visit, during 1981 and early 1982, I formed the impression that he had been occupying a somewhat uncertain political position.

During a General Synod debate on disarmament in November 1981, a motion was proposed urging the Government to appoint a Minister for Disarmament. 'The debate,' reported *The Times* (11 November) 'was full of evidence of great concern on the issues of arms control and nuclear weapons', and the loudest applause was for a member who insisted that the Church of England must rapidly make up its mind where it stood. At this point, to some surprise, Runcie got to his feet and made a speech in praise of the Foreign Secretary:

'I want to pay tribute to some of the recent speeches of Lord Carrington,' the Archbishop said, 'such as his initiative in the Middle East, his speeches as president of the Council of Ministers in Europe, and his more sympathetic attention to development policies.'

Dr Runcie recalled that on several recent issues, he had been at odds with the Government. But he went on: 'I believe at this moment we should welcome and support the statesmanlike way the Foreign Secretary wins respect as a genuine seeker for peace and international justice, within the present political realities.'

It was better to back the Foreign Secretary's efforts

[10]Duggan, p. 220.

than to divert attention with a proposal 'which might be merely cosmetic or might seem to be another contribution on the part of the church which is predictable, carping and complaining.'

This *Times* report (by Clifford Longley) said that Runcie's intervention had 'stopped' the debate – the Synod had 'proceeded no further' with the motion that there should be a disarmament minister.

Two months after this, in early February 1982, the Scarman Report on the Brixton riots was debated in the House of Lords. This time Runcie took an implicitly anti-Thatcher stance, stating (in the words of *The Times* report of 5 February) that:

the churches were determined not to abandon the inner city and retreat to suburbia. In the light of the report they would be seeking ways of extending and consolidating Christian work in education, youth, and voluntary services as well as helping to change the maligned stereotype impressions which groups had of each other and challenging the mythologies which had been created.

On 5 February 1982, several newspapers carried the headline 'Time for a black bishop – Runcie.' The *East Anglian Daily Times* reported:

The Archbishop of Canterbury, Dr Robert Runcie, believes it is time the Church of England had a black bishop. Churches had to 'do their bit' in seeing that ethnic minorities were represented in positions of authority, Dr Runcie said in an interview on a BBC TV programme for Asians yesterday . . . He says the Church should achieve more in combating racial discrimination . . . 'Instead of seeing the opportunities that come from having in our midst a rich diversity of people, we constantly see it as a problem. I don't. I see it as an opportunity.'

Yet little more than a month later, on 17 March 1982, the *Church Times* carried a report that Runcie had told a meeting of the National Society that he feared 'that this country's Christian tradition may be sacrificed on the altar of multi-culturalism'. The church must take care not to regard religion as the 'key to good community relations'.

Runcie himself says he does not see any contradiction in these four public pronouncements. In the disarmament debate, he was reacting against what he thought was a silly proposal that there should be a Minister for Disarmament. In the debate on the Scarman Report, he was merely reiterating the church's position. His hope that there would be a black bishop did not imply that Christian teaching in schools should be eroded by multi-cultaralism.

Argentina invaded the Falkland Islands on 2 April 1982, and a British Task Force sailed for the South Atlantic within a few days. On 14 April, Runcie made a speech in the House of Lords supporting military intervention, and he reiterated this in a statement quoted in *The Times* on 3 May:

There are those who believe that the task force should not have been sent to defend the Falkland Islanders from the armed aggression by the Argentine government. I do not hold with that opinion as I said in the House of Lords debate two weeks ago, and believe that within the complexities of an imperfect world, self-defence and the use of armed force in defence of clear principles can sometimes be justified.

The Times added: 'He repeated his call for prayers for all parties concerned, including the Argentines, and emphasized the need to search for a peaceful solution as a result of new British efforts at the United Nations.'

The argument that military action can sometimes be morally justified is an old one within the Christian tradition. Bruce Kent told me that he himself adheres to this 'just war' principle, rather than to strict pacifism, but he believes that, under modern conditions, war can almost always be avoided or postponed because of the possibility of negotiation.

On 8 May 1982 *The Times* published an article under Runcie's name, headed 'The Archbishop of Canterbury brings his statements on the Falkland lslands crisis up to date'. This referred to recent casualties on both sides, including the sinking of the *Belgrano,* but reiterated that Britain would have been 'gravely in breach of our moral duty' if no military action had been taken. The article asserted that the military commanders were in a better position than churchmen to judge what sort of strategy was necessary, and ended by anticipating that the conflict would be settled by 'UN mediation'.

It was a stiffly-phrased article, with none of Runcie's characteristic touches, and it was almost entirely the work of Richard Harries, one of his first Cuddesdon students, who in 1982 was Dean of King's College, London. The draft which he sent to Runcie on 5 May was scarcely altered before publication.[11]

Some newspapers had portrayed Bishop John Robinson (author of *Honest to God,* and now a Cambridge don) as opposed to Runcie's stance on the Falklands. Robinson wrote to assure Runcie that this was not so, and praised the *Times* article. Runcie replied on 11 May: 'I happen to believe that thoughtfulness and the attempt to state a reasonable case – as I attempted to do in *The Times* on Saturday – is better than falling for the temptation to make instant comment or join in self-righteous postering.'

Harries, who subsequently became Bishop of Oxford, sets out his own version of the 'just war' philosophy in his book *Christianity and War in a Nuclear Age* (1986).

[11]Harries has written that Runcie 'has for much of the time been dependent on drafts offered by others. More characteristic of the man we knew at Cuddesdon have been the innumerable "few words" at more informal gatherings, and after dinner speeches. Quite superb have been his short appreciations of General Synod members who were retiring.' *Robert Runcie: A Portrait by His Friends*, edited by David L. Edwards, Fount Paperbacks, 1990, p. 19.

This describes pacifism as a 'healthy' option for those who wish to take an extreme position (he compares it to monastic vows), but argues that the nuclear deterrent contains 'a strange mercy' because it has indeed deterred nations from war. His other books include *Is There a Gospel for the Rich?* (1992), which argues that capitalism and the creation of wealth is morally acceptable to Christians providing that it improves 'the quality of life' for everyone.

The fact that Britain was in military conflict with a Catholic country, Argentina, led the Vatican to state (by 23 May 1982) that the papal visit would have to be cancelled unless there was a ceasefire. This led to mutters at Lambeth about the Pope being under the control of Argentinian fascists, but the British Government now offered to withdraw from official participation in the visit, and the Vatican agreed that it could go ahead on that basis. The Pope landed at Gatwick on Friday 28 May, went to London for Mass at Westminster Cathedral and a private meeting with the Queen, and the next morning flew by helicopter to Canterbury.

Landing on a school playing field, he was welcomed by Runcie and driven into the city. The *Kentish Gazette* takes up the story:

> A great round of applause echoed through the Cathedral as soon as the Pope entered . . . The service was entitled A Celebration of Faith and began with the Cathedral Choirs of Canterbury and Rochester singing anthems . . . The Pope walked in procession with Dr Runcie to the altar in the Nave.
>
> The two men knelt together in silence . . . Afterwards, everyone said the Lord's Prayer before the Pope and Dr Runcie greeted each other with the kiss of peace. In his address of welcome, the Archbishop said: 'This is a service of celebration, but the present moment is full of pain for so many in the world . . . Our minds inevitably turn to the conflict and the tragic loss of life in the South Atlantic,

and we also remember the suffferings of Your Holiness' own fellow countrymen in Poland . . .'

In 597, Dr Runcie said, the Venerable Bede recorded that Pope Gregory sent Augustine . . . to preach the word of God to the English race . . . 'I rejoice that the successors of Gregory and Augustine stand here today in the church which was built in their partnership in the Gospel . . .'

The Archbishop and Pope then moved . . . to the High Altar. The Dean, the Very Rev. Victor de Waal, went . . . to St Augustine's Chair on which were placed the sixth century Canterbury Gospels . . . a gift from Pope Gregory to Augustine . . . The Pope and Primate kissed them . . .

The Archbishop of York, Dr Stuart Blanch, led the first intercession, followed by Archbishop Methodios of Thyateira, the Archbishop of Westminster, Cardinal Basil Hume, and the Moderator of the Free Church Federal Council, Dr Kenneth Greet.

Afterwards, the Pope delivered his 45–minute sermon in slow, but clear English. He said Christ prayed unceasingly for the unity of His Church . . . 'At the same time we are humbly mindful that the faith of the church . . . is not without the marks of our separation . . . My dear brothers and sisters of the Anglican Communion, whom I love and long for, how happy I am to be able to speak to you today in this great cathedral . . .'

The Pope appealed to all at the service, especially members of the Church of England and the Anglican Communion throughout the world, to accept the commitment to which Archbishop Runcie and he pledged themselves anew . . . 'May the dialogue we have already begun lead us to the day of full restoration of unity in faith and love,' the Pope added.

After the sermon, the Archbishop and Dr Greet moved to stand with the Pope for the renewal of baptismal vows . . . Everyone in the congregation followed the Pope's example and kissed their neighbours . . . During this came a moment few people who saw the service will ever forget. As the Pope approached former Primates Lord Coggan and Lord Ramsey there was a glance of recognition when he spotted them. He kissed Lord Coggan first, and then moved on to Lord Ramsey, both men seeming to give each other a great bear hug, and the crowd spontaneously reacted by applauding ...

The focus moved ... to the Chapel of Saints and Martyrs of Our Own Time, where the Pope and Archbishop were joined by representatives of the world-wide Church and placed candles in the seven-branched candlestick, naming a particular martyr ... First to place a candle was the Pope. He named Maximilian Kolbe, a Polish priest who took the place of a fellow concentration camp prisoner who was going to the gas chamber in World War II ... The Archbishop lit a candle for Oscar Romero, the Archbishop of San Salvador, who was murdered in his cathedral the day before Dr Runcie was enthroned ... [Afterwards] Primate and Pope prayed side by side just near the spot where Becket was murdered ...[12]

During the service, they both put their signatures to a Common Declaration, which referred to the publication of the final report of the Anglican/Roman Catholic International Commission, and continued: 'We are agreed that it is now time to set up a new international commission ... to examine ... the outstanding doctrinal differences which still separate us, with a view towards their eventual resolution ...'[13]

Following the service, the Pope met representatives of the British Council of Churches for a meeting which continued over lunch – a considerably abbreviated version of the

[12]*Kentish Gazette*, 4 June 1982.

[13]The most controversial finding of the report, published on 31 March 1982, was that a united church would need to have a universal primate, and that this person should be the Pope. Runcie commented that 'no one should leap to the conclusion that Anglicans are about to accept definitions of papal jurisdiction and infallibility made in the nineteenth century.'

'summit' which Runcie had hoped for.[14] A Catholic report of the proceedings noted that the question was asked, 'How can Church leaders encourage their more cautious followers to discover the deep spiritual communion that many of the leaders experienced?'

After lunch, Runcie persuaded the Pope to take a short rest in the Deanery; *The Times* reported that the Pope had responded to this suggestion: 'In Canterbury a Pope obeys.' He then flew back to London to conduct an open-air Mass at Wembley Stadium. During the remaining four days of his visit he went to Coventry, Liverpool, Manchester, Edinburgh, Glasgow and Cardiff, whence he flew back to Rome, saying goodbye in Welsh. *'A - men.'*

'The papal visit was totally surrounded by the Falklands,' Runcie told me, 'and it was difficult to put my mind to it. But I can remember driving into Canterbury, and the Pope comparing it to Krakow. He talked to me about how far the young people responded to the sort of romantic view that we had of either Krakow or Canterbury. And he talked about Taizé. Meanwhile he was taking it all in, and I remember that when we processed into the cathedral he did't bless anyone in the crowd – he expected me to do the blessing.

'One of the most moving moments of my life was entering the cathedral, and the enormous explosion of welcome and praise which drowned the choir. And I remember how good he was at lunch – and how envious I was of his valet, getting him everything, giving him his comb and that sort of thing. And he was very good with Lindy – he had a word with Lindy. It was a very happy day.

'The Prince of Wales asked whether he could come – he took the initiative, at the last minute, four days before. And he came and sat in the Dean's study, and you could see the

[14]Runcie says that another sort of 'summit' came out of the occasion. 'In the garden at Canterbury I suggested to the Pope that he call a summit of world religious leaders to pray for peace.' This took place at Assisi in October 1986, with Jews, Muslims and leaders of other religions participating as well as Christians.

Pope focusing on who this royal prince was. He hadn't been very well briefed. And Prince Charles was rather overawed, and didn't quite know what to say. It was a slightly awkward conversation. And the Pope was trying to work out how he fitted in – whether he'd come, as the representative of the royal family, to keep an eye on me! And Prince Charles feeling that it was going to be quite a big step to get on to sort of Laurens van der Post territory. So it didn't really gel!

'But the Pope was quite good with the ecumenical leaders, though we tended to misuse the time in pleasantries. And what was interesting was that the Quakers and the Protestants were amazingly deferential, and the man who was really pugnacious was the representative of the Episcopal Church of Scotland, the Bishop of Edinburgh! He asked the Pope some very direct questions about where he intended to take the church. That could have got something going, had we more time.

'Yet it did have a major effect around the Anglican Communion, because the service in Canterbury Cathedral was duplicated all over the world. In Sydney, for example, they had it with the head of the Catholic church in Australia. It created ripples. But it was always dogged by the ordination of women question.'

Meanwhile the Falklands was the backdrop to the papal visit? 'Yes. I was a hardliner, in Christian terms, and therefore I was conscious that I was not the flavour of the month.' I remarked that there had been a substantial piece of ghost-writing on his behalf by another hardliner, Richard Harries in *The Times*. 'Well, you are a writer, Humphrey. I was the holder of an office which required the best way I could manage to express the point of view which I held. Especially that was true under pressure. The use of a wordsmith is, to my mind, not only forgivable but sensible. You talk of "ghosting". I prefer "drafting". I needed to speak a word of authority based on consultation, and composed in the best possible style. Hence I frequently consulted widely, and members of my staff produced drafts. However, at the end of the day I always made myself personally responsible, and believe that I never gave any address on which I didn't lavish real care, and attempted to see that it was consistent with other statements. It would be an absurd caricature to suggest I was a passive plagiarist.'

Two weeks after the papal visit, with the Falklands conflict now over, Runcie issued a statement which included an expression of 'admiration for the courage and dedication of the Task Force'. This evidently pleased Mrs Thatcher, for her office sent him a circular letter which they were issuing to everyone who had written to congratulate the Prime Minister on the British victory. On the bottom she wrote in her own hand: 'I *had* to reply!'

She was, however, reported to be displeased by the planned content of a service of thanksgiving for the conclusion of the Falklands campaign, to be held at St Paul's Cathedral. Alan Webster, the Dean, was reputedly 'keen that the Lord's Prayer should be said in Spanish', to commemorate the Argentinian casualties (*Daily Telegraph,* 17 June), and the *Observer* (11 July) alleged that 'Mrs Thatcher is firmly opposed to any idea of mentioning, let alone remembering, the Argentine dead'.

The service was held on 26 July. Runcie preached the sermon. I could find no preliminary drafts or indication of authorship in the Lambeth files, but I remembered that Richard Chartres had told me that he had supplied a draft.

The sermon begins by giving thanks for 'the courage and endurance' of 'those who fought in the South Atlantic' (British troops are not mentioned specifically), and praises their lack of triumphalism: 'At the hard fought battle of Goose Green the reaction was not the conquerors' triumph, but "thank God it's stopped". It is right to be proud of such men.'

After mentioning the 'grievous losses' in the conflict, the sermon continues:

It is impossible to be a Christian and not to long for

peace ... This was one of the themes to which the Pope repeatedly returned during his visit to this country. His speech in Coventry was particularly memorable when he said, 'war should belong to the tragic past, to history. It should find no place on humanity's agenda for the future.'

I do not believe that there would be many people, if any, in this cathedral who would not say amen to that. War is a sign of human failure and everything we say and do in this service must be in that context ... Yet ... the great nations continue to channel their energies into perfecting weapons of destruction and very little is done to halt the international trade in arms ... War springs from the love and loyalty which should be offered to God being applied to some God substitute, one of the most dangerous being nationalism ...

In our prayers we shall quite rightly remember those who are bereaved in our own country and the relations of the young Argentinian soldiers who were killed. Common sorrow could do something to re-unite those who were engaged in this struggle ...

Ironically, it has sometimes been those spectators who remained at home ... who continue to be most violent in their attitudes ...

This was a clear reference to the *Sun* newspaper's jingoistic coverage of the war. It responded next day. Beneath the headline 'MAGGIE FURY AT RUNCIE'S SERMON: Insult to the heroes', it alleged:

The Prime Minister was last night 'spitting blood' over yesterday's Falklands service at St Paul's. Mrs Thatcher was said to be furious over the 'wet' sermon delivered by the Archbishop of Canterbury. And the controversial remembrance service led some Tory MPs to lash out bitterly at 'pacifists and cringing clergy'. They wanted the service to proclaim Britain's pride in a glorious victory. Instead the MPs saw it as an insult to those who fought and died ... Right-wing MP Julian Amery said angrily: 'The Archbishop would be better giving his service in Buenos Aires than in St Paul's ... Peace and reconciliation should be part of it – but not the whole story. There was no thanksgiving for the liberation of British subjects from the invaders. I thought it was a deliberate counter-attack against the mass of opinion of this country on the part of the pacifist, liberal wets.' ...

After a strenous behind-the-scenes struggle, Mrs Thatcher ... was still not happy with the final form that the service took ... Her husband Denis, when he had a chat and a drink with MPs on the House of Commons terrace after the service ... was said to have told them: 'The boss was angry enough this morning. Now she is spitting blood.'

Several Tory MPs, including Edward du Cann, wrote to Runcie to complain that the service was inappropriate, and the following Sunday, 1 August 1982, the Rev. Dr Edward Norman, Dean of Peterhouse College, Cambridge, and a well-known right-wing commentator on public affairs, contributed an article to the *Sunday Telegraph* in which he alleged that Runcie's sermon had been a 'calculated balancing act' designed to appease those liberals in the Church of England whose 'hatred of "Thatcherite" Conservatism' blinded them to the necessity of the Falklands war.

A Conservative councillor in Liverpool wrote to his MP:

'Is there no way in which Parliament can bring the Church of England to heel and stop it in its divisive liberalism? ... Many people, like myself, who were brought up with a love and respect for our country and what it stands for are becoming increasingly disillusioned and angry with the trendy clerics who seem to prefer to dabble in politics rather than the Bible.'

The MP (also a Tory) passed the letter to Runcie, saying that he agreed with it.

In the following weeks, Lambeth Palace received 244

letters criticising the service and the sermon, and 1,763 praising it, including this one from the Queen's private secretary:

> The Queen has asked me to thank you most warmly for preaching the sermon at St Paul's yesterday for the Falkland Islands Service. It must have been a daunting task for you and Her Majesty was full of admiration for the way in which you met this formidable challenge.

From the beginning of work on this book, I hoped to be able to interview Margaret Thatcher about her opinion of Runcie. I wrote to her late in 1994 asking if I could meet her, but was told by her personal assistant that 'due to her publisher's contract [for her second volume of memoirs] and the restrictions therein, she feels unable to contribute to your work'. A few months later, I met Lord Laing, to talk to him about Runcie, and happened to mention that Lady Thatcher had refused to be interviewed. Laing, a former joint treasurer of the Conservative Party, said at once: 'Has Margaret said no? That won't do. I'll tell her she *must* see you.' He rang me a day later. 'She won't meet you, but she'll speak to you on the telephone, if you ring to book a time.' He gave me the number of her office, and I spoke to the PA, Vivienne Kray, who arranged a date and time for me.

Looking back through my notes, I found that Lord Whitelaw, when I met him to ask about Runcie's army days, had said quite a lot about the Thatcher-Runcie relationship. I had asked Whitelaw if he thought she had any doubts about appointing him Archbishop. 'I should have thought she must have had. They were not compatible figures in any way at all. One has to remember that she has little sense of humour, and therefore if *you* have a sense of humour, you are always slightly suspect with her. Of course, if you're the Archbishop and have a sense of humour, that's even more the case. If she saw Bob and me standing together and laughing – which of course we frequently did – I think she thought, "This Mafia, what are they up to?"'

Above, John Mortimer interviews Runcie in the Runcie's flat in Lambeth Palace, 6 April 1982. *Below*, at the Kent Show, 1982. 'I said once to Jenny Boyd-Carpenter, "I'd like to keep a pig." Now, she was a lady who went into action . . .'

Lindy poses for the *News of the World* (issue of 26 September 1982). 'It was meant to be a serious article,' she says.

Above, Runcie with Hugh Montefiore, Bishop of Birmingham, at the 1985 General Synod. 'He was a great sitter on the fence,' says Montefiore. 'I always felt he would never say or do anything that would imperil his career.' *Below*, on a visit to Northern Ireland, Runcie is accompanied by Richard Chartres (third from left) and Terry Waite. 'Runcie has always gone for strong and distinctive personalities,' says Graham James. 'Terry Waite and Richard Chartres were hardly pushovers!'

Listening to a
debate in
General Synod,
February 1985.

Above left, Lindy conducts the Band of the Scots Guards, with vocal assistance from Terry Waite and Runcie, at a Lambeth Palace garden party, July 1985. *Above right*, Runcie, Waite and koalas in Australia, April 1985. *Below*, Lindy welcomes the Queen to Lambeth Palace, 19 May 1988.

Above, the shape of things to come: Runcie outside the Old Palace, Canterbury, with women deacons after their ordination, 27 February 1987. *Left*, Gareth Bennett in 1985, two years before his suicide following his *Crockford's* preface attacking Runcie. *Below*, Runcie and Pope John Paul II at the Vatican, autumn 1989.

The Runcies at Lambeth, 1988.

Runcie at the Lambeth Conference cricket match, July 1988, after umpiring the Church of England for eight years.

I remarked that Runcie is more conservative than he was popularly supposed to be. 'Well, he might be now,' replied Whitelaw, 'but he wasn't when Margaret was in power. She thought he was a liberal. She had this great thing of "If you're not for me, you're against me." They got on perfectly well when they met, but then she had scrupulously good manners, and was always polite, even though she might be cursing away in the background about some of the things he'd produced.'

Vivienne Kray told me to submit my questions to Lady Thatcher in advance. I consulted Runcie. 'Oh, you're going to speak to the Hacksaw, are you?' he said, and suggested some questions. Then (in late July 1995) I telephoned her.

Lady Thatcher: Hello?

HC: Oh, Lady Thatcher, hello, it's Humphrey Carpenter—

Lady Thatcher (interrupting): I'm afraid I can't help you very much, which is why I didn't offer, because I don't know Lord Runcie anything like the extent that you think I do. And I don't want to be anything other than very nice about him. He's a very nice man. We always had very good relations, and I had of course met him when Dennis and I were dining with the Laings. The Runcies were sometimes there. I don't remember him at Oxford.

HC: You don't remember him there at all?

Lady Thatcher: No, but certainly from the conversations which I've had with him, he's a very, very good mind and an extremely – well, as you'd expect from an Archbishop of Canterbury, a very nice man. A very modest man.

HC: I noticed you didn't mention him in your memoirs.

Lady Thatcher: No, well, there were no great church things during my time.

HC: Did you not feel any sense of the church being in opposition to you, when the press were making out that this was the case?

Lady Thatcher: The press sometimes will make out that that's the case. Then at other times they'll say that the

Church of England is the Conservative Party at prayer. Please understand: I did not read the press day by day.

HC: Could I ask you about the Falklands service of thanksgiving, in July 1982? You'll remember that Lord Runcie's sermon referred to the losses of the Argentineans as well as the British, and he called war 'detestable'. I think you congratulated him afterwards – he says: 'She didn't seem anything other than congratulatory to me.' But Lord Laing says that you did feel angry about the sermon. Do you recall your feelings?

Lady Thatcher: Well, I don't really want to say anything against Lord Runcie. Some people said that you shouldn't celebrate victory. I thought when you were celebrating victory over aggression, you should do it – first you should beat the aggressor, which we did, then you should give thanks for the sacrifices that people had made in order that aggression should *not* prevail. And don't forget that Bob Runcie was a very brave person in the last war, and he was decorated.

HC: But you felt that the emphasis was wrong, in the service and the sermon?

Lady Thatcher: I felt that we didn't give, perhaps, sufficient recognition to *all* of those without whose sacrifice, and the skill with which the campaign was fought, the Falklands would not be free. And I must say that I do think it is right to make it clear that an aggressor shall *never be appeased*. Never! And that was the first time in the post-war period that anyone had actually gone to fight an aggressor, and take back what he, by *evil,* by force, that is to say – had taken someone else's land, and tried to deny the freedom of its people.

HC: So you were not happy about a service that –

Lady Thatcher: You are asking me to make criticisms of Bob Runcie. I thought you would! And this is why I was not prepared to speak to you. I like Bob Runcie. He's a very, very good and honourable man, and I always enjoyed meeting him, and if ever we had genuine differences, they were differences between people who respected one another. And you're asking just exactly the sort of questions which I feared you would.

I had much more to ask Lady Thatcher, who was not such a co-operative interviewee as Runcie. But I will leave her replies to my further questions until later.

One danger of ghost-writing, I had suggested to Runcie when we were discussing the Falklands sermon a year before my phone call to Lady Thatcher, is that it can produce inconsistencies. The tone of the sermon seemed to me quite different from the *Times* article. He disagreed: 'It's all the same line, fundamentally, that I took over nuclear weapons. And although I used Richard Harries, and Richard Chartres, in this respect, I've redone the same sort of thing as recently as the D-Day sermon in Salisbury Cathedral in June this year [1994].' Which he wrote himself? 'Entirely. I've got time to, now.'

I said that Chartres had told me he played a large part in the Falklands sermon. Runcie agreed: 'He certainly did.' I asked him about his choice of ghost-writers, which seemed to me idiosyncratic; I suggested that he could have gone to somebody like Henry Chadwick, a man of immense learning and careful judgement, as opposed to a young and inexperienced figure like Chartres, or the eccentric and unpopular Garry Bennett. 'Henry did give me ideas,' he answered. 'The trouble was that someone who could serve up a complete draft for me proved, under pressure of events, more attractive than the person who could give me seminal points. I used to think, I'm afraid, that if I was going to be available for people, reasonably relaxed and not too tired and screwed up, I had to use a drafted address. Whereas I knew that I could do better myself – not always, but sometimes.' *And they call it the ministry of the Word?*

I said I found the use of ghost-writers very curious. He was one of the most conversationally fluent people I had ever met. After our sessions together for this book, when his remarks were typed out, it was sometimes hard to believe that they had not been written beforehand, so polished did they seem. And yet he claimed to have no self-confidence as a writer.

'It's a curious thing,' he answered, 'because Frances is the first secretary who's ever said to me, when I've had to write a foreword or something, "Just dictate it, and you can tidy it up afterwards." And when she's typed it out, I haven't needed to. It's been a great surprise to me.' Maybe he should have done this all along? 'When I'm confronted with a blank sheet of paper, I'm cautious. I write a sentence, and then alter it because I'm not pleased with it.' Yet paperwork – winning a scholarship and getting a First – had presented little difficulty in his early life. When did the anxiety begin? When he was a curate at Gosforth, for example, did he ever turn to anyone else for advice on what to say when preaching?

'Never!' he answered emphatically. And then, interrupting my next question: 'It never really started until, I think, Richard [Chartres] became my chaplain.' Ah, I said.

'I think that was the moment,' he continued. 'I suddenly found myself with a chaplain who I thought was more intelligent than I was.'

I said I found that fascinating. 'It's the first time I've realised it,' he went on. 'Quite a seminal discovery.'

I remarked, facetiously, on Chartres' physical resemblance to Svengali and Rasputin, and suggested (more seriously) that he was a very powerful person. Runcie agreed: 'Very powerful. He seemed to know what was going on in one's mind. I mean, if somebody had been to visit me, Richard would say four things about that person which I hadn't noticed at all. And for the first time in my life, perhaps, I had an inferiority complex, which I never overcame. Yes, I think that he did have a sort of mastery over me.'

I asked more questions about Chartres' drafting of speeches and sermons, but Runcie interrupted: 'First, I never wanted to be Archbishop of Canterbury. Second, I was very surprised when I was asked to be (I knew that sounds extraordinary). Third, we were having a degree of domestic crisis at the time. So my mind was preoccupied. And it was Richard, really, who convinced me that I could do it, because with him by my side, we would be able to sort of cope.'

I said, could I be cheeky and ask what sort of domestic crisis? 'Well, I think not – unless Lindy talked to you about it herself?' No, I said, she hadn't. 'I don't know whether you've had a really good talk with Lindy?' Runcie asked. I said I would take her out for another lunch.

Can one imagine Ramsey employing 'ghost writers'.

When Runcie addressed the [illegible] conference it was too full of the right [illegible] for Wainwright and others. [illegible] heart [illegible] Lis [illegible].

Will Charles succeed [illegible]?

14

A *very dirty business*

———◆———

But I didn't. For the first time a door had shut in my face and it seemed to be a significant one. The chances of getting Lindy to open it at the drop of a lunch didn't seem high.

'A degree of domestic crisis' sounded like something to do with the marriage. It was hard to imagine anything else that would suddenly make Runcie turn secretive. So I decided to pay another visit to the press-cuttings cupboard at Lambeth. I wanted to find the articles which I knew had appeared in the *Sun* and other tabloids alleging that the Runcies were on the marital rocks.

The first press attack on Lindy that I could find in the files dated from October 1983. In the summer of that year she had appeared in a BBC television programme, *Home on Sunday*, and in a *Sunday Express* article on non-supportive spouses (2 October) a journalist called Anne Edwards had recalled this:

How can a successful man gag a wife who seems hell-bent on making a fool of herself in public, and of him? . . . It cannot have done the Archbishop of Canterbury any good to have his wife explain on the box how much of his official life she found boring, how she detested the socialising where they were invited only because of his position, and how she loved to escape to her real friends.

Jonathan Mantle quotes from a *Times* article which Lindy herself wrote around this time (he gives no date): 'Clergy wives are people too ... So next time you meet one of us, do us a favour and treat us as individuals in our own right, will you?'[1]

The autumn of 1983 saw the publication of Margaret Duggan's *Runcie: the Making of an Archbishop*. A. N. Wilson used the occasion for a sustained demolition of Runcie in the *Spectator* (12 November 1983), mocking him as 'a travel bore' and adding, 'He seems to conceive his function as a sort of ecclesiastical foreign secretary, dashing about the world to attend boring conferences and spending most of his waking hours in airport lounges. Most politicians spend far too much of their time doing this sort of thing. But why should an Archbishop of Canterbury?'

Reading this, I felt that Wilson had a point. The overwhelming impression of Runcie's Archbishopric, apart from its crises, given by the press-cuttings and by Duggan's and Mantle's books, is of international travel. To take a passage almost at random from Mantle:

In late January 1984, the Archbishop, Waite and [John] Witheridge flew on their first overseas trip together, to Uganda ... The purpose ... was to bring encouragement and support to this beautiful and tragically afflicted part of the Anglican communion and to preach at the enthronement of the new Archbishop Yona Okoth near Kampala ... Runcie, Waite and Witheridge also travelled that spring to the West Indies ... The Archbishop gave fifty addresses in one month and travelled 2,000 miles, beginning in Belise and hopping down twelve islands.

[1] Jonathan Mantle, *Archbishop: The Life and Times of Robert Runcie*, Sinclair-Stevenson, 1991, p. 165.

Where is Mrs Runcie?' the local mothers' union would ask . . .[2]

Knowing how much of his retirement Runcie had already chosen to spend abroad, I wondered how much this feature of the Archbishopric had reflected his own taste for journeys, as much as the needs of the job. Could the foreign travel, usually undertaken without Lindy (as this passage points out) but with the supportive male company of his staff, possibly also have been partly motivated by a wish to be away from home?

I was eventually able to bring this up with Terry Waite, who had been responsible for organising many of the journeys. 'Well, I've been looking at the way Carey tears around,' answered Waite when we met to talk about Runcie, 'and I don't think we made as many journeys as he does. What we did at the beginning was say, "How many years have we got before the 1988 Lambeth Conference? Well, in those eight years we ought to try and get to as many parts of the Anglican Communion as possible." And also there were the journeys, organised by Christopher Hill, to churches other than the Anglican Communion – to South India, or the World Council of Churches, the Lutheran churches, and so on; and occasional journeys for other purposes. So when you put all of it together, it looks a tremendous amount.'

Surely a cynic could say it was a way of dodging issues at home, such as the ordination of women? 'The cynics *have* said that,' answered Waite, 'and I think they're wrong. He wasn't rushing to go overseas. He didn't dislike the foreign travel; he threw himself into it. But it was extraordinarily taxing.' Yet it's hard to see what all the journeys achieved, other than a general warming of relations between Lambeth and outlying places. Were there any specific victories? 'I think there were a number of instances of very considerable development. For example, Robert was the first Archbishop

[2]*ibid.*, pp. 179–81.

of Canterbury to visit China – at a time when the Chinese
church was struggling (and still is) to find a new identity
in a country that was gradually beginning to emerge from
the Marxist grip. The church there recognised that they had
to have a very distinctive and unusual relationship with the
state: on the one hand, to go along with certain aspects of
the situation, at the same time to have also a prophetic
ministry. A very difficult balance to achieve, because they
can so easily be seen on the one hand as quislings, and on the
other as extremist, people who just go on smuggling Bibles
in. And I think Robert helped them very considerably. Then
of course there was the Primates' meeting of the Anglican
Communion. I think that had the effect of giving people
from rather remote situations, like Burma, a feeling that they
belonged to a worldwide family.'

The visits certainly didn't achieve cohesion over the ordination of women, because the American Episcopalians and
the Canadians declared UDI in this respect, and ordained
them on their own initiative. 'I don't think it could have
achieved that,' answered Waite, 'given the nature of the
Anglican Communion. It is an association of sister churches,
under the moral and spiritual authority of the Archbishop
of Canterbury, a very different system from the Roman
Catholic church, as you will appreciate. So there was no way
of stopping it. Quite different social conditions in different
countries produce different results.'

After sneering at the foreign trips, A. N. Wilson's *Spectator*
article cited Runcie's shifting attitude to the ordination
of women. Wilson accused him of a 'slithery absence of
principle', giving as another example his statements on
marriage. According to Wilson, in 1981 he had praised
the engagement of the Prince and Princess of Wales as an
example of 'the respect in which the marriage bond is held
[by] the royal family', but two years later 'he appears to be
advocating divorce.' This referred to Runcie's support for the
General Synod's proposals for permitting the remarriage of
certain divorced people in church. In *The Times* (23 October
1983) he was quoted as observing that 'the church . . . found

itself in the midst of an epidemic of marital breakdown, and had a duty to help some of the casualties.' Runcie explains: 'I spent a great deal of time in many speeches and writings during the 1970s on the possibility of holding firm to the principle of lifelong union – and at the same time believing that exceptions should have special treatment. The Catholic and Orthodox churches have dealt with this matter, the one by the concept of "the death of a marriage", the other by "extended nullity", but we had refused to do either of these things. An important principle of moral theology was at stake here.' *[handwritten marginalia]*

There was no mention of Lindy in Wilson's article, but plenty in a *Sunday Times* piece in its 'Relative Values' series (7 August 1983) which featured James Runcie talking about his father, and vice versa. James said:

Before I went to boarding school at 11, we [the family] always had voluntary religion and compulsory music. (My mother's a music teacher.) I remember one Sunday I refused to go to church and everyone said that was fine. They all went off and I felt incredibly lonely. The next Sunday I was in church again . . .

With Christianity, I've wavered from the excessively charismatic to the excessively atheistic. I do believe, but I'm rather a lousy believer, a lazy believer . . . I've never rebelled against my parents. I used to play aggressively loud music and swear a lot when I was about 15 to prove that I didn't go to public school when I did.

I was 16 when my father was asked down to Marlborough to preach. That was excruciatingly embarrassing, because I thought he was going to cock it up . . . In fact he was brilliant . . . From then on I realised how exceptional a speaker he was, and how exceptional a thinker . . .

You may think that when he appears at public functions he's performing, but that's him. His doubt about certain strong political issues, or his difficulties in reconciling certain ideas or moral problems, are expressed totally clearly to everyone. He is presenting himself. He never pretends he can give black-and-white answers to grey problems. Obviously there are times when he's very tired and upset and lonely, rather beaten down by the pressure of work, and yet still there's that life, that ability to understand.

People say, 'It must be fascinating living with the Archbishop of Canterbury.' I say, 'He's not the Archbishop of Canterbury; he's my Dad, and my Dad is the same person.' . . .

When he was offered the job we spent two weeks discussing it with him. Every decision made has been very much a family decision . . .

These days, my father and I tend to talk more about art and literature, philosophy and falling in love. Over Christmas, I went through a very bad patch. My father was so receptive and gave me as much time as was necessary. He dropped things to talk to me and we went for lots of walks. It was wonderful and got me through a rather big depression. He didn't actually say, 'This is what you must do': he just asked the right questions. He helped me far more than anyone else and yet he was extremely busy with the church and bomb debate and other things . . .

I always want him to know where I am. I have this almost paranoiac closeness to him, which is extraordinary. He'll probably say something totally different!

When Runcie was given his turn, he said:

As a religious person I naturally believe that it's important for a child to be brought up with a sense of prayer, but we didn't ever teach James any prayers. I sometimes used to get him to kneel down when I was saying my prayers. There is an immense amount of hypocrisy and artificiality generated when parents feel a duty to teach a child prayers they never say themselves. For me religious education was taking him into church whenever I had some task to do like counting wafers or polishing the chalice – just letting him sit there to get some of the atmosphere of the place. I have always been strong on influence and weak on discipline.

I first became aware of [James] as an individual when we moved to Cuddesdon . . . I was conscious that he was a rather aggressive, quick-tempered character, and I used to wonder sometimes how far it was possible to cope with that directly, or whether it was more important for us just to be ourselves.

I had a friend who was a psychiatrist at Cambridge. We used to talk about the problems I had with students. I remember him saying that it doesn't matter so much if you have explosions between you and your wife in front of your children. He said that was far healthier than shoving arguments into the deep freeze and pretending that they didn't exist. Children are unnerved by artificiality most of all. That comforted me because we were a very open sort of household and there may have been a lot of flaws. Artificiality and contrived harmony was never something of which my wife approved . . .

Because James is gregarious like I am, he once said he might think of being a clergyman, if it wasn't for the difficulties about faith. I respected him and was rather pleased with his honesty. He wants to know about belief and its implications. He's the sort of person who says: 'How can you possibly preach Jesus Christ and support nuclear weapons?' I say it isn't quite as simple as that, and then try to give some theological explanation of support for multilateral disarmament.

A penetrating quickness, which goes along with a quick temper, is what he gets from his mother. He gets from me a love of human exchange and a sense of the dramatic. We often say in our family that my wife has a higher doctrine of justice than forgiveness and I have a higher doctrine of forgiveness than justice.

I test our understanding by the slightly painful things that we both leave unsaid. That is true of his understanding of how I feel about his Christian faith. He wouldn't want to express his disagreement because he respects my point of view. Some of the things which the young do nowadays – if I may put it decently and obscurely – I don't mention, because I know it would be painful for him to have a judgmental father.

James was then aged twenty-four, and working as a trainee theatre director. He later joined BBC Television's Music and Arts department, where he has made some notable programmes.

The next summer, of 1984, saw David Jenkins's election as Bishop of Durham, despite widespread protests from conservative Anglicans about his modernist interpretation of the resurrection and the virgin birth. He was consecrated at York Minster on 6 July. Two days later the minster was struck by lightning and seriously damaged. John Habgood, Archbishop of York, said that it was 'medieval' to regard this as a sign of divine disapproval; Runcie said that God was 'on the side of the men who fought the blaze'.[3]

In September, Britain's coal miners went on strike, and Runcie's first public pronouncement on the dispute was critical of the strikers. Referring to violence at picket lines, he said, in a sermon at Derby Cathedral: 'I have watched with dismay how some have taken law into their own hands and unleashed violence. This lawless behaviour . . . cannot be justified.'[4] A few days later David Jenkins, in his enthronement sermon at Durham, took a very different stance, calling for the resignation of the Coal Board chairman, Ian MacGregor, whom he described as an 'elderly imported American', and attacking the government for its indifference to poverty and social unrest.[5] Runcie was soon making similar remarks, telling *The Times* that he supported the Thatcherite aims of economic growth, higher pay, and

[3] *Sunday Express*, 15 July 1984.
[4] *Sunday Telegraph*, 16 September 1984.
[5] *Daily Telegraph*, 16 September 1984.

the recovery of national pride, but that 'if the human consequences of such aims mean unemployment on an unprecedented scale, poverty, bureaucracy, despair about the future of our communities, inequitable sharing of the sacrifice called for, then the objectives must be called in question'.[6]

Norman Tebbit, Mrs Thatcher's Industry Secretary, described these observations as 'a little woolly', and an unnamed minister added: 'What a cheek Runcie's got. He's been closing down uneconomic churches long before we were closing down uneconomic pits.'[7] Edward du Cann, chairman of the 1922 Committee, described Runcie and Jenkins as 'very naïve'.[8] *Jenkins always seemed to fight who owned gate to a supermarket.*

At Christmas 1984, Runcie gave an interview to Graham Turner of the *Daily Telegraph* in which he discussed Jenkins's demythologising of the New Testament:

In face of the sort of thing [Jenkins] was saying, it was a temptation for some to cluster behind the barricades of the old values, and for others to claim that Jenkins was leading them into a new world where they could retranslate the Christian religion. [Runcie] preferred to hold the middle ground 'where we have to attend to the *whole* Christian story . . .'

He recognised Dr Jenkins as a believing bishop, said Dr Runcie, 'but I think he's unfortunately' – and he hesitated, wanting to chose his words delicately – 'had my experience of being pushed out of one world into another and realised, painfully, that it's different.' Was he, I wondered, implying that the Bishop of Durham, having moved from a university . . . had rather let it go to his head? It seemed kinder not to inquire.

And what about Dr Runcie's wife, Rosalind? She had a reputation for being rather wild and unreligious, was she

[6]*The Times*, 7 October 1984.
[7]*Daily Mail*, 9 October 1984.
[8]*Daily Telegraph*, 9 October 1984.

a help or a hindrance to him? A tremendous help, replied the Archbishop. She, too, was reticent about her faith – he'd often watched her eyes grow leaden when someone was making a religious speech – but she had a very real one, and she did him a lot of good by cringing at any sort of pretentious piety. Their marriage was 'just splendid', nothing could ever break it up. On Christmas Day, the whole family would be taking Communion together, and it was genuine, and that genuineness made him happier than anything else.

As we said goodbye, I thanked the Archbishop for being so candid. 'I do try,' he replied with a faint smile, 'but I expect I shall suffer for it. Still, that's what we're here for, isn't it?' In a personal letter after our talk, Dr Runcie added a postscript in his own hand: 'Spare a prayer for me that I may speak with simplicity and wisdom at Christmas.' That, too, is the authentic Runcie.[9]

Four months later, in his 1985 Easter Day sermon in Canterbury Cathedral, Runcie took a firmly traditional theological line (reported in the *Daily Telegraph*):

The Archbishop of Canterbury, Dr Robert Runcie, yesterday made a personal declaration of his faith in the Gospel accounts of the Resurrection . . . Dr Runcie made no direct reference to the Bishop of Durham in his Canterbury sermon, but told the congregation that the Gospel stories were based on 'first-hand memory and firm tradition'.[10]

Private Eye printed its own version of this, beginning '"I BELIEVE IN GOD": ARCHBISHOP'S SHOCK CLAIM.' The cartoonist Cummings, in the *Daily Express*, interpreted Runcie's theological position rather differently, depicting him trundling into 10 Downing Street in a mobile pulpit, and saying to Mrs Thatcher: 'As we've taken up politics

[9]*ibid.*, 23 December 1984.
[10]*ibid.*, 8 April 1985.

because we don't know anything about God any more, can we mediate between you and Mr Kinnock?'[11]

He was now becoming a regular target for mockery in the right-wing popular press. When in March 1985 he compared Britain's inner city problems to the Ethiopian famine ('We do not have to look as far as Ethiopia to find the darkness of disease and death') the *Daily Express* headed its leader 'Some silly words from Dr Runcie',[12] and a Cummings cartoon showed Runcie in the pulpit of a crumbling ecclesiastical edifice, labelled 'Church of England', saying: 'We certainly don't have to look as far as Ethiopia to find the darkness of disaster – it's here on our doorstep!' The building is already going up in flames, ignited by David Jenkins, who is clutching a large matchbox.[13] The *Star* described Runcie's comparison with Ethiopia as 'Clerical claptrap'.[14]

However, the religious affairs correspondent of *The Times*, Clifford Longley, published an article headed 'Myth of Thatcher-Runcie quarrel':

> More headlines of the 'Runcie attacks Thatcher' variety may be confidently predicted in September, if not before. In that month the Archbishop's Commission on Inner Urban Areas will report . . . Dr Runcie . . . dealt with inner-city poverty in a sermon in St Paul's on March 6. He has since let it be known that he did not think he was attacking [Mrs Thatcher], and the Prime Minister has let it be known that she did not feel attacked . . .
>
> There are several right-wing Conservative MPs who are glad to oblige the Press with an insulting comment on almost everything Dr Runcie says or does . . . but the Prime Minister and the Archbishop of Canterbury have jointly decided to try to kill off the three-year media myth that they are sworn enemies (they had lunch recently).
>
> But it will not die so quickly, especially as some parts of

11*Daily Express*, 15 February 1985.
12*ibid.*, 7 March 1985.
13*ibid.*, 8 March 1985.
14*Star*, 8 March 1985.

the Press have evidently taken a dislike to the archbishop and will not want to let go too quickly one of the journalistic formulae that enables them to express it . . .'[15]

Longley observed that 'the nice people who staff church press offices' lacked 'the rarefied skills of higher news management', which he described as ultimately 'a very dirty business'.

A few weeks later, in a magazine profile, Runcie observed: 'Some of my predecessors have been polished off in different ways: one of them was beaten to death by mutton bones. I think I'm more likely to be battered by the media.'[16] Longley's prediction, that the Church of England report on the inner cities, *Faith in the City*, would reinforce the myth that Runcie was attacking the government, proved correct when it was published (later than expected, in December 1985). Under the headline 'Church report "marxist"', the *Sunday Times* (1 December 1985) stated that the government was preparing 'a strong counter-attack' on the report, which an unnamed cabinet minister had described as 'pure marxist theology'.[17]

The Commission on Urban Priority Areas had been instructed by Runcie, when he appointed it in the autumn of 1983, to 'look into ways in which the Churches can more effectively help those who live and work in our inner cities'. *Faith in the City* called for an increase in child benefit, positive measures against racial discrimination in employment and housing, the raising of the rate support grant, and an inquiry into mortgage tax relief on the grounds that it was unfair to subsidise the better off. These mildly left-wing proposals led even *The Times* (2 December) to headline them 'Church and state launched into new public quarrel'.[18] The *Observer* stated: 'C of E defies Thatcher again'.[19]

I raised the matter of *Faith in the City* in my telephone conversation with Lady Thatcher:

[15]*The Times*, 18 March 1985.
[16]*House Magazine*, 14 June 1985.
[17]*Sunday Times*, 1 December 1985.
[18]*The Times*, 2 December 1985.
[19]*Observer*, 1 December 1985.

Lady Thatcher: Faith in the City was very different from the later report of the Jewish community on *their* approach.

HC: Different in what way?

Lady Thatcher: The Jewish community, as you know, always stuck together, they always made a tremendous effort, they always look after their own, they never asked for – well, you go and read it!

HC: But you felt that *Faith in the City*, the Church of England report, was turning to the Government, and saying, 'You must do all the work'?

Lady Thatcher: Well, those are *your* words. I think it's a document that could have been written very differently.

HC: Lord Runcie was talking to me about this, knowing that I was going to be speaking to you, and he said that he feels, looking back, that the Government, or some people in the Government, did make rather a fuss about *Faith in the City*, but he said it started them on Michael Heseltine's inner city initiative.

Lady Thatcher: But the inner city initiative was long before *Faith in the City*. When did it come out?

HC: At the end of 1985.

Lady Thatcher: I think you'll find we were doing things in the inner cities long before that. Just check it up as a matter of fact.

HC: The other thing that he mentioned is the press campaign – it was scarcely a campaign, but you will, I'm sure, remember there was quite a lot of—

Lady Thatcher (interrupting): Incidentally, let me point out, you've still got problems in the inner cities. You look in today's papers. I've just been looking at some of the cuttings, at some of the council estates. The problems in the inner cities go back, I think, to putting people all together on those council estates, gradually getting a lot of people there, all of whom had the same problems.

HC: But did you feel the church was in any way interfering, by making that report?

Lady Thatcher: No, no. Look, I don't try to restrict what other people say. What we were doing was creating the wealth necessary to help many people out of poverty, and give them opportunities they wouldn't have had. And don't forget that in a way we won the ideological battle of the century. Don't forget the state of Britain when I took it over, as Prime Minister. Don't forget that. No one should. You just should remember what we actually did – pulled up the standards of living of Britain, gave many people a chance to own both capital or housing, property that they would never otherwise have possessed.

The press's stirring-up of supposed animosity between church and Government was nothing compared to the series of allegations about the Runcies which had begun to appear in August 1985. The *Star* led the way. Under the headline 'Family stir down at Lambeth Palace' it accused the Archbishop and his wife of 'living almost separate lives':

'She is rarely seen in Canterbury,' says our source there. 'On most occasions the Archbishop comes here alone.' Lindy stays on at Lambeth or in St Albans. She has constantly refused to kow tow to church authority, saying: 'Too much religion makes me go pop.' . . . Three years ago Mrs Runcie caused a stir by posing for a series of strange photographs which were little short of 'glamour' shots. In one she was draped across a grand piano. Another photograph shows her posing in a swimming costume.

The only reason she is with the Archbishop on part of his tour, we are told, is because she has been asked to play the piano in a number of concerts for charity. Otherwise, there is little doubt that she would not have gone.

Unlike their predecessors, the Coggans and the Ramseys, the Runcies are certainly not in the conventional devoted mould. But while close associates say their marriage is hardly a warm partnership, the union is unlikely to be rent asunder. Official separation is probably out of the question. 'I expect they will soldier on,' said one friend. 'At one stage there was a bit of a crisis. But I think they have learned to cope with the idea of leading separate lives and the relationship has become more mellow. It's rather sad, but in their own way they're making the best of it.'[20]

The *Star* had not printed any of the photographs referred to, which were published in *Sunday*, the magazine section of the *News of the World*, on 26 September 1982. The cover of the magazine shows Lindy in white tennis clothes, leaping exuberantly in the air on a tennis court, and is captioned: 'Meet the incredible Rosalind Runcie'. Inside, the article about her (chiefly an account of her childhood), is illustrated with shots of her playing croquet, ice skating, roller skating, drying her hair, and in a swimming costume (apparently a badly focused family snapshot). The article is preceded by a double page spread, captioned 'THE LADY LOVES TO PLAY', in which she is shown in a full-length red evening dress lying on top of a Bechstein grand piano, her face (with a half smile) turned towards the camera.

The *Star* printed a follow-up story next day, stating that its 'disclosure' about the Runcies' marriage was 'causing reaction within the Church' and that at present Runcie and Lindy were 'on holiday in Europe discussing the difficulties of their complex situation'.

The next day the *Daily Express* carried an angry denial of this from James (who was now a BBC radio producer) and the following Sunday, the *People* ran an 'exclusive interview' with him, in which he began by stating: 'Someone in the Church of England does not like my mother's independent way of life . . . I don't know who it is in the Church who resents my mother having her own career but it is about time they realised this is 1985. If they want her to behave like a vicar's wife of the 1870s they should pay her to do so.'

Two others were quoted by the *People*. Canon Michael Moore, formerly on the Lambeth staff, said: 'It cannot be good for any organisation if it is known or even thought that the man at the top has domestic difficulties.' Norman St John Stevas, described as 'a long-time friend of the Runcies',

[20]*Star*, 14 August 1985.

stated: 'The Runcies have a simply wonderful marriage – it is the best marriage I know.'

Nothing further about the marriage appears to have been published during 1985, but in September, *Woman's Realm* carried an article by Runcie about the church's attitude to marriage and divorce, in the course of which he wrote:

> Every marriage has its incompatibilities. Every couple has its ups and downs. But what people must understand is that very often by getting over the hump and working through the problem, you can produce a richer relationship. Some of the deepest experiences of life come not so much from neat harmonies but from something askew that is worked through together. You come out the other side feeling you've learnt something about yourself, about each other and the nature of your marriage.[21]

The press remained silent about the Runcies' private life for the first nine months of 1986; nor were their any further allegations about conflict between Lambeth Palace and Downing Street.

I raised the matter of the press nurturing a church and state conflict with Lady Thatcher.

Lady Thatcher: I think you think I take more notice of the newspapers than I do.

HC: Well, Lord Runcie said that Jim Prior said to him, 'She' – meaning you – 'could have called off that attack.'

Lady Thatcher (in her most emphatic manner): Is anyone suggesting that I could tell the press what to print?

HC: I think Lord Runcie felt that a word in the ear of David English [editor of the *Daily Mail*] might have had quite an effect.

Lady Thatcher: I did not read the newspapers day by day. I saw a digest. And I have never told the newspapers what to print. If they were doing things which were putting people's

---

[21] *Woman's Realm*, 14 September 1985.

lives at risk, then of course we had a D Notice provision. I don't think I ever interfered with the freedom of the press. Heaven knows, if anyone suffered from it, it was me!

The press campaign was renewed a year later. On 20 October 1986 the *Sun* front page carried the banner headline 'RUNCIE'S MARRIAGE SPARKS CHURCH CRISIS!' and quoted 'Senior Church of England men' as saying 'that unless the pair start acting like a proper married couple, Dr Runcie may have to consider quitting his post as head of the Church'.

The *Star* printed a similar story the next day. Though it was spread over five pages, it contained only one fresh allegation, from a Lambeth Palace gardener and his wife: that Lindy had taken clippings of plants for her garden at St Albans, and had bought a pair of secateurs on the Church Commissioners' account at the Army & Navy Stores.[22]

A day later the *Guardian* reported that the Runcies had issued a statement denying reports that their marriage was on the rocks:

> Dr Robert Runcie and his wife said they had been 'a happily married couple for nearly 30 years and we both look forward to our rewarding partnership continuing for the rest of our lives'. The reports were condemned as 'scurrilous, baseless and offensive' by the House of Bishops, convened to tackle a crisis involving the Bishop of London over church jurisdiction.

The article then turned to this other crisis:

> The bishops censured the Bishop of London, Dr Graham Leonard, for his recent offer to take a deposed Anglican priest under his wing ... Dr Leonard had offered 'help and communion' to the parishioners of St Michael's in Tulsa, Oklahoma, whose parish priest, Father John Pasco, had been deposed by his bishops. The American bishops

[22] *Star*, 21 October 1986. This referred to the garden of the house they bought in St Albans when Runcie became Archbishop. It was subsequently sold to James.

had described Dr Leonard's interference as 'deplorable, destructive and irresponsible'. Father Pasco is, like Dr Leonard, a traditionalist, strongly opposed to women priests, and to male priests who question the literal truth of the Virgin Birth and the Empty Tomb.[23]

Hugh Montefiore had written to me about what he called 'the Tulsa Affair' some while earlier in my researches, enclosing his own account of it in his Birmingham diocesan newsletter, just after it had blown up:

If I were asked: 'What has been the most dangerous development in the Church of England during your active ministry?', I think I would have to answer: 'The Tulsa Affair . . .'

Tulsa is a city situated in Oklahoma, a diocese of the Episcopal Church of the United States of America (ECUSA) . . . In 1978 the Rev. John Pasco signed an application in the name of St Michael's [his church] whereby he obtained from ECUSA $50,000 for the purchase of land and the erection of a building, and appropriated that money to St Michael's Church Foundation, over which . . . ECUSA has no jurisdiction. In 1984, when this was discovered . . . the Bishop removed Mr Pasco . . . [and] brought charges against him in the Diocesan Ecclesiastical Court based on his 'fraudulent acts'. Mr Pasco refused to attend his trial, and was convicted unanimously on all counts . . . The Bishop of Oklahoma deposed Mr Pasco from the ministry of the Episcopal Church.

There is no reason to doubt that Dr Graham Leonard, the Bishop of London, has a genuine pastoral concern for the people of St Michael's Tulsa [who had supported Pasco] . . . He issued a statement to the effect that he would take them under his protection, acting not as Bishop of London but as a Bishop of the universal Church . . . The House of Bishops of ECUSA reacted strongly. No

[23]*Guardian*, 22 October 1986.

doubt there were some historical factors involved. Way back in 1634, the Bishop of London ... was given jurisdiction over English congregations resident in foreign countries including America; and this lasted until the War of Independence ...

On September 25th [1986] the Bishops [of the Church of England] took unprecedented action. Upon the receipt of news about the Bishop of London's proposed visit [to Tulsa], they issued a unanimous statement: '... We regard ... [Dr Leonard's] activities [as] deplorable, destructive and irresponsible ...'[24]

Later, the Archbishop [of Canterbury] had an interview with the Bishop of London and expressed his disapproval of a visit to Tulsa. But the Bishop went, and confirmed 24 candidates ...[25]

When I received this article from Montefiore, I wrote to ask whether he thought there was any connection between the Tulsa affair and the smear campaign against the Runcies. He answered:

I certainly heard rumours of a tie-up between Anglo-Catholics, the media and the government at those times when there was a concerted media effort to make things too hot for Bob and Lindy. However I never was given a shred of evidence to back this up. I think that you should ask Bob about it; and I will tell you why.

For some reason I was admitted to an inner counsel at Lambeth Palace held before a meeting of the House of Bishops: it consisted of the Archbishops, the 'Prince Bishops' [Winchester, Durham and London] and myself (I was said to be included because I was chairman of the Board for Social Responsibility). On one occasion when there was a nasty press campaign, I remember saying: 'Archbishop, can't we do anything to help you?' Bob

[24]Graham Leonard says it was not quite unanimous; the Bishop of Edmonton (Brian Masters) voted for Leonard, and the Bishop of Chichester (Eric Kemp) abstained.
[25]*The Bishopric*, December 1986.

paused a long time before answering, and then said 'No', and as we were going out he said to me that he daren't say anything else because the Bishop of London was present.

I said that surely he hadn't been party to the efforts to get rid of him. He said, no, but Leonard was in touch with people who were. [Graham Leonard comments: 'Who? I do not know of any.'] However next morning there was that awful story in the tabloids about Lindy lying on a grand piano,[26] and as Bob came into the House of Bishops, he passed me a note saying that he had changed his mind. He must have done the same to others, because the Bishop of Winchester, I think it was, (John Taylor), who composed and proposed a strong statement of support for the Archbishop, which was passed by the House of Bishops and published.

The statement by the House of Bishops was carried in the *Daily Telegraph* on 22 October 1986: '. . . the House of Bishops took the unusual move of publicly criticising attacks on the Archbishop and Mrs Runcie, condemning them as 'scurrilous, baseless and offensive'.

The following weekend the *Mail on Sunday* published this story:

RUNCIE TARGET OF WHISPERERS

A bitter Church of England row over women priests is thought to be behind last week's allegations about the Archbishop of Canterbury's marriage. Some opponents of the ordination of women are believed to have been conducting a whispering campaign against Dr Robert Runcie and his wife Rosalind. They are angry because they think Dr Runcie is too sympathetic towards those campaigning for women priests.

Last week's stories . . . are not new. In August last year,

[26]In fact this had been published in 1982, but smear stories about the marriage were appearing during the Tulsa crisis.

an almost identical story appeared in the *Star* ... the day before a new organisation opposing the ordination of women was launched and coincided with the beginning of a crucial election campaign for the Church's General Synod.

This year, the same allegations surfaced just a week before the House of Commons is due to vote on a Synod motion backing the idea of women deacons ... Tory MP Peter Bruinvels, a member of the General Synod, said: 'This has got something to do with the ordination of women.'[27]

The conspiracy theory seemed plausible. But should one therefore dismiss all the allegations about the marriage, and the recognisable echoes, in some of the press reports, of Runcie's words to me – the unnamed friend who had recalled 'a bit of a crisis' at one stage in the marriage – and Runcie's own allusion, in his *Woman's Realm* article, to 'something askew'?

I arrived in St Albans in November 1994 armed with notes on the cuttings about the marriage, feeling distinctly nervous about tackling such a sticky subject. When Runcie answered the door, he surprised me by saying: 'Lindy will make you a cup of coffee.' She was not only there (unusual for a weekday morning in term time) but didn't seem in a hurry. I asked if she had time to sit down in front of the tape recorder. 'Not really. I want to take three cracked eggs back to Sainsbury's and complain to the manager.' But I persuaded her.

I asked how the grand piano photograph in the *News of the World* had come about. 'Well,' she answered, 'it was meant to be a serious article, and somebody else got hold of it, I don't know how.' But how did the photographer persuade her to lie on the piano? 'He was a friend – I wouldn't have done it otherwise – and it was going to be a serious thing about my life.' How did she come to know him? 'He was a journalist

[27]*Mail on Sunday*, 26 October 1986.

here, in St Albans. It was meant to be very serious.' Runcie made a sceptical face at this.

I asked whether she had contemplated legal action when the press began to publish insinuations about the marriage. 'I couldn't sue at first (though I was terribly upset, as you can imagine), until it came to some things that I was purported to have said, in quotes. Then I sued, because I had never said them. I was supposed to have said awful things about Princess Diana. She and Prince Charles came for a wedding talk, and I had kids taking piano exams that day, and there was a state banquet in the evening, and I couldn't go to the exams the day before, because there was a Church of England Children's Society fete, or something, that I had promised to do something at. So Buckingham Palace were rung up and asked if they minded if I wasn't there at the lunch. And Prince Charles said, "The children's exams are more important than I am." He was very nice about it. So I left at six o'clock in the morning, to teach these kids before the exams. I got to St Albans at eight, and after the exams I went and had my hair done for the banquet, and I saw Prince Charles there, and he said, "I hope the children did well." Well, they all got distinctions, actually. But allegedly I had refused to have lunch with Princess Diana, and as she arrived for it, I supposedly swept out of the house saying, "I really can't be bothered to talk to that frivolous girl." Well, I know who said that.' She named the wife of a member of the Lambeth staff, who she said had not been allowed to wait at table.

What about the gardener and his wife who had reported her for buying secateurs at the Army & Navy? 'And plants!' Lindy responded. 'They'd never seen our little garden. I have a good friend called Graham Bridgstock, who now I think writes for the *Evening Standard*. He used to take me out to lunch, and I said, "If anybody could bother to come and see the garden, it's mostly paving, and it's twenty-one yards by seven!" It was ridiculous.'

I asked if there had been a gossipy, slightly bitchy atmosphere at Lambeth. Lindy alleged that two people in particular 'were determined to have us both out on the street. And my lawyer said, "They're not really going for you, they're going for Robert," which made me feel worse.'

Eventually she sued the *Star*. 'I wanted an open apology, and damages to a charity of my own choice, and my legal expenses paid. And then of course came more filth, because they tried to stop me by frightening me.' By printing more of it? 'Yes. "Twenty Things You Don't Know About Rosalind Runcie." Drinking in the kitchen – "Tiddly as a newt." And lifting my skirt above my head to show the shocked maids my suntan.' (Runcie laughed at the idea that they had had maids.) 'And my language would shock a stevedore. And I love men. I surround myself with men, young men, and rich men. And going to gay sleazy night clubs with my homosexual friends.'

'You've got a lot of homosexual friends,' remarked Runcie in response to this.

'Of course I've got a lot of homosexual friends,' his wife replied. 'Why shouldn't I?'

'Much to your credit now,' Runcie agreed, slightly sarcastically.

'Jeffrey Archer did me a good turn,' continued Lindy, 'because his libel thing got in before mine – I don't know how, because it happened after – and he won half a million, and I think they got a bit ratty, because I said, "I want to see, in court, whoever said that I'd said these things." Nobody wanted to show their face.' How much did the charity get when she won the case? 'Well, first of all they offered two thousand pounds. And I said, "If you think I'm going to take that, it's insulting." And then it came to five thousand, and I said, "Well, I've proved my point, I'll take that." But my lawyer said, "We can get a bit more, I think." So then it went up to eight thousand five hundred, and we wouldn't settle. Because the apology was going to say "She may have suffered embarrassment", and I said, "Not may, *did*." And it went up to ten thousand pounds. There's an extremely nice statue in Lambeth Palace garden, a mother and a child. That's what the *Star* paid for.' The statue cost ten thousand? 'By the time we'd put it up. It was eight thousand plus the putting up. It was done by a very nice girl, Emma Pova or something like that, and it's a lovely statue, bronze. Frightfully expensive.' She wanted that rather than an actual charity? 'That was my charity, the Lambeth Palace garden. Because I was raising money for it at that time, and it's open for charity.'

I mentioned that the second batch of press insinuations was just as the Tulsa business had blown up. 'Oh, that,' answered Lindy. 'We came back from the States, having had a fabulous holiday with friends, and there was all this about our marriage being in ruins, and James didn't have us there to field it. It was so awful when I read it at the airport that I had a double brandy. We'd stayed three weeks with friends in the States. Now, if you've got an unhappy marriage, you can deceive somebody for about two days when you're staying with them, and then the tension starts – I've seen it with other people. Three weeks, laughing and joking – I mean!

'I have raised over a million pounds for charity playing the piano. You don't do that staying in Lambeth Palace. I thought that, married to somebody famous, I could use his name and make money for all these charities. Most weekends I had been booked out two years ahead to play in concerts. All right, that's separate lives, if you like, but it isn't really.'

I said that my eye had been caught by the remark by somebody unnamed: 'I expect they will soldier on, but at one stage there was a bit of a crisis. But I think they've learned to cope with the idea of leading separate lives.' Lindy began to make guesses as to who had said this. I asked if the reference to 'a bit of a crisis' might have had some basis in truth (Runcie himself had used similar words to me).

'I was extremely unhappy at Lambeth at first,' answered Lindy. 'They were rewiring it for three and a half years. The dirt and everything else was dreadful. I did actually run away at the beginning. Because we were in this tiny little flat – our flat wasn't ready. So I went and stayed with a woman friend who lives in Hereford Square.' How long was she away? 'Oh, about a week. I came back, but I thought, I want to get away from this. Do you blame me?' But this could have been remembered by certain people, and interpreted as her walking out on Robert? 'Yes, perhaps.'

I mentioned what Runcie had said about Richard Chartres' influence on him. Did that worry her? 'I thought he was fabulous. He was the kindest man. He helped me when I was doing my A Levels, with my essays.' I said I had no idea she had done A Levels. 'I did my Italian A Level when we were at St Albans. Because Robert said I had one of the most acute untrained minds he'd ever met. So I thought, well, I'll try and learn Greek. There was nobody to teach it, but there was an Italian who taught at St Albans High School. So I was allowed to join the lower sixth for O Level. And in the upper sixth you did A Level in one year. My God, it nearly killed me! Five set books, and the vocabulary. And Richard helped me. And he said, "This is a very good essay, but you haven't actually answered the question." So I wrote it again. He said, "This is not such a good essay" – because I found Fascism so boring – "but you have answered the question." And I respected him.'

I reminded Runcie that he had talked of 'having a degree of domestic crisis' when he was being offered the Archbishopric. What did this mean?

Runcie: Well, there was a—
Lindy (interrupting): I didn't want to go.
Runcie: Yes, that was the thing.
HC: That was all? You made it sound terribly mysterious.
Lindy: I loved being here [St Albans]. And I just thought, why should I bother with all this? Because I would not go to York. And I said to Robert, 'If you really want to go to Lambeth, I will go with you. But you know *I* don't.'
HC (to Runcie): Why did you consider this to be something that you shouldn't tell me on Lindy's behalf?
Runcie: I think that there was, for the first time, and the last time, really, a degree of Lindy having buddies who were closer to her than I was. Because she needed support for herself, as somebody who was reluctant to come.
HC: You felt she was crying on other people's shoulders?

Runcie: That's right.

Lindy: That's such an isolated position to be in. You're right up there, and you daren't talk to anybody.

Runcie: The thing is that – how shall I put it? – in retrospect you realise how lonely Lindy must very often have been. After all, there weren't too many people to whom she could talk when I was busy, either at Cuddesdon, or at St Albans. I think that made for a degree of estrangement. Here's me thinking that this is the greatest decision of my life; and here's somebody lamenting the loss of piano pupils. That's the sort of scale of the thing.

I asked whether, looking back now over the Lambeth years, it was worth it in the end? Lindy admitted, 'It seems like a sort of fairy story now. We met wonderful people, and we had lots of lots of lovely dinner parties; people asked us to marvellous things. I thought the moment we left there, they would never speak to us again. But a lot of them still ask us out, and that's rather nice.' Runcie added, 'We're going to have lunch with the Queen Mum. And I've just been invited to John Birt's Christmas drinks.'

Lindy was indignant, 'You've been invited and not me again?'

Some months later, when looking through Garry Bennett's papers, I came across a Christmas card from the Runcies, which presumably dates from December 1986, a few weeks after the second round of press insinuations about their marriage. On the front was a photograph of them both standing together, smiling. Inside, Runcie had written: 'Apologies for the pagan card – to convince the doubters.'

15

Liberal subjectivist?

I thought it was time to write to Graham Leonard. He replied on 17 November 1994, from the address not far from Oxford, where he lives in retirement:

> I appreciate your invitation to talk about Robert Runcie for your biography of him. I must say that I would prefer not to do so, especially when he is still alive. What I would have to say would not be uncritical. We differ a good deal on some principles, especially the relationship between authority and freedom. I do not want to be unhelpful and I am willing to talk. I would, however, want there to be a clear understanding that you distinguish between material which I would provide for you to use and direct quotations of anything I might say, the latter being only included with my agreement. If you are happy to talk on this basis, I would suggest that you telephone to arrange a time.

Runcie had described Leonard to me as 'a jolly sort of youth chaplain kind of man in his early days. He was at Balliol and he married the daughter of a Fellow of Caius. She used to genuflect when he processed past her in church as Bishop of London, which was an embarrassment to Henriette Santer and Sally Thompson,[1] who stood bolt upright!

'I think he thought he could have done the job of Archbishop much better, and in a way that's true! Because he would have taken all the small print very much more seriously. I wanted him to give time to the House of Lords, but although he doggedly argued his way there, he never endeared himself to them as did Gerald Ellison [Leonard's predecessor as Bishop of London]. He built up with Garry Bennett the myth that I headed the Liberal Establishment.'

I asked about Leonard's own social background. 'Well, I should have thought slightly better than mine. He was an army officer in the war, and a scientist at Balliol.'

I met Leonard on 29 November 1994.

His house is superficially much like the Runcies – plain and modern, in a suburban-style side-street – but the study to which he led me reminded me more of my father than of Runcie. Leonard smokes a pipe, as my father did; his shelves are crammed with the sort of theological books that my father had. His public image as Bishop of London and unofficial leader of the hard-line Anglo-Catholics was both flamboyant and authoritarian. The person I now met, on the other hand, seemed a quietly conventional Anglican clergyman – though he is now a Roman Catholic.

From the outset, he was friendly, relaxed and chatty. He had his own recording machine ready, and switched this on when I switched on mine, as Tony Benn is said always to do, to guard against misquotation; but he alluded to this in a slightly embarrassed fashion: 'It just helps me because afterwards I forget what I've said.'

I began by asking when he first became aware of Runcie. 'When he was at St Albans. Not before then.' Which theological college had he himself been at? 'Westcott. That's one of the problems. He's too much Westcott.' Too much the liberal

---

[1] Wives of Mark Santer and Jim Thompson, then suffragan bishops in the diocese of London.

side of Westcott? 'It's not quite that. My time at Westcott, which was after I'd come out of the army at the end of the war, was really the only unhappy time of my life. What really got under my skin was the Westcott syndrome – "We don't have any rules, but this is what we all do." Particularly coming from the army, where you knew what the rules were, it came across to me as a kind of moral blackmail; the club mentality. You know my Tulsa expedition?'

Absolutely, I answered. And I wanted to talk about it. 'I'm sure you do! When I came back, there was a press conference, and one of the journalists said, "Have you broken the law?" And I said, "No, I've upset the club."[2] And this was one of the things which got under Bob Runcie's skin. The House of Bishops, when I was in it, was run very much like that – very much the Westcott syndrome.'

And yet, I said, Runcie himself was made very uncomfortable by the Westcott syndrome. 'Really? I never knew that.'

I asked Leonard when he felt that he and Runcie had diverged. 'Well, I became Bishop of Willesden in 1964, and went to Truro in 1973. He became a diocesan first. And then he'd already gone to Canterbury when I went to London. We got on perfectly well personally; we enjoyed meeting each other. But I never knew what line he was going to take over anything. And he always seemed to me to confuse fundamentals and fundemantalism, which are quite different things. He always seemed to me to take the line that, if you accepted any degree of fundamentals or absolutes, this would automatically mean that you would try and ram them down people's throats. That's exactly the opposite to what I've always thought, which is that it's precisely when you know you are living under judgement that you are able to have some degree of sensitivity towards others. It's your liberal subjectivist who is liable to be very tyrannical. Bob

[2]Leonard later wrote to me: 'I was most careful not to act over Tulsa until St Michael's [Fr Pasco's church] had ceased to be part of the Episcopal Church. See Halsbury, *Ecclesiastical Law*, para. 319, which states that a priest, though ordained for a particular jurisdiction, is justified, when abroad, in ministering to any congregation which is not under the jurisdiction of a bishop.'

objected to the title of my lecture at Fulton, Missouri [in September 1987]: "The Tyranny of Subjectivism". It comes out in this book.' At which point he picked up a copy of an SCM Press paperback with Runcie's name on the front cover, called *Authority in Crisis? An Anglican Response.*

Leonard opened it and read from it: ' "It is all very well to speak, as some have, of 'the Tyranny of Subjectivism'. But to suggest a simplistic return to commonly agreed moral 'absolutes' is not really as helpful as it at first sounds. They are not to be had. Even if the human race could universally agree on what is good or evil, right or wrong, we would still be left with the problems which arise when we try to find an agreed application of these insights." I didn't advocate that, actually. But at the bottom of the page, when he's talking about the weaknesses of liberalism, he says: "Authority comes back in unacceptable and indeed frightening forms, because liberals have consistently failed to realise that liberalism can only thrive in a society which holds strong common moral assumptions." Now, how you relate the top and bottom of that page, I find it difficult to see.'

Runcie had not mentioned that book to me. 'It's very illuminating,' said Leonard. 'It was lectures he gave in New York. But one doesn't know whether he wrote them himself! Have you talked, for example, to Ruth Hook, wife of Ross Hook? She was very steamed up, because things she wrote were incorporated in things without any acknowledgement at all.'

I said I had seen the name 'Ruth' in his correspondence about drafts of sermons and speeches, and wondered who it was. Subsequently I wrote to her about this, and she replied:

Yes, from time to time I wrote newspaper articles which went out under the Archbishop's name, and also some scripts for his broadcasts. Robert sometimes gave me notes for these, and sometimes inserted a sentence of his own in my completed text; sometimes they were mine alone. I liked writing these things, but I did in the end find lack of acknowledgment a bit of a stumbling block.

'Richard Chartres used to tell me what he'd written,' continued Leonard. 'He was very loyal to Bob, but nevertheless he was quite open about it to me on one or two occasions. And the other one, of course, was Garry Bennett. I wrote all my stuff, though I did rely on people to brief me – I had researchers. But I wouldn't be prepared to put something under my name that was somebody else's work.

'I used to go to Bob, before some debate in the Synod, and say, "How are you going to vote, Bob?" "Well, I *think* I'll vote this way . . ." And I remember one occasion, I said, "It's now five o'clock, and the debate's tomorrow. You're saying that now, but are you going to say the same thing at ten o'clock tomorrow morning?" One never knew. It was extraordinary. He'd laugh about it!'

I had noticed in the Lambeth press cuttings files a series of news items reported at the beginning of July 1982. That summer, General Synod were debating the Covenanting proposals which had first come before them two years earlier. Adrian Hastings, in his book on Runcie writes:

The Bishop of Guildford, David Brown, had been the Anglican leader within the discussions with the other participating churches and he had, therefore, the responsibility of presenting the Covenant to Synod. Naturally enough, he wished to know in advance the mind of the Archbishop and what he now intended to say. He asked Runcie but was able to obtain no clear reply.[3]

The *Daily Telegraph* report of the debate (7 July 1982) notes:

[3]Adrian Hastings, *Robert Runcie*, Mowbray, 1991, p. 127. Christopher Hill remembers working with Runcie on his speech for the Synod until late into the night.

The Archbishop voted for the covenanting proposals but with reservations. He was unhappy that the prayers for reconciling the ministries of the participating churches did not specifically incorporate Free Church ministers into the historic priesthood. Dr Runcie said: 'I am only sorry that we have not been able to find the means to make improvements at this stage so that we could have carried more of the Synod and so that I myself could be more unqualified in my enthusiasm.'

When the vote was taken, the proposals failed to obtain the necessary two-thirds majority among the clergy. 'It is arguable,' writes Hastings, 'that if Runcie had spoken more enthusiastically it might have passed . . .'[4] Seven days later, the *Guardian* reported:

The Right Rev David Brown, Bishop of Guildford, collapsed at Church House, Westminster, where a week ago he unsuccessfully pleaded with the General Synod to adopt the Proposals for a Covenant between the Church of England and Free Churches. An ambulance was called after his suspected heart attack . . . but he was found to be dead on arrival at Westminster Hospital . . . A statement by the Churches Council for Covenancy said Bishop Brown 'suffered personally at the failure of the proposals because he had given himself wholeheartedly to them.' . . . The Archbishop of Canterbury, Dr Robert Runcie, said he was personally stunned . . .

I told Graham Leonard I had often heard it said that he had been very upset not to be chosen as Archbishop of Canterbury himself in 1979.

'Oh, I never expected it at all. It never entered my head. I knew perfectly well that there wasn't a chance. And in any case, things had gone so far in the Anglican Communion by that time that I think it would have been a quite impossible

[4]*ibid.*, p. 128.

job. They'd already ordained women in America, I think. I would have found myself in an impossible position. I never had any illusions about that at all – in fact, I never thought I'd go to London. I thought I would remain in Truro. Ramsey was very cross with me over my attitude to the Anglican-Methodist discussions. I, in a sense, led the campaign against it, though I wasn't in the Synod then. (I was disfranchised, in those days, as Bishop of Willesden.)'

But was he expecting someone other than Runcie to get Canterbury? 'I don't think I was. I thought he was reasonably orthodox; I always found this laid-back unwillingness to commit himself a bit trying, but I'd seen a lot of him, because he was chairman of the Anglican-Orthodox discussions, of which I was a member for, I think, seven years, and so we travelled together – we broadcast together on Radio Tashkent!'

I mentioned the story that Runcie was the second choice for Canterbury, but Downing Street had intervened. 'Well, that, of course, is said about my appointment to London. Which is untrue. The two names that went up were Habgood and me. The Crown Appointments Commission had decided that it would not put the names in order unless there was a two-thirds majority, which would have meant eight to four. And in my case it was seven to five. So the names went up side by side. And it is not true to say that Thatcher took the second name.'

Leonard became Bishop of London in 1981. When did a sense of conflict with Runcie begin? 'Well, one of the things that came up – I forget how many times – was the remarriage of divorced persons. We could never understand each other over that. Over the ordination of women, of course, he was initially against it.

'The only two occasions when he got really cross with me were the one I've mentioned, when I said, "I've upset the club!", and the other was after I'd come back from Tulsa, when he tried to maintain that he'd told me not to go. And I said – I can see it now; it was in the corridor at Church House – I said, "You know perfectly well you didn't. I asked you repeatedly; I said, 'Are you telling me not to go?' And you said, 'No, I'm not. I'd prefer that you didn't, but it's your decision.'" If he had told me not to go, I don't think I'd have gone. When it came up at the House of Bishops, I discovered subsequently that the paper on it which had been written for the Archbishop and the House was in fact written by Garry Bennett. Though *I'd* talked to Garry, who had agreed that I had a case.'

Was he using Tulsa as a stick with which to beat the Runcie establishment? 'No. I can honestly say that I went to Tulsa as a purely pastoral act, in response to the letters I got from John Pasco. I just felt, here's a man who's suffering. The way he was being treated was so appallingly un-pastoral. I didn't see it at the time as a great gesture of my attacking the establishment. I was a little surprised at what was read into it. I knew they wouldn't like it, of course.'

To some people, I said, it looked a remarkable coincidence that the second bout of press insinuations about the Runcies' marriage happened just at the time of Tulsa. 'Do you know, I've never noticed that,' answered Leonard. 'I kept totally out of that.' People had been mentioned (I said) who might have put the press in touch with disaffected members of the Lambeth staff – his own press secretary, for example. Leonard told me that this job had been held by the Rev. Norman Hood, now dead, who had previously worked for Mervyn Stockwood.

Mark Santer, whom I had seen recently, had said to me that he thought it was rather strange that Leonard should have a press secretary all to himself, when the area bishops in the London diocese didn't have any press staff. 'Well,' answered Leonard, 'they could have had them if they wanted them. They were perfectly adequately provided with expenses.' But the implication is that he himself took the press very seriously? 'I did. But only because of the pressure of the press on me. I just had to have a buffer between me and them. Norman Hood was extraordinarily good. He was a great friend of a lot of journalists – Ian Walker, who was one of the deputy editors of the *Mail on Sunday,* was one of

Norman's great friends. And – what was that chap's name on the *Mail* itself? He often rings me up at intervals still. I could look him up.' He went to the telephone and picked up a list. 'I've got all my press numbers on here. But Norman was very good at establishing relations with the press. And I found when I retired that not having a press secretary was a very great loss.'

He believed in working with the press rather than against them? 'Oh, you've got to.' The implication, I said, was that Hood might have been one of those who was quite keen, at the time of Tulsa, to divert attention from Leonard by pointing a finger at the Runcies. 'I didn't realise it was simultaneous,' Leonard answered. 'I've got all the press cuttings here, but I haven't looked at them, and don't care to, actually. But I hadn't realised that they were at the same time. Certainly there was no link in my mind at all. And I must say I don't think for a moment that Norman would have been part of that at all. All his friends in the press were what I would call the more responsible ones.'

Looking at George Carey's time in office so far, I asked, did Leonard begin to see virtues in Runcie that he didn't perceive earlier? 'I'm not sure that I've ever consciously thought of comparing them. George Carey I find quite incomprehensible! But if I'd written that book [pointing to ✱ *Authority in Crisis*] I would have referred to "Our Lord" throughout. But Bob never does. It's always "Christ".This was rather symptomatic. Do you see what I mean? There was a kind of distancing from the person of Christ, in a way. If I'm doing Biblical scholarship, that's a different matter. But I can't talk about Our Lord as if he weren't here, wasn't alive. The idea of talking about him objectively is alien to me.

'I was very seldom able to talk theology with Bob. And one found that the kind of books he'd been reading were not recent theology. Our style was very different. I would go straight in on the theology in a sermon. He would spend his time establishing a link with the people there, in a different kind of way. He desperately wanted to be loved. But when he became Archbishop, he faced an impossible situation. The

✱ *Our Lord* is a very Anglican phrase *only*.

Anglican Communion was showing all the signs of becoming like the British Commonwealth – all the signs of breaking up. I couldn't have coped – I couldn't have accepted that situation – but he did keep it together.'

I said to Leonard that the popular caricature of him, by the end of his time as Bishop of London, was as somebody poised on the starting line, ready to lead the breakaway anti-ordination-of-women church. 'No,' he responded, 'I've never wanted to break away. I've said this repeatedly – as I read church history, the story of breakaway churches is uniformly dismal. I don't quite know what my mind was then. But I became a Roman Catholic this year not just over the ordination of women, but on the whole question of authority. I retired in 1991, when I was seventy, and I joined the Roman Catholic church in April 1994. It seemed to me that, if it proved impossible to remain in the Church of England, that was the only sensible place to go.'

I reported much of this to Runcie when I went to St Albans two weeks later, on 12 December 1994. His first words when he opened the door were: 'Mark says you've been taken in by Graham Leonard.' I had written to Mark Santer saying I had found Leonard likeable, and wondered whether he had mellowed since retiring.

The sitting room was full of piles of Christmas card, many for overseas, which Runcie was signing under Lindy's direction (a pile for each country). These occupied the sofa, where Runcie usually sat, and our different position in the room (he in an armchair) drew my attention, as never before, to the large portrait of him in cope and vestments which hangs by one of the doors. I found myself wondering whether I would be able to live with a large painting of myself – especially one, like this, entirely lacking in humour; the painter had interpreted him solely as a figure of sanctity and extreme seriousness.

I also took a good look, for the first time, at the books on the two smallish built-in bookshelves on either side of the fireplace: mostly coffee-table works of one sort or another.

The only title I could read from my chair was an edition of Saki.[5]

'Personally,' Runcie continued, 'I've always got on with Graham. Voices have never been raised between us, and there have been moments when I've enjoyed his company, and defended him against other people. And Graham's Anglo-Catholic world was my Anglo-Catholic world. But the thing I found irritating about him was that he was such an enthusiast for the ecclesiastical small-print – ecclesiastical politics seemed to motivate and excite him in a way that I found rather tiresome. And I think Jim Thompson and Mark Santer would be better able to tell you the degree to which he chose to regard being leader of the Catholic party in England as more important than running the diocese of London. He was clearly the odd one out among the bishops, and he reacted to the sense of being marginalised, in the inner councils of the church, by regarding himself as responsible to another constituency. And also he was unflinching in moral rectitude, and yet allowed the diocese of London to be packed with campaigning homosexuals.' (Reading this remark later, Leonard responded: 'How could I have stopped them being appointed? The Bishop of London has very little patronage, and I inherited the practice by which area bishops nominated for their areas. In any case, which "campaigning homosexuals" is he referring to?')

Runcie continued: 'I've never felt personally as strongly about Graham as the people who were always warning me about him – and therefore I was, in a sense, double-faced, because I treated him as a friend, and yet knew that I was being told by people whose judgement I trusted to employ a long spoon.

'Now,' he changed the subject, 'I don't usually give you my own plugs, do I? But I've had a very remarkable fan-letter.' He picked it up from the floor. It was from Dr Gordon Wakefield, a distinguished elderly Methodist theologian,

[5]Runcie comments of this: 'It is Lindy's room rather than mine.' Lindy says it is by her choice that the portrait hangs there.

who had been listening to Runcie deliver the Gore Lecture in Westminster Abbey two weeks earlier. 'I heard several Gore lectures in the 1960s,' wrote Wakefield, 'but not MacKinnon, Nineham, Nuttall, Dillistone, nor Owen Chadwick could rival you. It is a very important piece and should have wide dissemination. You were fairer to Gore than some, spoke with a more sensitive understanding and confronted the most serious issues.' Runcie gave me a typescript of the lecture to take away.

The annual Gore Lecture commemorates Charles Gore, Bishop of Oxford from 1911 to 1919, and a prominent Anglo-Catholic. Reading it when I got home, I realised that it ought to provide Runcie's answer to the charge that he was simply a 'liberal subjectivist'. Ostensibly writing about Gore, Runcie seems in fact to be anatomising himself – or at least, making plain what he would like to be:

> Always within him, was a tussle between the radical, sceptical, creative mind, and the tough seeker after clarity and control in the Church's behaviour in the world. The radical thinker in him had little patience with the idea that the Church's discipline was one of unbending rules ... Yet ... there was a difference between casting a sceptical eye on the pronouncements of authority, and rejecting the disciplinary claims of authority altogether.

Near the beginning of the lecture, Runcie quotes Gore's remark 'I have always thought that the only very difficult dogma of the church was the dogma that God is love', and comments:

> This statement ... was written in the immediate aftermath of the First World War ... The Christian tradition ... has boldly asserted creation by love as its foundation doctrine. Gore makes us understand what a hard doctrine this is ... One sort of doctrine of creation is comparatively easy to formulate: the idea of a neutral, amoral creator and a neutral, amoral creation ... the spiralling abstract

beauty of chaos theory on the computer screen . . . What is harder to assert is that the pattern is one of benevolence . . . structured by a loving creator . . .

Any theological training which is any good will set its students thinking about the problem of evil – not that it will expect them to achieve any more than the Church's greatest minds of the past. What will the new curate say the first time that he or she takes the funeral for a deeply-loved child, or comforts someone who has seen a parent's personality disappear into the void of Alzheimer's disease? Where is the love in creation then?

I was particularly interested to find him referring to this age-old theological dilemma, since I (like many others) find it an insuperable barrier to Christian belief. I read on eagerly:

As Gore says, 'this is a tremendous question indeed', and it would distort my theme and be a misuse of my time to attempt to answer it. Sufficient to remind you that in its first two centuries, the Church rejected one alternative and tempting answer . . . that . . . creation was in fact evil, and everything good, including Jesus Christ, was wholly separate from it . . . The faith which calls itself Catholic is committed to Gore's 'very difficult dogma' that God is love.

This dogma cannot be proved by reason . . . [but] needs to be approached, entered into and eventually made our own by the harnessing of the will that the Church calls faith . . . Once this harnessing of the will in faith is begun, the exploration of the Christian life can start . . .

So no glib answer to the problem is offered, simply an honest acceptance that it *is* a problem; and then he goes on to ask what sort of 'discipline' is defined by this central tenet of faith, that there is a loving God. 'Love,' he asserts,

cannot be an unchanging system of rules . . . Jesus Christ is not frozen in the first century . . . he is part of an infinite variety of human experiences, which alter from age to age. To imitate him will be to find out what the contemporary age is like, and how love is best expressed in it.

This imitation of Christ our contemporary is of course a more complex and challenging business than the obeying of ancient precepts. It requires the discipline of thoughtful holiness or it will end in shipwreck ... We may have to accept that the discipline ... may be radically different from discipline labelled Christian in other periods of history ...

Charles Gore is recorded as emerging from a performance of a Brandenburg Concerto and remarking 'If that is true, everything must be all right' (which seems to me rather an improvement on Mother Julian's 'all shall be well, and all manner of things shall be well'). The point about the discipline of music is that it is strict within its own terms but infinite in its variety over time ... The Brandenburg Concerti are completely true to their own rules of harmony, rhythm and structure, and lie within those rules in a wonderful freedom because their composer knows the rules so well. Yet the rules are not the same as those to which Monteverdi wrote his Vespers ... [or] the rules used by composers of the twentieth century ... Yet we can view these varieties of musical discipline as related to each other; each composer is within the Western musical tradition, and sometimes consciously echoes earlier rule-systems in a particular context, as indeed is the case with both Stravinsky and Tippett.

I thought this impressive, but began to suspect multiple authorship. Did Runcie really know enough about music to write such a paragraph unaided? Were the unseen drafters at work again? I telephoned; he was out, so I left a message on the answering machine, and went on reading the lecture.

It goes on to tell how Gore, in the years after the First World War, was bitterly opposed the spread of artificial contraception, deeply resenting even the 1930 Lambeth Conference's cautious approval of its use within marriage.

'At first sight,' Runcie writes, 'Gore's attitude might seem to be an instance of . . . myopia.' But he continues:

> Of course Gore was absolutely correct. His historical sense had allowed him to detect what his more worldly episcopal colleagues missed, that the acceptance of artificial contraception represented and indeed continues to represent a revolution in the Church's attitude to sexuality . . . because its effect is to separate sexual enjoyment from procreation and set the two impulses on divergent paths. That has affected the whole of Western sexuality . . .

It may be that we come to different conclusions from Gore's about this and other issues. What we can take from his life is a refusal to over-simplify, to make things tidy. There is a phrase at the end of his book *Jesus of Nazareth* which is worth remembering . . . 'O yet consider it again!' – consider your defiant reassertion of old certainty, or your brash affirmation of iconoclastic novelty. It could almost serve as the motto of thoughtful holiness. With this as our motto, we can insist on keeping the 'tussle' in focus, and accept that to be honest, to be mature in the Christian life, is to accept complexity, diversity, even the insolubility of some of the questions which face us . . .

Discipline in Christian life does not consist of a rulebook . . . Its context is the changing flow of time . . . The Church needs people to lead its thinking in suggesting new paths . . . But almost by definition, because he is the guardian of tradition, the bishop must say to the Church or to the world, 'Wait a minute. Think carefully about what you are doing' . . . A traditionalist will preach a sermon at this point on the dangers of liberalism: give them an inch and they take an ell. Liberals must learn a sadder but allied lesson: that the moderate reformer generally goes under. Time and again, liberal-minded people build safe-guards into their arrangements, only to see them swept away . . . Gore knew . . . what happens when floodgates open. Did he know equally clearly that sometimes the pressure is such that floodgates have to be opened? . . .

So I present you with a two-fold discipline which goes to make up thoughtful holiness . . . on the one hand the attentive discipline of the innovator who has the courage to think new thoughts and face up to the likelihood that this may bring failure . . . on the other the attentive discipline of the church leader who is the guardian of the tradition . . . If Christian faith is to be true to its master and if the Church is to find the new shape of its identity for the sake of God and of humanity in every age, these two disciplines are tied together, so long as the world shall endure.

The morning after I had finished reading the lecture, Runcie returned my phone call. ' Yes, I got about five people to help me with ideas for it,' he told me. 'The stuff about music was Helen Oppenheimer or someone. But I reworked everything into my own words. That's my way of doing things. Oh, and another of the people who gave me suggestions was Gordon Wakefield, who wrote the fan-letter.'

A few months later, I went to see Mary Cryer, who had been on the Lambeth staff for most of Runcie's archbishopric, and to whom Hugh Montefiore had directed me. She spoke quite affectionately about both Runcies, though with a certain detachment. She had previously worked as Mervyn Stockwood's secretary, and he had used her as a confidant. She found that Runcie did not want her to repeat this role, and she soon passed on the secretarial work to others, herself concentrating on the running of the Palace, including the petty cash. She says that Runcie would often come to her asking for money, since Lindy usually kept him short of it, believing that he would waste it. 'What he really wanted was to go off and buy books.' She describes him as often irritable to his staff (which surprised me), and she felt that Lindy was not giving him the support he needed. 'He couldn't go and discuss his problems with her in the evening.' She adds that the two of them would sometimes snap at each other in front of the staff. She could see that Lindy's jaunts to concerts with unattached male friends were misinterpreted by some. But she also had the firm impression that it was, in its unusual way, a successful marriage.

When I brought up the perennial matter of Runcie's dependence on others to write drafts of his sermons and speeches, she agreed that this had caused huge problems, not least because the material produced by the ghost-writers was often quite untrue to his own character. But she concluded our conversation with this story:

'When dear old Mervyn died, in January [1995], we had a big requiem, and we asked Michael Mayne to preach, because he'd been Mervyn's first chaplain when he became Bishop of Southwark, and now he's the Dean of Westminster. Then we decided that we must have a memorial service, and we wanted Robert Runcie to preach at that one. So we asked him, and he said yes. In fact he came to the requiem, to see what it was all about, to get the feel of it, do some research, so to speak. He took a lot of trouble, even though he was frightfully busy going to and fro to America in the meantime. He wanted a list of people he should speak to about Mervyn. Well, on the day, he looked quite nervous as he got up into the pulpit. But he was brilliant. Absolutely marvellous. So good that, at the end – and I've never heard it before in a memorial service – we all clapped. And I'm certain that he'd written every word of it himself. And of course, when he really does do that, he's superb.'

I think we have to exonerate the ghost writers!

16

'St Terry'

———————

I first met Terry Waite on a railway platform in December 1994, when we were both to appear on BBC Radio 4's *Any Questions*. I knew he was a big man, but was not prepared for his actual size – he towers above everyone, and is broadly built to match. At times he indulges in the relaxed bullying that a very big man can afford. During the programme, when I produced some statistics about the Government's education cuts and earned a round of applause for them, Waite jabbed in with: 'Humphrey's had that up his sleeve all evening – he was determined to get it in somewhere!' I liked this side of him, but was less comfortable with what I soon found myself labelling his 'holy' aspect – a solemn and (it seemed to me) self-consciously 'religious' manner into which he was always slipping, quite unlike anything that I had experienced with Runcie.

We arranged to talk together for this book, and in February 1995 I travelled to Suffolk, where he had bought a cottage in a village not far from Cambridge. He had chosen it because, when not otherwise engaged, he liked to spend one day a week in Trinity Hall, Runcie's old college, where he had lived while writing his book about his captivity, *Taken on*

Trust. At the cottage, he was working in an outbuilding that looked rather like a signal box (he explained to me that it had once been a wheelwright's shop). We settled down in the main living room of the house, in front of a real log fire.

I asked him about Runcie's dependence on his ghost-writers, saying that I thought it was a cop-out – though a cop-out Runcie probably had to make, given the sort of person he is. 'Remember,' said Waite, 'that the pressure of work in that job is enormous – just the sheer volume of mail, and the decision-making, and the number of people you have to see. It's very difficult for anyone from outside to understand just how much work there is. And therefore, if I were in the job, I would want to get rid of as much of it as I could do to somebody else. Now, having said that, my feeling is that Runcie underestimated his own ability as a writer. I've always felt that, when he sat down and put his mind to something, he could write far better than anybody around him. He's got a very distinctive style – he's very witty, he's trenchant, and he says some important things. And I think that it's regrettable that he's never really applied himself to do more writing.'

I said that Runcie had come to realise that, when Richard Chartres was his chaplain, he was actually rather frightened of him. 'Richard is very penetrating,' said Waite, 'very able to make an accurate analysis very quickly. If you're surrounded by someone like that, there's a tendency to depend on them more and more. And I think Richard could make many people feel quite considerably afraid. *I* have never felt that; I've always had tremendous respect and admiration for him, and he was utterly loyal (in my estimation) to Robert. But I could see how the relationship developed. Although it would be unfair to suggest that Richard was doing anything other than his job.'

It had become clear to me that Chartres had the huge advantage that Lindy approved of him. Waite agreed, adding: 'You either hit it off with her or you don't. I tried to keep out of her way. I don't believe that she and I saw eye to eye; I think we were very different people. I'm sure she's told you that.' She had indeed expressed her discomfort about Waite to me, without being able to explain it. I said to Waite that I could not see why she should approve of Chartres and disapprove of him. 'I think it's an initial chemistry,' Waite answered. 'When I first met her at St Albans, I just don't think she cared for me at all. It was just instant.' On both sides, presumably? 'Yes, absolutely. I think it's that curious vulnerability that she has, and almost an intuitive, though unexpressed, understanding that one can see behind the front that she puts up. I mean, if ever I have had any ability [laughs], it's been a certain intuition – which has sometimes alarmed me – to be able to see more deeply into situations, into people. And that can be an uncomfortable thing to live with.'

Though tempted to pursue Waite's claim of intuitive powers, I turned instead to the Runcie marriage, and said I had gathered that they went through a bad patch around the time that the archbishopric was on offer, but that things had healed by the time the press began to print allegations. Did that tally with Waite's own observations? 'Oh, I think so. I tended to stay at quite a distance from all that. And also she rarely came on any overseas tours, which were my prime responsibility. And who can ever understand the relationship of any couple in any marriage?'

I asked Waite why he had never been ordained. 'For a very simple reason. I don't believe I have a priestly vocation. I have valued the freedom to move and work in a variety of ways. And I suspect that a number of people have gone forward for ordination who should never have been ordained, because they've really wanted to exercise a different kind of ministry.' Did he feel, early on, that some great task was waiting for him, did he have a sense of looking for a dramatic role? 'I don't believe so, although I've always been drawn towards situations that are very difficult, virtually impossible. I and my wife went off to Africa with three young children. I remember at the time being sick in the stomach about that decision. And yet I felt it was something I must pursue, never knowing where it would lead.'

With hindsight, his extraordinary career as a Superman lib-
erator of hostages begins to look like a calculated reaction to
Runcie's fence-sitting, or at least his very carefully balanced
policies. 'I'd never thought of that,' said Waite. 'If we look
at the three hostage episodes, it was quite clear that we ought
to do something in the Iran case, and we did. The second one,
Libya, was less clear, insofar as the individuals concerned had
no direct church involvement.[1] On the other hand, there was
a point of very considerable principle. When the relative had
turned to us, I had directed them to the Foreign Office. And
it became clear over Beirut that the Foreign Office was not
getting anywhere, and knew very little, and would value an
involvement by us. It seemed to me that if we claimed to be
the Church of England, and not a sectarian group – if we
claimed to be at the service of all people in this land – we
ought to do it. And if we were to do it, we ought not to
turn back when the going got tough; we ought to go through
with it.

'Well, Libya turned out all right. But I was genuinely very
reluctant to be involved in another one, in Beirut. We only
picked it up after persistent pressure from the Presbyterian
church in America. And what is often forgotten is that my
involvement in these crises was only a part-time job. I mean,
between going out to Libya, and Lebanon, and dealing with
that mass of complex material, often single-handed, I was
in China, I was in Australia and New Zealand, I was in
Canada. Looking back, I honestly don't know how I did it
all. I really don't.'

Which was the point at which he felt Runcie's support for
him was waning? 'Well, we were not having early successes.
We got Ben Weir out, and then Jenco came out,[2] and I was

[1] In 1981 Waite effected the release of three Anglican missionaries taken hostage
in Iran. Three years later he intervened successfully in the case of four
Britons – two teachers, an oil engineer and a telephone engineer – held
captive in Libya.
[2] Benjamin Weir, an American missionary held hostage in Beirut, was released
in September 1985, and Martin Jenco, a Catholic priest detained there, in
July 1986.

doing my damnedest to get into Kuwait. We were in touch
with Syria, we were in touch with the Lebanese, we were in
touch with, oh, dozens of people, but nothing really seemed
to be moving, and it was a case of my having constantly to
explore this avenue, that avenue, see another avenue. And I
think Robert felt, look, we're not really getting far. This is
taking up far too much of your time, because the Lambeth
Conference is approaching, and you weren't appointed to do
this job of hostage work. But there was the media interest.
We deliberately chose the strategy of going public, of giving
myself a public profile, in order to get a response from
kidnappers – which we actually got, because a letter was
received. And once you've done that, you can't turn back.
If you do pull out publicly, what do you do to the hostages?
But I think Robert thought I was making it too much of a
personal crusade. And that would be a fair criticism.'

I told Waite what Runcie had said to me:

> Waite was initially a good friend and a good companion,
> and we worked well together. But he always enjoyed
> centre stage; he was what Oliver North once called 'a
> grandstander' – but forgivably so. Of course it was totally
> absorbing to him, but if he was going to be an international
> negotiator he oughtn't to be on my staff.

Did Waite think this was fair comment? 'No, I don't think it
is, entirely. If he didn't want to get involved in it, he ought
to have said so very clearly. In which case I could have said,
"Very well, in that case I resign, and I'll do it from another
base." I was quite prepared to do that. Once the Iran-Contra
business broke, I had to go back to Beirut, to demonstrate my
good faith to the kidnappers.[3] And what would it say to men
who were in prison (they actually wrote to the Archbishop
of Canterbury saying, "Please help us") if we said, sorry,
we're pulling out because it's too tough? What would that

[3] The American arms-for-hostages deal was publicly exposed in November
1986.

say about the resilience of the church, and its ability to stick with something and really stand by people, to pay the price personally? So I went back. I said, "I damn well will, even if this costs me my life." Now, that may sound terribly arrogant, but I was willing, because it was so important.'

In a sense, the half-heartedness of Runcie's support had made him go even further? 'Absolutely. I admit to certain uncharitable thoughts, when I was absolutely alone in the Lebanon, surrounded by sharks, by the most dreadful people. There were journalistic sharks, and people out for this, that and the other. It was exceptionally difficult. And my life was on the line every day. And I thought, am I really supported from home? And I wasn't.'

Runcie had gone on to say, in that conversation with me: 'I don't think he knew about the Irangate thing, but I think he would not recognise that he was being used by the Americans.' Waite's response when I read this to him was: 'Well, I mean, I think it must be clear to everybody now that we had no dealings with Iran. No, there was certainly no knowledge at all about American arms dealing, none whatever. I can say that quite categorically.'

In his review of Waite's *Taken on Trust*, Robert Fisk, who had been *The Times* correspondent in Beirut during the hostage crisis, and a friend of Waite's, is very sceptical about Waite's position over Irangate. He writes: 'After talking to the State Department he [Waite] banged down the phone with the word: "Bastards!" Even at that early stage, it seems, the Americans were two-timing Terry Waite. Did this not raise the smallest suspicion in his mind about his friend Colonel Oliver North?' And Fisk also writes, a couple of paragraphs later:

In early 1986, an American-crewed aircraft was detected by Turkish radar returning from Iran to Tel Aviv. From sources in Beirut I was told that the plane had taken military spare parts to Tabriz ... Not long afterwards, intrigued by this aircraft's strange journey to Iran, I visited Waite at Lambeth Palace and mentioned that I had heard

there were 41 pallets of spares for Iranian fighter bombers
on the plane. I remember Waite replying: 'So you know
about that!'[4]

I read these passages to Waite. His response was: 'Well,
I mean, so what? Honestly, I've no recollection of that. I
remember him telling me the story. I honestly do think that's
a bit of journalism. I really do. Because it meant absolutely
nothing to me, that particular flight – I can say that quite
honestly and categorically. I mean, I genuinely didn't know
about the arms for hostages, genuinely.' But he might have
had suspicions? 'No, there were no suspicions about arms.
There were various theories. I was the only person to be
in face-to-face contact with the Lebanese kidnappers. I
understood that Kuwait was the key.[5] But we also knew
that Syria had a certain degree of influence, and we were
in touch with them through the Roman Catholic church. I
was also told that Iran had a key, and I actually went to
the Iranian embassy, or to its representatives – there was no
embassy in London. I visited them on a couple of occasions,
and tried to see if I could get some leverage there. I got
absolutely nowhere with them.

'Now, whenever there's a hostage situation, there will be
those who have directly taken the hostages, who will have
their own agenda. Secondly, there will always be others
who gather round the hostage crisis, to take advantage
of it, for one reason or another. If I, as an independent
negotiator, am able to establish contact with those who'd
directly taken the hostages, discover their agenda, work on
it, and be successful, all right, then we're clear. That does
not mean that there aren't others around who have their
own agendas, and who've been pushing them at the same
time, claiming that they, too, have total influence.

'Now, whilst I'm looking on at the Kuwaiti agenda – which

[4]*Independent*, 22 September 1993.
[5]The Islamic Jihad had negotiated with Waite on the understanding that he
would plead for the lives of comrades sentenced to death in Kuwait for terrorist
bombings.

is extraordinarily complicated, very frustrating – Iran has a relationship with the Lebanese Shiites; it's financing them. Iran has two agendas: developing the Islamic revolution throughout the Middle East (using the Lebanon as a back door); and fighting the Iran–Iraq war. Oliver North comes in from the American administration, and the Iranians tell him, "If you'll supply us with arms, we'll put pressure on the Lebanese Shiites to get some hostages freed."

'All right, there are two agendas, and I'm caught in the middle. It doesn't necessarily mean that, because I know North, who was appointed by the American administration, that they're going to tell me everything they're doing, not for one moment. And if you're caught between the agendas, then you're caught. And when it broke, that's the point when I had to make the decision, do I pull out now – implying by pulling out that there was complicity, the game's up – or do I go back and say, I am willing to face these fellows, these Lebanese, face these kidnappers?'

I asked Waite what his feeling had been when the Irangate story broke. The picture he paints of North in his book is so cloak-and-dagger that it can scarcely have surprised him to see North's double-dealing revealed. 'Well, after a while things don't surprise you, do they, when you hear of the double-dealings that go on in the political realm? My feeling was one of absolute sickness, because I realised that there was a chance here of myself being compromised, of the whole thing collapsing totally. And I felt it was a terrible thing. I mean, that's why I got on the phone to him immediately.' He actually phoned North? 'Yes, and asked him what the hell was going on. He simply said, "Oh, don't worry, it'll be all right." Something of that nature.' He wasn't going to discuss it at all? 'No.'

I asked Waite how much he had seen Robert Fisk when they were in Beirut together. 'Well, Fisk was a friend of Terry Anderson [one of the American hostages], and I depended on him for a lot of local knowledge. And Fisk makes a point [in his review], which I really think is not very worthy of him, that I had claimed to have seen the hostages, when I brought the photographs back, but this wasn't true.[6] The kidnappers had asked me to be very, very careful with the photographs; and I was damn careful. And I was torn here between a double loyalty. Fisk claimed – as I think was right – to be a personal friend of Terry Anderson, and wanted to know how he was. And he had local knowledge and was helpful. On the other hand, he was a journalist, and a journalist is a journalist!

'Fisk asked me, had I seen the hostages? And I was very cagey. I was debating in my mind whether or not even to show him the pictures. And I showed him the pictures under absolute secrecy. And then, naturally enough, he began to question me more about the circumstances; and out of protecting the hostage-takers, I gave no more information away. Fisk interprets this as me being unduly manipulative.' But did he tell Fisk he'd met the hostages? 'I didn't say that at all. I just would not say what had happened. I was deliberately evasive. Because if, for instance, I'd said I had met them or I hadn't met them, all Fisk had to do was to work out how long I'd been away, how long it had taken me to give the camera to somebody, come back with the pictures, and he could put together where the people were. Now I didn't want a journalist printing this stuff, endangering life. And in my estimation it was totally right, not to be untruthful, but to be evasive. Later on, what do I come back to? I find the book reviewed, and my actions are totally misinterpreted, misrepresented.'

I said that it was a very striking review. By the end, Fisk has turned completely against Waite, and writes sarcastically: 'So is it "St Terry" we must examine?' I suggested to Waite that it was fair to say that he had left a lot of questions unanswered

[6]Fisk writes, in the same review of Waite's book: 'Waite said he had met the four men [the hostages], very briefly. Both Gumucio [a Bolivian-American journalist] and I were nursing the unpleasant suspicion that Waite had not actually seen the four men. And sure enough, in his [book], Waite makes it clear that the kidnappers had simply taken his camera to another location where the men were being held, then returned with their snapshots. So why did Waite not tell us this? Why was it necessary – after his bravery in meeting the captors – to fantasise about his experience?'

in the book. 'Of course. And I don't feel any necessity to answer certain things. Lots of points that have been made against me, I actually don't feel under any compulsion to answer. You take your stand, and you say, "I can live with my own conscience."'

I told Waite that Runcie had said to me: 'Since he's come out, we've got on better than we ever did, because he's come through the incarceration in a remarkable way [and] he's united to his family, which he wasn't before . . .'. That seemed to imply that he and Runcie had not really got on when Waite was working for him. 'I don't think that's true,' answered Waite. 'I'm also not sure about "He's united with his family, which he wasn't before." I'd put it in a very different way. In family life, you go through strains, ups and downs, and you get to new levels and new depths; and that's certainly true. I think that could be misinterpreted in a very wrong way.'

It was something he had left completely out of the book – his marriage, and his relationship with his family. He didn't even say he was going to leave it out; it was a silent omission. 'No,' he answered. 'I mean, why should I? Frances [Waite's wife] took the deliberate line of cutting herself off from the press. She didn't give interviews, and she's never done. She was respected for that in my opinion. And if that's the way she wants it, that's the way it should be. And I think we've been extremely fortunate, the way we've gone through and grown up together – very fortunate.'

The fact that his book was written on that premise, of not discussing this area of his life, was one of the things that had led to unflattering comparisons being made between it and Brian Keenan's and John McCarthy's books, which were much more personally revealing. Did this worry him? 'No. I've said what I wanted to say. And it certainly hasn't worried people who've read the book. Look at the enormous correspondence which it's engendered – tremendous – and the way in which it's sold! It must have sold half a million in this country.'

I said I felt there was another area of omission: that while

Waite fully described the physical discomforts of captivity, and the psychological uncertainty, I didn't get the feeling of absolute and utter despair which he must, surely, have felt at least from time to time. 'No, I didn't. I don't think I did feel absolute and utter despair. I mean there were times when I was very, very low but not utter despair. I felt terrible agony, terrible misery, but I don't recollect ever feeling total absolute despair.' If that was true, then was he possibly someone who had never felt despair in his life at all? 'I've had to live with a degree of vulnerability. I certainly felt the agony of spirit in captivity. I said to myself, as I say in the book, death would be preferable to this living death. But I didn't particularly want to die in those circumstances, with my family and friends not knowing how I died.'

He was not somebody who by nature experiences total despair, a total loss of faith in himself? 'No, not total. Very, very low, undoubtedly. But not total.'

The other area he didn't go into in the book was his relations with the other hostages, when he was confined with them. 'I have two reasons for that,' he explained. 'One is that the book was written in my head, in captivity; it's primarily a book written from solitary. And when you move from solitary to be with others, a very different process takes place – you're into personal communication. The book, in a sense, ends when I join the others. The second thing is, I have very strong reservations – it took me a long, long time to put in what I wrote about Tom Sutherland.[7] And I only put that in because he said such remarkable things when he came out. When men are locked up together, with only two

[7] A brief passage in *Taken on Trust* describes mutual irritation between Waite and Sutherland. John McCarthy writes of Waite that he was 'a bluff companion, but moody and changeable after the long years alone. He would punctuate his conversation with anecdotes about his VIP status. I never knew how much irony there was in the pomposity with which he described his various comings and goings. He was great fun to be with when he was in good spirits, but he needed a lot of attention . . . He was desperately worried about what his actions had done to his family, but resorted to self-justification in order to overcome this, rather than a straightforward acceptance of his own fears and failings.' (John McCarthy and Jill Morrell, *Some Other Rainbow*, Corgi, 1994, p. 448.

or three feet between them, they are at their most vulnerable. And because you are thrust together in that particular form of relationship, where man is so very vulnerable, I almost regard that – and this may sound silly – as having a sacred quality, a set-apart quality. I don't think it's for me to point at that, or write about that, or make assumptions about the other man. It's for him to say what he has to say about himself.'

I could understand his not wanting to write about the others. But clearly there must have been quite a lot of conflict between them all, and surely that was when he must have learnt most about himself, seeing himself as they saw him? 'Yes,' he agreed, 'there was conflict, but I don't think it was necessarily the conflict that one could really get hold of, because almost for the whole of that final year I was chronically sick with a bronchial infection. And a chronic irritation to the others because of it. Also, as Terry Anderson said, a very big man comes in, very noisy – true! Thirdly, the fact of having to learn to communicate again after four years' solitary – pretty terrific. Fifthly, probably a guilt factor, a certain unconscious recognition that "We asked this man to come out here" – because they signed the letter to the Archbishop – "and he's come out, and he's captive with us now!" And if you ever try to do something for people, never expect thanks, because they're always in a very ambiguous relationship with you. I've made a point with all the previous hostages of leaving them alone. They don't owe me anything.'

But did he have the experience, when he was confined with the other hostages, of seeing himself through other people's eyes? 'Oh yes, of course. It's the most terrible thing. I'm not blind to that. I know my own failings. I know that, if you're the build and personality that I am, can severely threaten and irritate people. Size threatens, a certain ability with words threatens.'

I said I was interested in Fisk's 'St Terry' jibe, because I did think there was now an undercurrent of that feeling about him and his motives. His book had taken the line of not laying himself bare, and of not admitting follies and mistakes. Did he feel that he might have overstepped the line of sympathy with some people because of this? 'I think there are people who will view these things cynically,' he answered. 'But that's up to them. That's their judgement. For someone to be able to tell me what my motives are, when I struggle to understand them myself, is supremely arrogant.'

I said that he struck me as in some ways two people. First, there was an enormous energy, and a ruthlessness which went with it. 'There has to be,' he answered, 'if you're going to work in that field – there has to be an enormous energy to keep going.' I said I found that side of him more attractive than the aspect which Fisk calls 'St Terry'. 'Well, I'm not a saint,' was his response. 'I never have claimed it, have I?'

What was he going to do with the rest of his life? Did he not feel the danger of being trapped inside the St Terry image? Wouldn't he want to go off and do something completely different? 'Oh yes, let life unfold. One step at a time. But I am not ambitious in that sense. I like to spend quite a lot of time alone, because I think in solitude there are many learnings to be made; and if you're in solitude, it enables you to be more effective in relationship with other people too. It's a matter of finding the balance between solitude and community.'

Did he enjoy solitude before he had experienced captivity? 'No, not at all.' So he had simply developed a taste for it, having experienced it for so long? 'Yes, it's something that's very remarkable and good, and enables you to deepen and develop perspectives on yourself and, hopefully, to be a little more human in relationship with other people.' He didn't feel he was trying to develop a different personality that wasn't really him at all? 'Not at all. I think what one has to do in life is grow up into oneself, and begin to make the discernment in practice of distinctive spirituality. And I still struggle with that, to understand what the whole thing means. And now is the time to continue the exploration which was set off by an extraordinary chain of events – to explore the solitary side, to discover the riches of that, having had thirty active years of chasing around.'

I said I could imagine Lindy remarking, 'Well, he's got all

that money from his book, so he can afford to do that.' Waite answered: 'Well, I came out without a penny. And I had to make my own way. And from it springs things you can do for other people as well as for yourself. At least a third of the time goes in charitable work, and a lot of the income.'

Had he expected the Church of England to have a job waiting for him when he got out? 'Not at all. And I certainly didn't want to go back to a job with the church. Because of the nature of my own particular vocation, which I'm still trying to understand and to work out, I don't think I fit easily with the structure of the church.' Was any job offered to him? 'Oh yes, there were several. I was asked to look at several things, and I declined them all. I knew it was necessary to sit down, have those couple of years, and actually do that writing.'

He had been talking a lot about the spiritual life. In practical terms, what did this mean? Was he somebody who says the offices of the church every day? 'No. I like the quietness of an early morning Communion service. I find it very difficult to go into the so-called "family services", happy-clappy things of that nature.' When he was living in Trinity Hall, writing his book, how often in the week would he make his communion? 'I'd go on Sundays.' He wasn't a weekday communicant? 'No.' And what about prayers – I was interested in how much the spiritual life involved formal observance for him? 'Well, that's the very question that I struggle with at the moment. I don't normally speak about these things. But what does it mean to be contemplative in contemporary society, and what is the nature of contemplation? How does a contemplative vocation find its fulfilment through lay ministry? It's almost arrogant even to ask the question, but that's what I work at, at the moment. It's a question of trying to find an understanding which goes beyond form and structure, but which doesn't despise form and structure.'

How old was he now [1995]? 'Fifty-six. And from the middle twenties I was bang into it all. For the moment, I have this degree of independence.' He had told me that his next major project was writing a book on solitude; would there be other books after that? 'I think I will, but that's enough for the moment.' And charitable work, how many organisations was he involved with at the moment? 'The Butler Trust, which is to improve the quality of service of those who work in prisons – not only the prison officers, but others. And Victim Support – I've been a trustee of that for a long time. And Y-Care, the development movement of the YMCA. And I have an active involvement in hospice work. And then, it's almost like being an independent agony aunt, because of the number of people who arrive with personal problems.'

I said he had been very kind in putting up with my questions. 'I actually thought it was turning out to be a biography of myself,' he laughed, 'not of Robert! I would hope that I have a very minor part in this whole story. Looking back at the Lebanese business, we ought to have had a better team, with a better evaluation process as we went along, step by step. But where do you get that team from?' There should have been a team, rather than just him? 'Yes. But where do you get the resources?'

I sent a transcript of this interview to Robert Fisk. He telephoned me and said that it did not change his feelings about Waite. 'I think he became very caught up in the dramatic romance of what he was doing,' he remarked of Waite's behaviour over the photographs of the hostages. And of Oliver North's Irangate deal: 'My feeling is that Waite must have known that something was very wrong.' But again and again, Fisk emphasised Waite's courage: 'He was very brave. I'm not sure I'd ever do what he did.'

I asked Runcie about the efforts to get Waite released. He recalled Sir Robert Armstrong, Cabinet Secretary, saying to him: 'I hope you're not going to get too involved with the Americans on this question, because it can't be assumed that our policy is the same as theirs.' Did this sound as if the British Government was aware of Irangate before it blew up publicly? Or was it merely a le Carré-esque reflection of the usual Anglo-American security relationship?

Runcie said that the attempts to get Waite released 'occupied, of course, an enormous amount of energy. Almost the day after Waite went, John Lyttle joined my staff,[8] as Secretary for Public Affairs – to advise me about political and parliamentary matters, and to cope with Ma Thatcher and all sorts of things like *Faith in the City*. He got sidetracked on to Waite, and never really managed to get off it. He was a very skilful tactician, he worked day and night at it. He established connections with people who were not so favourable to Waite.

'And there was the business of looking after Waite's family. In the old days, Waite had become a big man who didn't appear much on the family scene. And not once *ever* did Frances Waite say, "You ought to be doing more to get him released." There wasn't a hint of a Jill Morrell.

'She got a job, working in an old people's home, and enjoyed it enormously. Lindy took her to Wimbledon. Our press officer Eve Keatley looked after her a lot, made sure she came to Christmas parties and things like that. And one would say to her, "I'm frightfully sorry there's still no news – we're doing all we can." And she'd simply say, "Oh, I *know* you are – you're marvellous."

'John Lyttle sent me a memorandum about Waite almost every day. And there was one character we were in touch with, a Kurd living in Iran. I've never been able to check out his exact relationship with Rafsanjani [President of Iran], but he claimed that it was his mission to keep in touch with us – he was an agent who moved between Iran and this country at a time when we had no diplomatic relations with them. He would turn up; John Lyttle would meet him at Victoria station, there was never any official appointment. Just so that he could tell Rafsanjani and his masters that he really was in touch with me, I saw him twice in a flat which we arranged.

[8]He came straight from working on the Police Complaints Board. Earlier he had been political agent both to Roy Jenkins and Shirley Williams.

And he did give us a certain hope – he told us that Waite was alive.

'Waite, I think, has sensed that the more John Lyttle discovered about the Irangate story, the more he built up an intense dislike of him! And in some ways perhaps it is best that poor old John died just before Waite returned, though I longed for the two to meet.'

I said that Waite's own defence was that he had had to work alongside other people's agendas, which may not have been very savoury, but it was necessary. 'I think that's true. But John held it against him that he enjoyed their agendas too much.'

I told Runcie I was puzzled that Waite could convince himself that he could spend the rest of his life sitting in his cottage in Suffolk writing books. Runcie replied: 'He wants to be in action again.'

17

'My God, what a mess'

On 25 November 1986, shortly before Waite's disappearance, the Rev. Gareth Bennett of New College, Oxford, wrote in his diary:[1] 'A letter marked "Strictly Personal" turned out to be from Derek Pattinson [Secretary-General of the General Synod of the Church of England] asking me whether I would write the anonymous preface to the next *Crockford*! He wants it by the end of May. I do not think that I can face the work.'

On the same day, Bennett heard that Richard Harries was to be the next Bishop of Oxford. He remarked in the diary: 'I suppose I had thought they might ask me.'

Crockford's Clerical Directory, the Church of England *Who's Who*, had been published every few years since 1858, and by tradition carried an unsigned preface which commented, sometimes acidly, on current ecclesiastical events. A few years earlier, its proprietorship had passed from Oxford University Press to the Church Commissioners and the Central Board of Finance of the Church of England. They decided to continue with the anonymous preface, despite the

[1] Kindly made available by his executor, the Rt Rev. Geoffrey Rowell.

fact that, as the Bishop of Rochester put it, '*Crockford* is now inevitably seen as an official in-house publication.'[2]

Bennett discussed Pattinson's invitation with the Rev. Philip Ursell, Principal of Pusey House, Oxford. 'We were coming back from Chichester,' recalls Ursell, 'and he said, "I've been asked to write the *Crockford's* preface. Do you think I should?" And I said, "Yes, of course." Garry said: "It won't be the sort of liberal, bland preface that we've had so many times. If I'm going to be honest, it'll be very forthright." I said, "That's all right. Do it." But he didn't make up his mind then.'[3]

Bennett's part in Runcie's story – and Runcie's in Bennett's – needs to be traced from the beginning of Bennett's life, which it can be, thanks to an autobiography that he started to write not long before his death, in minute, fastidious handwriting. Gareth Vaughan Bennett was born in 1929 in Westcliff-on-Sea in Essex. An only child, he saw little of his father, who commuted to a London office, but he was (as he puts it in the autobiography) 'utterly guarded and cosseted' by his mother. 'I was never allowed out with other children, and I used to sit at the window, watching other boys . . . walking by in gangs or groups.'[4] This feeling of being excluded from gangs of powerful people continued to the end of his life.

His parents did not take him to church, but he began to attend services when his school was evacuated to Buckinghamshire during the war. He was rejected as unfit for National Service, and won a place at Christ's College, Cambridge in 1948, achieving a First Class in the finals of the History Tripos.

After taking his Cambridge degree, he proceeded to do a Ph.D. on an eighteenth-century Bishop of Peterborough, (White Kennett)

[2]Rt Rev. David Say to Sir Douglas Lovelock, 4.12.87 (Lambeth Palace).
[3]This and subsequent quotes from Ursell are from an interview with the author, 23.5.95.
[4]The autobiography was kindly made available by the Rt Rev. Geoffrey Rowell.

He was a pupil of Sykes a year before me and did Sir the same subject! Never met him.

and was awarded a doctorate when only twenty-four. He accepted a three-year appointment to lecture at King's College, London, where the Dean, Eric Abbott, encouraged him to be ordained. He signed up for three long vacation terms at Westcott House, while Runcie was its Vice-Principal.

> Bob Runcie was the one member of staff who actually seemed to think it was a good thing that I was an academic, and we had a number of humorous conversations . . . He had a kind of benevolent oversight of me which was more that of equal to equal than I deserved. He was always cheering me up by asking my advice on this or that theological problem. I became quite devoted to him . . . He had intelligence, wit and style. But I can scarcely have realized that I was laying the foundations of a friendship with a future Archbishop of Canterbury.

Bennett was ordained to a part-time curacy in his parents' village in Essex, and continued to lecture at King's, where he began work on the life of the eighteenth-century Tory High Churchman, Bishop Francis Atterbury. One of Bennett's New College colleagues, Tony Nuttall, points out the resemblance between Bennett's *Crockford's* preface and his portrait of Atterbury; for example in this passage: 'Atterbury . . . was clear what his goal was: not just to harass the Archbishop but to make Convocation [predecessor of the General Synod] an instrument by which urgently needed measures could be taken to restore the authority and status of the Church.'[5]

In 1959 Bennett applied successfully for the Deanship of Divinity of New College. Runcie tells an anecdote about this: 'When Garry was being interviewed, Warden Hayter opened the proceedings in his agreeable diplomatic way: "I hope you were comfortable last night, Dr Bennett." And Garry replied [Runcie slips into a whining, Kenneth Williams voice]: "Well,

[5] G. V. Bennett, *The Tory Crisis in Church and State 1688–1730: The career of Francis Atterbury Bishop of Rochester*, Clarendon Press, 1975, p. 57.

When I read the Times Version of the Preface on the train to London, I believe it was Bennett.

no, I wasn't really, because the bed was very lumpy." And the Fellows decided at that moment to elect him, because he would obviously be anti-Hayter, as most of them were – typically Oxford!'[6]

The Dean of Divinity had charge of chapel services. Bennett's predecessor had let things run down badly, so that, although New College possessed a celebrated choir, there was little in the way of a congregation. Bennett was made uncomfortable by the supercilious anti-Christian attitudes of many of the dons, and realised that his manner of speaking was being mocked by the choirmen. Many of the undergraduates were ex-public schoolboys who ignored his greetings in the quadrangle. All this left him feeling 'very solitary'. But he managed to build up 'a little clientele' at services, with several ordinands. 'There was never a religious revival, but when I introduced a terminal "corporate communion", with buffet supper afterwards, I often found that I had seventy or more communicants, including fellows and wives.'

Allen Warren, who was an undergraduate at New College during these years, notes that, though the *Crockford's* affair led Bennett to be characterised as a defender of the Anglo-Catholic tradition, his churchmanship at New College was 'without extravagance and unaccompanied by "bells and smells" . . . I remember Garry saying to me that he wished [the chapel] to be a place which all college members could enter, whatever their commitment or otherwise . . .'[7] Philip Ursell of Pusey House describes Bennett as 'a classic High Churchman [who] always said the daily offices without fail – the Book of Common Prayer Matins and Evensong'. Ursell, for whom Bennett often preached at Pusey House, admired many of his performances in the pulpit. 'Some of his sermons preached here were absolute gems. They were very simple, spiritual sort of things. You could see the progress of the

---

[6]Quotes from Robert Runcie in this chapter; are taken from an interview with the author on 1.6.95.

[7]Allen Warren, 'The *Crockford's* Preface: an Historian's Perspective', in Allen Warren (ed.), *A Church for the Nation*, Gracewing, 1992.

man towards a greater holiness in just the few years that I heard him preach.'

In 1968 it was Bennett's turn to act as Sub-Warden of New College, and there arrived to relieve him of some of his chapel duties a young ex-Cuddesdon student named Geoffrey Rowell, recommended by Runcie. Bennett's autobiography praises Rowell's achievements in the college, and adds: 'he has remained one of my closest confidants.' Rowell, now Bishop of Basingstoke and Bennett's executor, says he was astonished when he read this: 'I had no idea at the time how much my friendship mattered to him. He simply couldn't express affection, except to his cat Tibby – I once went to supper with him, at his house [in New Marston, an Oxford suburb], and after the meal he stretched out on the sofa with Tibby lying on his stomach. Garry went all gooey over the animal.'[8] Bennett's diary for 15 July 1987 mentions 'A quiet evening with Tibby.'

Like Geoffrey Rowell, Philip Ursell, Bennett's only other close confidant, did not realise how much his friendship mattered to Bennett: 'I got on extremely well with him. I don't know why, because we weren't very similar. He was a very sophisticated and very shy man. And one of the things that came out after he died, which shocked me a great deal (because I always assumed that Geoffrey and he were very close friends), was when we went over to his house to sort things out, and Geoffrey said, "You know, this is only the second time I've ever been here." And that astonished me. Because I had thought nothing of phoning Garry, if I got fed up, and saying, "I'm coming over for a drink." Perhaps once a week I might have been there, simply calling in for a glass of whisky with him, and a chat.'

During the 1970s, Bennett began to withdraw from New College, eventually giving up the deanship, largely on account of the admission of women. 'He thought that New College

---

[8]Quotes from the Rt Rev. Geoffrey Rowell are taken from an interview with the author, 6.5.95.

had joined the mad rush [to admit women],'[9] says John Cowan, who was then fellow and tutor in German at the college, and who, with Rowell and Ursell, was a third friend and confidant. Bennett retained a lectureship in history, but had not managed to get a readership or professorship in either the Theology or History faculties – church history (his specialisation) fell rather between the two. Reaching his fifties, he realised that he was professionally at a dead end.

For a while, the General Synod of the Church of England seemed to offer a way out. In 1975 Bennett was elected to it as a representative of Oxford University. 'At first,' he wrote in his diary,[10] 'I found it difficult to speak or take part, and became rather frustrated.' But eventually he 'surprised myself by becoming a leading speaker'. He was asked to serve on various synodical bodies – the Doctrine Commission, the Faith and Order Advisory Group and the Board for Mission and Unity. Once a left-winger – during the 1956 Suez crisis he had taken part in an anti-Government demonstration in Whitehall – he now began to ally himself, 'not without some reservations', with the right-wing Anglo-Catholics.

Philip Ursell says that he took great trouble with his Synod speeches: 'They were always written out – he would think, before going to the Synod, about whether to speak on a subject or not. And I think people respected the fact that he would analyse something with a razor-sharp mind, and show up the weaknesses, rather like a don marking somebody's essays. For example he attacked the bad logic and sentimental reasoning of the *Faith in the City* report.'

During 1980, he began to contribute material to Runcie's speeches and sermons. He carefully kept all Runcie's letters to him in a file neatly labelled 'Archbishop of Canterbury'.[11] What seems to be the earliest of these, dated 'October 11th', reads as follows (like most of them, it is hand-written):

[9]Quotes from John Cowan are taken from an interview with the author, 9.5.95.
[10]In an entry for the beginning of 1985.
[11]The letters were kindly made available by the Rt Rev. Geoffrey Rowell.

My dear Garry,

Congratulations on your return to the Synod ... We shall need all the voices of Anglican moderation and sanity which we can muster!

Since you are one of the few consultants that I can rely on for sound and disciplined drafting I am likely to trouble you even further.

I thought that I might float before you some of the varied engagements on which you might be able to assist ...

Runcie then lists three forthcoming speaking engagements with which he wants help: the annual commemoration sermon at All Souls, Oxford; a speech (following the Prime Minister's) for the Lord Mayor's Dinner; and the Presidential Address, introducing the Queen, to the General Synod. The letter continues: 'I am staying in Oxford on the nights of November 1st and 2nd so that we might have a chance to talk together ... my tiresome diary ... needs refreshing with a gossip about Oxford, Deaneries and the like ... Yours ever, Bob.'

In March 1981, Bennett drafted for Runcie a talk on 'Church and Nation' for the Free Church Federal Council (at two days' notice), and a sermon for the centenary of Westcott House. There were many others, but the requests from Runcie usually came by telephone, and Bennett was not keeping a diary at this period, so his contributions are not recorded.

Runcie says that he had asked for Bennett's help occasionally before he became Archbishop: 'From time to time, if there was anything historical to be written, I would ask his opinion – not very often until I went to Canterbury. Then, if we had something like the centenary of the House of Laity of the Church Assembly, Garry would write me a draft. Sometimes it was no use, but he usually wrote very good little historical things, which would start off a speech. I remember he was rather a master of quotations from Sydney Smith. He was a great help to me.'

Of course, Bennett was by no means the only speechwriter

working for Runcie behind the scenes. Gerald Priestland, then the BBC's religious affairs correspondent, and himself a Quaker, writes in his autobiography:

> My relations with Robert Runcie became very close and there was a time when he cherished the hope that I might eventually come and work for him at Lambeth Palace. Quakers, in my view, should be ready to serve wherever they are needed; but I do not think it would have done Runcie much good if it had leaked out that I was drafting speeches and sermons for him. I helped him *ad hoc* on one or two scripts . . .[12]

If eyebrows might have been raised at a Quaker ghost-writing for the Archbishop of Canterbury, even more surprise would have been expressed that, by 1985, Runcie was also using the services of a Roman Catholic, Peter Cornwell. Formerly on Runcie's staff at Cuddesdon, Cornwell had felt the necessity in 1984 of renouncing the Anglican Church for Rome while he was vicar of St Mary the Virgin, Oxford, the University church, whose previous incumbents had included John Henry Newman.

Cornwell says that Runcie was 'deeply hurt' by his decision – he had been very close to Runcie, and was a member of the Cell – but, after the crisis had passed, Runcie did not hesitate to ask Cornwell to ghost-write for him: 'It was mostly uncontroversial stuff, but I knew him well enough to guess what he would think about something. And I would try to slip in a few ideas of my own! There were other Roman Catholics writing for him – including John Harriot, an ex-Jesuit who had a column in the *Tablet* – and also a Methodist, Gordon Wakefield. Gordon and I used to compare notes, because a thing would come out, and I'd say, "That must be a bit of you there, Gordon, and this is a bit of me!" I remember there was a great sermon he preached in St Mary's on Newman, which

[12]Gerald Priestland, *Something Understood, an autobiography*, Andre Deutsch, 1986, p. 264.

was a mixture of our bits – bits of Methodist and bits of Papist! But when you see the awfulness that can result from people writing their own stuff, you can understand Robert's desire not to say silly things. And I think he probably found it hard to express the things which really mattered to him, so he looked round for other people to package it a bit.[13]

Like Cornwell and Wakefield, Garry Bennett took pleasure in hearing his own words from Runcie's mouth. His New College friend John Cowan recalls watching one of the royal weddings on television with Bennett, who proudly identified part of Runcie's sermon as his own work.

Priestland, Cornwell and the other ghost-writers were happy to help Runcie and expected nothing in return. For Bennett, however, the working relationship with Runcie raised his hopes that his career might take a favourable turn. The reference in Runcie's 'October 11th' letter to having a 'gossip' about 'Deaneries' suggests that he was dropping hints to Bennett that he might be appointed dean of a cathedral. Bennett's 1985 diary shows Runcie seeming to take a great interest in his career:

3 January: [At the Standing Committee of the General Synod, to which Bennett had been elected] At the sherry before lunch I had a talk with Bob Runcie. He said that he wants us to have lunch later in the month and a serious talk. Again he pressed me about Jack McManners's chair [of Ecclesiastical History, at Oxford, which had been frozen, like other vacant professorships at the time]. What was happening? I said I did not know. He said that he has had a talk with the Prime Minister; she was possessed of the notion that the bishops were 'wet' and did not believe enough. She said to him 'I hear there is a man called Bennett at New College.' Bob said he said 'A very good man.' What did I feel about a church job? I said that I was in a very open state. I did not want to stay much longer at New College; I needed a change and a

[13]The Rev. Peter Cornwell interviewed by the author, 19.8.93.

refreshment. Did I want to stay at the university? I said 'not necessarily'. He said he had to get this clear 'if I am to promote your cause . . .'

4 *January:* . . . My mind has been very uneasy today about yesterday's conversation with the Archbp. I could be letting myself in for a great deal of worry and upheaval. Perhaps after 25 years in Oxford I am not fit for anything else, and bachelors do have to be careful about the domestic situation.

Philip Ursell says, of Runcie's hints that Bennett might be chosen for a senior job: 'He'd have made an awful bishop. He wouldn't have been any use at all. He didn't have the common touch, the small talk – and the thought of him going around, night after night, in church halls, at bunfights, at confirmations – he couldn't have done it. And he had no broad experience of the church. He'd never been properly trained; he'd just spent the summer terms at Westcott, and that's not real training for the priesthood. He used to talk about his curacy in Essex, but that was just taking Sunday services, and next day he was on the train going up to London to lecture at King's.'

Runcie himself says that Bennett constantly fouled his chances of advancement through ill-judged behaviour. 'I began to promote him as a person to be taken seriously. I put him up for several jobs. I tried to get him a canonry at Canterbury. But I remember John Baker [Bishop of Salisbury] saying: "Anyone who's ever sat on a committee with Garry Bennett will run a mile at the thought of promoting him for anything." Runcie adds that Bennett made himself almost as unpopular on the Standing Committee of the General Synod. 'He saw this as his arrival at the place of power. Now, it was a tiresome committee – and he made it not only tiresome; he wrecked it! And it seemed to me that a man I had originally regarded as someone of scholarship, with a bit of intellectual clout, who might have become a Canon of Canterbury or a Dean of Winchester, was gradually getting sucked into the vortex of this terrible argumentative synodical committee

work. I couldn't believe that Garry could take it seriously
– but he went to all the sessions.'

Graham Leonard was well aware of Bennett's ambitions,
and his dependence on Runcie for fulfilling them: 'A number
of us used to say to him, "Look, if you want to move
anywhere, you've got to give up writing Bob's speeches and
sermons. Because otherwise he won't let you go; he relies on
you too much." But Garry wouldn't do this.

'Now, I remember putting him up to be Dean of Winchester, which he'd have done very well. And I talked to Bob,
who said, "It's not on the cards; he's going to be the new
Professor of Ecclesiastical History at Oxford." A post that
had been frozen. So I rang Garry and said, "Congratulations,
I hear you're going to get the Ecclesiastical History chair."
"Nonsense," he said. "It's still frozen." Now, that happened
more than once, and there were various appointments where
Bob would say that Garry wasn't available.'

Another year passed, and Bennett's hopes were still being
disappointed:

1 January 1986: ... I had half expected to be offered some
    kind of senior church job but again *nothing* happened. A
    whole series of possible deaneries and bishoprics went by
    and often were filled with second-raters. The professorship
    has receded out of sight, and I become increasingly uncertain whether I should be appointed to it, even if it were
    released ... Of course, during this year I have become
    closer to the Archbishop and clearly he owes me something
    and needs me in the present situation of the Church ...

Several letters and postcards from Runcie indicate the
extent to which he now depended on Bennett for material
for sermons and addresses on topics from clergy charities to
his presidential address to Synod. 'I don't know whether you
would like to have a shot at something to help me, or to talk
sometime by telephone or face to face ... You are the only
person to date who in my present naked state has produced
a brief which I could actually use!'

Runcie admits, however, that he had little wish for personal contact with Bennett: 'He was a menace on the telephone, because he would never get off it. He would go on and on; he never wanted to end the conversation. I realise in retrospect how he must have craved this sort of conversational exchange.'

Another undated letter from Runcie shows that he was still fueling Bennett's hopes of a deanery or bishopric: 'I only wish that I could do more from you. Rest assured that I will not cease from promoting the cause.' And again on 16 July 1986:

I continue to ponder your future, and wonder whether it might be worth promoting your name for the Deanery of Winchester. This does not mean that my word will count; but contrary to popular belief her Ladyship [Mrs Thatcher] does consult me at *most* times, listens to what I have to say. It would seem to me to fit, and I would be happy to see you there – the connexions are obvious – Not a bribe [the letter had asked for material for a speech], just a Thought for the Day.

At the end of 1986, Bennett found once again that all the hints had come to nothing. Yet he still went on writing for Runcie:

6 *February 1987*: [At Chichester Cathedral.] Bob's sermon was entirely mine for the first paragraph, though he bungled some of the quotations . . . As we walked back various people said they had recognized my style!

Philip Ursell, who had driven to Chichester with Bennett that day, and had been given a preview of the sermon during the journey, comments on Runcie's frequent suggestions that Bennett would be given a top job: 'That was very naughty. I said to Garry, "It's not in the interests of Bob Runcie to put you into anything, because his source of writing is going to disappear."' Runcie, however, emphatically denies that this was so: 'I never thought of saving him to be a supplier of scripts. There was no reason why a dean should not be able to do that – he might have had more time than a busy teaching don.'

Bennett now realised the futility of his position. 'Up at 7.45 after a restless night,' he wrote in his diary on 20 February 1987.

> The ineffable Richard Harries [the new Bishop of Oxford] filled the religious slot [on Radio 4] with honeyed vacuity. What do I do? The prospect of staying on in the C of E as I am, a fish-out-of-water in a church dominated by the liberal establishment, is not inviting. I am now excluded from any real place in its leadership, only in its opposition.

It was in this state of mind that he accepted Derek Pattinson's invitation to write the anonymous preface to *Crockford's*.

Pattinson himself had done duty as a ghost-writer for Runcie. Asked whether former Archbishops used ghost-writers, Pattinson says: 'Donald Coggan would have had ideological, spiritual and logical objections to doing such a thing! Michael Ramsey didn't need it; he knew what he wanted to say. Geoffrey Fisher was well organized; it may be that chaplains were required to get an abstract from *Who's Who* or something, but I think he wrote it all himself.' On the other hand he emphasizes that Runcie 'transmuted' what was written for him.[14]

Pattinson does not give the impression that his choice of Bennett to write the preface to the 1987 edition of *Crockford's* was motivated by malice towards Runcie. For the 1983 and 1985 editions, the anonymous preface-writer had been David L. Edwards, Provost of Southwark, who told Pattinson that he had felt inhibited in what he could say now that the church itself had taken over publication of the book. Pattinson found Edwards's 1985 preface 'very dull', and was

[14]Quotes from the Rev Sir Derek Pattinson are taken from an interview with the author, 26.6.95.

determined to liven up its 1987 successor. 'By that time,' he says, 'Garry had got very much into the Synod. He was on the Standing Committee, on every committee, it seemed, and was making very lively, vigorous, sharp, shrewd comments. One knew that he would write something very pungent, striking, direct, and well written. So we thought we would ask him to be the preface writer.'

On 26 November 1986, the day after he had received Pattinson's letter, Bennett wrote in his diary: '. . . as an old man [he was fifty-seven] I am anxious for a bit of recognition before I retire! It would be nice to make *Who's Who* one day . . .' And on 27 November: 'I begin to think that I *may* write the *Crockford's* preface.'

He invited Pattinson to lunch at New College. 'He was obviously very keen to have a go,' says Pattinson, 'but he wanted an absolute assurance that I would print what he wrote – that I wouldn't fiddle with it. He was very suspicious of the bureaucrat with his blue pencil. And not only mustn't I fiddle with it myself, but I must not take it to anybody, to get them to vet it. Well, with the backing of Jim Shelley [Secretary to the Church Commissioners], I promised that there would be no interference, no censorship.'

Asked if he knew that Bennett was going to be critical of Runcie in the preface, Pattinson says: 'I knew from general conversation with him, then and on other occasions, that his view of Robert was (a) very affectionate, and (b) very critical, both at the same time.' In fact Bennett's emotions about Runcie were being affected by events since he had accepted the commission. On 1 February 1987 he went to Bushey Heath in Hertfordshire to preach for its vicar, George Austin (now Archdeacon of York). After lunch, according to Bennett's diary, Austin produced 'an interesting computer read-out which showed how virtually every episcopal or decanal appointment was Bob R's nepotism. I must say it shook me, and I began to see I had really no chance.'

The print-out, which is among Bennett's papers, lists men who had been Runcie's pupils at Westcott House or Cuddesdon; it also demonstrated that, on the whole, liberal churchmen had been preferred to Anglo-Catholics and evangelicals.[15]

Bennett's diary for 9 February shows that he and Pattinson lunched together again that day, and 'Derek . . . was very open in his opinion about the Archbishop and encouraged me to write about his leadership'.

On 19 February, Bennett tried putting his viewpoint directly to Runcie:

> At 9 the Archbishop rang. He thanked me for my Chichester contribution and asked me what I thought about the Bishops' report [on the ordination of women]. We had a very vigorous argument. It got on to the Crown Appointments Commission [which appoints bishops and archbishops]. I said it had become an instrument to exclude Evangelicals and Catholics. He said it was the diocesan representatives [on the Commission] who did it. I asked what use it was to have such a Commission if it did not assure a balanced episcopate.

On 23 February, at a meeting at Church House, 'The Archbishop came up and foolishly I snapped at him a bit. He must now have got the feeling that I am angry. I am!' The next day he was told, by some unidentified person, that his name had been put up as one of four diocesan recommendations for the new Bishop of Birmingham – Hugh Montefiore was retiring – but he had been 'turned down by the archbishops supported by [Alan] Webster . . . That vexed me a great deal – but I admit I would not wish to be a bishop of *that* diocese.'

[15] Yet 3½ years later, Michael Baughen, Bishop of Chester, himself an evangelical, wrote: 'Appointments to bishoprics have been far fairer than Gary Bennett suggested in his *Crockford's* Preface . . . The mix is far more representative now than eight years ago, and approximately a quarter of the House of Bishops would be considered Evangelical in the full or broad sense of that term. It was certainly not so when I became a Bishop in 1982.' *Robert Runcie: A Portrait by His Friends*, edited by David L. Edwards, Fount Paperbacks, 1990, pp. 113–4.

Runcie, meanwhile, was as friendly as ever to Bennett. In March he spent some weeks at All Souls, Oxford, on a brief sabbatical (to prepare for the 1988 Lambeth Conference), and one of his first actions was to telephone Bennett, who invited him to dinner at his house in New Marston on 12 March. The diary records the evening:

> Bob ... was wearing a collar and tie. We drove to New Marston, and the meal seemed to go well, though I could see that he wanted to go easy on food and drink. We chatted about Oxford and individuals. I pointedly did not bully him. He mentioned the Birmingham appointment, and he was surprised when I said we were waiting to learn whether it was Jim Thompson or Mark Santer if Mrs T. turned him down! He said I had good information. I got the impression it was to be Santer. [He was correct.] We talked about George Austin. I spoke kindly of him but I could see some steel in Bob's eyes ... He left at 10.15 ... I had kept things at an easy level.

Philip Ursell comments on Runcie's behaviour towards Bennett: 'He can flirt with men as well as women – there is that side to him.'

Ursell was now trying to persuade Bennett to give up hopes of bishoprics and deaneries, buy a house in Chichester (where he held a canonry, and which he loved), and drive up to New College for a couple of days' teaching each week. He could have afforded to live there in style; his diary for 2 March 1987 noted that he had nearly £75,000 in savings; later he found he had another £26,000 in a deposit account. His Oxford house was probably worth about £125,000. Ursell remarks that he was very good with money: 'When Garry bought a new TV set, it had Teletext, and I remember one evening having to sit there drinking whisky with him while he went through his shares on it – "Look, it's gone up! You can see them moving if you watch carefully." And you could indeed see the figures altering.'

Money frequently came into the conversations between

Bennett and Ursell, because Pusey House, of which Ursell was Principal and Bennett a Governor, was in serious financial difficulties. Bennett told Ursell that, in his will, he had left most of his estate to Pusey House. 'He told me this in passing,' says Ursell, 'but people often do tell you things like that, and they don't actually mean it. He said it in front of John Kelly [former Principal of St Edmund Hall, Oxford], at a time when he was trying to persuade him to leave his money to Pusey House as well.' *Kelly died 1997.*

Bennett found the *Crockford's* preface very hard to write. On 27 March, he noted: 'I stayed in trying to work on *Crockford*, which is beginning to be a worry.' Philip Ursell, the only person outside Church House who knew that he was writing it, lent a hand: 'He showed me several drafts of it, and there were one or two bits that I added for him – the bit about the Book of Common Prayer being a unifying force, and a lot of the American stuff; I fed him up to date information about the American church.'

Bennett had just finished the first section, on the Anglican Communion, when he read in the *Church Times* that Alan Webster was to retire as Dean of St Paul's. 'I suppose I might be thought of,' he wrote in his diary, 'but I just do not trust Bob Runcie!' He had now put himself up for election to the Crown Appointments Commission: 'I must take it that there is now no likelihood of my being a bishop, so why not take a hand in choosing bishops?'

The preface was finished on 9 July, well after Pattinson's original deadline. 'I shall have to brace myself for its publication next December. It could cause an explosion! And I shall certainly be suspected! But now I do not care!' He let Geoffrey Rowell (now chaplain of Keble College) in on the secret: 'He read my piece for Crockford and said it was very good; it ought to be published as a pamphlet.' This was the sole occasion on which Rowell was invited to Bennett's house in New Marston; he says that Bennett gave him the preface to look at while he was cooking the meal, so that he scarcely had a chance to take it in properly.

Bennett sent the text off to Church House, and on 22 July noted that Pattinson had written saying it was 'very good'. Bennett was displeased that the letter 'was typed by a secretary and sent from Church House'; he was becoming very anxious about secrecy. On 24 July: 'I am afraid I shall . . . be detected. But my hopes of any job are now void, and I really am not at all sure at my age I even want a different job.' Meanwhile acquaintances were asking 'if I was going to be Dean of St Paul's. It is misery this kind of rumour . . .'

Pattinson says that he had been 'hounding' Bennett to get him to deliver the preface. 'He eventually gave it to me on the first night of the July Synod. I had to trail with him back to his rooms after the evening session, and he put it into my hand and I took it back to my room and poured myself a glass of whisky and read it. And my first reaction was, "Oh, this'll sell!"'

As to the criticisms Bennett had written of Runcie, Pattinson says: 'There was nothing about Robert that wasn't part of the gossip one heard over glasses of wine. And I would submit that, if publication had occurred the moment it was handed to me, the whole atmosphere would have been very different. But we were beginning to have the great attack from the hard-line evangelicals, the Tony Higtonites and so on [Higton, an Essex vicar, was a leader of the conservative evangelicals in the Synod], who were determined to get their own back on the bishops for a whole lot of reasons. By the time the preface appeared, the atmosphere had changed – it was poisoned.'

Asked if it was not irresponsible to allow a personal attack on the Archbishop of Canterbury to appear with the apparent sanction of the Church of England itself, Pattinson says: 'We should have perhaps perceived that, and not been quite so naïve.'

That autumn Bennett found himself in the familiar galling position of being an also-ran in the odds for the deanery of St Pauls. On 30 November advance copies of the preface were sent out to the press.

Some twelve thousand words in length, it began by declaring: 'These are critical times for Anglicanism, and now more than ever there is need of an informed and critical account of the state of the Anglican Communion in general and the Church of England in particular.' The first section contained nothing controversial; it was a shrewd summary by an accomplished church historian of the predicament in which the Anglican Communion currently found itself. Some overseas provinces were ordaining women priests on their own authority; the Book of Common Prayer had been 'virtually eliminated', depriving the church of a common liturgical base; and traditional Anglican theology and church history were no longer taught to ordinands. 'It would seem that modern man must live amid the ruins of past doctrinal and ecclesiastical systems.'

Then the preface turned to the head of the church:

Robert Runcie has been Archbishop of Canterbury since 1980 and has already established himself as a notable holder of the primacy. He has intelligence, personal warmth and a formidable capacity for hard work. He listens well and has built up a range of personal contacts among clergy and laity far wider than that of any of his predecessors. His speeches and addresses are thoughtful, witty and persuasive.

There were other compliments; and then:

It would therefore be good to be assured that he actually knew what he was doing and had a clear basis for his policies other than taking the line of least resistance on each issue. He has a major disadvantage in not having been trained as a theologian, and though he makes extensive use of academics as advisers and speechwriters, his own position is often unclear. He has the disadvantage of the intelligent pragmatist: the desire to put off all questions until someone else makes a decision. One recalls a lapidary phrase of Mr Frank Field that the

archbishop is usually to be found nailing his colours
to the fence.

This, asserted the preface, made Runcie 'peculiarly vulnerable
to pressure-groups'. As someone trained in 'the elitist liberalism of Westcott House', he displayed 'distaste for those
who are so unstylish as to inhabit the clerical ghettoes of
Evangelicalism and Anglo-Catholicism', preferring 'men of
liberal disposition with a moderately Catholic style which is
not taken to the point of having firm principles', especially
if 'they have a good appearance and are articulate over the
media'.

The preface then turned to other targets. The General
Synod was 'virtually powerless and consistently ineffec-
tive'; most of the debates were merely for show. Real
power lay not, as some believed, in the hands of Derek
Pattinson ('an immensely dedicated and hardworking civil
servant') but with the diocesan bishops. Since 1977 these
had been chosen by the Crown Appointments Commission,
in which the Archbishops of Canterbury and York had a
'predominant influence'. This had led to 'a virtual exclusion
of Anglo-Catholics from Episcopal office and a serious
under-representation of Evangelicals'.

Here, the attack on Runcie resumed:

One thing cannot be doubted: the personal connection of
so many appointed with the Archbishop of Canterbury
himself. A brief biographical study will reveal the remarkable manner in which the careers of so many bishops have
crossed the career of Dr Runcie: as students or colleagues
at Westcott House and Cuddesdon, as incumbents or
suffragans in the dioceses of St Albans or Canterbury, or
as persons working in religious broadcasting at the time
when he was chairman of the Central Religious Advisory
Committee of the BBC and IBA . . . Though one may accept
that an archbishop should have influence on appointments,
it is clearly unacceptable that so many are the protégés of
one man and reflect his own ecclesiastical outlook.

After this, the preface had little more to say. It praised
Graham Leonard: 'He has not always been particularly
adroit in the presentation of his case ... but ... his ideas
on faith and order place him securely in the mainstream
of Anglicanism.' It sneered at David Jenkins, Bishop of
Durham: 'the appointment of a man of such imprecision
of mind and expression under the guise of being a theologian
was a minor Anglican disaster'. And it concluded by hoping
that the Church of England could be rescued from 'its present
suburban captivity' and become 'once again a Church for the
English people'.

When he saw the preface in print for the first time, Philip
Ursell noticed that 'little paragraph headings' had been added
in the margin by somebody at Church House, 'which meant
that anyone not knowing very much about church matters
would look at them and see the one about "An Archbishop in
toils"' (the first paragraph to attack Runcie). Derek Pattinson
denies that he added these headings ('If they weren't there in
the typescript, they would have been put in by Robin Brooks,
our publications manager'). Another of his staff, John Barton,
the Church House broadcasting officer, was so outraged by
the preface that he initially refused to distribute copies to
radio and television, despite instructions from Pattinson and
John Miles. Pattinson says of this: 'John Barton wanted
to engage in one of those bureaucratic evasions, which I
myself have done on the odd occasion, of not wishing to
give it official backing. But clearly one couldn't do that
with *Crockford,* particularly when we were publishing it.
And this is one of the places where the whole business leaves
its scar; John Barton and I meet pleasantly, and so forth, but
we would never seek each other's company now.'

Advance copies of the preface (but not of the remainder
of the book) had also been sent out to the diocesan bishops,
thereby alerting them at the same time as the press to the
attack on Runcie. Bennett, meanwhile, had not received a
copy. On Tuesday 1 December, anxiously awaiting publication, he wrote in his diary:

Graham Leonard rang up to ask whether he could congratulate me as the author of the *Crockford* preface! He
had an early copy and it is to be published on Thursday. I
swallowed hard and decided to deny it! He said it sounded
like me, and I was one of the few people he could think of
who could write it! He was highly pleased at the references
to himself and read bits out to me. I said it sounded good
and I would look forward to reading it in full! Help! I
expect that, come Thursday, I shall have an awkward
time with the Press on to me, and much speculation
about authorship. I shall have to deny it through thick
and thin because it will be highly unpopular in certain
exalted quarters.

Lambeth Palace apparently received a copy on Wednesday
2 December, the day after the diocesan bishops. Runcie's
current chaplain there, Graham James, read it at once, and
wrote Runcie a memo about it:

An odd piece. Some useful *historical* analysis in the first
half, but it becomes increasingly incoherent [as] the writer
succumbs to what are clearly deep frustrations about
his own lack of preferment ... *Overall* I think he's
just as confused as the rest of us about the nature of
the Anglican Church ... I think you *are* vulnerable
upon the Appointments issue, but *not* on the grounds of
ecclesiastical nepotism, but simply because this is a small
country, with a limited pool of proto-episcopal talent, and
a relatively restricted intelligence gathering apparatus in
the dioceses.

James himself had come to Lambeth via a curacy in the St
Albans diocese and the Senior Secretaryship of the Advisory
Council for the Church's Ministry.

Runcie recalls that he first heard of the preface from Eve
Keatley, the Lambeth press officer: 'She said, "I'm very
worried about this." I said I hadn't seen it – and it was
already in circulation.' When he read it, 'I think I spotted it

was Garry at once.' But he was not particularly disturbed by the preface. Attacks on his style of archbishopric had become commonplace, and 'I thought, "Garry's said these sort of things to me before." I didn't take it all so seriously.'

One of the first journalists to see the preface was Reg Evans of the Press Association, who was a member of the Church House Communications Committee. This was due to meet, and on the morning of publication, Thursday 3 December, Evans wrote some notes of what he intended to say at the meeting:

> 1 Move suspension of agenda to discuss *Crockford's* preface.
>
> 2 I was the 1st journalist on to this story. Incredible that attack of this nature shd bear imprimatur of church. Like a white paper attacking Mrs Thatcher . . . or . . . a report on a company with a preface rubbishing the managing director. I rang Church Commissioners and then Church House: a) who wrote it? b) who commissioned it and knew identity of writer? Expected refusal to question a) but was even refused information on question b) Mice scurrying into wainscot. Lambeth Palace dignified no comment . . .
>
> Last night I discussed this preface with an experienced libel lawyer: he posed the question what would happen if the archbishop sued? The defendants would be the publishers and the author. The identity of the author could not then be hidden . . .
>
> The hunt is on for the author. Be sure he will be found.[16]

The first paper off the mark was the *Evening Standard,* on the eve of publication, Wednesday 2 December. Reporting the 'extraordinary personal attack' on Runcie, it said that Church House refused to identify the author beyond stating that he was 'a person of distinction in the church'. Lambeth

[16]Typescript by Reg Evans, 3.12.87, Lambeth Palace.

Palace had said there would be 'no statement from Dr Runcie', but his successor as Bishop of St Albans, John Taylor, was quoted describing the preface as 'a cowardly and disgraceful attack by a writer who has abused the privilege of anonymity'. The article observed: 'The question now is how long the writer will be able to hide behind his anonymity.'

During the day before publication, Bennett, in his room at New College, received

> a series of telephone calls from various newspapers asking if I were the author of the *Crockford* preface. They concentrate on it entirely as an attack on the Archbishop, ignoring all the rest of it. I simply denied that I was the author! When asked who could be, I said I had not read the text. Clifford Longley [of *The Times*] unnerved me most of all; he said he thought it was I because of the theology, the style and attack, and because I had the experience of the Church's admin. which the preface revealed. I said I had not written it. What was the alternative? . . .
>
> I listened to the radio news which had . . . Bishops of Peterborough and St Albans saying it was disgraceful and a cowardly use of anonymity. It was also on the six o'clock TV news . . .
>
> Home at 8.40. Philip [Ursell] came round to discuss the situation. He seemed quite cheerful but I suspect he thinks I may be smoked out! I must cover my tracks as well as poss. but it may be the Abp. will read between the lines. A Lambeth Palace spokesman emphasized he did not reply to everyone's contributions! P. left at 11.30 and soon to bed, a bit agitated and rather alarmed!
>
> *Thursday 3 December:* A very restless and sleepless night, consumed with anxiety and regrets over this wretched article. Up at 7 and to the shop to buy up the papers. A great spread in *The Times* with a full page of quotations. The general view was that the Archbishop has been 'savaged'. I suppose I was naïf not to anticipate this furore!

The *Times* article, by Clifford Longley, speculated that,

in view of the fact that Runcie was now sixty-six and had said he would retire before his seventieth birthday, the preface marked 'the opening round in a battle over the succession. An obvious candidate it seems designed to harm is the Archbishop of York, Dr John Habgood, who is coupled with Dr Runcie in several passages.' Runcie himself, meanwhile, was maintaining a 'dignified silence'.

Bennett could not rely on this. His diary for the 3rd continues: 'The telephone rang at 8.45, the archbishop's time, and I did not answer.' Runcie himself says that he did not make any telephone call to Bennett: 'It wasn't me. That's one thing I can categorically say.'

On the morning of publication, the Tory papers were inclined to agree with the preface-writer in their estimate of Runcie. 'It is unlikely that Dr Runcie's authority can now be re-established after such a blow,' asserted the *Daily Telegraph* leader writer, suggesting that he should resign. But the *Daily Mail* disagreed: 'The Archbishop is no saint. But anybody with that number of arrows sticking in him can't be all bad!'

The *Mail* added: 'Early suspicions of authorship fell on Dr Gareth Bennett, a High Church academic of New College, Oxford. But Dr Bennett said yesterday: 'I have not seen the preface and I can assure you I did not write it.'

After buying the papers and avoiding answering the phone that morning, Bennett went into New College and tried to conduct tutorials, 'with my mind abstracted'. He walked to Blackwell's bookshop, 'but no copies of *Crockford*'. Clifford Longley's assistant at *The Times* telephoned him 'to say that Lambeth Palace was saying "off the record" that I am the author! That will get the Press on me! I sat and pondered on a scene of disaster. Obviously the Archbishop thinks it is me, and has set his dogs on me. So I am right out of the Church of England. I shall linger on and not put up again for the Synod.'

He held more tutorials, then went back home and turned on the six o'clock radio news. He wrote in his diary: 'The Archbishop of York was denouncing the "scurrilous"

[handwritten annotations in top margin]

anonymous contribution.' (It was the first of several such statements by Habgood). Later that night, Bennet received a telephone call from a *Daily Mail* reporter asking to come and talk to him.

I agreed for Monday [he wrote in the diary] but instantly regretted it! My God what a mess and basically my own fault. I shall be lucky to weather this business through without disaster and some kind of public exposure. I rang back to the *Mail* and cancelled the appointment. George Austin rang to say it was not he, and to repeat that Lambeth was giving out that it was me. I rang Derek Pattinson but got an answer-machine. Very low indeed. The more I think about it the more bloody foolish I know I have been. But the pressure of last summer was very great and other people ought to have warned me. Derek rang back at 12 midnight to say that I must persist in denial; we would keep in touch. He said it would blow over after the weekend. He was obviously a bit shocked by news of the Lambeth 'off-the-record' disclosure.

The newspapers continued to give the story prominence on the Friday morning, 4 December. In *The Times,* Hugh Montefiore defended Runcie against the charge of nepotism:

I wonder if the anonymous author would include Dr Graham Leonard among the 'Westcott House elite'. A survey of recent appointments to important sees shows many with no previous connection with Dr Runcie – Norwich, Salisbury, Chelmsford; or from a different Anglican stable – Chester, Lichfield or St Albans [all evangelical]. Others were consecrated before Dr Runcie became archbishop.

The *Guardian* suggested several possible authors of the preface, including Henry Chadwick and Edward Norman, but it, too, included Bennett in the list.

Bennett, who had spent 'another wretched night', bought

the newspapers again: 'A reporter from the *Mail* rang up to offer me £5,000 if I was the author and wished to go public with them. He said it was rumoured that an announcement was to be made in the next 48 hours.' Bennett's diary ends here.

That morning, Pattinson forwarded to Bennett a letter from Roderick Gilchrist of the *Daily Mail* (who had been covering the story) addressed to 'the Author of the Preface'. It offered 'a very generous sum of money' to be paid to 'any charity, or the Church, or any other concern of your choice' if Bennett would admit to authorship. Geoffrey Rowell found it among Bennett's unopened mail some days later.

On the Friday night, Bennett and John Cowan were to represent New College at a dinner at King's College, Cambridge. Philip Ursell and another member of the Pusey House staff, the Rev. Stuart Dunnan, also had a Cambridge engagement, at Emmanuel College, so it had been arranged that Bennett would drive them all there. Ursell recalls that the preface was the topic of conversation for the entire journey; because of the presence of Cowan and Dunnan, he and Bennett 'were talking about it as though we didn't know who had written it!'

On the Saturday morning, Bennett arrived at Emmanuel to collect Ursell and Dunnan. 'He came up to the breakfast room,' says Ursell, 'and picked up the papers. He hadn't seen them till then. He picked up the tabloids, which were saying that the Establishment was hounding this man, and was determined to get him, and the *Daily Mail* saying "all fingers now point to Garry Bennett". And he was very quiet on the way back, in quite a different mood.' John Cowan noticed that Bennett had tucked one of the newspapers into the outside of his suitcase.

When Bennett's car reached Oxford, he dropped Ursell and Dunnan at Pusey House. 'When he dropped me,' says Ursell, 'I said, "I think I'd better call round this evening," which was not in the least bit unusual. And he said, "Yes, I think you'd better."' He then drove to New College, picked up his letters, declined Cowan's suggestion that they should lunch together, dropped him at his house near the college, and said: 'I must get back to feed my cat.'[17]

At some point that afternoon, he telephoned Derek Pattinson, leaving a message on his answering machine asking him to call urgently. Pattinson took the message at six, and telephoned Bennett at once. There was no reply. William Oddie, a former member of Pusey House staff and author of a book on Bennett and the preface, observes of this: 'If Garry had been expecting Pattinson to return his call, he must at that stage have expected to be alive to receive it.'[18]

Later that Saturday, after Evensong at Pusey House, Ursell drove to New Marston, keeping his promise of calling on Bennett. He turned into Moody Road, the hillside cul-de-sac at the end of which stood Bennett's house with its attached garage. Bennett always kept his car in the road.

> And as I got to the end, I noticed there was no car at the side. He never put the car away [so] I assumed he was not back. I turned the car at the end of the road and began to drive out . . . Mr [Harold] Cooper [Bennett's next-door neighbour] came out of his house as I was doing that and we had a conversation and both of us concluded that [Garry] had not returned. The curtains of his house were open and his car was not there and there were no lights on and it showed all the signs of not having been entered, certainly after the hours of darkness.[19]

Ursell drove back to Pusey House, and kept phoning Bennett throughout the evening, in case he had gone off for a drive and come back.

> I was a bit concerned – not concerned that anything had gone wrong, but I thought it curious that, having made an

[17]William Oddie, *The Crockford's File*, Hamish Hamilton, 1989, p. 51.
[18]*ibid.*, p. 52.
[19]*Gareth Vaughan Bennett* . . . Transcript copy shorthand notes taken at HM Coroners Court, Oxford, on 16th March 1988, made available to Bennett's executor by N. G. Gardiner, HM Coroner, Oxfordshire. (Hereafter referred to as 'Inquest'.)

arrangement to meet, he hadn't phoned to say, 'Look, I'm going off.' I was telephoning him all through the weekend, to see if he'd come back.

He didn't appear at Evensong at New College on Sunday evening, which was unusual, because he always did, and dined afterwards. All of which added to my thoughts that he'd gone away for the weekend.

Pattinson, too, was telephoning Bennett's house. 'I know what I would have said to him – "Look, I think we'd better go public, and I'll stand by you." But I couldn't get him. I tried again on the Sunday, and still got no answer. I thought, oh well, perhaps I've got it wrong and he's in Cambridge for that dinner.'

By Monday evening, there began to be some concern in New College at Bennett's non-appearance – he was supposed to be conducting the entrance examinations for History candidates – and John Cowan, after consulting Ursell by telephone, decided to go to New Marston. Reaching 15 Moody Road, 'I knocked on the door, or rang the bell, and got no response. I could see there was no car on the drive.'[21] Cowan therefore called on Bennett's next-door neighbour, a retired engineer named Harold Cooper, who had Bennett's door-key because he was often asked to feed the cat. 'We had a short discussion,' said Cowan.

> Between us we felt that entry into Dr Bennett's house was warranted . . . We opened the front door . . . As we went in we saw first of all [Bennett's] suitcase on the stairway with the newspaper still tucked in. This appeared to have been just placed there, untouched otherwise. Then we saw the cat was dead in the sitting room.[20]

Harold Cooper said of this: 'We looked into the lounge and the dining room and when I looked into the lounge I saw the cat lying dead on the carpet.' He had fed the cat 'late Friday morning' when it came round to his house – 'he was looking for food so I gave it to him'.[21] (Asked about the cat's appearance, Cowan says that it was stretched out peacefully on the carpet, with no mess of any sort around it'. He adds: 'It looked very old.'[22]) Cooper observed: 'The cat appeared to have died peacefully, it looked very normal lying on the carpet.'[23]

Cooper continued: 'I immediately ran upstairs into all the other rooms to see if there was any sign of him there.' Cowan was 'rather surprised how untidy the house was',[24] and Cooper thought it more chaotic than usual (though Bennett was not tidy by nature). Then, explains Cooper:

> We thought, well, we would look into the garage, and went through the kitchen where the entrance to the rear of the garage is . . . I looked into the garage. The first thing I saw was the car. It was not very light, the lights are not very good in the garage, it was half-light. We put the light on. I was a bit surprised to see the car [because Bennett did not put it in the garage]. I looked into the car. We saw Dr Bennett stretched out in the passenger seat. We opened the door and Dr Cowan felt his hand and I held his hand and shouted 'Garry, Garry', and there was no response. I realised that he was dead.

Cowan added:

> As we went closer I saw Dr Bennett in the front passenger seat. He was in a reclining position. It was one of the seats that tips back. We opened the door and called his name and there was no reply, and established that the body was cold to the touch, so we left everything as it was and I called immediately the ambulance service and the police.
>
> When I was in the garage I saw the hosepipe. I saw that the back window of the car had been turned down slightly and a hosepipe pushed in there and then jammed between the window and the top of the door.[25]

[21] All quotes from Harold Cooper are taken from Inquest.
[22] John Cowan interviewed by the author, 9.5.95.
[23] There was no post-mortem on the cat, so the cause of its death is uncertain.
[24] Inquest.
[25] *ibid.*

Philip Ursell was still telephoning Bennett's house at intervals, and finally on Monday evening the phone was answered, by a policeman, who told him that Bennett had been found dead. 'My immediate response was to ring Geoffrey [Rowell]. In fact, I went over to Geoffrey straight away.'

Rowell immediately telephoned Lambeth Palace; he was told that Runcie was in Canterbury, entertaining the Patriarch of Constantinople and other Orthodox clergy. Runcie eventually received a message to telephone Ursell, which he did shortly before midnight. Ursell gave him the news, and there was a long silence before Runcie spoke. 'He was very shocked,' says Ursell, 'and at the same time very concerned for me. It was an astonishing side of Runcie the pastoral priest – he was more concerned that I should not feel any guilt; did I know that Garry had written the preface? And I wasn't, even then, prepared to admit that I knew he had. But he spoke for about twenty minutes or half an hour, reminiscing and saying of course he realised that Garry had written it, "and he never said anything in it that he hadn't said to my face". That was a splendid side of his character.'

Next morning, Tuesday 8 December, the *Sun* led with the banner headline 'RUNCIE ROW AUTHOR KILLS HIMSELF: Oxford don in fume-filled car.' It quoted Thames Valley Police as saying, 'We are treating it as suicide.' That day, Pattinson and James Shelley of the Church Commissioners wrote to Runcie:

Dear Robert

Crockford's

Now that the facts regarding the preface to Crockford's have necessarily had to be made public, we are free for the first time to tell you directly how deeply we, as responsible for having invited Dr Bennett to write the preface, regret the manner in which this affair has developed. In following, earlier this year, the procedures previously adopted for the preface, neither of us imagined for a moment that the outcome could have such appalling consequences.

We both wish to say how saddened we are by Garry
Bennett's death. We are also anxious to say how sorry
we are that the preface and its reception by the media
should have caused so much hurt to you personally. We
wanted you to know that we felt this as soon as we were
free to do so.
Yours ever
Derek   Jim[26]

That day, there was due to be a meeting of the Policy
Sub-Committee of the General Synod (of which Bennett had
been a member). Alert to this, the press were able to photograph Pattinson and Shelley arriving for it. The meeting was
held in private; at its conclusion, a coolly-worded statement
was issued expressing 'grief' at Bennett's death, exonerating
Pattinson and Shelley – 'they acted strictly in accordance with
precedent' – and deploring 'the various pressures to which Dr
Bennett had evidently been subjected following the preface's
publication'.[27]

Runcie, who was present, recalls the meeting: 'Everybody
was waiting for this statement, and one nice member of the
committee said, "Oughtn't we to couple it with a statement
of our loyalty to and affection for the Archbishop?" And one
by one by one these characters said, "I don't think so, that's
another matter. If we were to say we supported the Archbishop, that would suggest that there was a question of people
not supporting him." I suppose I felt a bit hurt. I thought,
I've devoted hours to these piddling meetings, and they're
not prepared to put up some little statement of support.'

At the end of the meeting, the Rev. David Holloway, an
evangelical from the Newcastle diocese, made a separate
statement to the press, saying that he had 'not been allowed
to raise in the sub-committee points concerning the content of
the preface', and that he believed Bennett had been 'speaking
a word of prophecy'.[28] He was not the only person to feel that,

[26]Pattinson and Shelley to Runcie, 9.12.87, Lambeth Palace.
[27]*Independent*, 11.12.87.
[28]*Times*, 11.12.87.

in consequence of Bennett's death, the arguments advanced in the preface were not receiving proper consideration. Henry Chadwick, who was concluding a distinguished church and academic career as Master of Peterhouse, Cambridge, tried to initiate a discussion of the contents of the preface in General Synod, but found it impossible to divert the debate from the question of whether the preface should have been commissioned.

A few of the letters that Lambeth Palace was now receiving took the same line as Holloway, but most were in support of Runcie. 'We survive cheerfully,' Runcie wrote to the Bishop of Rochester on 15 December. 'I only hope that I can live up to the amazing trust placed in me by so many loving letters.'[29] In contrast, John Habgood was being widely attacked for his role in the affair. Peter Bruinvels, a former Conservative MP and a member of General Synod, spoke of 'the total witch-hunt spearheaded by the Archbishop of York to find the guilty man which hounded him . . . to such an extent that he could not take the pressure'.[30]

On Tuesday 15 December, a requiem for Bennett was held in New College chapel. The *Independent* quoted a 'spokesman' as saying: 'There is no difference in the ceremony because he committed suicide. His ashes will be buried in consecrated ground.' Ronald Gordon represented Runcie at the requiem and Graham Leonard gave the Absolution for the Dead.

Asked about the details of Bennett's will, Ursell says: 'There was a bequest to Geoffrey, in consideration of his being executor, and a bequest to Garry's cousin, but the rest of it came to Pusey.' The sum, not far short of £250,000 after the sale of Bennett's house and some valuable pictures, played a considerable part in restoring Pusey House's financial stability.

Derek Pattinson says: 'The real tragedy of the Bennett affair was that John Habgood went out of the running for Canterbury, because of his part in it.'

Is that really the case? I think not. John Habgood is now (1997) 70 and would have retired. He Lambeth confused it 1958 [handwritten annotations]

[29] Runcie to Rt Rev. David Say, 15.12.87, Lambeth Palace.
[30] *Observer*, 13.12.87.

The Jennett affair was a
Monumentally sad affair.

I always felt that Jennett was
overshadowed at Oxford by John Walsh   (another
Sykes
pupil!)
who worked also on Cer and had a
Fellt A research student which the more
angular Jennett never had.

Jennett was incredibly Naïve ~not to
realize he'd be wrong he recognized
— he'd seek imitate Attenboro's letter a
Convocation Man.   Religiously Jennett was
not in any
a classic High Church Man
Was odd:— He had respect in must have
Jenkins Very poor "Henson lecture   A Course
infuriated him with his remark that
Cleull Lelisans "make it up"   au followers/2
Several Historical School Boy howlers!
I fear he was probably right about Runci
But could fairs Used "Leitosas"
irony. Rather
Hence
vitriol!

18

A *classic Anglican*

------◆------

Tracing the thwarted career of Garry Bennett underlined for me once again the chance element in Runcie's success, the fact that he had been the right face in the right place at the right time, rather than an outstanding individual whose eventual supremacy in the Church of England could have been at all predicted.

If Bill Vanstone was Runcie's 'good' *alter ego*, a man of perhaps greater spirituality and intellect who had spurned public achievement, wasn't Bennett in some respects a negative version of Runcie? He had come from a similarly unsmart social background, and had achieved academically like Runcie, but had lacked the Runcie charm and performing skill, and had sunk into a well of envy and despair while Runcie rose inexorably to the top.

Also, Bennett's story was a companion piece of Waite's. Waite had been allowed to run off the rails with disastrous consequences for himself. Bennett had been encouraged by Runcie to hope for a deanery when few others believed there was a chance for him. Moreover Bennett had been a powerful analyst of Runcie's archbishopric. Somewhere in this biography there had to be a devil's advocate, an exposer of its subject's fundamental weaknesses; and Bennett, give or take a few exaggerations and distortions, had played that role effectively.

But I had to admit that with Waite and Bennett I had sidetracked myself. I also knew from long experience that there often comes a point in the writing of a biography when I (so to speak) fall out with my subject. I think it is probably a necessary step towards the balance and impartiality which one must finally achieve, but it does not feel like that while it is happening. The sensation is of suddenly perceiving some huge truth which darkens the whole picture.

From the outset with Runcie, I had feared that I might write not hagiography, but something superficial, cheery and anodyne. Confronted with such a highly accomplished anecdotalist, I knew it was vital that I should get behind the façade of the performer to the 'real' man, who must be flawed like every other I had written about. Consequently I had looked hard for the feet of clay. Did he play around with women? Could he have been in the know about Irangate? Wasn't his use of other people's drafts for his public utterances dishonest? Was he terminally indecisive and weak? Had the tabloid press been right in asserting that his marriage was a sham? Was his encouragement of Garry Bennett's hopes an unfortunate error of judgement?

One by one, I had pursued these leads, and found myself up a blind alley. I had become convinced that there were no women in Runcie's life apart from Lindy, and that, whatever difficulties their marriage may have been through, it was now as successful a partnership as I had ever seen in action. The Irangate notion had long ago vanished. Waite had clearly been naïve about the Americans, but I doubted whether he had really known what they were up to. I could not imagine him imparting a high-level international secret to Runcie, whom he thought was not giving him proper support. My doubts about the drafts and the indecisiveness remained, but as for Bennett, Runcie had clearly been unaware of the depths of the man's misery when preferment failed to materialise. Was it reasonable to blame someone who had to oversee thousands of clergy around the world for failing to know the inner feelings of just one of them? For the rest of the time, Runcie had been extraordinarily shrewd and good at human relations. Cynics might say that he was a man who wanted to be loved by everyone, but he had come very near achieving that among those who knew him well. Even Graham Leonard had spoken of him with affection. Everywhere I went, people had been highly critical of Runcie's successor at Lambeth; but to be honest, the only voice raised against Runcie himself had usually been his own – he was constantly self-critical.

By the summer of 1995, I had been working on the book for more than five years. I decided to show Runcie the text that then existed – a rough draft of everything up to and including the Bennett chapter, with the interviews Runcie had given me remaining largely unedited.

He told me he would read it during an American trip. 'Thank you very much for the dreaded sealed box,' he wrote to me on 5 October. 'I can assure you that it has not been opened and it will not be until I am, perhaps, in Californian sunshine.'

I heard nothing more until the end of November, when Frances Charlesworth rang me to say that Lindy had read the typescript, 'and as you may guess she's not happy about all of it!' Was she happy about *any* of it? 'I don't know,' said Frances. And what about Runcie himself? 'He's been dipping into it. Lindy has told him he *must* read it properly. He says he will – and he'll write you a letter.' He did, a few days later. After apologising for the delay, he registered their joint and unqualified dismay. 'Lindy is horrified and remains visibly upset . . . I am also astonished at the extent to which you have baldly used the tape recorder.' He described the result as 'a kind of ecclesiastical Alan Clark Diaries.'

I wrote back immediately, saying I was sad that he had reacted so strongly against the first draft, and assuring him that it was meant to be an affectionate portrait. We agreed to meet and discuss it when he returned from a trip to China. He had been invited back by Chinese Christians who remembered him affectionately from his 1982 visit.

On 25 January 1996 I arrived at his front door. He gave me a warm welcome but looked anxious, and said: 'I don't like confrontations or arguments.' Over the next hour and a half, he reiterated what he had said in his letter, and added: 'It's a very good bit of journalism, but it isn't what I wanted and had in mind. But I can see that to alter it would be to reduce its impact.' Typically, I noted, he appreciated its saleability.

We agreed that I would show the text – which I had already revised considerably – to Peter Cornwell, the former member of Runcie's Cuddesdon staff who was now a Roman Catholic priest, and to Jim Thompson, Bishop of Bath and Wells and another ex-member of the Cuddesdon team.

Thompson wrote to me in late February, saying he had found the book engrossing, but thought its characterisation of Runcie quite unfair:

> I do believe he is an outstanding person who has qualities which together amount to a special brand of holiness. This quality is not diminished by his weaknesses but is somehow carved out of them . . .
>
> To those who have worked close to him through the years your portrayal of a person pushed here and there, depending on other people's leadership and decision, does not do justice to the qualities of leadership, decision and conviction which he possesses. He had the guts to give the church space to come to its conclusions on issues which were splitting it. He was often able to see both sides of an argument, and the issues we were facing were not susceptible of absolutist answers. At Cuddesdon we saw him as a directive and strong Principal who made plenty of decisions. When I was on the staff we used to call him 'unilateral' Runcie, and he exercised there his authority, humour and intellect . . .
>
> I can see why people think that Liberal Catholics don't have clear manifestos, because of their tolerance and flexibility. But is is a real mistake to think there is no creed, no passionate commitment to a set of beliefs . . .

Cornwell's response was much the same:

> As a papist, I have to say that I find something more heroic
> in Robert's performance than you found – a flawed hero,
> but a hero nonetheless. So I resist the impression you may
> give that he is a weak person pushed around by tough
> characters. In my experience he can prove himself to be
> quite a tough old egg. There are countless examples of his
> spurning the advice of his staff at Cuddesdon, and then
> emerging triumphantly vindicated.

Both Thompson and Cornwell had ghost-written for
Runcie, and felt my treatment of this was unfair. 'He made
material his own,' Thompson told me, 'often dug out nuggets
from stuff that was not so good, and moulded it into his own
beliefs and conviction.' Similarly Cornwell wrote:

> My experience was often to find my own sentences bent
> and used in a way that I certainly did not intend! ...
> You are of course right that Robert has a strange lack
> of confidence in his own material, which is invariably the
> best. It is this diffidence, this continuing incredulity that
> he is actually Archbishop of Canterbury, which charms
> and which indicates what I would call his 'spirituality'.
> The fact that he never took himself seriously can be said
> to be a mark of 'godliness', or, in secular terms, a sense
> of perspective.

I wrote to several people suggested by Jim Thompson –
three of Runcie's former staff at Lambeth, and John Habgood
– asking them for the assessments of him. Meanwhile, during
another visit to Runcie to discuss the book, I recorded his own
memories of the final years of his archbishopric.

He told me that planning for the 1988 Lambeth Conference
had begun two years ahead of it. 'By 1987 I was beginning to

work out, with the help of the Anglican Consultative Council in London, the logistics of it all. I employed a phrase which I had plucked from our discussions with the Orthodox. When we talked about making decisions on the basis of church leaders and without any laity present, they always used to say: "A bishop brings his diocese with him." And that became a phrase of mine for the Lambeth Conference.

'It was our intention to start a process whereby, in the dioceses around the world, people would discuss what the issues were, as seen by them in Sydney or in Chicago or in Fiji or in Ireland. This would determine the agenda; and after the Conference, the bishops would need to report back to their dioceses; so that the Conference would be part of, or the climax of, a larger process. It also helped with getting the Conference expenses of each bishop paid, because if the people of his diocese thought that, in a sense, *they* were getting to the Lambeth Conference, and being let in on it, and they had an expectation of it finding its way back into the life of the diocese, then it became reasonable for them to pay the expenses. (It was a very expensive business.)

'Then we began to split the Conference up into four sections: one on unity and ecumenical matters; one on doctrine and mission; one on liturgical and spiritual things, and pastoral measures; and one on issues of social justice. And we appointed chairmen of each section. Then we had a very important meeting of the chairmen and the secretaries, a residential conference at Blackheath, so that we could begin to form the detailed agenda. And although it probably doesn't compare with the present preparations for the 1998 Lambeth Conference – because they've learnt from us, and have spent even more time preparing for it – it was a very well prepared conference in terms of participation and understanding, and this principle of bishops bringing their dioceses with them.

'It was less able to produce documents of intrinsic worth, on issues at stake – the whole question of the ethics of the family, marriage, embryo-research, abortion, that cluster of issues, which might have merited weighty papers from theologians, into which the Lambeth fathers could get their teeth. That's what the previously best Lambeth Conference had done, the Conference of 1958, which recognised the possibility of artificial contraception; there was a fine paper written in preparation for that. Now, we didn't have impressive papers, but we did have much more participation from people.'

To what extent, I asked, was the ordination of women debated? 'That was a big issue,' said Runcie. But the debate presumably couldn't be conclusive? 'No, because the Americans were already ordaining them. And there was a small party that was going to condemn this, but the Conference wouldn't have it. There was another party that felt that, on a matter so fundamental as that, no province should move autonomously. But in general the provinces of the Anglican Communion were reluctant to be subject to central control. And who can blame them, since – and this is something that I used to say to Graham Leonard – "the trouble is that the Anglican Communion was started by the Church of England taking independent action from the Church of Rome, which was the then centre, and was founded on the principle of the autonomy of cultural disparates. So who are we to condemn the Americans?" But of course it's also a principle of Anglicanism that nobody acts independently; we're all inter-related. Yet there's a difference between independence and autonomy. The law allows a particular province to act without reference to the centre, yet there would come a point where the rest of the Communion would disown a province. But the principle is of being in partnership with each other.'

So it was a successful Lambeth Conference rather than a memorable one? 'I think that would be generally true, though it was memorable in the human relations that were built up. And there had been so many predictions that it would be a failure, that the Anglican Communion couldn't really hang together, with some provinces ordaining women and some not. There was a really serious effort to work out how we should defend this interim stage, and we particularly made much of the principle of "reception", that there is a time when a new step forward in the church is being tested, before it's fully received.

'Some people complained that matters were put on the agenda, and decisions made about them, when they couldn't possibly have been addressed in detail. The Brazilian rain-forests, for example. Yet it may have been this item which, simply because it was on the agenda, enabled the Anglican bishops in Brazil to claim that they'd brought their dioceses with them.

'The official report of the Conference[1] looks very arid, and of course many of the peace and justice issues – the problems of the Polynesian peoples, tourism damaging traditional ways of life in the Pacific, or even the dental problems of Eskimos – didn't get full plenary discussions. But that's why the organisation of the Conference was so important, and these different reports represent quite detailed discussion. Because if you were in a sub-section of the section on peace and justice, you might have spent most of the time on that particular issue. No previous Lambeth Conference had been so skilfully planned, and had such a molecular structure.

'And the worship was very well arranged, and there was good well-arranged daily prayer and daily readings. Every day started with the Eucharist, before breakfast, and then there was an hour of Bible reading, done in the various sections that were doing the business. So you got to know people devotionally as well as in debate.

'And there were the big moments, which they enjoyed – the opening service in Canterbury Cathedral, the visit to St Paul's, and the garden party at Buckingham Palace. Then there were moving days, like Hiroshima Day – August the

[1] *The Truth Shall Make You Free: The Lambeth Conference 1988. The Reports, Resolutions & Pastoral Letters from the Bishops*, Church House Publishing, 1988.

6th – when the Japanese bishops planted a tree. There was a cricket match between Australia and the rest of the world. And some of the relationships that were made were very important; for example, in South-East Asia the bishops of Singapore and Malaysia have now formed themselves into a province.'

I asked to what extent the Conference had been over-shadowed by the twin crises of Waite and Bennett, which had erupted in the year preceding it. (Waite was captured in January 1987 and Bennett died in December that year. The Conference was held in July 1988.) Indeed, how had they affected his final three years as Archbishop?

'Well, not really so much. Waite took time, but not time that occupied all the days. I was conscious of Waite, but many other things had to be done, and the Lambeth Conference took more time. The Lambeth Conference, of course, paid no attention to these things.' Did Garry Bennett's death cloud things over? 'Surprisingly little.'

I asked when he had decided on the date of his retirement (31 January 1991, some months before the mandatory retiring age of seventy). 'I think not until about 1989, when I became aware that beside my own fairly imminent retirement, the Bishop of London [Graham Leonard] and the Bishop of Durham [David Jenkins] were both going to retire soon. It was clear that I should retire, or at least announce my retirement, in good time, so that Canterbury could be filled before they had to fill London and Durham. Otherwise, of course, they might have put somebody who would have been right for Canterbury into London. And when I saw that this had to be done, I was quite grate-ful to decide to retire, though the press distorted it. I remember that there was one headline, "Archbishop to Quit Early".'

I said I had the general impression that, after the Lambeth Conference, the last eighteen months of his archbishopric seemed to have been quieter than the earlier years. In particu-lar, there weren't the same struggles with the Government? 'Yes, I think that that was so. Though there was quite a lot of activity with the creation of the Church Urban Fund.[2] And I also went to Rome in 1989, stayed at the English College and went to the Vatican. But I think a lot of the things we'd fought for were now established. The things that I wanted to do had been done. Though we had not settled the ordination of women, which began to take over everything else. That was the boil that we had not lanced by the time I left.'

He didn't want to preside over the final vote? 'I didn't, because I felt it was important to hold on board as many people as we could. And I'm sure that we'd have lost more and better if we had gone for it too precipitately.'

Had he been consulted about the choice of his successor? 'No, there were no consultations. And his appointment was a complete surprise to me. I thought it might have been John Habgood, but there was no sense in which I was running anybody. And I was very surprised when Carey was chosen, because he'd only been a bishop for a very short time.'[3] And because of his evangelical position? 'I suppose so.

[2]Sir Richard O'Brien, Chairman of the Crown Appointments Commission which had put Runcie's name forward for the archbishopric, and of Runcie's Commission on Urban Priority Areas which had written the *Faith in the City* report, wrote to me: 'Robert responded quickly to the suggestion [in 1982] from the urban bishops and Eric James that some form of Urban Commission should be established. He helped to recruit the members, and from the start he took a close interest in what came to be known as the Archbishop's Commission on Urban Priority Areas. He never interfered with its work. He offered me an open door at any time; but I did not have to use it. I always knew he was *there* in support. He took the chair for the press conference to launch the report [*Faith in the City*] and continued solidly in support throughout the period when the report was the subject of lively debate and discussion.

'After publication it was invaluable to know – and to have others know – that he was always available for particular gatherings and meetings. I am not implying that he necessarily agreed with every detail. It was Robert's *general* backing for *Faith in the City* together with his *specific* support for the Church Urban Fund which were so important.'

[3]Graham James, who was there when the news came of George Carey's appointment, confirms that Runcie was astonished. Another source told me the rumour that Carey's name had been put forward to Mrs Thatcher by the Crown Appointments Commission very much in second place to that of Habgood, but that she, as so often, had rejected their first choice almost on principle.

But there were people who'd always been keen to get an evangelical as archbishop, because they're the growing edge of the church.'

I told him I had been listening to an Oxford vicar, a liberal churchman in middle age, who was very gloomy about the future, and felt that the Church of England would gradually be torn apart by the extreme wings. Did he share this fear? 'I don't think I do. But I think the church may have to make all kinds of changes, for changing times. And it will need to take much more seriously the fact that religion is pretty weak in western countries. I think it was Gellner who called our culture Consumer Unbeliever International.' The Pope fights against that – what other strategy is there for the church than aggressive conservatism? 'It's got to have more spiritual discipline, doctrinal flexibility.' *What Does that mean?*

But that, I said, was middle-of-the-road liberalism, and surely such appeal as the church still has comes almost entirely from the conservative wings, the Catholics and evangelicals? 'The difficulty about the conservative wings,' Runcie answered, 'is that they tend to be literalist, either about the scriptures or about church traditions. The church should be more conservative in its spiritual roots and liturgical expression, but more capable of the risks necessary in translating the doctrines into the new world. The new must grow out of the old and not replace the old, that's very important. But the new must grow.'

Was there, I asked, going to be any place in the future for the sort of figure he had been – the Catholic liberal? 'I think it's going to be quite difficult for the Archbishop to carry with him enough spiritual clout to be taken seriously at the centre of the nation's life. Because there is a distancing of church from state, I think. There are fewer and fewer people who are involved in what makes the nation tick, either politically or culturally, who have their roots in the life of the church and the Christian faith.' But could he imagine a liberal like himself – sceptical, with a sense of humour – rising again to the archbishopric? 'It's difficult to imagine that. And I know that people like John Witheridge and Graham James say that I'm the last.'

* * *

Graham James, Runcie's last chaplain, is now Bishop of St Germans in the diocese of Truro. I met him in London, having explained that people to whom I had shown my first draft felt I was putting too much emphasis on the ghost-writing, and on Runcie's lack of decisiveness.

James reminded me that I was not the only person who had made him out to be indecisive: 'His public image was particularly bad on television, where he came across as weak and unsure. Yet there needs to be an element of lack of confidence in all the best people, because it prevents the arrogance that leads to the second-rate.

'I agree that he's not a man to make the instant decision. He's a man of a historical cast of mind, and he's got the historian's rather sceptical approach to things, which means that he's never one to take up great causes. If you look at his speeches and lectures, they generally begin in the past and lead to the present. That's not the product of people putting those words into his mouth; it's the very nature of the man. He surrounded himself with people of a historical cast of mind – my own degree's in history, and so was Richard Chartres'.'

James was not surprised that I had made a beeline for the ghost-writing. 'People do find it odd, because preachers are meant to preach from conviction. But actually I'm against a too personalist view of ministry. And Robert had a very high sense of the public office of Archbishop – at a time when offices such as the Prime Minister were becoming more and more identified with the personal holder. Everyone spoke of "Mrs Thatcher" rather than "the Prime Minister", but Robert represented and embraced an older tradition of public office. I call him "Robert" now, but it was noticeable that even those who were close to him at Lambeth referred to him as "Archbishop" rather than using his name.'

James emphasised that this identification with the public office was in marked contrast to Runcie's two immediate predecessors. 'Michael Ramsey had been theologically brilliant, an original preacher and thinker, but an administrative shambles, and was almost completely uninterested in ecclesiastical government. Donald Coggan's exercise of the office of Archbishop, during his five years in it, had been a very personal one. In 1975 he launched a Call to the Nation – a personal initiative, inadequately resourced and researched, and it was inevitably a dampish squib. (He had had more success with a Call to the North when he was Archbishop of York.) And when he went to Rome, Coggan pleaded for inter-communion, against all advice and as a personal initiative (which failed, of course). You could call this brave and prophetic, and certainly there are times when the Archbishop ought to go out on a limb in his leadership, but personal convictions alone are not enough. Contrast the Call to the Nation with the much greater impact made by Runcie through *Faith in the City* and the subsequent establishment of the Church Urban Fund.'

The use of a supporting team of writers (James went on) reflected this view of the office of Archbishop: 'It wasn't just overwork, and the fact that he hadn't got time to write all his own stuff. When Robert spoke on any public occasion, he wanted to present not just his own feelings, but a message that people would recognise as expressing the mind of the church.

'This made him a very demanding person to work for. You worked long hours, and there wasn't much division between job and private life. On the foreign trips, we weren't allowed to relax, even when sightseeing. I remember on a visit to Central Africa, we had a day off to look at the Victoria Falls, and while the rest of us were gazing at the rainbows dancing around our feet, the Archbishop turned to me and said, "What are you doing about that sermon for Surrexit?" – a big conference at which he was due to preach as soon as he got back. And he'd be fulfilling an engagement in Australia on one day, back at Lambeth twenty-four hours later, and go straight to his desk and expect us to do the same. You had to live the work with him.

'You were at it most of the time, because there was a great deal of agonising over the material that was going to go out. And much more was written in-house than people sometimes recognise. There's this impression of a worried Archbishop who was trawling in things from all sorts of quarters. In fact the number of outside people whose material was used was not very great.

'He didn't usually swallow someone else's draft whole. He was a great critic of what you produced. He had an eye for the weak argument, the clumsy turn of phrase, the cliché. And you will find a common style and themes, and certainly a common language, in what he delivered. That's because all the speeches and sermons were worked over so carefully by him, even if he hadn't drafted the original material. Before every engagement, however small or insignificant you might think it, he'd be sitting in the car and going over the script yet again, scribbling in the margin, and there'd be a tremendous build-up of tension. He was never blasé about going into the pulpit even in the smallest church. And I remember a state banquet in Lusaka, with television cameras, and quite without warning, at the end of a speech by Kaunda, the President, the Archbishop was called upon to respond – and we hadn't been told, and no speech had been written. And he got to his feet, and was brilliant. It was better than any draft we could have produced for him!'

James gave me an example of 'the sort of thing Runcie was willing to do which a weaker person would have steered well away from'. It was during the tension immediately after the *fatwah* on Salman Rushdie had been declared, in 1989. 'The politicians couldn't deal with it at all. But Runcie, together with John Habgood and the Bishop of Bradford, held a meeting at Lambeth, when leaders of sections of the Muslim community came together for an afternoon. The discussion centred on possible changes to the blasphemy law, to protect religious minorities in Britain. This came to nothing, but it did mean they felt they were being taken seriously. And it was an initiative in inter-faith relationships which has been followed up since by George Carey.'

On the question of weakness, James added: 'Genuinely weak people tend to appoint weaker and more colourless people around them. I need to be careful saying this, having been on his staff myself, but I think Runcie has always gone for strong and distinctive personalities – Terry Waite and Richard Chartres were hardly pushovers!'

I told James I was beginning to feel I had been wrong, in this book, to characterise Runcie as a liberal. James agreed that he was far more conservative than many people had supposed: 'He's a traditionalist, not a reformer; he's on the side of established institutions, and he tries to make them work without always seeking to reform them. Also, he wanted to be essentially in solidarity with Government; he used to say that the natural place for the Church of England and the Archbishop was to be in "critical solidarity" with Government. That's the reason (he said) why the bishops always sit on the Government side in the House of Lords, which ever party it is. And I think he veered much more towards the solidarity than the criticism. And such left-wing initiatives as *Faith in the City* and the setting up of the Church Urban Fund weren't natural things for him at all; they reflected, rather, his habit of consulting people of different views, and of wanting to take whatever line these people felt the church as a whole ought to be taking, even if it was not personally attractive to him.'

I mentioned A. N. Wilson's sneer about Runcie's innumerable overseas trips. James said he thought these journeys had achieved a great deal: 'Between the Lambeth Conferences each ten years, the Anglican Communion is held together largely by the ministry of the Archbishop of Canterbury. And there were plenty of reasons – pastoral, theological and organisational – why it could easily have fallen apart in the 1980s. Some provinces were already ordaining women, while others didn't want that to happen. Certain parts of the Anglican Communion found Runcie's style irritatingly patrician (I'm thinking of New Zealand and Canada especially), but the Americans appreciated him, and Africa enjoyed him, though there was sometimes puzzlement at his characteristic manner of understatement.

'He took trouble on these trips over what might seem rather trivial local problems, which he would spot brilliantly, using his characteristic method of picking the right person to go to a place, report back to him, and make constructive suggestions. The time he devoted to something like the attempt to appoint the first native Bishop of Bermuda, or the efforts to establish the first Province in South-East Asia, could look out of all proportion to the scale of the Anglican Communion as a whole. Yet it bore enormous fruit at the 1988 Lambeth Conference. The conference opened in the wake of Waite's disappearance, the *Crockford's* affair, and all the press attacks on *Faith in the City* and the Runcie marriage. And I think the English bishops were surprised by the respect and affection in which he was held by those who had arrived from overseas.'

James's judgement of the 1988 Lambeth Conference was much the same as Runcie's: 'The weakest thing was all the resolutions, which were then ignored, because the Church of England has no executive authority to carry them out. Its strength was the quality of the relationships achieved between the bishops taking part.'

I told James that Runcie denied that Waite's disappearance had overshadowed the remainder of his archbishopric. He agreed. 'It wasn't the cloud over every activity that's some-times been painted – life was just too full. And he was always at his best, I thought, when the press were most hostile. At the time of the *Crockford's* preface, I was astonished by his apparent invulnerability against the arrows that were being aimed at him. He could be very anxious about what he might say in some speech that was coming up. But when things were directed against him as a person, he could cope with that. You see, he's a man without much interest in himself.

'He's much more interested in the foibles of the human condition as displayed in others, than in himself. When I think of his room upstairs in the flat at Lambeth, it was bare. He wasn't troubled by his surroundings very much. He's remarkably lacking in interest in his surroundings, and all the paraphernalia of contemporary life. If it wasn't for Lindy, he'd live in rather spare circumstances. What fascinates him is other people. He attends to them, notices them, and finds in the foibles of human behaviour an endless supply of humour. After a public engagement, he'd invariably start describing all the things he'd noticed about people who were there. And he'd usually have picked up material for some anecdote, which would get polished up and used in letters, and maybe even in a speech or a sermon.

'He was a brilliant observer. And not just of other people. Sometimes I thought, here's a man who's got a high sense of public office, but he's almost like an observer of himself, watching himself exercising the office.'

John Witheridge, Runcie's chaplain from 1984 to 1987, left Lambeth to be Conduct (senior chaplain) at Eton College. Over lunch in a wine bar in Eton High Street, he told me that Runcie had greatly discouraged this move. 'He didn't want me to come here – it was embarrassing for him, in the middle of all the church's emphasis on Urban Priority Areas. I said in my leaving speech, "I'm going instead to an *Urbane* Priority Area!"' Runcie warned him that, if he went to Eton, he would not get a good job in the church thereafter, but Witheridge stuck to his guns and, after nine years, has now moved from Eton to be Headmaster of Charterhouse.

Witheridge makes no bones about his own conservatism, and sees Runcie as essentially of the same persuasion: 'Richard Chartres and I were widely recognised as ecclesiastical Young Fogeys, anti the liberal establishment in the Church of England. And it's curious, if he's really a liberal, that he chose us as his chaplains. Graham James is more of a liberal, but that was much less a personal appointment – he came via Ronald Gordon, who knew him very well.

'I think Robert's a profoundly conservative man, but he allowed himself to be deflected by the 'sixties and 'seventies liberals. Yet that's impressive, in a way, because it tells you how ready he was to listen to a younger generation, despite his own deepest instincts. And he genuinely listened to what I had to say when I joined his staff. I was barely thirty, and he'd been Archbishop for four years or so, but he genuinely wanted to know what I thought about things. That sort of openness is a sign of his real interest in other people, and concern for what they think and feel.'

Shortly after Runcie had announced the date of his retirement, Witheridge contributed an article to *The Times* (7 May 1990), in which he argued that the job of Archbishop of Canterbury was, in its present form, unworkable:

As it stands, the task that [Runcie] will bequeath is an impossible one. It has been so for at least a hundred years ... Randall Davidson said it was 'an impossible job for one man', and Cosmo Lang complained that his work-load was 'incredible, indefensible and inevitable'. William Temple did 'the work of a Prime Minister with the staff of a Head Master', and Geoffrey Fisher believed 'that the first requisite of an Archbishop is to be as strong as a horse'.

Witheridge wrote that Runcie had shown 'determination to devote himself to all aspects of his office', which had meant enlarging the Lambeth staff and delegating more than his predecessors; but he had still been under 'immense and unrelenting pressure of work'.

Talking to me, Witheridge recalled that, despite supposedly delegating responsibility for the diocese of Canterbury to the Bishop of Dover, Runcie had still tried to be its diocesan bishop: 'He aimed to spend every other weekend in Canterbury, and all the major church festivals. And on Monday morning he would sit in on diocesan staff meetings. He wasn't somebody of the temperament which could say, "I'm not going to bother with this or that aspect of the job." He's a perfectionist, he has a fear of criticism, and he instinctively wanted to do everything that was expected of the Archbishop – and to do it better than it had ever been done before. There was a huge cost to his own energies, and he had to delegate a lot to his staff, and to increase their numbers; but of course, paradoxically, if you have a bigger staff, you create more work.'

Witheridge was impressed by Runcie's physical stamina,

particularly on overseas trips: 'The strain of those overseas tours, for a man in his sixties, must have been almost intolerable. I don't know how he did it. I, aged thirty, was often utterly exhausted! But he's a man of considerable physical strength, and he seemed able to recharge himself – and he got a lot out of it. He'd get a particular boost from the acclamation of the crowds. He's a man who needs to be loved – that's a major part of him, and it refuels him, recharges the batteries. I used to find it a pain in the neck, all that pressing the flesh on those trips, and we used to try to drag him away from it to give him some rest. But he'd stay to the very end.'

I said that, for a man who needs to be loved, he had seemed fairly resistant to the press attacks, and to the *Crockord's* preface; I mentioned that Graham James had thought him fairly invulnerable on these occasions. Witheridge disagreed. 'I remember when he read the attacks in the press on what he'd said about the miners' strike he was obviously quite worried about it. I think it really threw him. Graham may be right, but it doesn't fit my picture of him. He doesn't have the inner self-confidence to cope with people disliking or opposing him. You have to be very sure of yourself to live with that. I think he was very good at concealing his feelings on that sort of occasion. He never *really* unburdened himself to me – I don't remember him telling me anything really personal, or letting off steam.'

What about the indecisiveness, the apparent weakness, or at least the unwillingness to make decisions quickly? 'His style of leadership had its own strengths,' said Witheridge, 'but that wasn't obvious to a nation that had Margaret Thatcher as Prime Minister. There was so much fuss about "strong leadership", and Robert's style of listening to people, taking his time to make decisions, and leading from behind, was simply not in fashion.

'He clearly likes to have strong people around him. I'm a more confident person than he is, more certain of my own opinions, much more able to make up my mind and stick to it. And Richard Chartres very much encouraged me to behave like that. "You must take a stand," he said. And of course Lindy has *very* firm views on things; there are no grey areas in her approach to life.'

We turned to the ghost-writing. 'I was in charge of all the sermons and speeches,' Witheridge explained. 'I had to make sure that there was something prepared for every occasion. There were some things he would write, a lot were written by me or someone else on the staff, and a lot were farmed out by him. And he would sometimes ask more people for drafts than I was aware of. Their contributions would come in, often at the last moment, and I was left doing the editing, because it was my responsibility to hand him a draft from which he could actually speak. It was embarrassing, of course, to reject totally any material that had been sent, particularly if it had come from somebody distinguished. So you were sometimes faced with quite a difficult editorial problem. And then the style had to be made to match his manner – I used to call it "Runciefying".'

Why should the ghost-writing have remained publicly unacknowledged by Runcie and his staff? 'The church wasn't used to it,' answered Witheridge. 'People expect (perhaps a bit naïvely) that a sermon should come from the heart, and be a personal statement. His predecessors probably wouldn't have been terribly worried if they did come out with platitudes which they'd written themselves. Robert was determined not to do that, and wanted to be professional. He wanted to drag the church out of its rather amateur corner. But he knew people would have been very quick to judge him harshly if they realised he hadn't written it all himself. And the magic would have been spoilt. So he was caught in a real dilemma.'

Christopher Hill, who was Runcie's Secretary for Ecumenical Affairs, had just been consecrated Bishop of Stafford when he received my letter asking him for his summing-up of Runcie's strengths and weaknesses. On the telephone, he told me that he began to work at Lambeth at the end of the Ramsey days, and served under Coggan before Runcie's arrival. He agreed with Graham James that Runcie had more consciousness of the public nature of the archbishopric than his two predecessors. 'Also, Donald Coggan saw Canterbury as in some ways an enlarged archbishopric of York. I think Robert saw it as a quite different job to anything else in the Church of England, and he was probably the first Archbishop to feel that; largely because he was unusual in not having previously been Bishop of London or Archbishop of York, the then usual route to Canterbury. And the job had grown over the years, so that it *was* different. The responsibilities had increased hugely. And he styled his Primacy on that assumption.'

Did Hill agree with Graham James's belief that Runcie had leant so heavily on a team of speech-writers because he was acutely conscious of the public nature of the office? 'Yes. Coggan saw his public speeches as personal sermons – that may be part of his evangelical background. Whereas Robert wanted a kind of ministerial team, that would give him expertise, and a wider net of communications through the members of that team, and through his personal contacts outside – the people he would ring up for drafts and advice. They gave him a different insight on key issues, theological and public. It was much more profound than just needing someone to write this stuff. He saw the job at a world level, and needed tools to do it properly. And, as Graham says, he particularly feared the meaningless cliché.'

Hill travelled with Runcie around the ecumenical world, and was with him at a number of key Anglican Communion meetings. He came to admire Runcie's ability, mentioned by Graham James, to identify local problems almost in an instant. 'He would go into a room and within ten minutes he would have picked up, in a conversation, what was wrong. And I could brief him on really tricky issues, and he'd lead the talk round to key issues almost without anyone noticing. He hated direct confrontation; he'd much rather have a quiet conversation with someone about a problem.'

I asked Hill if he saw Runcie as liberal or conservative. 'Many of his friends were liberal, as you know,' he answered, 'but he also retained deep friendships with people who would have objected to that title. Garry Bennett is the obvious case, but there were many others. And I think that he was struggling for an orthodoxy that could be critically engaged with the times.'

Why did Hill think Runcie's public image was so poor? 'It's difficult to say, but going back, one remembers how poor Michael Ramsey's image was. I think it's a recurring pattern. All the frustration that people feel about the church is, these days, focused on one person. Also, I think the Catholic-minded traditionalists within the Church of England saw him, understandably, as one of them – and then felt let down by him. One hesitates to bring George Austin's name in again, but he was typical of a certain strand.'

What about John Witheridge's conviction that the job of Archbishop of Canterbury is impossible? 'One way of doing it,' answered Hill, 'would have been the obvious decision to cut out the diocese of Canterbury. But Robert was unhappy at the American and Canadian models, where the Primate has no see. Even the Pope has his own diocese, in Rome. It's an old patristic principle, and Robert saw Canterbury as his little local church.

'I think the Archbishop of York and the Bishop of London could have been used much more to share the work, but there was enormous resistance from "Little Englanders", who resented the time any Archbishop must now spend in the Anglican Communion. Yet John Habgood did more and more, and came into his own towards the end of Robert's ministry, and then the stature of this less flamboyant and more philosophical man became clearer. They got on very well, mind you, and respected each other's talents.'

John Habgood, living in retirement in Yorkshire, replied by return of post to my request for his views on Runcie. (I had offered him the choice of paper or the telephone, and he said he would rather write, 'as this method gives one slightly more time to think.') He, too, emphasised Runcie's 'consciousness of history' and his 'love of style, especially in speaking'. He felt that Runcie's restructuring of the Lambeth staff, to free himself for the exercise of his personal strengths, had been 'frustrated by the Terry Waite saga which took up a huge amount of staff time, and occupied John Lyttle when his skills were badly needed for advising on political issues nearer home. It was also emotionally demanding on Robert himself, and if I had to pick out a major mistake made during his primacy, I think it would be his failure to control Terry Waite's activities at an earlier stage.'

In Habgood's eyes, Runcie had treated 'the more mundane tasks of an archbishop, like chairing meetings' as 'an unwelcome chore'. Habgood recalled:

> He usually came well prepared with advice from others, but it was not always clear that he had read the main documentation, and he was apt to state his own conclusions before there had been any discussion. In summing up, however, his shrewdness stood him in good stead, and our joint contributions (with myself usually having read the papers) were more often than not helpfully complementary. In fact for most of the time we found it easy to work with one another.

Graham James's impression that Runcie did not mind the press attacks on him was not shared by Habgood: 'I know from our telephone conversations during the worst times what a lot these cost him emotionally. This is one reason why I deliberately drew the media away from him during the *Crockford's* affair.'

What about the accusation that he could not make up his mind? Habgood wrote that this was

> only half true. He certainly took a long time to do it in many instances – not least in making appointments – and he certainly agonized over major decisions. But I always saw this hesitancy as a measure of his sense of responsibility for the church as a whole, and his desire genuinely to represent its breadth. We were living in times

when everything seemed to be going through a process of change, so caution was not out of place.

Habgood added that Runcie's indecision over the ordination of women 'was actually helpful in enabling the Church of England and Anglican Communion to stay together as the process moved towards its climax'.

He praised Runcie's mixture of 'holiness and humour, breadth and seriousness of purpose', and concluded:

> I do not know how history will evaluate his primacy. There was nobody better suited for the job available at the time, and he had the stature for it. It was his bad luck that he had to do it during an exceptionally difficult period, and that he was to some extent damaged by the vicious campaigns against him. As I saw him, he was a classic Anglican, who managed to maintain his balance against all the odds.

On 21 March 1996 I wrote to Runcie, sending a draft of this chapter (he had now read the revised text of the rest of the book). He telephoned to say he was just off to St Louis, 'with eighteen addresses to give, and not a ghost in sight!' A few days later I received a note promising 'a little postscript' to the book – to which he now seemed resigned – and adding ironically: 'The way you have ghosted this [last] chapter – using your tape recorder and bending other people's views to your own ends – is an interesting example of what was often my own method.'

Four months later, after he had read the proofs, he sent the postscript:

Mr dear Humphrey

I have done my best to die before this book is published. It now seems possible that I may not succeed. Since you know that I am not enthusiastic about it you are generous to give me space for a postscript.

One of my predecessors at Canterbury on being shown his portrait and asked whether he thought it did him justice, replied 'It's not Justice I need, but Mercy.'

There is much that is just and more that is merciful in your story but I am afraid that they do not add up to my original idea for a biography. It is certainly not a hagiographical 'stocking filler' but it is yet another personal investigation heavily dependent on the skilfully edited tape recorder. Burbling into it for background, I find it reproduced for substance. It is not only the syntax which makes me wince. There is much that I never imagined I would see in print.

The 'mischievous journalist' has plenty of material for a Sunday paper Profile and enticing sentences to be chopped up for promotion; but the writer of the *Inklings* who brilliantly evoked the atmosphere of Oxford in the 40s does not seem to me to have fully grasped what it was like to be Archbishop of Canterbury in the 80s. Maybe some distancing is essential if all the evidence is to be gathered in. I can imagine an historian in the distant future, fascinated by your words, saying 'But surely there was more to it than that.'

Meanwhile I shall try to keep my sense of humour and the perspective of eternity. I am sorry that you have had such difficulty in 'pinning me down'. Indeed I have a strong suspicion that the whole experience has made you the Reluctant Biographer of

Yours truly

All biographies are relationships. They are created by the interaction of two people, writer and subject. When the subject is dead, the writer can happily pretend to reanimate him or her, and to create an idealised relationship, in which the 'partner' is in fact an entirely passive puppet, performing whatever tricks the biographer chooses. The result is in effect a cunningly disguised work of fiction.

Living subjects refuse to respond so passively. Biographers who tackle the living embark on real human relationships with them. It is as risky as any other sort of relationship. If the biographer hopes to achieve the same degree of pretended intimacy as with the dead subject, he or she will probably be disappointed. Boswell seems to have managed it, but then one remembers that he did not publish until Johnson was dead.

In the past, I have been slightly embarrassed at not having known my subjects. I never met W. H. Auden, Benjamin Britten, or most of those I have written about. Now I realise it was an advantage; my personal feelings did not get in the way. I could have written two books about Runcie: one, an affectionate portrait based on personal observation; two, a detached and critical biography examining every weakness as well as strength. I tried to write both. In the process, I have certainly learnt a great deal more about the biographer's trade.

I can't see Runcie as a great Archbishop.

Adrian Hastings' Robert Runcis

(1991) is much more significant.

What a pity Owen Chadwick could

not equal his fine life of Michael

Ramsey, with a life of Runcie.

Index